Normal Organizational Wrongdoing

Normal Organizational Wrongdoing

A Critical Analysis of Theories of
Misconduct in and by Organizations

Donald Palmer

OXFORD
UNIVERSITY PRESS

OXFORD
UNIVERSITY PRESS

Great Clarendon Street, Oxford, OX2 6DP,
United Kingdom

Oxford University Press is a department of the University of Oxford.
It furthers the University's objective of excellence in research, scholarship,
and education by publishing worldwide. Oxford is a registered trade mark of
Oxford University Press in the UK and in certain other countries

First Edition published in 2012
First published in paperback 2013

Impression: 1

Published in the United States of America by Oxford University Press
198 Madison Avenue, New York, NY 10016, United States of America

British Library Cataloguing in Publication Data
Data available

ISBN 978–0–19–957359–2 (Hbk.)
ISBN 978–0–19–967742–9 (Pbk.)

Printed and bound by CPI Group (UK) Ltd, Croydon, CR0 4YY

For Kim, I promise to take off more time to ski next winter.

Preface

This book has its origins in a quantitative empirical analysis of corporate illegality that I never completed. I spent my first twenty years as a sociologist of organizations conducting quantitative empirical studies of overlapping corporate boards of directors. Corporate boards overlap when the same individual simultaneously sits on the boards of two firms. My early studies examined the factors that lead firms to become interlocked. My later studies examined the consequences of interlocks for firm behavior, such as the adoption of the multidivisional form and the pursuit of hostile takeovers. In 2004, I began designing a quantitative empirical analysis of the impact of interlocks on the likelihood that firms would pursue anti-competitive acquisitions. But before I made much progress towards implementing the design, I read a book that reoriented my thinking about organizational wrongdoing, most importantly about the factors that cause wrongdoing and the best way to study it.

Alan Draper, a good friend who is Professor of Government at Saint Lawrence University and an expert on the American labor movement and comparative politics, sent me James Stewart's *Den of Thieves*. Alan thought that Stewart's well-researched chronicle of insider trading on Wall Street in the 1980s might serve as an interesting supplement to the quantitative data that I was planning to analyze. As it turned out, Stewart's book did more than this. It led me to question my assumptions, based on a superficial reading of the business press, that the typical instances of wrongdoing were clearly aberrant and that the perpetrators of wrongdoing were unquestionably abhorrent. Even more important, it led me to suspect that the same structures and processes that I covered in my core course on organizational behavior as facilitators of efficiency and effectiveness (i.e. right-doing) in organizations were also crucial facilitators of wrongdoing. Finally, it led me to suspect that the best way to understand the structures and processes that gave rise to organizational wrongdoing was to accumulate detailed qualitative information on individual instances of wrongdoing.

I have spent the better part of the last six years trying to develop the implications of these insights. My efforts in this regard have been shaped by a number of other people. The most important of these were my three doctoral dissertation advisors. While my dissertation was a quantitative empirical investigation of interlocking directorships and was completed in 1981, my advisors imparted more encompassing and enduring outlooks that influenced me in ways that I have only recently fully realized. Charles Perrow introduced me to a journal article by David Sudnow titled "Normal Crimes" (Sudnow 1965). The central idea of this article, as I remember Perrow characterizing it, was that violations of the law were commonplace and that police officers did not enforce every infraction, but rather selectively enforced the law so as to construct social order. Later, Perrow wrote a highly influential book titled *Normal Accidents*. The central idea of that book is that under certain conditions (system complexity and tight coupling), organizational accidents are inevitable. As will soon become clear, *Normal Organizational Wrongdoing* is inspired by Sudnow and Perrow's fundamental insights, and Chapter 10 of the book is a direct extension of Perrow's accident analysis.

Mark Granovetter introduced me to a way of conceptualizing the vast area separating economists' undersocialized conception of human beings and structural functionalist sociologists' oversocialized construal. Granovetter's "Economic action and social structure: The problem of embeddedness" (1985), gave birth to the embeddedness perspective. And this perspective has come to provide an umbrella for a wide range of sociological scholarship, from network research to new institutional theory. The distinction between under and oversocialized conceptions of human beings provided me with a way to distinguish between the two dominant approaches to explaining organizational wrongdoing presented in the first chapters of this book: the rational choice (undersocialized) and culture (oversocialized) accounts. It also provided me with a way to distinguish between these two dominant explanations of wrongdoing and the alternative (embeddedness) accounts that form the balance of the book.

Finally, Michael Schwartz provided a model of how to use popular reports for sociological analysis. Schwartz was the founder of the MACNET research group at SUNY Stony Brook, to which I was a latecomer in 1975. MACNET stands for Mathematical Analysis of Corporate Networks, and the MACNET group was formed with support from the NSF to map the network of interlocking directorates among large U.S. corporations in the 1960s. Michael, despite being the mathematical brains behind the project, was consumed with reading business press reports about large firms. He accumulated an immense pile of *Fortune, Business Week, Wall Street Journal,* and *New York Times* articles that he ripped from their original sources and that he thoroughly underlined and extensively annotated. Michael often used references to these articles when making points in project group meetings, at the same time reminding the group that good sociologists read and observed broadly (i.e. they did not just read the work of other sociologists). He and Beth Mintz later used references to these articles in their highly influential book based on the MACNET project findings, *The Power Structure of American Business* (Mintz and Schwartz 1985). Without a doubt, my enthusiasm for reading as much as I could about as many instances of organizational wrongdoing as I could locate has its origins in Michael's passion.

This book also was inspired by the work of three more contemporary colleagues. Dick Scott's classic, *Organizations: Rational, Natural, and Open Systems* (2002), provided an exemplar of a book that critically characterizes an entire field. Jeffrey Pfeffer's widely read *Managing with Power: Politics and Influence in Organizations* provided a prototype of a book that is both intellectually rigorous and accessible to practitioners. Finally, Jerry Davis' award-winning book, *Managed by the Markets: How Finance Re-Shaped America*, provided a model of a book that is both scholarly and politically relevant. Clearly my book does not live up to these books' standard of excellence. But it does aspire to their accomplishments.

More immediately, this book benefited significantly from an article by Ashforth and Anand (2003) and a chapter by Brief, Bertram, and Dukerich (2001) on organizational corruption. I was not aware of these theoretical statements when I began my work on organizational wrongdoing. But after I learned of these pieces and read (and re-read) them, my work came to be defined by my incorporation and reaction to the ideas they contained. This book also benefited from two edited volumes on ethical decision-making, *Codes of Conduct* (Messick and Tenbrunsel 1996) and *Social Influences on Ethical Behavior in Organizations* (Darley, Messick, and Tyler 2001). I was not aware of either of these volumes when I began the book, but I drew inspiration from them as the project progressed. While they focus on a somewhat narrower topic than I consider here (ethical behavior as opposed to wrongdoing), they investigate many of the same social structures and processes that I examine.

Even more immediately, this book builds on my collaboration with Michael Maher. This collaboration produced a preliminary statement of the book's main idea, "Developing the process model of collective corruption in organizations," which appeared in the *Journal of Management Inquiry* (Palmer and Maher 2006). Chapter 10 draws heavily from another article I co-wrote with Michael titled "The Mortgage Meltdown as Normal Accidental Wrongdoing," which appeared in *Research in the Sociology of Organizations* (Palmer and Maher 2010). Initially Mike and I planned to pursue the topic of organizational wrongdoing together, but other commitments took Mike in a different direction. The book also builds on a subsequent collaboration with Henrich Greve and Jo-Ellen Pozner. Our partnership, which substantially broadened my view of the field, resulted in a review chapter titled "Organizations Gone Wild," which appeared in the *Academy of Management Annals* (2010). I owe Mike, Henrich, and Jo-Ellen a huge debt of gratitude.

This book also benefited from the contributions of several other colleagues. Chris Yenkey and Michael Schwartz provided an incisive reading of Chapter 2, which lays out the book's main argument. James Detert drew my attention to (indeed, gave me his copy of) Walter Pavlo and Neil Weinberg's book *Stolen without a Gun*, upon which I draw heavily to illustrate my extension of ethical decision theory in Chapter 6. Kristin Smith-Crowe and Ann Tenbrunsel gave me invaluable input on Chapter 6, which helped me avoid mischaracterizing this literature into which I am most definitely an interloper. Art Brief and Jeff Pfeffer offered crucial comments on Chapter 9, which examines how power facilitates wrongdoing in organizations.

In addition, Mike Lounsbury and Paul Hirsh provided excellent criticisms on the preliminary statement of the book's main idea, the *JMI* article mentioned above. Art Brief and Barry Staw provided input on a more developed but still provisional statement of the book's main idea, published in *Research in Organizational Behavior* (Palmer 2008). Lounsbury and Hirsh, as well as Marc Schneiberg, Tim Bartley, Mauro Guillen, and Charles Perrow, also provided crucial input on the *RSO* chapter I co-authored with Michael Maher on the mortgage meltdown, which laid the foundation for Chapter 10 of this book. I have also benefited from feedback that I received when delivering talks based on this book at the business schools of the University of Alberta; Boston College; Harvard University; the University of California, Berkeley; The University of California, Irvine; Simon Fraser University; Cornell University; Northwestern University; The University of Chicago; and INSEAD in Fontainebleau. The inputs of several people at these stops stand out in my mind: Royston Greenwood, Dev Jennings, Mary Ann Glynn, Chris Marquis, Doug Guthrie, Mike Tushman, Matt Bothner, Jean Bartunek, David Strang, Brian Uzzi, Mark Mizruchi, and Linda Johanson.

I also owe thanks to a large number of other people, some of whom I will undoubtedly inadvertently overlook. Erica Palmer conducted preliminary research on the mortgage meltdown, upon which I drew in Chapter 10. She also prepared the references. In addition, Erica and Anthony Palmer read a preliminary draft of the first half of the manuscript and alerted me to inconsistencies and ambiguities that smart non-technical readers would find disconcerting and that very much required fixing. Anthony's persistent questioning of my point of view played a major role in the development of my ideas. Patricia Odean read the entire manuscript and offered editorial suggestions that rid the manuscript of innumerable incomprehensible passages, awkward constructions, and grammatical errors. Mathew Zafonte and Kim Pawlick provided invaluable encouragement. Matt periodically reassured me that my perspective on wrongdoing would resonate with readers. Kim intermittently issued guarantees that I would eventually get the book done (all the while nudging me to take note of the vast literature in psychology that I was ignoring and on occasion providing me with useful points of entry into this literature). Their timing was impeccable. Four years of students who took my course on the causes of organizational wrongdoing at the UCD/GSM provided criticisms and suggestions that shaped the book as it evolved. Finally, David Musson and Emma Lambert at OUP offered expert scholarly and editorial advice and demonstrated uncommon patience as I developed the manuscript. I am very lucky to have been the beneficiary of all these gifts, which I will do my best to reciprocate.

Contents

List of Figures and Tables

Figures

Table

List of Abbreviations

ADE	Adverse drug event
ASPD	Antisocial personality disorder
CDO	Collateralized debt obligations
CPA	Coalition Provisional Authority
DEA	Drug Enforcement Agency
FDA	Food and Drug Administration
FERC	Federal Energy Regulatory Commission
FTC	Federal Trade Commission
GAAP	Generally accepted accounting principles
MIC	Methylisocyanate
NAACP	National Association for the Advancement of Colored People
NHTSA	National Highway Transportation Safety Agency
NSF	National Science Foundation
PRC	Performance Review Committee
PSC	Private security contractor
SEC	Securities and Exchange Commission
SPE	Special purpose entities

1

Introduction

Wrongdoing perpetrated in and by organizations has dominated the news periodically over the past decade. The most prominent case involved energy market manipulation, fraudulent accounting, and special purpose entity conflicts of interest at Enron Corporation. Other cases included the fraudulent billing practices at Worldcom, the inappropriate use of company resources for top management perks at Tyco, and the post-dating of stock options at Waste Management. Much of the highly publicized organizational wrongdoing has been collective in nature, involving the interaction of many people in the same or interdependent organizations. Each of the recent instances of wrongdoing cited above fits this description.

Organizational wrongdoing can have significant consequences for its victims. It can be injurious to customers. The women who used Wyeth Pharmaceutical's drug fenfluramine, the active ingredient in the prescription appetite suppressant cocktail Fen-Phen, were not fully warned of the drug's dangers. As a result, many took the drug and unsuspectingly experienced elevated risks of primary pulmonary hypertension and heart valve disease, painful and incapacitating conditions that in many cases resulted in death (Mundy 2001). The agribusinesses that purchased Archer Daniels Midland (ADM) lysine shouldered substantially higher costs because ADM conspired with other lysine producers to fix the price of the cattle feed additive at above-market levels (Eichenwald 2000).

Organizational wrongdoing also frequently is injurious to investors. Many of the elderly men and women who bought shares in Prudential Bache's deceptively risky, and in some cases entirely fictitious, limited partnerships lost their life savings when these mischaracterized and bogus financial instruments went belly up (Eichenwald 2005). The community members who placed deposits and bought stock in local thrifts lost their nest eggs in the 1980s when their savings and loan institutions went bankrupt after engaging in a variety of fraudulent dealings (Pizzo, Fricker, and Muolo 1991).

1

Organizational wrongdoing also can be injurious to employees. The workers and managers who invested their pensions in Enron saw their retirement savings evaporate when the company, buffeted by charges of extensive top management financial and accounting fraud, went bankrupt (McLean and Elkind 2004). Finally, organizational wrongdoing can be injurious to communities. In the 1970s, the women who lived in the vicinity of Love Canal experienced elevated incidence of miscarriage, and their children suffered above average incidence of defects at birth and serious illnesses in childhood, presumably because toxic waste dumped into the canal by Hooker Chemical contaminated the upstate New York community's water supply (Verhovek 1988). A decade later, the families who lived in the vicinity of the Union Carbide chemical plant in Bhopal, India, suffered blindness, respiratory illnesses, and death, when the plant released toxic gas into the atmosphere surrounding the plant (Shrivastava 1991).

Organizational wrongdoing also can have significant consequences for its perpetrators. For many years, prosecutions of companies and their leaders were rare, and punishments were mild. But in 1991, more stringent sentencing guidelines for organizations were issued in the United States. These and other subsequent legal changes in the United States and abroad have rendered organizations and their leaders more vulnerable to prosecution and punishment. In recent years, civil judgments of $100 million or more against wayward corporations have become common. Moreover, significant fines and jail terms have been meted out to convicted corporate and white-collar criminals. It can be argued that the punishments dealt to organizations and their leaders are still insufficiently frequent and severe, and that as a result, wrongdoing often does not harm and sometimes very much benefits, perpetrators. But the significance of the increasingly severe punishments for the firms and individuals who receive them cannot be denied. To be sure, all of these consequences, whether experienced by the victims or the perpetrators of wrongdoing, amount to personal tragedy and economic waste.

This book is a critical review and extension of theories about the causes of organizational wrongdoing. I primarily examine theories at the individual level of analysis and almost exclusively focus on collective wrongdoing. Further, while I consider wrongdoing in many different types of organizations, from government agencies to financial institutions, I largely focus on private-sector organizations. Put succinctly, I analyze theories that explicate the factors that lead directors, top managers, middle managers, and line employees to either initiate wrongful behavior that initially or ultimately involves multiple individuals, or that cause these organizational participants to join others engaged in wrongdoing already in progress. I do not seek to identify factors that make some subunits, organizations, industries, or higher levels of social organization prone to misconduct. I do not focus on white-collar crimes such as embezzlement, which tend to be perpetrated by solitary individuals.

My critical analysis of theories offers six contributions to the literature on organizational wrongdoing. First, I distinguish between two overarching *perspectives* on organizational wrongdoing. These perspectives present different outlooks on the nature of wrongful behavior, the characteristics of wrongdoers, and the range of causes of wrongdoing in organizations. One perspective, the conventional view, conceptualizes wrongdoing as an abnormal phenomenon. The other perspective, a contrasting outlook, conceptualizes wrongdoing as normal.

Second, I identify two ideal-typical *approaches* to analyzing the causes of organizational wrongdoing. One approach, the more longstanding and widely accepted "dominant" framework, assumes that wrongdoing is produced by mindful and rational actors who deliberate in social isolation, make discrete decisions, and develop positive inclinations to engage in wrongdoing. The other approach, a more recent and increasingly popular "alternative" framework, assumes that wrongdoing is sometimes produced by mindless and boundedly rational actors, who formulate their behavior in an immediate social context, in a temporally protracted escalating fashion, and who never develop positive inclinations to engage in wrongdoing.

Third, I elaborate eight specific *explanations* of organizational wrongdoing. Two of these explanations follow from the perspective that views organizational wrongdoing as an abnormal phenomenon and embrace the dominant approach to explaining wrongdoing: the rational choice and cultural accounts. Five of these explanations follow from the perspective that views organizational wrongdoing as a normal phenomenon and embrace the alternative approach to explaining wrongdoing: the administrative system, situational social influence, power structure, accidental behavior, and social control accounts. One of these explanations, the ethical decision account, bridges the two perspectives and approaches. The relationships between the two overarching *perspectives* on organizational wrongdoing, the two dominant *approaches* to analyzing the causes of wrongdoing, and the eight specific *explanations* of wrongdoing are depicted in Figure 1.

Fourth, I contribute to the elaboration of the one bridging and five alternative explanations of wrongdoing. I believe that all eight explanations of organizational wrongdoing are valuable and can be considered complementary. But as will become clear in the next chapter, I champion the normal organizational wrongdoing perspective on wrongdoing and the alternative approach to explaining wrongdoing. Thus, I do not just review the explanations of wrongdoing associated with the normal organizational wrongdoing perspective and the alternative approach to explaining wrongdoing. I try to advance these explanations as well.

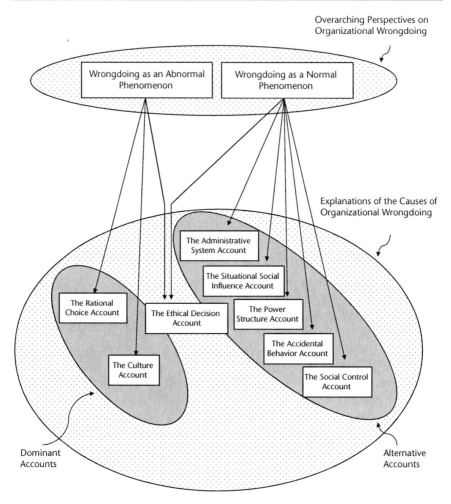

Figure 1. The Relationship between Perspectives, Approaches, and Explanations

Fifth, I illustrate the eight explanations of organizational wrongdoing using rich case study materials. Much of the research on organizational wrongdoing uses quantitative empirical research methods, in particular laboratory experiments and field surveys. These methods have proved useful, especially in elaborating the dominant explanations of wrongdoing. But I believe that qualitative case analyses of the sort presented here are useful and in some respects necessary if we are to fully understand the causes of wrongdoing, especially those causes apprehended by the one bridging and five alternative explanations of wrongdoing favored in this book.

Finally, I consider the practical implications of the full range of explanations of wrongdoing examined in the book. Most organization scholars consider the study of organizations to be an applied one and thus believe that they have an obligation to study organizational phenomena with an eye to developing practical applications (Thompson 1956). For the most part, organizational scholars have studied phenomenon with an eye to improving organizational efficiency and effectiveness (March and Sutton 1997; Augier, March, and Sullivan 2005; Khurana 2007). But the earliest scholars exhorted organizational scientists to conduct work that can reduce the incidence of corruption (Boulding 1958). And many who study wrongdoing offer prescriptive suggestions. I will lend a hand to this effort.

In the next chapter, Chapter 2, I elaborate in more detail the two overarching perspectives on organizational wrongdoing and the two approaches to analyzing the causes of wrongdoing. I also articulate more precisely the relationship between these perspectives and approaches and the eight specific explanations of organizational wrongdoing considered in the book. In Chapter 3, I develop the definition of wrongdoing that guides my examination of the causes of wrongdoing. I also explain how theory was developed and data were analyzed in the course of writing the book. In order to understand the causes of a phenomenon, we must have a clear definition of the phenomenon, a strategy for developing theory, and a method for marshalling evidence to do so. I present the eight specific explanations of organizational wrongdoing in Chapters 4–11. In the final chapter I consider the practical implications of the explanations of wrongdoing considered in the book.

2

Two Perspectives On Organizational Wrongdoing

Organizational wrongdoing can be viewed from two contrasting *perspectives*: one which views organizational wrongdoing as an abnormal phenomenon and one which views it as a normal phenomenon. Further, the causes of organizational wrongdoing can be understood from two approaches: a dominant outlook and an alternative one. Finally, there are eight different specific *explanations* of wrongdoing. Below I outline the two contrasting perspectives on wrongdoing, elaborate the two different approaches to understanding the causes of wrongdoing, and foreshadow the eight explanations of wrongdoing. I also indicate why I believe the explanations of wrongdoing that flow from the normal organizational wrongdoing perspective and that embrace the alternative approach to understanding wrongdoing are particularly worthy of greater attention and development.

Following my discussion of the perspectives, approaches, and explanations that form the core of this book, I present a detailed description of an instance of organizational wrongdoing that illustrates the two different approaches to understanding the causes of wrongdoing. This description will serve both to solidify my characterization of the difference between the two approaches and introduce the type of evidence upon which I will draw when elaborating the explanations of wrongdoing considered in the book. I end the chapter with a few remarks about what I consider to be the book's main message and my overarching objective in writing it. I suspect that some of the arguments that I develop in *Normal Organizational Wrongdoing* will run against the grain. So I will try to clarify my outlook and goals right from the start.

The two contrasting perspectives

Organizational wrongdoing as an abnormal phenomenon

Most popular and much scholarly thinking about organizational wrongdoing implicitly considers it to be an abnormal phenomenon. Wrongful behavior is viewed as aberrant—a clear departure from the norm and thus implicitly rare. Further, wrongdoers are seen as abhorrent—extraordinary in a malevolent way, sometimes characterized as "bad apples." Some view wrongdoers as possessing despicable personality traits, such as excessive greed. Others view them as holding deplorable attitudes and beliefs, such as a reckless disregard for the welfare of others. Finally, the causes of wrongdoing are believed to be a narrow range of flawed or distorted organizational structures, sometimes characterized as "bad barrels." Some focus on misaligned organizational incentive systems that motivate people to pursue illicit objectives. Others focus on perverse organizational cultures that condition people to think and act in deviant ways. Sometimes these analyses are explicit. Often, though, they are only implied in exhortations to improve governance controls and to upgrade ethics programs, which are intended to correct misaligned incentive structures and perverse cultures. Popular and scholarly authors sometimes draw a sharp distinction between focusing on "bad apples" as opposed to "bad barrels," favoring one orientation over the other. But I consider this a family quarrel rather than a fundamental dispute.

Thomas Stewart, one-time editor of the *Harvard Business Review*, embraced the "wrongdoing as an abnormal phenomenon" perspective when offering his assessment of the general state of global business (2004). In an opinion piece in the *Financial Times,* he wrote:

> Post-Enron, post-Shell, post-WorldCom, post-Parmalat, the collective knickers of the business world are in a twist about ethics, and rightly so. Deals are the building blocks of business. Enormous sums are at stake and the money belongs mostly to strangers, not neighbours. Without ethics to define deals and fair dealing, business will not get done. Rightly, therefore, regulatory bodies have yanked the chain. Rightly, business schools throughout the world have given more prominence to ethics in their curricula. Rightly, also, once-malfeasant companies such as Tyco have developed impressive safeguards to keep themselves straight. One day this horse will bolt again—greed is a clever animal—but it should not be for want of new locks on the stable doors.

Robert Shiller, a distinguished professor of economics at Yale University, also implicitly embraced this perspective when assessing a specific instance of wrongdoing at the New York Stock Exchange. In an op-ed piece for *The New York Times,* Shiller (2005) commented on the widely criticized pay package granted the NYSE's chairman, Dick Grasso, which provoked a New York State

Attorney General civil law suit against both the Exchange and Grasso. Shiller expressed outrage at the magnitude of Grasso's compensation package, approximately $187 million, asking, "Why did nobody on the exchange's board look at that astronomical sum and feel some personal responsibility to find out what was happening?" After briefly referring to the "ineffectiveness of the safety controls" in place at the NYSE, he turned his attention to what he considered the primary cause of this instance of egregious behavior and of organizational wrongdoing more broadly. In his words, "I can't read minds, but I think it is fair to say that to some extent the players in this drama—as well as those in the ones now being played out in the courtrooms and starring former executives of Tyco, WorldCom and HealthSouth—have been shaped by the broader business culture." Shiller located the origin of the broader business culture in our graduate schools of business, whose courses "often encourage a view of human nature that does not inspire high-mindedness." He substantiated his assessment with a penetrating analysis of the standard business school curriculum, which extols the virtue of self-interested behavior. The overall message of Professor Shiller's column was clear: Grasso's compensation package obviously was excessive and those who approved it clearly were delinquent. Further, the excessive package was approved because the culture in which the NYSE board and business more generally is enmeshed is one-sided and thus distorted.

Organizational wrongdoing as a normal phenomenon

Although most who write about organizational wrongdoing implicitly consider it to be an abnormal phenomenon, a growing number of scholars implicitly regard it as normal. This contrasting perspective assumes that wrongdoing often is not much different from organizational right-doing. This is partly because in most advanced societies, whether capitalist or socialist in character, competitive pressures often require people working in organizations (hereafter, "organizational participants") to operate close to the line separating right from wrong (Coleman 1987, 1988; Braithwaite 1988). Those who operate at a safe margin from the line are disadvantaged in their competition with other economic actors. The immediate vicinity of the line separating right from wrong, though, typically is a grey area. And organizational participants operating in this area are faced with significant cognitive and behavioral challenges in their efforts to approach, but not cross the line. These cognitive and behavioral challenges play an important role in many of the explanations of organizational wrongdoing examined in this book.

Further, the normal organizational wrongdoing perspective assumes that many wrongdoers are ordinary; that is, people who do not possess unusual human traits (e.g. sociopathic tendencies) or typical human traits that are allowed to develop in the extreme (e.g. unusual greed or ambition). Organizations are great levelers. The structures and processes that regulate behavior tend to reduce the significance of individual differences (Pfeffer and Davis-Blake 1989; but see House et al. 1996). This speaks to a major implication of the analysis that follows; namely, that even the most ethical, law-abiding, and socially responsible organizational participants are at risk of engaging in wrongdoing.

The normal organizational wrongdoing perspective also assumes that wrongdoing can be the product of the full range of structures and processes that shape behavior in organizations. Further, it assumes that these structures and processes can give rise to wrongdoing in a fashion that sometimes is incidental to the production of right doing. The full range of structures and processes that shape behavior in organizations and that can facilitate wrongdoing include administrative systems, situational social influence, power structures, and the routine technological processes that are susceptible to accidents.

Finally, the normal organizational wrongdoing perspective assumes that wrongdoing is ubiquitous. Many scholarly articles and popular books on organizational wrongdoing begin as this book did, with a recitation of the several most prominent recent cases of wrongdoing with which readers are likely to be familiar: Worldcom, Tyco, Waste Management, and Enron. But there is a plethora of less prominent prior and recent cases, many of which will be examined in this book, including the quiz show fraud of the 1950s, the B.F. Goodrich brake fraud case of the 1960s, the Colonial Pipeline bribery case of the 1970s, the insider trading schemes of the 1980s, the Fen-phen appetite suppressant tragedy in the 1990s, and the mortgage meltdown and subsequent financial crisis of 2008. Indeed, organizational wrongdoing has a history dating back to the emergence of large organizations, including religious orders, nation states, and business enterprises. The first reported case of financial fraud, which resulted in the South Sea Bubble, and that precipitated a global financial crisis, occurred at the dawn of the joint stock company in 1711 (Carswell 2001).

Emile Durkheim, one of the founders of modern sociology, was among the first to address the ubiquity of wrongdoing in society (Durkheim 1984, 1997). He argued, to put it simplistically, that societies must create wrongdoing in order to survive. Societies are groups of people who share the same definition of acceptable behavior. But they cannot define acceptable behavior without at the same time defining unacceptable behavior. Further, societies benefit from singling out and punishing those who engage in unacceptable behavior. Doing so reminds members of society of the views regarding acceptable behavior that they share. And this reinforces social solidarity. In advanced societies, specialized organizations assume the necessary responsibility of drawing and policing the line separating right from wrong. These specialized organizations, whom sociologists call social control agents, effectively create wrongdoing, albeit in a fundamentally different way than the perpetrators of wrongdoing do.

Taking stock

I have argued that two broad perspectives apprehend organizational wrongdoing, a well-established framework that views wrongdoing as an abnormal phenomenon, and a still embryonic framework that views wrongdoing as a normal occurrence. I think the perspective that views wrongdoing as an abnormal phenomenon has merit. Thus, I devote time to elaborating the explanations of wrongdoing to which it gives rise: the rational choice and culture accounts. These explanations are covered in Chapters 4 and 5. But, I also think that the perspective that views organizational wrongdoing as a normal occurrence has merit. Further, I think that this perspective takes into account a broader range of less explored causes of wrongdoing. For this reason, I devote time to both elaborating and developing the explanations that flow from the normal organizational wrongdoing perspective: the administrative systems, situational social influence, power structure, accidental, and social control accounts. These explanations are covered in Chapters 7 through 11. There is one additional important explanation of organizational wrongdoing that I have not yet mentioned that represents a bridge between the two main perspectives on organizational wrongdoing. I describe and extend this account, the ethical decision explanation, in Chapter 6.

Figure 2 depicts the characteristics of the two perspectives on wrongdoing and the relationship between these perspectives and the eight explanations of wrongdoing. The first seven explanations of organizational wrongdoing focus on the perpetrators of wrongdoing. The eighth explanation, the social control account, focuses on those who draw the line separating right from wrong. Following the normal organizational wrongdoing perspective, I conceive of the first seven explanations as being rooted in different explanations of behavior in organizations more generally. Thus I begin my elaboration of each of these explanations by noting its roots.

Two ideal-typical approaches to understanding the causes of organizational wrongdoing

There are also two contrasting approaches to analyzing the causes of organizational wrongdoing. The first approach assumes that wrongdoers deliberate mindfully and rationally on the merits of engaging in the wrongful course of

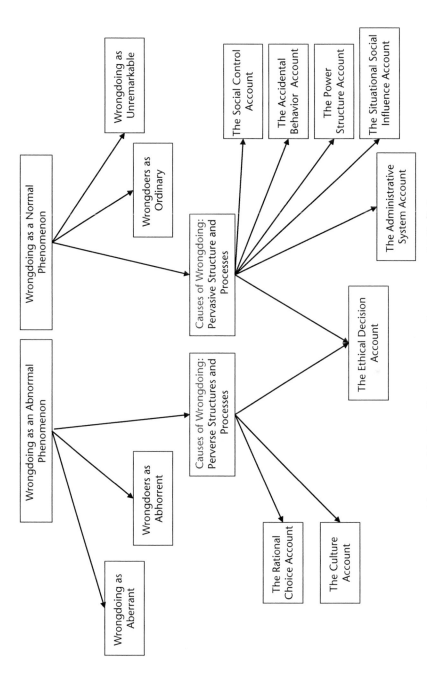

Figure 2. The Two Perspectives on Organizational Wrongdoing

action in question. It also assumes that wrongdoers largely are uninfluenced in their deliberation by their immediate social context. It also assumes that wrongdoers make discrete decisions to engage in wrongful behavior. Finally, this approach assumes that once people make a discrete decision to engage in wrongdoing, they develop a positive inclination to engage in the behavior in question. Because this is the most frequently employed outlook, I refer to it as the dominant approach.

The second approach to analyzing the causes of organizational wrongdoing embraces diametrically opposed assumptions. It assumes that wrongdoers often embark on organizational wrongdoing without engaging in mindful and rational deliberation. It also assumes that wrongdoers often embark on organizational wrongdoing under the influence of their immediate social context. It also assumes that wrongdoers often embark on organizational wrongdoing in a crescive fashion, that is, over a protracted period of time, during which they become increasingly embroiled in the wrongful behavior. Finally, this contrasting approach assumes that wrongdoers often embark on organizational wrongdoing without first developing a positive inclination to engage in the wrongful behavior. Because this outlook is less frequently but increasingly employed, I refer to it as the alternative approach.

While the two approaches to understanding the causes of organizational wrongdoing do not follow directly from the two perspectives on organizational wrongdoing characterized in the previous section, they are associated with the same groups of specific explanations of wrongdoing. The rational choice and culture accounts tend to embrace the dominant approach to analyzing wrongdoing. The administrative systems, situational social influence, power structure, accident, and social control accounts tend to embrace the alternative approach. Finally, the ethical decision account once again occupies a bridging position, spanning the two approaches. The fundamental characteristics of the dominant and alternative approaches to explaining organizational wrongdoing are represented in Table 1. I presume that the distinction between discrete decisions and crescive processes is obvious. But I suspect that the other three distinctions between the dominant and alternative approaches to explaining wrongdoing are less transparent. Thus, I explain them in more detail.

Mindlessness and bounded rationality

According to Langer and Moldoveanu (2000: 1–2), "mindfulness . . . can be best understood as the process of drawing novel distinctions" and "the process of drawing of novel distinctions can lead to a number of diverse consequences, including (1) a greater sensitivity to one's environment, (2) more openness to new information, (3) the creation of new categories for structuring perception,

Table 1. The Two Ideal Typical Approaches to Explaining Organizational Wrongdoing

	The Extent and Character of the Potential Wrongdoer's Deliberation	The Potential Wrongdoer's Immediate Environment	The Temporal Character of the Potential Wrongdoer's Transition into Wrongdoing	The Extent to which the Potential Wrongdoer's Transition into Wrongdoing is Intentional	The Explanations that Employ the Approach
Dominant Approach	Mindful and Rational	Situational Vacuum	Discrete Decision	Positive Inclination	Rational Choice, Culture, and Ethical Decision Theory
Alternative Approach	Mindless and Boundedly Rational	Situational Embeddedness	Crescive	Absence of Positive Inclination	Administrative Systems, Situational Social Influence, Power Structure, Accidental Behavior, Social Control, and Ethical Decision Theory

and (4) enhanced awareness of multiple perspectives in problem solving. The subjective 'feel' of mindfulness is that of a heightened state of involvement and wakefulness or being in the present." Importantly, mindfulness includes an attention to intuition and emotion. As Langer and Moldoveanu (2000) put it, "mindfulness is not a cold cognitive process. When one is actively drawing novel distinctions, the whole individual is involved." Weick and Roberts (1993: 361), who draw on Ryle (1949), have offered a very similar concept, "heedfulness." According to them, "people act heedfully when they act more or less carefully, critically, consistently, purposefully, attentively, studiously, vigilantly, conscientiously, pertinaciously." Because mindfulness and heedfulness are virtually identical concepts, and because the term *mindfulness* is more familiar to the average reader, in this book I will use mindfulness exclusively.

The dominant explanations of organizational wrongdoing assume that organizational participants are mindful. But the alternative approach that I champion in this book assumes that organizational participants often embark on wrongdoing in a mindless manner. In Langer and Moldoveanu's words (2000: 2), when we behave mindlessly "we rely on distinctions and categories drawn in the past (and) rules and routines are more likely to govern our behavior, irrespective of the current circumstances." In Weick and Robert's words (1993: 362) heedless behavior is "careless, unmindful, thoughtless, unconcerned, indifferent" and represents "a failure to see, to taken note of, to be attentive to."

Rationality has been defined in many ways. In this book I employ a commonsense definition of rationality that equates it with the thorough analysis of complete data pertaining to alternative courses of action. There are two types of rationality. Substantive rationality is the thorough normative assessment of complete data pertaining to the ends one seeks to attain. Formal rationality is the thorough cost-benefit analysis of complete data pertaining to the means used to attain chosen ends (Schroyer, 1975).

The dominant explanations of organizational wrongdoing assume that organizational participants, when mindful, deliberate in a rational way. But the alternative approach that I champion in this book assumes that organizational participants, when mindful, often embark on wrongdoing in a boundedly rational manner. Bounded rationality is mindfulness that is compromised by the limited capacity of human beings to accumulate and process information. Put crudely, the world is a complicated place and, as a result, the information required to conduct thorough cost-benefit or normative deliberations about behaviors and their consequences often is extensive. Further, people are boundedly rational, that is, cognitively limited in their ability to make thorough cost-benefit calculations, normative assessments, or ethical decisions even when the amount of information needed to conduct a thorough analysis, assessment, or decision is modest (March and Simon 1958).

Mindlessness is well illustrated by the tendency to react automatically to one's environment, following innate predispositions, learned social codes, or organizational rules and protocols. For example, Langer and associates (Langer, Blank, and Chanowitz 1978) conducted a study that showed that students waiting in line to use a photocopying machine were more likely to let another student "cut ahead" of them if the other student provided a reason for requesting to cut ahead, even when the reason the other student supplied simply restated his/her request to cut ahead (i.e. the student justified their need to cut ahead by saying, essentially, that they needed to cut ahead). Langer contends that human beings have an innate tendency or internalized social code that dictates we accept requests that have justifications.

The complex world/bounded rationality dilemma is illustrated well by Dennis Gioia's description of his job as Ford Motor Company's Field Recall Coordinator. Gioia writes, "It is difficult to convey the overwhelming complexity and pace of the job of keeping track of so many active or potential recall campaigns. It remains the busiest, most information-filled job I have ever held or would want to hold. Each case required a myriad of information-gathering and execution stages. I distinctly remember that the information-processing demands led me to confuse the facts of one problem case with another on several occasions, because the tell-tale signs of recall candidate cases were so similar" (Gioia, 1992: 382). I will return to Dennis Gioia and Ford in the next chapter because Gioia was one of the safety coordinators who recommended against recalling the Ford Pinto, despite mounting evidence that the compact car was susceptible to bursting into flames when impacted from the rear at relatively slow speeds.

The immediate social context

All human behavior is, fundamentally, social action. The human experience consists largely of exposure to socially constructed input. For example, the words we hear and speak are interpretable only in the context of a shared language. And the objects we see are acquired, manipulated and appreciated, and exchanged only within the context of markets, scientific systems, and cultures. The dominant explanations of organizational wrongdoing assume that wrongdoers are influenced by their social context in this way. But the alternative approach that I champion in this book assumes that organizational participants also are influenced by their social context in a more immediate way. Specifically, it focuses on the administrative structures (e.g. rules and standard operating procedures), situational social influence processes (e.g. small-group dynamics), power structures (e.g. formal authority and resource dependence), technological systems (e.g. task interdependencies), and social control relationships (e.g. interactions with law enforcement officials) in which organizational participants are typically embedded. And it considers how these structures and processes can influence how people think and behave in the moment.

The absence of positive inclinations

A positive inclination to engage in a course of action represents a state of mind in which a person views the course of action as desirable, in particular, relative to available alternative courses of action. It is important to distinguish a positive inclination to act in a particular way from a disposition to act in a particular way, because psychologists use the term *disposition* in a very precise way. Inclinations to engage in a course of action are psychological states that are *produced in the situation* (Pfeffer and Davis-Blake 1989). Dispositions are psychological states that, by contrast, *people bring to situations* and that influence the way they think and act in situations. Dispositions include personality characteristics, need states, attitudes, preferences, and motives or goals (House, Shane, and Herold 1996). Dispositions are relatively stable; that is, they tend to persist over time and across situations. But they can vary in stability and even can be influenced by experience. For example, personality characteristics generally are understood to be relatively immutable, but need states are recognized to vary according to need satisfaction.

The dominant explanations of organizational wrongdoing assume that organizational participants develop a positive inclination to engage in a wrongful course of action before embarking on the course of action. The prototypical dominant explanation assumes that positive inclinations to engage in a course of action are produced by some type of deliberation. Regardless of their origin, though, positive inclinations to engage in a behavior are the precursors to intentions to act and actual action. The alternative approach to understanding organizational wrongdoing that I advocate assumes that people do not always develop positive inclinations to engage in wrongdoing before they embark on it. The prototypical alternative explanation of organizational wrongdoing assumes that people sometimes embark on wrongful behavior mindlessly, and as a result never develop a positive inclination or even an intention to act. Instead, action is, for lack of a better word, automatic. In fact, the alternative approach allows that organizational participants sometimes embark on wrongful courses of action even though they are negatively inclined to engage in the behavior. Such instances involve some form of compulsion or coercion.

Taking stock

I have argued that two approaches have been used to understand the causes of organizational wrongdoing, a well-established dominant outlook and a newer but increasingly popular alternative one. I think the dominant approach to explaining organizational wrongdoing taps an important dimension of wrongdoing in organizations. Certainly, people sometimes deliberate mindfully and rationally, in relative social isolation, make discrete decisions, and develop positive inclinations to engage in wrongdoing. But I also think that the alternative approach to explaining wrongdoing is valid. That is, I believe that people sometimes slip into wrongdoing over time, in a mindless and boundedly rational fashion, influenced by their social context, without ever developing a positive inclination to do so. Further, I believe the alternative approach captures complexities that sometimes characterize organizational wrongdoing that the dominant approach does not tap. And this belief reinforces my motivation to not only elaborate but develop the administrative systems, situational social influence, power structure, accident, social control, and ethical decision explanations of organizational wrongdoing—accounts that to varying extents embrace the alternative approach to explaining wrongdoing. It also leads me to complete my presentation of each of the eight explanations of organizational wrongdoing with an assessment of the extent to which it embraces the alternative assumptions about how organizational participants come to engage in wrongdoing. Signs that explanations of wrongdoing fail to embrace the alternative assumptions provide impetus to move on to other theories that embrace the assumptions more consummately.

An illustration of the two ideal typical approaches to understanding the causes of organizational wrongdoing

In this section I draw on Paul Krimmage's account of his experience with banned performance-enhancing substances (i.e. doping) as a professional bicycle racer to illustrate the two ideal typical approaches to explaining organizational wrongdoing elaborated above. I also draw on his account to introduce the reader to the sort of evidence that I will use to illustrate the ideas presented in the book. Krimmage is a controversial figure in professional bike-racing circles. When he left professional cycling, he embarked on a career in journalism. And since then, in print and public forums, he persistently has questioned not only the cycling community's commitment to eradicating doping but also the purity of the sport's leading cyclists, most notoriously, Lance Armstrong. Some question Krimmage's motivation for zealously pursuing the doping issue. But as far as I know, no one has questioned the veracity of his account of his own experiences.

Paul Krimmage began bike racing as an amateur in his home country of Ireland when he was 10 years old and jumped to the professional ranks when he was 24. He rode as a professional from the winter of 1986 through the summer of 1989, eventually competing three times in the Tour de France (being one of only a handful of Irish professionals to have ridden in the famous multi-day race at that point). He ended his career on the twelfth day of the 1989 Tour de France, when he, like many who start the race, fell behind and was forced to abandon the contest.

Professional cyclists used a variety of substances believed to enhance performance, including nitroglycerine, cocaine-based substances, and strychnine, as early as the last years of the nineteenth century. Officials and the general public only became seriously concerned about the use of performance-enhancing substances in 1967, when a rider died from ingestion of amphetamines during a race. Around this time, various governing bodies, most notably the International Olympic Committee and the International Cycling Union, began establishing rules that prohibited the use of specific substances. Nevertheless, use of performance enhancers in cycling continued and is believed to be prevalent even today. This is partly because it has proven technically difficult and politically problematic to develop and institute reliable methods of detecting banned substances. But, it is also partly because enterprising members of the cycling community have developed new performance-enhancing substances, when technical advances and political will has allowed for the design and implementation of rigorous methods of detecting existing banned substances.

When Krimmage entered the ranks of the professionals, many cyclists were using amphetamines (as a stimulant on race days) as well as cortisone and testosterone (to aid recovery during training and after races). And some riders were experimenting with a wider range of steroids, hormones, and more exotic chemicals such as erythropoietin (EPO) that became a part of the regular training and racing regimen of many riders in the 1990s. Krimmage wrote a memoire of his cycling career, *Rough Ride*, in which he frankly discussed his experience with banned performance enhancers. He raced clean for most of his career, but used amphetamines on three occasions in 1987.

Some of Krimmage's recollections appear consistent with the dominant approach to explaining organizational wrongdoing, recollections that suggest he engaged in focused and clearheaded deliberations, in the context of little consequential social interaction with others, over a relatively short period of time, and that this for the most part led to a positive inclination to eschew the use of banned performance-enhancing substances. For example, Krimmage recalls contemplating the use of banned performance enhancers during his first Tour de France in 1986. The Tour includes over 20 stages (separate component races), most of which cover more than 100 miles, and some of which include the summiting of multiple steep mountain peaks, all within a period of a month. For the first eight days of the race, Krimmage rode strong and performed well. But on the ninth day, severe fatigue set in. And this led him to contemplate doping. In Krimmage's words, "I was knackered. My batteries went completely flat. With fourteen stages still to race, I had a decision to make. A big decision. The biggest decision of my life. Did I want them re-charged (pp. xv)?" After contemplating the question, he decided against doping. As he put it, "On the Tour's ninth day, sport betrayed me. I was not prepared to take drugs to further my career in the sport (pp. xvi)." He would go on to recall that his decision was partly a matter of principle, but also partly a matter of fear, two factors upon which he elaborates later in his memoire.

Other of Krimmage's recollections, though, appear more consistent with the alternative approach to explaining organizational wrongdoing. Some of these recollections indicate that he revisited the issue of using banned substances many times, and that his behavior evolved over time, partly as the result of his many decisions. When Krimmage began his career as a professional cyclist, he considered the ingestion and especially the injection of any substance (legal or banned) to be doping. He declined offers of completely legal vitamin B-12 injections. He even declined offers of legal oral vitamin supplements and caffeine pills. But over time, he incorporated these and other legal chemical aids (such as those that aided digestion) in his training regimen and pre-race preparations. And eventually, on three occasions in a two-week period, he took banned amphetamine injections. In the two years following this relatively short period of doping, though, he remained "clean."

Further, some of his recollections suggest that the deliberations that led to changes in his behavior were on occasion compromised, short-circuited, and even post hoc. For example, during the 1987 Tour of Italy, a doctor entered his room after a very tough stage and offered him an intravenous feeding of glucose. Team doctors and trainers had offered him pills and injections on numerous previous occasions, but he had always declined the offerings, worrying that the pills or injections might include banned performance enhancers. But on this occasion, Krimmage recalls that he simply offered his arm, having too little energy to question what other, possibly banned, substances might be in the drip.

Later Krimmage recalls his state of mind just before he decided to use amphetamines for the first time. He fell behind and was forced to abandon the 1987 Tour de France and, in a state of depression, suspended training. Weeks later, he was scheduled to ride in the first of the series of day races known as the "French Classics" that follow the Tour. Professionals were paid on contract by race organizers to ride in these day races, also called criteriums, which were more performances than competitions. While most bike race courses are open and spectators can watch the action for free, the French Classic courses were closed and spectators were charged admission. Further, the leading veteran riders covertly predetermined the outcomes of these day races, awarding victory to the cyclists who had recently distinguished themselves in the Tour de France. Krimmage worried that he might not be able to "perform," by which he meant keep pace with the other riders, most of whom he knew would be "charging," that is, using amphetamines. And he worried that if he did not perform, he might not get paid. But his reasoning was anything but cool and collected. As Krimmage recalled:

> Today is different: today they are paying to see a spectacle, and therefore we are obliged to perform. What if I can't? What if I'm unable to follow the others? ... Will the manager still pay me my contract? Will I have the neck to approach him for it? I shouldn't have come here—but hell, I need the money. Ann (Krimmage's fiancée) is living with me now. There's more expense, more responsibility. . . . I sit on the bed watching the others get ready, waiting for the moment. I know it has to happen. I'm waiting for it to happen. Fuck it, I want it to happen. The pressure—I can't take this pressure. It happens: the smiles. . . . a bag is produced. In it small white ampoules of amphetamine and a handful of short syringes. A glance is thrown in my direction. My 'chastity' is well known within the team but it is only polite to offer. I scratch my head and breathe in deeply. If I walk out through the door with only the hotel lunch in my system I will crack mentally. As a result I will probably be dropped (off the back of the main pack of riders) and ridiculed after two laps. I can't face any more humiliation. The pressure. I need the money. I nod in acceptance.

After Krimmage returned home from the race, he revisited his "decision" to use amphetamines earlier in the day. But again, his deliberations were anything but organized. As Krimmage recalls, "The events of the day are turning in my head, the arguments for and against crossing my head like a tennis ball in a seemingly never-ending rally. The 'againsts' are hitting beautifully. . . . But the 'fors' return with some lovely volleys." Some of his vacillation likely was due to the amphetamine molecules still coursing through his system hours after the race. But some likely was due to the complexity of the decision. Over the course of his memoire, Krimmage considers the many pros and cons of doping.

The pros were relatively straightforward. Banned substances could not make him a winner. But they could help him become an effective *domestique* (a rider who helps the team's best riders win) and thus could earn him the admiration of his fellow riders and the approval of his *directeur sportif* (team manager). The admiration of his fellow riders could bring him acceptance: he could become "one of the boys." And the approval of the directeur sportif could mean survival as a professional cyclist, and survival meant a modicum of acclaim (and, perhaps more importantly, escape from derision), as well as subsistence for himself and his family. Finally, once he took the plunge, he learned that the use of performance enhancers provided him with a sense of self efficacy that fortified him for competition. And when he rejected doping, he experienced a disheartening sense of futility. Races that he had previously contested successfully, he now entered anticipating defeat, believing that it was impossible for him to surpass riders who had charged.

The cons were also numerous and possibly more difficult to weigh. He feared the guilt that he expected to experience in the wake of doping, as doping violated closely held values that were internalized as a child. He also feared detection and the repercussions of detection. He idolized his father, who had been a successful amateur cyclist. And he relished the admiration of his Irish compatriots, who followed his career closely. He knew he would suffer great embarrassment if he used banned substances and his doping was detected and made public. More practically, he feared the effects of doping. He had heard that the use of steroids, hormones, and other chemicals could result in physical harm and even death. Further, he feared that the use of these substances might be addictive. Finally, he found the very act of injecting substances into his body repulsive.

Krimmage used amphetamines twice more in the following two weeks. He recalled that it was "easy to slip into a routine," which suggests that he did not deliberate much, if at all, before using amphetamines on these occasions. Further, he wrote, "my new habit started to worry me. I was losing control of my ability to say no." This suggests that he found it difficult to deliberate on these occasions or perhaps to act on his deliberations. As a result, he decided never again to put himself in the position of entering a race without adequate training, and he remained clean for the remainder of his four-year career.

Krimmage also provides recollections that suggest that others in his immediate environment played an important role in his decision making or lack thereof. When recounting his decision not to dope during his first Tour de France, Krimmage made reference to the possible influence of others, which he did his best to resist. He wrote, "I had witnessed abuse of drugs on a number of occasions after joining the professionals, I tried to block out the fact that you could break the rules in this sport and get away with it (pp. xv)." But the widespread use of banned substances among professional racers was impossible to ignore. Krimmage described feeling that fellow riders and team officials expected him to use performance-enhancing substances because doing so would increase his capacity to contribute to the team effort. As a *domestique*, it was his job to help the team's better riders get and remain in a position to win races. And Krimmage's ability to do this hinged on his physical condition. As a result, on the occasions when he refused to use performance enhancers, he felt "embarrassed" (p. 125) and even "guilty" (pp. 113–114). Ultimately, Krimmage's refusal to use performance enhancers limited the degree to which his teammates accepted him into their inner circle. And he very much wanted to be "one of the boys" (pp. 91, 98, 146, 150). So Krimmage began to avoid situations when he might be asked to participate in doping. Finally, when he accepted amphetamines for the first time, he remembers thinking, "I have joined the club and it feels almost satisfying to have done so (p. 147)." But he still needed his teammates for one very practical reason. As already noted, Krimmage found injecting himself with any substance (legal or banned) repulsive. As a result, he relied on his teammates to perform the injections on the three occasions on which he used amphetamines.

Finally, on several occasions, Krimmage seemed not just to feel pressure to use performance enhancers but to feel compelled to do so. His decision to use performance enhancers seemed to be as much the result of coercion as it was the result of weighing of pros and cons: He doped despite being *disinclined* to do so. Krimmage recalls a teammate who put pressure on him to "toe the line" at a particular race. The teammate said that it was Krimmage's "duty" to defend the team's leading rider, which was an obligation that Krimmage willingly accepted. Further, he added that doping was just "part of the job," which was where Krimmage drew the line. Remembering that day, Krimmage wrote, "I felt he was putting a gun to my head (p. 114)." Ultimately, Krimmage placed the blame for doping on the sport's power brokers: the team sponsors, the team officials, the race organizers, and even the sports media. He felt that they created a coercive system in which riders had no choice but to dope or leave the sport. Indeed, towards the end of his career, his anger at the power structure became an additional factor strengthening his resolve to remain clean.

How can we make sense of Paul Krimmage's general abstinence from performance-enhancing substances between 1986 and 1989, and his isolated use of amphetamines during a three-week period in 1987? And more importantly, how can we make sense of what Krimmage tells us about his thoughts, feelings, and actions in regards to doping throughout his professional career? In *Normal Organizational Wrongdoing*, I will attempt to show that the dominant approach to explaining organizational wrongdoing and the specific accounts of wrongdoing that employ it, provide a useful, but incomplete, picture of the factors influencing Krimmage's (and other wrongdoers') behavior. I will also attempt to show that the alternative approach to explaining organizational wrongdoing and the accounts of wrongdoing that employ it provide a useful complement to the dominant approach, filling in important parts of the picture that otherwise would remain obscured from sight. Before embarking on this effort, though, a few words about the book's message and my overarching objectives are in order.

The book's message and my overarching objectives

I have outlined two overarching perspectives on organizational wrongdoing. I have also elaborated two approaches to understanding the causes of wrongdoing. Finally, I have said that while I believe both perspectives and approaches are valid, I favor the normal organizational wrongdoing perspective and the alternative approach to explaining organizational wrongdoing. This stance implies two messages, one of which might be considered optimistic and the other of which might be considered pessimistic. The optimistic message is that the number of bad apples in organizations, people who intentionally engage in wrongful acts, is small relative to the number of good apples, people who strive to pursue rightful behavior. The pessimistic message is that a large number of structures and processes without which organizations could not function can cause a significant number of the many good apples to embark on wrongful behavior or to join the few bad apples intentionally pursing wrongful courses of action. On balance, the book's pessimistic message drowns out its optimistic one. To put it another way, this book dwells on the dark side of organizations more than it does the bright side.

I do my best to represent the determinants of organizational wrongdoing, especially the factors that lead good apples to become involved in wrongdoing, in a dispassionate manner. That is, I try to withhold moral judgments of organizational wrongdoers. This is partly because the book is a social scientific analysis, not a normative commentary. It is also partly because my analysis leads me to conclude that the labeling of acts as wrongful and of individuals as culpable is one of the dimensions through which wrongdoing is created. But, I must admit, I also withhold moral judgments partly because I sympathize with many organizational wrongdoers. They face a complex world that their limited cognitive resources leave them ill equipped to navigate. Moreover, intransigent organizational structures, strong social psychological processes, daunting power dynamics, and other formidable aspects of their immediate social context influence their thoughts and actions. Finally wrongdoers' behavior evolves in ways that are difficult to track and is subject to constraints that are difficult to overcome. As I dug deep into the actual instances of organizational wrongdoing recounted in this book, I came to the conclusion that even the most ethical, socially responsible, and law-abiding people are at significant risk of becoming entangled in wrongdoing when placed in an organizational context.

I do not, though, think that most people who engage in wrongdoing in organizations should be absolved of guilt and punishment. While I sympathize with many of the wrongdoers described in this book, for the most part

I do not consider their behavior to be acceptable, nor do I consider the consequences of their behavior to be tolerable.[1] It is true that attributions of cause can be used as the basis of attributions of responsibility and blame (Margolis 2001). Those who see organizational participants as subject to powerful external forces might be more inclined to give them a free pass. This is not, though, my inclination. I hope that by contributing to understanding of how organizational participants come to engage in wrongful behavior, I provide insights that can help organizational participants who might otherwise engage in deplorable forms of wrongdoing avoid becoming ensnared in such behavior.

But, the first order of business is to address some technical matters. In the next chapter I present the definition of right and wrong that I will use, the theory building approach that I will follow, and the research methods that I will employ in this book. Once that is done, I can begin to elaborate the eight explanations of organizational wrongdoing that I believe organize thinking on this subject. Only after I have considered the eight explanations of wrongdoing can I return to thinking about how wrongdoing in and by organizations might be curbed.

---

[1] I intentionally hedge when stating my personal opposition to organizational wrongdoing (implicitly allowing that I find some forms of wrongdoing acceptable) because, as will become clear in Chapter 11, I also think that the labeling of behavior as wrongful is influenced by interests and power.

3

Definitions, Theoretical Development, and Method

Introduction

I have to address two matters, before I can begin elaborating the eight specific explanations of organizational wrongdoing. First, I need to delineate the definition of organizational wrongdoing that I employ in this book. I begin by elaborating the three underlying criteria according to which organizational behavior can be considered wrongful: the law, ethics, and social responsibility. Then I outline two alternative approaches to defining organizational wrongdoing that capture these three underlying criteria: the exegetical and sociological approaches. After considering the advantages and disadvantages of each, I opt for the sociological approach and describe it in more detail. Then I delineate the kind of organizational wrongdoing that will be the primary focus of my attention: collective wrongdoing.

Second, I must describe the nature of both the theoretical explanations of wrongdoing that I develop and the empirical evidence that I present. The remainder of this book is structured as an elaboration of eight explanations of organizational wrongdoing, illustrated with descriptions of actual instances of wrongdoing. But it is based on two separate interrelated types of analysis: a theoretical analysis of prior theory and research on organizational wrongdoing, and an empirical analysis of actual instances of wrongdoing. I conclude the chapter by describing how I conducted these two types of analyses so that the reader can critically evaluate the basis of the arguments I develop in the course of the book.

Defining wrongdoing

Three underlying criteria used to characterize behavior as wrongful

THE LAW

Three types of standards can be used to evaluate whether a behavior crosses the line separating right from wrong: the law, ethical principles, and social responsibility doctrines. The law consists of written guidelines or prohibitions. Conformity to these guidelines or prohibitions is monitored and adjudicated by full-time law enforcement professionals employed by local, state, or federal governmental agencies. Organizational participants can run afoul of two types of law: criminal and civil law. Criminal and civil law differ in the types of behaviors to which they pertain, the kinds of law enforcement professionals who monitor compliance to their provisions, the procedures used to adjudicate transgressions of those provisions, and the kinds of penalties applied to transgressors. We occasionally will refer to these differences.

Scholars who study illegal behavior in organizations distinguish between two kinds of illegal behavior. Illegal behavior that benefits employees at the expense primarily of their organization is called white-collar crime (e.g. embezzlement). Illegal behaviors that benefits the organization at the expense primarily of buyers, suppliers, competitors, and other third parties is called corporate crime (e.g. illegal dumping of toxic waste). I will not observe this distinction for two reasons. First, illegal behavior can benefit both the organization and the organizational participants who perpetrate it. In many of the instances of wrongdoing described in this book, such as the illegal special purpose entities at Enron discussed at length in Chapter 9, this was the case. Second, the distinction between white-collar and corporate crime rests partly on assumptions about wrongdoers' motivations: specifically, whether wrongdoers seek to advance their firm's or their own interests. But not all behavior can be considered, strictly speaking, motivated. The argument that much organizational wrongdoing cannot be considered motivated behavior is among the central claims of this book.

ETHICAL PRINCIPLES

Ethical principles consist of written or unwritten guidelines and prohibitions. Conformity to ethical guidelines or prohibitions can be monitored and enforced by a collegial body or can be policed more informally. Some ethical principles are embodied in official professional codes of ethics, such as those that cover certified public accountants. Conformity to these codes of ethics tends to be monitored and enforced by professional societies, such as the American Institute of Certified Public Accountants. Failure to conform to such codes of ethics can be punished by official sanctions, such as prohibition from serving as a public accountant. Other ethical principles, though, are embodied only in widely shared understandings, such as those that proscribe lying. Conformity to these ethical principles is monitored by self-appointed evaluators, such as representatives of the mass media. Failure to conform to such ethical principles tends to be punished by general approbation.

Business ethics scholars distinguish between two broad types of ethical views: utilitarian and deontological perspectives. Utilitarian perspectives focus on the likely consequences of a prospective behavior. The most rigorous utilitarian view takes into account the interests of all those who might be affected by a prospective behavior and factors in whether their interests are served or harmed by the behavior in question. It considers actions that provide the greatest good for the greatest number to be the most ethical. It is difficult to identify all the people who might be affected by a prospective behavior, to determine the interests of all these people, to quantify the benefits and harm that a prospective behavior might generate for them, and then sum these benefits and harms across all potentially affected people. For this reason, simplified versions of the utilitarian view typically are employed. The most popular simplified version of the utilitarian approach considers an action to be ethical if it leads to greater benefit than harm. But even this simple rule of proportionality can be difficult to apply because it requires that very different benefits and harms be compared with one another in a quantitative fashion. Consider, for example, the issue of whether to allow forestry companies to log an area that provides the habitat for an endangered species. Application of the simplified utilitarian approach requires that policy makers weight the benefits of preserving the livelihood of a relatively small group of forestry workers against the harm of eliminating a rare species to a larger community of citizens.

Deontological perspectives evaluate prospective behaviors on the basis of their alignment with fundamental principles regarding right and wrong. There are two main deontological views. The human rights view assumes that all human beings have, by virtue of birth, the same basic privileges and protections. And it considers any action that violates a person's basic human rights to be unethical. The U.S. Bill of Rights often is used as a guide when enumerating the basic human rights that organizational participants possess. These rights include the right to free speech, the right to privacy, the right to due process, the right to free consent, and the right to follow one's conscience. Of course, one could (and many have) posited other basic human rights, such as the right to a safe workplace and the right to adequate health care. The right to free consent, which can be thought of as the right to be fully informed of the conditions surrounding one's existence, is thought by many to be the supreme employee right. Indeed, some believe that most of an employee's basic human rights can be abrogated, as long as the employee is informed ahead of time that, if hired, this would be the case. Thus it is generally believed that workers' right to privacy can be abrogated (e.g. by random drug testing), as long as employees are informed when hired that this right will not be respected after they are hired.

The justice norms view assumes that all social groups are regulated by norms of fairness that pertain to the distribution of rewards, the allocation of punishments, and the enforcement of regulations governing behavior more generally. And it considers any action that contradicts these norms of fairness to be unethical. There are three types of justice norms. Distributive norms pertain to the criteria according to which benefits are distributed in an organization. For example, in the U.S., it generally is considered unfair if workers are promoted according to criteria (such as skin color) that do not pertain to their ability to perform the job into which they might be elevated. Compensatory norms pertain to how punishments are meted out in an organization. For example, in the U.S., it often is considered unfair if lower-level workers are asked to pay (in layoffs and salary reductions) for the strategic errors of top management, especially when the top managers continue to enjoy salary increases and bonuses. Administrative norms pertain to the criteria according to which any organizational policy is applied in specific circumstances. In the U.S., it typically is considered unfair to apply an organizational policy selectively so as to advantage one person or group to the disadvantage of others. For example, it would be considered unfair to circumvent an organization's stated policy to promote from within in order to give a friend of the boss who is not currently employed by the organization the inside track for a job.

SOCIAL RESPONSIBILITY DOCTRINES
Social responsibility doctrines also consist of unwritten guidelines and prohibitions. Conformity to these guidelines or prohibitions, though, is exclusively monitored and enforced informally. Socially irresponsible behavior consists of actions that are believed to damage society in a material way. For example, organizations that rely primarily on non-renewable sources of energy can be considered socially irresponsible insofar as their behavior can be said to undermine the ability of the Earth to sustain human life in future generations. Social responsibility doctrines typically are used to evaluate the performance of private-sector organizations. The two most popular doctrines used to evaluate business organizations are the shareholder and stakeholder approaches.

Most business leaders and many management scholars employ the shareholder model to identify socially irresponsible behavior. The shareholder model conceptualizes the firm as a collection of people or entities that provide capital to the firm. The most important capital providers are the people and institutions that own stock in the firm. The other major capital providers include financial institutions that lend money to the firm. According to the shareholder model, managers' primary responsibility is to maximize share-holder wealth. Any behavior that managers pursue that does not maximize shareholder wealth is socially irresponsible. The shareholder model is rooted in the belief that in a free-market economy, the pursuit of self interest on the part of owners results in the greatest good for the greatest number.

Many management scholars and an increasing number of business leaders, though, use the "stakeholder model" to identify socially irresponsible behavior. The stakeholder model conceptualizes the firm as a coalition of groups who stand to benefit from or to be harmed by the firm. For example, public corporations typically are conceptualized as coalitions that include, at a minimum, shareholders, employees (perhaps represented by unions), governmental bodies, and the communities in which they are situated. According to the stakeholder model, it is the firm's responsibility to balance the interests of all members of the coalition that supports it. The stakeholder model is rooted in the belief that because all companies must obtain charters from the government in order to incorporate themselves, they have a responsibility to operate in ways that serve the public interest.

Two alternative ways to define wrongdoing

One can readily elaborate the three general criteria used to evaluate whether behavior crosses the line between right and wrong in the abstract, as I have done above. It often is difficult, though, to apply these general criteria to specific behaviors. As a result, scholars who study wrongdoing often do not define their object of inquiry precisely. One can use two alternative strategies to define wrongdoing in terms of the three general criteria discussed above. One can take an exegetical approach, which entails analyzing works in the fields of philosophy, theology, and social criticism, and using that analysis to develop a unified understanding of wrongdoing. Tenbrunsel and Smith-Crowe (2008) recently recommended that ethical decision theorists take this approach, advocating that theorists take advantage of the extensive literatures in philosophy and theology on the topic of ethics to develop a definition of unethical behavior that all researchers can embrace. Alternatively, one can take a sociological approach, which entails adopting understanding of the law, ethics, and social responsibility that are in use in society. Among several sociological approaches from which one could chose, the most common define wrongdoing as any behavior that those responsible for monitoring and controlling wrongful behavior, called social control agents, label as wrongful. Below I consider the advantages and disadvantages of both approaches, ultimately opting for the second.

THE EXEGETICAL APPROACH

The exegetical approach has at least two important advantages. First, it possesses the potential to produce a definition of wrongdoing that would be temporally and spatially invariant. Because this approach entails using a single body of thought produced by legal scholars, philosophers, and theologians from around the world, it could produce a definition of wrongdoing that would only change as this body of thought evolves—something that occurs slowly over time. And insofar as this approach could produce a definition of wrongdoing that is stable, it could increase the likelihood that theorists and researchers would focus on the same empirical phenomenon, and thus increase the likelihood that their scholarly endeavors would generate cumulative knowledge.

Second, the exegetical approach allows for the explicit integration of normative and social scientific concerns, which both the pioneers of organizational science and some recent critics of the field might welcome. The founders of organization science explicitly characterized organizational science as an applied enterprise (Litchfield 1956; Thompson 1956). They likened organization science to engineering and medicine, contending that it marshaled knowledge generated by multiple disciplines to solve practical problems. Engineers synthesize knowledge from mathematics, chemistry, and physics to solve problems such as the design of bridges and chemical manufacturing processes. Organizational scientists integrate knowledge from economics, political science, sociology, and psychology to improve the efficiency and effectiveness of organizations. It is most definitely true that over time, theory and research in organization studies has focused increasingly on improving organizational efficiency, studying problems such as those related to worker motivation and group decision-making. But the earliest organization studies scholars explicitly recognized the furtherance of democracy and the suppression of corruption as goals that the new field of organization science should pursue (Boulding 1958). Rakesh Khurana's book, *From Higher Aims to Hired Hands* (2007), charts the changing focus of management education and research from broader societal concerns to narrow organizational ones, and implicitly endorses a return to the former.

As the field of organization science developed, though, practitioners have come to see it as a discipline rather than an applied field. And progressively they have embraced the Weberian notion that science should be "value-free" (Weber 1946). Recent critics of contemporary social science have argued that social scientists necessarily infuse the theory they develop and the research they conduct with the values that they hold. These critics maintain that social scientists who believe and assert that they theorize and research in a value-free way are imbuing their work implicitly with dominant and possibly oppressive values. These critics thus advocate that social scientists consider the value stance they bring to their work, incorporating values that have the potential to liberate and facilitate social change rather than dominate and reproduce the status quo (Van Maanen 1995a, 1995b). When applied to theory and research on wrongdoing, this perspective might entail defining wrongdoing in ways that depart from existing definitions, perhaps defining behavior that social scientists consider abhorrent as wrongful, even though contemporary social control agents do not concur. In this way, research on wrongdoing might bring to light and increase understanding of forms of behavior that many would consider objectionable but that dominant elements of society unintentionally or willfully ignore.

The exegetical approach, though, has one major disadvantage. It is unlikely to fulfill its potential to produce a single widely accepted definition of wrongdoing. Ultimately, whether a particular behavior is right or wrong according to the three criteria elaborated above is subject to dispute. The line distinguishing between socially responsible and socially irresponsible behavior is debatable because people differ in the social responsibility doctrines they embrace. The line distinguishing between ethical and unethical behavior is debatable because people differ with respect to the ethical principles to which they subscribe. Even the line distinguishing between legal and illegal behavior is debatable because legal scholars differ with respect to their views of the law and its interpretation.

THE SOCIOLOGICAL APPROACH

The sociological approach has three notable advantages. First, it offers those who embrace it a good chance to produce a single widely accepted definition of wrongdoing. If one adopts the sociological approach, the problem of defining wrongdoing becomes, to a significant extent, an empirical question. One must identify the entities that will be considered valid social control agents. Further, one must delineate the social control agent actions that will be considered bona fide labels. But once social control agents are identified and social control agent labels are delineated, then one need only observe social control agent actions to determine what behaviors are wrongful. I think there is a good chance that we can record and interpret observations of social control agent actions with reasonable unanimity.

Second, the sociological approach is well suited to addressing managerial concerns. As indicated above, the earliest organizational scientists viewed the field as an applied one, devoted to solving organizational problems. And for much of the field's history, for good and for bad, organization scientists have considered the field's primary constituency to be managers, and have focused on helping managers solve practical problems (Hambrick 1994; Bartunek 2003). Managers, by virtue of their pressing need to attend to market pressures, are most concerned with matters related to the success of their firms.

31

Thus, for good and for bad, they should be most interested in the causes of behavior that run afoul of social control agents, because such behaviors can result in sanctions that are costly to the organizations they lead. Finally, in contrast to the exegetical approach, the sociological approach aspires to separate normative from social scientific considerations. Most social scientists are committed to a value-free stance, famously articulated by Max Weber (1946). Thus, many social scientists will likely prefer this approach, although the possibility of a truly value-free social science admittedly is open to question.

The sociological approach does, though, suffer from two significant disadvantages. First, even if successful, it produces a definition of wrongdoing that is something of a moving target. The same social control agent over time can alter the criteria by which it judges behavior as wrongful. For example, the Supreme Court recently altered the range of behaviors covered by the honest services statue, which federal prosecutors have been using to pursue purported white-collar criminals (Connor 2010). Similarly, social control agents embrace different criteria to judge behavior as wrongful, depending on their societal context. For example, the same type of monetary exchange might be viewed as a gift in one country but a bribe in another. More vexing, different social control agents situated in the same time and place can embrace different criteria for labeling behavior wrongful. Thus, purported wrongdoers might be found guilty of crossing the line separating right from wrong in a civil court, but absolved of guilt in a criminal court, as recently was the case in connection with Blackwater Worldwide's involvement in the Nisoor Square killings in Iraq (Wilber 2010; Zucchino 2010).

Second, the sociological approach appears to exclude from analysis behaviors that might be considered objectionable, simply because they are not labeled wrongful by social control agents. As a result, the sociological approach might be considered to implicitly defend the status quo. If true, this would be a particularly serious disadvantage. For example, consider what most would regard as the objectionable behaviors perpetrated by private-security contractors in the early years of the Iraq War that were not labeled as wrongdoing by social control agents. Journalists reported instances in which security contractor employees killed or injured Iraqi citizens, sometimes while "on the job," but were in no way held responsible for these acts. An agreement negotiated by the U.S. government and the Iraqi Provisional Authority exempted private-security contractors from Iraqi law and placed them under U.S. military oversight. Further, the U.S. government instituted few formal regulations delineating appropriate private-security contractor behavior and provided minimal enforcement of those few guidelines. As a result, private-security contractor employees followed what they referred to as "big boy rules," a set of loose informal guidelines that only dictated that employees look out for themselves and refrain from engaging in behaviors that might jeopardize the safety of their co-workers. In this social control environment, private-security contractors essentially could do no wrong, because there were few rules to break and almost no one to enforce the few rules in place (Fainaru 2008).

THE APPROACH I TAKE

I adopt the sociological approach to defining wrongdoing in this book, primarily because the disadvantages of the exegetical approach are more significant than the disadvantages of the sociological approach, given the objective of this book. If I elaborated my own personal definition of wrongdoing, based on my reading of philosophy, theology, and social criticism, I would run a significant risk that my elaboration of the causes of organizational wrongdoing would be considered irrelevant by readers who do not share my definition of wrongdoing. By adopting the sociological approach to defining wrongdoing, I reduce that risk, because my personal views on this subject do not factor into my definition of wrongdoing. There is an important implicit fine-grained distinction here that bears explication. I do have strong personal beliefs about where the line between right and wrong should be drawn. But for the purposes of this book, I do not use those beliefs to inform my definition of wrongdoing. Instead, I use the definition of wrongdoing in practice as the definition of wrongdoing in this book.

I also adopt the sociological approach to defining wrongdoing because I think one of the potential disadvantages of this approach can be worked around and even turned into an advantage. As noted above, the sociological approach excludes from analysis behaviors that are not labeled wrongful by social control agents, even if many believe those behaviors are objectionable. But while the sociological approach prohibits study of such behavior as wrongdoing, it does not prohibit studying this behavior altogether. Such behavior can be analyzed using theories that have been employed to analyze right-doing, some of which we will consider in this book. For example, one can study the factors that cause private-security contractor employees to commit unprovoked violent acts against Iraqi citizens, even if this behavior is not classified as wrongful. Such a study might focus on the kinds of people recruited to work for private security contractors, some of whom struggled to succeed in peace-time settings and had prior records of wrongdoing (such as former policemen who had been terminated for the use of excessive force). It also might focus on the incentive structure inherent in the extremely chaotic and dangerous environment that characterizes modern-day Iraq, in which threats to one's safety can materialize unexpectedly and with substantial ambiguity.

More importantly, by defining wrongdoing as behavior that social control agents label as wrongful, the sociological approach implicitly recognizes that social control agents are as responsible for creating wrongdoing as are the perpetrators of wrongdoing, albeit in a fundamentally different way than the perpetrators of wrongdoing create wrongdoing. This implication of the sociological definition of wrongdoing dovetails with the final implication of the normal organizational wrongdoing perspective, elaborated in the previous chapter. By recognizing that social control agents create wrongdoing, the sociological approach opens up a line of inquiry that is largely ignored by organization studies scholars: the examination of the factors that cause behaviors to be labeled as wrongful. For example, in the case of private-security contractor misbehavior, the sociological approach to defining wrongdoing encourages social scientists to ask why private-security contractors were essentially unregulated in the opening years of the Iraq War. I will address this topic and this specific example in greater depth when I discuss the social control account of wrongdoing presented in Chapter 11.

Elaborating the sociological approach to defining wrongdoing

Now that I have chosen the sociological approach to defining wrongdoing, I need to elaborate it in two respects. First, I need to identify the entities that I will consider valid social control agents for the purposes of this book. Many entities exert social control over organizations and organizational participants, and thus could be considered valid social control agents. These entities vary in the formality of their constitution, the breadth of their jurisdiction, and the severity of the punishments that they can administer. Some social control agents are formally chartered, having legal standing and employing full-time professionals, while others are informally constituted, having no legal standing and relying extensively on volunteers. Some social control agents make credible claims to represent the broad public, while others make credible claims to represent only a restricted segment of the public (credible claims being those validated by a social control agent's constituency). Finally, some social control agents can imprison and fine wrongdoers. But others can only restrict wrongdoers' sphere of economic activity or tarnish wrongdoers' reputations. Social control agents that are formally constituted, have broad constituencies, and that wield the most significant punishments, enjoy the greatest primacy, that is, they command the most attention from potential organizational wrongdoers.

Managers are most concerned with governmental bodies, collectively referred to as "the state," because they are formally chartered, make credible claims to represent the broad public, and can impose significant punishments on wrongdoers (e.g. imprisonment and fines). But managers are also concerned with professional associations, interest groups, and the media. Professional associations such as the American Medical Association are formally chartered but can only make a credible claim to represent members of the profession and can only impose modest sanctions on wrongdoers (e.g. restriction of employment). Interest groups such as Mothers Against Drunk Drivers

[MADD] typically are even more informally constituted, relying primarily on a sea of dues-paying volunteers, and electing or appointing a small number of paid staff to fill administrative offices. They often make claims to represent an ill-defined subset of the broad public (e.g. in the case of MADD, those who oppose driving under the influence of alcohol and other substances believed to undermine driving acuity). And they can impose only weak sanctions such as product boycotts. Finally, the media generally is informally constituted (i.e. anyone can create a media organization). Media organizations can make claims to represent the broad public, but these claims are validated only weakly (e.g. indicated by readership or viewership). And media organizations can only hope to influence public opinion.

I primarily focus on the state in this book, because it enjoys the greatest primacy. Thus, I define organizational wrongdoing as any behavior that organizational participants perpetrate in the course of fulfilling their organizational roles (e.g., as directors, managers, and/or employees) that the state judges to be wrongful. I employ this conservative operationalization of the sociological approach because I want to reduce the chance that readers will think that I am not examining *real* wrongdoing. With this said, almost every instance of wrongdoing described in this book was labeled wrongful by multiple social control agents. Further, in many cases, the actions of non-governmental entities contributed to the state's decision to label the behavior as wrongful. And in some instances, one could argue that the non-governmental actors' labeling activity was more consequential for the wrongdoers than was the state's labeling actions.

For example, I will discuss the Enron debacle in considerable detail. The state played a central role in labeling behavior associated with Enron's collapse as wrongful. The U.S. Congress held hearings on Enron and various legal organizations indicting and prosecuting the firm and its officers. But the accounting profession and the media also played important subsidiary roles. In fact, *Fortune Magazine*'s investigative reporting on Enron provided a significant impetus for state intervention in this case. I will also discuss the rigging of television quiz shows in the 1950s at some length. The state played a somewhat smaller role in this case. The U.S. Congress held hearings on the fraud, and the New York Attorney General's office convened a grand jury to investigate it. But the media's actions proved more consequential. Newspapers, news magazines, and television news programs produced an avalanche of coverage that publicly shamed the participants to such an extent that they were unable to work in the industry for many years to come.

Second, I need to delineate the state actions that will be considered bona fide labels. I will consider an act to be wrongful if the state makes a concerted effort to designate the act a violation of the criminal or civil codes and/or imposes on the perpetrator some form of punishment. The state need not, though, be successful in its effort to label the act or impose punishment on the wrongdoer. In common parlance, I consider behaviors to be wrongful if the state labels the behavior as wrongful, even if that label does not subsequently "stick." For example, I consider the manufacture and sale of the Ford Pinto, which tests and subsequent customer experience revealed to be prone to bursting into flames when impacted from the rear at low speeds, to be wrongful behavior. Even though no one was convicted of a crime and only a handful of civil awards were upheld in connection with this case, a deluge of civil complaints were filed against Ford, and criminal indictments were handed down against several of the firm's executives. Similarly, I consider the rigging of television quiz show contests in the 1950s–1960s to be wrongful. Even though the authorities eventually concluded that the deception broke no federal or state laws, Congressional hearings were held and a grand jury was convened to look into the case.

Collective wrongdoing

Now that I have presented the definition of wrongdoing that I employ in this book, I need to define the type of wrongdoing on which I focus primarily. There are two broad types of organizational wrongdoing: wrongful behavior perpetrated by individuals and wrongful behavior carried out by collectivities. Individual wrongdoers work alone to perpetrate wrongful acts. For example, individuals are the principal embezzlers of organizational funds. Collectivities consist of two or more people who work together to carry out wrongful acts. For example, collectivities are required if prices in a market are to be fixed.

Further, there are two kinds of individuals within collectivities: initiators and recruits. Initiators are the first persons to pursue a particular wrongful course of action. Recruits are persons who join a wrongful course of action already in progress. Thus, a particular wrongful course of action might be initiated by a single individual or by a collectivity. Further, a particular wrongful course of action, once initiated by an individual or a collectivity, might attract other participants. If an individual initiates a wrongful course of action and then recruits others to join the pursuit, the wrongdoing evolves from an individual into a collective enterprise.

In this book I am interested primarily in wrongful courses of action that are perpetrated by collectivities. I think that most wrongful courses of action require at least the tacit cooperation of others and thus are at least nominally collective. Further, I think that collective wrongdoing wreaks more damage on organizations and societies than individual wrongdoing, because the more people involved in a wrongful course of action, the more it can accomplish. The most recent highly publicized cases of organizational wrongdoing appear to bear out this assertion. When ruling on a motion related to the Enron debacle, the Texas Court of Appeals noted, "the fall of Enron is not about one person or even a few people; it is the story of a host of actors.... asking the jury, or us, to look only at Lay, Fastow, Skilling, (Arthur) Anderson, and some of its partners, is like asking someone to look only at the eye of the hurricane and to ignore the furor surrounding it" (McLean and Elkind, 2004: 411). However, even older, less dramatic cases of organizational wrongdoing are consistent with this assertion. Later in the book I will refer to an instance in 1963 in which Colonial Pipeline Company made cash payments to two Woodbridge, New Jersey, public officials to secure building permits and right-of-way access to construct petroleum storage tanks on city property. This rather mundane instance of wrongdoing required orchestration by more than fifteen top and middle-level executives in four different companies (Mintz 1972).

Further, I am interested particularly in the processes through which wrongful courses of action that are initiated by individuals or groups attract recruits. I think that the vast majority of employees and managers are law-abiding, ethical, and socially responsible people who, left to themselves, would not initiate wrongful courses of action. I believe that most people who participate in wrongful courses of action are good people who are recruited to participate in bad behavior. Hence, much of this book is motivated by the desire to answer the question: Why do good people join others already embarked on a wrongful course of action?

Theoretical and empirical analyses

This book elaborates eight explanations of organizational wrongdoing and illustrates each with descriptions of actual instances of wrongdoing. I elaborate the eight explanations of organizational wrongdoing at the individual level of analysis. That is, I spotlight people as opposed to groups, organizations, industries, and larger social aggregates, and investigate the I that lead them to engage in wrongdoing. With that said, I take into account interpersonal interaction and small-group dynamics, as well as organizational and higher-level social structures and processes, because people are embedded in and influenced by these social structures and processes. While some theories of organizational wrongdoing take into account the socially embedded character of individual behavior, others do not. For example, much of the theory and research on ethical decision-making considered in Chapter 6 analyzes wrongdoing as if it does not occur within the context of organizations (or, as if the fact that it occurs in an organizational context does not matter). To remind readers that I am focusing on people who work in organizations and that I think people's organizational context impacts their behavior, I generally (but not exclusively) refer to them by the cumbersome moniker "organizational participants."

My presentation of individual-level explanations of organizational wrongdoing proceeds from dominant to alternative explanations, moving in the direction of explanations that increasingly embrace the notion that wrongdoing often is mindless and boundedly rational, shaped by the social context, temporally crescive, and devoid of positive inclination or intent. I do not, though, attempt to provide a comprehensive review of every individual-level theory of organizational wrongdoing. Instead, I strive to present the contours of the main approaches. The book is a product of two interrelated analyses, one theoretical and the other empirical. In the next two sections I explain the method underlying these two different, but in my case very much complementary, types of analyses.

Theoretical development

This book is largely the result of an extensive, although admittedly not exhaustive, critical reading of prior theory, and research on organizational wrongdoing. I explored the prior theory and research with two goals. First, I sought to distill the multitude of individual studies into a relatively small number of general explanations that differed from one another along a few significant dimensions. In the process, I concluded that the literature could be grouped reasonably into eight explanations, seven of which focus on the potential perpetrators of wrongdoing and one of which focuses on those who seek to control them. I suspect that most of the groupings will seem entirely predictable to specialists on the subject, although some (such as my grouping of strain theory under the umbrella of the rational choice account) will seem unconventional. I also concluded that the eight explanations of organizational wrongdoing could be characterized as differing from one another in the extent to which they implicitly assume that wrongdoers deliberate mindfully and rationally, are unaffected by their immediate social context, make discrete decisions, and develop positive inclinations to engage in behavior consistent with those decisions. This determination, I think, is somewhat novel.

Second, I sought to identify weaknesses in prior theory and research on organizational wrongdoing and to formulate ways to address them. In the process, I concluded that prior work on the role that decision-making, administrative systems, situational social influence, power structures, accidents, and especially social control agents play in wrongdoing was underdeveloped in one way or another, and I devised ways to extend this work. These efforts are most evident in Chapters 6–11.

Empirical method

This book is also the result of extensive reading about multiple instances of organizational wrongdoing. At the same time that I immersed myself in prior theory and research on wrongdoing, I read about as many instances of collective organizational wrongdoing as I could find. Thus, this book is also a multi-case study in which the cases are instances of wrongdoing (Platt 2009). Most individual-level research on organizational wrongdoing is based on carefully controlled experiments or surveys. Such studies are useful because, when well executed, they generate results from which relatively clear inferences can be drawn. But experiments and surveys prove cumbersome tools when used to elucidate the alternative approach to understanding organizational wrongdoing that I champion in this book.

Experiments tend to expose subjects to simple ethical, legal, and social responsibility dilemmas, with few dimensions along which there is uncertainty, in contexts that are relatively free of social influence and organizational constraint, and for which, perhaps most importantly, the need to deliberate generally is telegraphed to the subject, and the opportunity to do so in a consummate fashion is, for the most part, provided. Surveys can take into account the social and organizational context in which wrongdoers are embedded but tend to capture this context in a relatively restricted set of timeless quantifiable variables. Qualitative case studies allow for the examination of how unethical, illegal, and socially irresponsible behavior evolves over time, in the presence of organizational structures and social relationships, in decision contexts that are complex, fraught with uncertainty, and compromised by information deficits, and in which the need to deliberate sometimes is not recognized, and the opportunity to do so in a consummate way is not available.

With this said, the qualitative case analyses that I present in this book do not resemble the rigorous case analyses found in most scholarly journals, which are formulated according to stringent guidelines of data collection, manipulation, and interpretation (Eisenhardt 1989). Such case study methods have many advantages. Most important, they allow researchers to develop theoretical ideas that are more likely to be "valid" and to be easier for other researchers to "validate" or "invalidate." But such methods are useful, particularly when researchers are interested in a narrow range of postulated theoretical relationships. And, for better or worse, I am interested in a very broad range of theoretical relationships. So I have elected to use a less disciplined approach.

I identified the instances of collective organizational wrongdoing that shaped the development of this book through a wide variety of means that included citations in scholarly and popular work on wrongdoing, reports in the media (print and electronic), and the suggestions of colleagues, friends, and acquaintances. Often the identification of an instance of wrongdoing via one method (e.g. the suggestion of a colleague) led to research that resulted in the identification of other instances of wrongdoing (e.g. citations in a scholarly work) such that I became aware of instances of wrongdoing in a snowball-like fashion. I refer in the book to only a fraction of the instances of wrongdoing I studied.

The extent to which I pursued an instance of wrongdoing depended largely on the degree to which I could obtain detailed information on the wrongdoing in question. I focused primarily on cases for which I could obtain information that allowed me to construct a narrative in which organizational participants, rather than social science variables, were the primary actors (Abbot 2009). This reflected my desire to develop theory at the individual level of analysis that might be useful to executives, managers, and employees, as well as academics. And I focused particular attention on cases that provided information on the thoughts, behaviors, and emotions of organizational participants, as well as the history and structure of the social relationships in which they were embedded. This reflected my increasing desire to investigate the alternative explanations of wrongdoing in which these features of a wrongdoer's social context play such an important role. Over time, I adjusted my focus on instances of wrongdoing so as to increase the diversity of types of wrongdoing and organizational settings in which they were manifested. This reflected my desire to develop ideas on wrongdoing that were robust from the standpoint of type and context (Vaughan 2009).

The information that I uncovered on wrongdoing varied considerably from instance to instance along two dimensions. First, the information varied on the level of remove from the action. Some of the information came directly from participants in the wrongdoing, as was the case in Paul Krimmage's book on his experience in professional cycling (2007) and Kermit Vandivier's article on his time at B.F. Goodrich Corporation (1972). Other information came from detailed interviews with participants in wrongdoing, as was the case with Kurt Eichenwald's books on Prudential Bache (1996) and Enron (2005) and Alicia Mundy's book on the Fen-phen debacle (2001). Finally, other information came from news reports that were based on a smattering of sources, many of which were secondary (i.e. documentary) or even higher order in nature.

Second, the information varied with respect to the level of prior processing. Some of the information was obviously extensively processed, as in the case of critical commentaries such as Michael Lewis' writing on the mortgage melt-down (2008). Other information was less obviously, but still significantly processed, as in the case of investigative journalist accounts, such as those on the Enron debacle (McLean and Elkind 2004; Eichenwald 2005). Finally, some information was relatively unprocessed, such as stories filed by reporters.

In some cases, these stories came from a single reporter or team of reporters employed by the same news organization (e.g. the *Boston Globe* articles on the Big Dig ceiling collapse). In some cases, these stories came from a plethora of reporters at a number of different news organizations (e.g. the articles covering the newly invigorated investigation into Lance Armstrong's possible use of banned performance-enhancing substances).

I analyzed each instance of organizational wrongdoing with two goals in mind. First, I sought to determine how the instances might be characterized in terms of the explanations of wrongdoing that I was identifying in the course of my reading of prior theory and research. Second, I sought to remain open to the possibility that the instances of wrongdoing might suggest the operation of theoretical mechanisms not exemplified in prior theory and research, and in need of explication and development. This dimension of my empirical analysis is reflected most in the theoretical development presented in Chapters 6–11. As I proceeded with my analysis of the cases, I found that most of the instances of wrongdoing exhibited signs that multiple theoretical processes were at work. In the end, I concluded that no single theory of wrongdoing is sufficient to explain all wrongdoing. And few instances of wrongdoing can be explained by a single theory. Thus, unlike some prior work, this book does not argue for a single theory of organizational wrongdoing, although it does champion the five accounts that fall under the rubric of the alternative approach. This is reflected in the fact that the same instances of wrongdoing are mentioned in connection with several different explanations of wrongdoing.

In a sense, I have attempted to do what Professor Shiller, quoted in Chapter 2, says he could not do, that is, with the help of wrongdoers and those who tell their stories, I try to "read minds." There are, of course, many weaknesses of this approach. Two weaknesses are particularly glaring and must be acknowledged right from the start. First, these case studies do not provide independent tests of my arguments. Second, these cases are open to multiple interpretations, most importantly interpretations that differ from the ones I provide here. I consider the issue of alternative interpretations of the illustrations in the conclusion of the book.

With these preliminary issues out of the way, I am ready to begin elaborating the eight explanations of organizational wrongdoing identified in the book, beginning with the first of the two dominant explanations: the rational choice account.

4

A Rational Choice

Introduction

The rational choice explanation is the first dominant account of wrongdoing in and by organizations. It is rooted in a theoretical perspective that views each organization as a nexus of contracts linking multiple stakeholders (e.g. employees, managers, buyers, suppliers, etc.) and views organizational participants as cost-benefit calculators. Organizations are populated by people who interact with one another via exchange relationships, engaging in behaviors in return for the provision of rewards and the withholding of punishments. People scrutinize alternative courses of action with an eye to determining whether the benefits they generate outweigh the costs they entail. In this view, organizational wrongdoing arises when an organization's incentive structure becomes misaligned and motivates wrongdoing.

This chapter describes the basic rational choice explanation of organizational wrongdoing and presents the two most influential rational choice theories: agency and strain theory. It then develops an overarching rational choice framework that incorporates these two specific theories and other rational-choice-related models of organizational wrongdoing. I briefly consider the conditions that give rise to rational-choice inspired wrongdoing and detail the policy prescriptions intended to eradicate those conditions. I also discuss recent work in cognitive psychology that suggests how rational choice can go wrong, leading people to embark on wrongdoing when it runs counter to their interests. I conclude with an overall assessment of the rational choice account.

The basic rational choice explanation

The rational choice explanation of organizational wrongdoing assumes that people calculate the costs and benefits of pursuing a wrongful course of action and only decide to pursue the action if they conclude that the likely benefits of the wrongdoing outweigh its potential costs. Numerous instances of wrongdoing appear to have their origins in such calculations. And if one does not have the details through which people become involved in wrongdoing, it is easy to retrospectively construct a favorable calculus for almost any instance of wrongdoing.

The most infamous instance in which cost-benefit calculations are believed to have led to wrongdoing involved Ford Motor Company's decision to proceed with the manufacturing and sale of its Pinto subcompact car, despite increasing awareness that the car was susceptible to burst into flames when impacted from the rear at relatively low speeds. The Pinto was designed so that its gas tank was positioned between the rear bumper, which some have described as ornamental, and the rear axle assembly, which was attached to the chassis by protruding bolts. Tests conducted by Ford while the car was in pre-production revealed that when the Pinto was struck from behind, even at low speeds, its gas tank became compressed against the rear axle and its protruding bolts. And in many instances, the compression of the gas tank against the bolts caused it to rupture and erupt in flames.

Mark Dowie (1977) contends that Ford executives calculated the costs and benefits of fixing the Pinto gas tank problem soon after they discovered it. Specifically, Dowie maintains that Ford executives knew that injuries, deaths, and associated civil law suits could be reduced by a number of possible modifications to the car's rear-end section, some of which would have required major changes (the repositioning of the axle), but some of which would have necessitated only small alterations (the lining of the gas tank with a rubber bladder). But the executives also knew that any modification of the rear-end section would increase costs and that some alterations would decrease trunk space. Further, they believed that customer preference for safer cars was not as great as customer preference for low-cost cars with ample trunk space.

According to Dowie, the firm ultimately decided to forgo modifying the Pinto's rear-end section because it concluded that a redesign would cost the company more in reduced car sales than it would benefit the company in decreased civil suits. Dowie also contends that Ford executives engaged in a cost-benefit analysis soon after the first law suits related to the gas tank problem began to trickle in. According to him, "The cost of retooling Pinto assembly lines and of equipping each car with a safety gadget like that $5.08 Goodyear bladder was, company accountants calculated, greater than that of paying out millions to survivors like Robbie Carlton or to widows and widowers of victims like Sandra Gillespie." In his words, "The bottom line ruled and inflammable Pintos kept rolling out of the factories."

The belief that the Ford Pinto's rear-end design was unsafe was upheld by the National Highway Transportation Safety Agency (NHTSA), which conducted an investigation into the Pinto's design. NHTSA's findings and its stated intention to institute a mandatory recall prompted Ford to recall the car voluntarily for retrofitting. Further, several Pinto fire victims successfully sued Ford for punitive damages, based largely on the contention that Ford's design of the Pinto was guided by a cost-benefit calculation that prioritized profits ahead of human safety.

The victims' lawyers discovered an internal Ford document in which a company engineer advocated delaying redesign of the Pinto's rear-end section to save the firm money. But the memo did not explicitly state that safety concerns provided the impetus for a potential redesign of the rear-end section, thus it did not provide incontrovertible evidence that Ford executives had engaged in a trade-off between safety and profits when they decided against redesigning the car. Further, no other evidence was produced to validate the contention that Ford executives decided to design the Pinto's rear end in an unsafe way or failed to redesign the rear end when problems surfaced, in order to save money (Schwartz 1991). In fact, it is generally hard to find concrete evidence that people engage in explicit cost-benefit calculations before engaging in wrongdoing. The existence of such calculations is typically inferred after the fact on the basis of circumstantial evidence. But in isolated incidents, evidence of explicit cost-benefit calculations has surfaced.

Kurt Eichenwald (2000) describes an instance in which Archer Daniel Midlands (ADM) executives Mark Whitacre, Terry Wilson, and Mick Andreas were captured on an informant's tape recording, engaging in an explicit cost-benefit calculation before deciding to approve a campaign contribution that exceeded legal limits. Whitacre, president of ADM's bioproducts division, told the other two executives that Howard Buffet, assistant to the chairman (and son of the well-known investor Warren Buffet), asked him for company funds to support Wisconsin Governor Tommy Thompson's re-election campaign, but that he declined Buffet's request because the company was at its legal campaign contribution limit. On hearing this, Mick Andreas, ADM's vice chairman, gave Whitacre approval to release the funds saying, "You can go over the limit. Just a small fine." To which Terry Wilson, another division president, chimed in, "If they want a thousand dollars, you give a thousand dollars. So it costs us nine thousand," adding the estimated cost of fines for violating campaign-finance laws. Whitacre then corrected Wilson, "Twelve thousand after tax." Andreas nodding in agreement said, "That's true." Then he added, referring to his father and chairman/CEO of ADM, "You make sure Dad is behind it. Is Dad asking for 'em?" When Wilson answered, "Oh, yeah," Andreas responded, "Okay."

Two rational choice theories

A number of specific theories of organizational wrongdoing fall under the rubric of the rational choice explanation. Below I discuss two such theories: agency theory and strain theory. Agency theory is rooted in the field of economics, while strain theory originates in sociology.

Agency theory

Agency theory is an outgrowth of economic thought on the separation of ownership from control in private enterprise that occurred in the early part of the twentieth century. As firms grew in size in the early 1900s, ownership became dispersed among a large number of unrelated stockholders, and leadership fell to professional managers. As these developments intensified, a group of economists known as managerialists became worried that the interests of dispersed stockowners and professional managers were misaligned. The former were presumed to seek profit maximization, the classic capitalist imperative, while the latter were thought to favor a variety of parochial interests, including the divergence of company assets to top management perks. Managerialists also worried that owners' ability to monitor and control managers' behavior was compromised because owners were removed from the day-to-day control of the firm and separated from each other, thus allowing managers to pursue their parochial interests (Berle and Means 1932; Galbraith 2007).

Agency theory addresses managerialist concerns about the relationship between owners and managers, but offers a broader framework within which those concerns can be elaborated. It posits a relationship between principals, who compensate others for work performed on their behalf, and agents, who perform that work. And it focuses on situations in which the quantity and quality of agents' work is difficult for principals to assess because the outcomes of agents' work (i.e. their performance) is the product of not only the quantity and quality of agents' work, but also a host of other factors (e.g. market forces) over which agents have little control. In such situations, agents have an incentive to engage in opportunistic behaviors (some of which might be wrongful) that advance their own interests at the expense of principals' interests.

In the case of owner principals and manager agents, wrongful agent behaviors include earnings manipulation and the diversion of company resources to personal use (Fama 1980; Fama and Jensen 1983). Agency theorists have proposed a number of ways to align the interests of managers and stockholders, such as the use of stock options (Dalton et al. 2007). And they have proposed a number of ways to control managerial opportunism, such as the use of independent boards of directors (Hillman and Dalziel 2003). But managers have found ways to circumvent these devices, such as stock option post-dating and director co-optation (i.e. providing directors with benefits that compromise their independence). Thus, agency theorists characterize the relationship between owners and managers as a continual struggle in which owners strive to encourage faithful behavior on the part of managers and managers seek to pursue malfeasance of one kind or another.

Agency theory can be used to explain some of the fraud that contributed to the savings and loan crisis of the late 1980s which followed deregulation of the savings and loan industry (also referred to as the thrift industry) at the beginning of the decade (Pizzo, Fricker, and Muolo 1991). From an agency theory standpoint, thrift managers were agents, and thrift depositors and stockholders were principals. Deregulation increased the gap between thrift manager interests and thrift depositor and stockholder concerns. It also undermined the capacity of thrift depositors and stockholders to monitor thrift manager behavior.

Even before deregulation, the interests of thrift managers diverged from the concerns of depositors and stockholders. On the one hand, thrift managers sought to expand the volume of their institutions' deposits, which they only could do by promising high interest rates, and sought to grow the size of their loan portfolios, which they only could do by making risky investments. Managers whose thrifts had large deposits and loan portfolios enjoyed higher salaries and enhanced social status. On the other hand, depositors were not particularly interested in increasing the volume of their institution's deposits, and stockholders were not particularly interested in expanding the size of their institutions' loan portfolios. Depositors just wanted their thrifts to remain solvent, and stockholders only aspired to stable returns on their investments. This conflict of interest was attenuated, though, by federal and state regulations that restricted thrifts from obtaining large blocks of deposits at high interest rates and constrained thrifts to invest only in low-risk residential housing.

Industry deregulation widened the gap between the interests of thrift managers and the concerns of depositors and stockholders. Thrifts were permitted to invest in a wider range of business enterprises, including relatively high-risk commercial real estate projects. Thrifts also were allowed to obtain large blocks of deposits from institutional investors, for which they were permitted to pay high interest rates. This provided thrift managers with an additional incentive to solicit borrowers engaged in risky and thus high return enterprises, such as commercial real estate. In addition, real estate developers were permitted to establish thrifts. As a result, thrift managers now had an interest to lend to commercial land development projects in which they had a financial stake.

Further, even before deregulation, depositor and stockholder monitoring of manager behavior was problematic. Due to the separation of ownership from control, depositors and stockholders found it difficult to stay informed about managerial lending practices. The difficulty of monitoring thrift manager behavior was attenuated, though, by extensive federal and state monitoring of thrift manager investment decisions. After deregulation, depositor and stockholder monitoring of thrift manager behavior became increasingly problematic. There were fewer federal and state examiners than before, and the examiners that remained were instructed to scrutinize thrifts less stringently. In addition, the number of thrifts dramatically increased. Thus, thrift examiners had less time to visit thrifts and less time to scrutinize the thrifts they visited.

These conditions gave rise to a tidal wave of organizational wrongdoing. The most mundane form of wrongdoing entailed thrift managers' issuance of loans to less than reputable borrowers who they knew would eventually default on their loans. A more egregious form of wrongdoing entailed thrift managers' issuance of loans to enterprises in which they had a direct or indirect business interest. The principal–agent relationship promulgated by deregulation gave rise to this organizational wrongdoing in two ways. First, it caused previously law-abiding thrift managers to turn to wrongdoing. Second, it attracted a variety of questionable characters to the S&L (savings and loan) industry. Some appeared to be simply more ambitious and unscrupulous than the average business executive and thus more susceptible to the perverse incentive structures. But others were convicted criminals, a few of whom had organized crime connections, who were looking for illegal business opportunities.

Strain theory

Strain theory was developed by Robert Merton (1938), a key figure in the evolution of American sociology, to explain the fact that lower-class populations exhibited higher crime rates. Merton maintained that the imperative to achieve social mobility was pervasive in American society (exemplified by the "rags-to-riches" saga), but the ability to move up the social ladder was limited in lower-class populations. Strain theory's fundamental postulate is that people tend to pursue illegitimate means of achieving their aspirations when legitimate means are blocked. This postulate has been refined and extended by a series of other sociologists, most notably Robert Agnew (1985, 1992).[1]

---

[1] Some will consider the discussion of strain theory under the rubric of the rational choice account inappropriate. Strain theory is considered a sociological approach because it was formulated and refined by sociologists to explain how variation in the conditions of social groups generates variation in crime and deviance rates across groups. And some consider sociological explanations to be antithetical to explanations that focus on individual-level rationality. But strain theory implicitly assumes that individuals develop rational responses to the social situations in which they find themselves. And many sociologists who draw on strain theory to develop hypotheses about the causes of organizational wrongdoing, including those discussed in this chapter, have based their hypotheses on explicit assumptions about individual-level rationality.

Strain theory's fundamental postulate serves as the basis of a number of more specific hypotheses about the causes of wrongdoing in and by organizations. Some strain theory-inspired hypotheses focus on the nature of the environments in which organizations and people are situated, predicting that firms and individuals situated in milieus where resources are scarce, such as competitive environments, find it difficult to achieve their aspirations and thus are more prone to engaging in wrongdoing. Consistent with this hypothesis, several studies show that firms are more likely to engage in wrongdoing if they are located in industries where average profitability is low, or during times when aggregate stock prices are depressed (Staw and Szwajkowski 1975; Simpson 1986, Simpson 1987).

Paul Krimmage's decision to use amphetamines illustrates the impact that blocked aspirations might have at the individual level. According to Krimmage, the professional bicycle-racing environment was extremely competitive in the 1980s. All professional sports are highly competitive. But the extreme physical demands placed on professional road cyclists, especially in the major multi-stage races, are unique. Krimmage recalls that the bulk of his career was dominated by the single-minded, almost desperate attempt to simply "survive." Professional cycling appears to have remained highly competitive at least through the 1990s. Frankie Andreu and Steve Swart, teammates of Lance Armstrong on the Motorola and U.S. Postal teams, recently admitted that they used erythropoitin (EPO), a banned performance-enhancing substance that boosts the number of red blood cells in the blood stream, during the Tour de France in 1999. Both riders testified that they felt that they had to take EPO to be included in the subset of their team's riders selected to compete in the Tour. Andreu testified that some of the team's riders felt that they could no longer compete with some European teams that had rapidly improved and were rumored to be using EPO. Andreu's wife claimed that after the 1999 tour, he told her, "You don't understand. This is the only way I can even finish the Tour (Macur 2006)."

Other strain theory-inspired hypotheses focus on organizational and individual performance, predicting that organizations and people who experience performance shortfalls are more likely to engage in wrongdoing. Poor performance might be an indicator of an organization or individual's ability to reach their aspirations. Or it might constitute one factor limiting an organization or person's ability to achieve their goals, insofar as poor performance sometimes limits an organization or individual's ability to obtain resources needed to meet long-run performance expectations. Consistent with this hypothesis, several studies suggest that poorly performing organizations are more likely to engage in wrongdoing (Clinard and Yeager 1980; Agnew et al. 2009). Numerous instances of wrongdoing at the individual level have been chalked up to performance shortfalls that either indicate or contribute to blocked aspirations. As noted in the introduction, Paul Krimmage began his limited use of amphetamines immediately after his first failed attempt to complete the Tour de France in 1987.

The case of investment banker Joseph Jett provides a similar example in a more traditional business context (Freedman and Burke 1998). Jett earned an undergraduate engineering degree from Massachusetts Institute of Technology and an MBA from Harvard Business School. But his first two jobs on Wall Street, at Morgan Stanley and CS First Boston, did not go well. In each case his performance was judged by his superiors to be deficient and in each case his employment ended in relatively short order. His third job on Wall Street, at Kidder Peabody, began in a similarly disappointing fashion. After six months of employment, he received a warning that if he did not improve his performance, he would be dismissed and out on the street again. In response, Jett removed all of the furniture from his New York City apartment and slept on the floor in order to (by his own account) punish himself for his poor performance at First Boston and his poor start at Kidder. Under this extreme performance crunch, Jett developed a method of trading government scripts that generated apparently real but actually fictitious enormous profits for the firm, which he cashed in for huge bonuses for himself.

Firms and individuals are particularly likely to face blocked aspirations when they are asked to meet unrealistically high performance standards. McLean and Elkind (2004) and Eichenwald (2005) contend that Enron pursued questionable accounting and finance practices because Wall Street had unrealistically high growth expectations for the firm. Wall Street had unrealistically high growth expectations for Enron, partly because it perceived the firm to be an energy trading enterprise capable of dramatic expansion, when in fact it was fundamentally a public utility with relatively modest growth opportunities. At the end of each quarter, top managers feared that they would fail to hit Wall Street earnings targets and that failure to hit those targets would undermine investor confidence in the firm and ultimately erode the price of the company's stock, upon which the feasibility of some of the firm's key financial transactions depended. As a result, as the time to report quarterly financial numbers approached, Enron executives performed a variety of questionable accounting maneuvers and completed an assortment of dubious financial transactions, later determined to be fraudulent, in an attempt to remove debt from, and add revenue to, the firm's balance sheet.

Firms and individuals also are particularly likely to face blocked aspirations when obstacles arise that impede achievement of reasonable performance expectations. In the immediate post-WWII period, Ford Motor Company's top management established aggressive production goals to meet the dramatically expanding demand for new automobiles. At the same time they negotiated generous labor contracts with the United Auto Workers Union to reduce the likelihood of work stoppages that might slow the flow of cars off the firm's assembly lines. Some provisions of these contracts reduced plant managers' control over the speed of the assembly line, which made it more difficult for them to meet the new aggressive production goals. So the plant managers covertly shaved inches off the sticks used to separate chassis on the assembly line, in violation of the UAW contract, to surreptitiously speed up the pace at which cars came off the assembly line each day (Halberstam 1986).

Sometimes employees can inadvertently create their own barriers to goal attainment, thus increasing the pressure to engage in wrongdoing. As noted above, Paul Krimmage embarked on a short period of amphetamine use after failing to complete the 1987 Tour de France, fearing that a similar poor performance in the upcoming French Classic criteriums would jeopardize his ability to support himself and his family. But he feared performing poorly in the French Classics, not just because he had performed poorly in the Tour, but also because he had suspended training in the wake of his failure to complete the Tour. And his resulting diminished physical fitness exacerbated his fears of performing badly in the French Classics.

An overarching rational choice framework

The rational choice explanation assumes that people are cost-benefit calcula- tors and thus only engage in wrongful behavior when they believe that the benefits of wrongdoing outweigh its costs. Agency theory and strain theory build on this basic concept to develop more specific hypotheses about the causes of wrongdoing in and by organizations. In this section, I present a more encompassing rational choice framework that builds on the basic tenet that people are cost-benefit calculators and subsumes many of the key agency and strain theory hypotheses. I begin by outlining the general structure of the framework, which draws its inspiration from the expectancy theory of employee motivation. I then consider how this framework conceptualizes individual differences and situational variation as causes of organizational wrongdoing. My goal is to indicate the richness and power of the rational choice account and provide a jumping-off point for the other accounts of wrongdoing considered in the book.

The basic expectancy theory argument

Expectancy theory was developed by two management theorists, David Nadler and Edward Lawler (Nadler and Lawler 1977). It holds that workers are motivated by the desire to obtain "outcomes" for which they have a "positive valence" (i.e. rewards) and to avoid outcomes for which they have a "negative valence" (i.e. punishments). But the theory also holds that two "expectations" regulate the extent to which workers are motivated to complete a task that promises rewards and avoids punishments. The first is a worker's expectation that he or she can successfully complete the task: the "effort–performance expectancy." The second is a worker's expectation that he or she will receive promised rewards or avoid potential punishments upon task completion: the "performance–outcome expectancy." Put succinctly, expectancy theory assumes that workers are motivated to engage in courses of action that promise rewards and avoid punishments only if 1) they believe that they can accomplish the task and 2) they believe that if they accomplish the task, they will receive the promised rewards and sidestep potential punishments.

Expectancy theory is broader than most previous theories of motivation in three important respects. First, previous theories of motivation assume that workers' motivation is independent of their abilities, with highly motivated workers making better use of their abilities than less motivated workers. Expectancy theory assumes that workers' ability to accomplish a task partly determines their motivation to complete the task. Second, most prior theories assume that worker motivation is determined primarily by internal states, with some workers being inherently more motivated than others. Expectancy theory assumes that workers' motivation is influenced by the nature of their environment, insofar as the nature of workers' environments can influence both their ability to accomplish tasks and the likelihood that they will be rewarded or punished for task completion. Third, most prior theories of motivation assume that workers' motivation to accomplish a task is not influenced by other people in their environment. Expectancy theory allows that workers' motivation can be influenced by other people in their environment insofar as other people can influence workers' ability to accomplish a task and receive rewards or avoid punishments associated with task completion.

Paul Krimmage's decision to use amphetamines before the French Classic criteriums in 1987 provides a straightforward illustration of the basic expectancy theory argument. Krimmage's effort–performance expectancy associated with the use of amphetamines was relatively high at the time. He admitted that he eschewed the use of amphetamines partly because he feared that if he acquired and stored the drug in advance of a race, he might get caught. But this obstacle was overcome by the fact that many of his teammates acquired amphetamines and offered them to him during pre-race preparations. Krimmage also admitted that he eschewed use of amphetamines because he found injecting them repulsive. But this obstacle was overcome by the fact that his teammates offered to inject him with the amphetamines. Krimmage's performance–outcome expectancy associated with the use of amphetamines also was high, at least on the occasions when he used them. Krimmage used amphetamines in the French Classic criteriums that followed the 1987 Tour de France. He noted that amphetamine usage was particularly high in the post-Tour criteriums because there was no drug testing at these races. The absence of doping controls reduced to near zero the likelihood that his use of amphetamines would be detected and punished.

Enron's manipulation of the electric power market in California provides a more complex illustration of expectancy theory in action (McLean and Elkind 2004). California policymakers attempted to deregulate the state's energy sector in the 1990s, but the attempt was influenced (some would say perverted) by the intervention of political interest groups. As a result, the deregulation effort produced a set of rules that was ripe for exploitation, providing numerous opportunities for questionable behavior.

Enron's lead West Coast energy trader, Tim Belden, was an expert on California energy policy and devoted long hours to studying California's newly deregulated system in search of loopholes. When he found an apparent loophole in the new system, he conducted experiments to verify his analysis. He went ahead with schemes to manipulate the energy market only after his experiments confirmed that the loopholes were exploitable. In the words of expectancy theory, Enron traders' effort–performance expectancy was high because the California system was ripe for gaming and because the traders possessed the knowledge, in some cases produced by careful hypothesis-testing, needed to game it.

Also important, Enron's schemes were highly sophisticated—so sophisticated that Enron's own lawyers found them difficult to comprehend. As a result, it was unlikely that the public and even government investigators would uncover the schemes. Further, the electrical power industry's main watchdog organization, the Federal Energy Regulatory Commission (FERC), shared Enron's enthusiasm for energy market deregulation and Enron's assessment that California had botched its effort at deregulation. As a result, FERC was not sympathetic to calls to investigate and punish Enron's trading activity. In the words of expectancy theory, Enron traders' performance–outcome expectancy was high because the likelihood of detection and punishment was small. In the wake of Enron's collapse, though, its trading operation was subjected to considerable legal scrutiny. And in light of this scrutiny, three of its traders were indicted and ultimately pleaded guilty to market manipulation.

Expectancy theory locates the causes of wrongdoing in the individual and in the situational context. Individuals have preferences for rewards and aversions to punishments. Situations present possibilities for task completion as well as reward and punishment allocation. A number of theories focus on the characteristics of individuals and situations, some of which explicitly consider wrongdoing. These theories can be used to extend the expectancy theory explanation of organizational wrongdoing. I review a few of these theories below.

The role of individual differences

Expectancy theory allows that people vary in the valence they attach to different outcomes. Different people value the same rewards to dissimilar extents, just as different people loathe the same punishments to dissimilar degrees. Thus a person's propensity to engage in organizational wrongdoing should depend partly on the extent to which the person values the rewards and loathes the punishments with which a particular type of wrongdoing might be associated.

The idea that a person's preference structure explains a person's propensity to engage in organizational wrongdoing provides the foundation for the most frequently invoked explanations of wrongdoing offered in the popular and business media. The most superficial accounts characterize wrongdoers as possessing exaggerated ambitions, without presenting supporting evidence. For example, investment bankers thought to be responsible for the questionable practices that precipitated the mortgage meltdown and subsequent financial crisis of 2008 have been repeatedly characterized as "greedy" (Fleming 2009).

More sophisticated accounts document behaviors that appear to testify to wrongdoers' distorted preference structures. For example, several media outlets reported that Bernard Madoff, who orchestrated an elaborate Ponzi scheme that defrauded investors out of hundreds of millions of dollars, sported an extravagant lifestyle that included expensive in-house manicures, but was stingy when it came to providing service workers such as waiters with gratuities (Lysiak and McShane 2009).

The most sophisticated accounts, though, delve into wrongdoers' backgrounds to find sources of their distorted preference structures. Barry Minkow used a variety of frauds to transform his small carpet-cleaning business, ZZZZ Best, into a large publically traded restoration company. Joe Domanick (1991: 10–11), drawing partly on a book Minkow wrote to celebrate his meteoric rise to fame and fortune, maintained that the fraudster experienced significant economic uncertainty as a child. According to Domanick, Minkow's memories of his adolescence were dominated by the "shame he felt at his family's sporadic poverty." Minkow suffered from attention deficit hyperactivity disorder and his parents attempted to channel his "compulsive wild energy" by enrolling him in an exclusive military academy. But they withdrew him from the academy when they could no longer afford to pay the expensive tuition. While at the academy, Minkow became aware of the difference money could make. By the time he left the exclusive private school, he possessed a powerful desire "to be superior."

The idea that a person's preference structure explains his or her propensity to engage in organizational wrongdoing also provides the foundation for scholarly explanations of wrongdoing. Sociologists Hirschi and Gottfredson (Hirschi and Gottfredson 1987; Gottfredson and Hirschi 1990; but see Simpson and Piquero 2002) contend that people who have "low self-control" are more likely than people who have "high self-control" to pursue white-collar crime. People with low self-control place a greater value on immediate rewards and exhibit less concern for more distant punishments than other people. Gottfredson and Hirschi contend that such people are more likely to engage in white-collar crime because such crime tends to generate more immediate rewards than does acceptable and even exemplary job performance, even though it runs the risk of subsequent detection and punishment. David Levine, the central figure in the largest insider trading conspiracy of the 1980s, resembled the prototypical low self-control white-collar criminal. Levine frequently complained about what he believed was his slow progress up the corporate ladder at the investment banks where he worked. At one point he even fumed about a $500,000 year-end bonus, which he took to be an insult (Stewart 1991).

Gottfredson and Hirschi believe that people with low self-control are attracted to the immediate excitement and pleasure that wrongdoing can produce, as well as the pecuniary gain it can generate. This idea dovetails with psychological theory on crime, in particular, theory about the effects of antisocial personality disorder (ASPD). People with ASPD, commonly referred to as sociopaths, are believed to exhibit a disregard for the rights of others, as indicated by impulsivity, recklessness, lack of remorse, and a variety of related characteristics, making them more likely to engage in a variety of forms of wrongdoing. Michael Rapp, a thrift manager convicted of fraud during the 1980s savings and loan crisis, appears to fit the description of a wrongdoer with a high need for excitement. As described by Pizzo et al. (1991):

> He (Rapp) loved to spend his days figuring out schemes. A brilliant man, he could have been successful as a legitimate businessman, but the excitement of swindles held too powerful an allure for him, as did the vast sums of quick and easy money they produced. From the day thrifts were deregulated, it was inevitable that Rapp would loot them. Opportunities of that magnitude could not possibly go unnoticed by swindlers like Rapp.

Several of the participants in David Levine's insider trading schemes found participation in the conspiracies exhilarating. Indicative of this, a number of the participants referred to the schemes as "the game." One of David Levine's co-conspirators, Robert Wilkis, appeared to get caught up in the excitement. As recounted by Stewart (1991: 67–68):

> Wilkis was nervous at first, afraid that the weak link in the scheme was the possibility that his relationship with Levine might be detected. So Levine suggested that they speak in code, using false names when they called or left messages. Wilkis became 'Allan Darby'; sometimes Levine used the same name or 'Mike Schwartz.' Using codes was fun; it gave their insider-trading scheme the aura of a Hardy Boys escapade. Soon they were engaged in conversations so riddled with codes they would have seemed ludicrous to any listener. Levine—'Mr. Darby'—would call on the phone. 'Hi, Bob. We've got to talk company business.' Company business meant the trading scheme. 'I'm taking a peck at Jewel' meant Levine was accumulating a modest position in Jewel Companies. 'Textron is looking OK' meant Wilkis should pay more attention to that situation, gleaning additional information for Levine.

The role of situational variation

Expectancy theory also locates the cause of wrongdoing in the situation. It predicts that wrongdoing will emerge in situations that promise abundant rewards and few punishments for wrongdoing, and a corresponding dearth of rewards and potential punishments for alternative right-doing. It also predicts that wrongdoing will emerge in situations where the effort–performance and performance–outcome expectancies associated with wrongdoing are high and the effort–performance and performance–outcome expectancies associated with alternative right-doing are low. The idea that situations determine the rewards and punishments associated with wrongdoing and the opportunities to engage in and reap benefits from wrongdoing is at the heart of much sociological thinking about crime of all kinds, beginning with work on juvenile delinquency (Cloward and Ohlin 1960) and extending to work on what is known as routine crime (Cohen and Felson 1979; Clarke 1995), and most germane to this book, white-collar crime (Coleman 1995).

The television quiz show frauds of the 1950s illustrate the role that situational variation can play in stimulating organizational wrongdoing (Stone and Yohn 1992). The quiz show frauds entailed television producers' careful control of the outcome of on-air contests through the selective advance provision of questions and answers to contestants, all the while maintaining the illusion that the contests were fair. Evidence of the fraud generated considerable public outcry (as reflected in newspaper and magazine editorials denouncing it), stimulated several New York State grand jury and district attorney investigations, and eventually gave rise to a U.S. congressional committee hearing. It did not, though, result in criminal convictions or civil judgments (at least not for contest-rigging). Thus, the 1950s quiz show fraud was an instance of organizational wrongdoing, insofar as it led social control agents to investigate and try to eliminate it. However, it was not illegal behavior, insofar as law enforcement officials determined that the fraud did not break any standing laws.

In the 1950s, quiz shows were created by independent production companies in conjunction with specific advertisers (e.g. Geritol and Revlon Cosmetics), and were aired by the broadcast networks for a fee paid by the producer–advertiser partnerships. Under this arrangement, advertisers had an incentive to increase the popularity of the programs with which they were associated, because the more popular the programs were, the more potential customers they could reach. Further, the quiz shows were broadcast live. Thus, producers had little control over the dramatic character of their shows (and thus the audience appeal of the shows) once a broadcast began. Under this arrangement, the producer–advertiser partnerships had a substantial incentive to do whatever they could before a broadcast began to control how a show's action would unfold during the broadcast. Finally, in the 1950s, the quiz show formula entailed asking difficult questions, giving contestants ample time to provide answers, and inviting winning contestants back for subsequent rounds of competition, all in the hope that audiences would develop admiration for, and emotional attachment to, the quiz show winners. Indeed, winning contestants found their pictures on the covers of major periodicals of the time, such as *Life Magazine*. Under this arrangement, producers and advertisers had a substantial interest in ensuring that the "right" contestants won.

The producers responded to this situation by establishing what they called "controls." Under pressure from the advertisers, they tried to influence whether one of the contestants would win the matches (i.e. whether or not the contestants would tie), which contestants would win the matches (e.g. whether a new champion would be crowned), and how they would win or lose the matches (i.e. the dramatic tension of the contest). Indeed, several producers claimed that under the quiz show regime of the 1950s, it would be impossible to produce a successful quiz show without using controls of some kind. Without providing contestants with the questions in advance, the contestants would not be able to answer the questions on the air (because, as dictated by the quiz show formula of the day, the questions were typically difficult). If the contestants could not answer the questions on the air, they would not be revered by the audience. Further, without providing the contestants with questions in advance, the producers could not coach the contestants on how to answer the questions. If contestants could not be coached, their on-air performance would not generate the theatrical tension needed to entertain audiences and keep them watching. Finally, without selectively providing contestants with questions and answers in advance, the producers could not determine who would win. In short, without using controls, the producers could not regulate the dramatic tenor of the programs and create popular heroes.

After the quiz show fraud was uncovered, the rigging of shows was made a federal offense. This undoubtedly reduced producers' incentive to rig their shows, because they were now at significant risk of punishment for doing so. Further, after the quiz show fraud was revealed, the industry altered the structure of quiz show production. Beginning in the 1960s, producers created game shows on their own and then sold them to the networks. To finance the shows, producers and/or networks sold a show's commercial time to advertisers, who paid in proportion to the show's popularity. Under this arrangement, advertisers had little incentive to pressure producers to alter the programs on which they advertised so as to increase the size of the programs' audience. It made more sense for advertisers to simply take their advertising dollars elsewhere.

In addition, beginning in the 1960s, the quiz shows were pre-recorded. This allowed the producers to alter the dramatic character of a segment after it was filmed and before it was broadcast by editing the recording of the segment. Finally, the quiz show formula changed. The producers now used easy questions, ones that most audience members could answer. As a result, show popularity hinged not on audience adoration of, and attachment to, brilliant contestants, but rather on audience involvement in the contest. Audience members could now play along at home, because they often could answer the questions themselves. In fact, some quiz shows even incorporated audience participation in their broadcasts, in some cases nominally (as when studio contestants "played for" a home audience member) and in other cases actively (as when home audience members wrote or phoned in their answers to questions used in broadcasts).

How misaligned incentive systems develop and how they can be eradicated

The rational choice explanation of organizational wrongdoing locates the causes of wrongdoing in the individual and the situation. When organizations incorporate individuals who have preference structures that make them prone to engage in wrongdoing, then the organization is filled with bad apples. When organizations present their members with rewards and punishments and associated effort–performance and performance–outcome expectancies that leave them inclined to engage in wrongdoing, the organizations are bad barrels.

Organizations can come to employ bad apples in two ways. First, those who wish to engage in wrongdoing can intentionally employ other likeminded individuals. Second, those who wish to engage in right-doing can fail to conduct adequate due diligence when hiring new employees. Both dynamics appear to have been at work in the U.S. savings and loan crisis. One of the consequences of cutbacks in the number of savings and loan examiners and the concomitant increase in the number of savings and loan institutions during the 1980s was a decrease in the scrutiny of people submitting applications to found thrifts. As a result, there was an influx of convicted felons into the savings and loan industry. And once these individuals gained entry into the industry, they arranged for other crooks to join them.

Organizations can develop incentive systems conducive to wrongdoing in two ways. First, those who wish to engage in wrongdoing can design incentive systems that motivate employees to engage in wrongdoing. Barry Minkow relied on an inner circle of co-conspirators to pull off the ZZZZ Best fraud. And he kept these co-conspirators in line partly by offering them salaries that were much larger than they could earn elsewhere and by promising them large bonuses to pull off particularly audacious scams, one of which I will describe in detail below. Second, those who wish to engage in right-doing can inadvertently create incentive structures that give rise to wrongdoing. It is generally thought that managers inadvertently create incentive structures conducive to wrongdoing when they fail to establish clear rules separating appropriate from inappropriate behavior, and when they fail to devote sufficient attention to monitoring and punishing wrongdoing.

The rational choice explanation of organizational wrongdoing implies clear and actionable managerial policies for curbing wrongdoing. It suggests that managers should be careful to hire employees with favorable preference structures, such as those with high self-control. Further, it suggests that managers should institute governance structures that make clear both the boundaries separating acceptable from unacceptable behavior and that make sure that employees are rewarded promptly and invariably for acceptable behavior and punished swiftly and with certainty for unacceptable behavior. However, at least two reasons explain why this simple prescription for reducing wrongdoing is unlikely to be completely successful; and thus, why wrongdoing is likely to be endemic or normal even in organizations that embrace these prescriptions.

First, it is extremely difficult to devise incentive systems that do not have unintended adverse consequences. In fact, the creation of incentive structures that inadvertently give rise to undesirable behavior is so well documented, it has been given a name, "rewarding A while hoping for B" (Kerr 1975). For example, Wall Street investment bank Kidder Peabody rewarded its managers partly on the basis of their subordinates' performance, presumably in the hope that this would motivate managers to invest time and effort in developing their subordinates. But this incentive structure might have rewarded managers for turning a blind eye to their subordinates' malfeasance when it redounded to their benefit. As described above, Joseph Jett generated unusually high profits at

Kidder Peabody after notable failures at two other investment banks and a disappointing start at Kidder. But his supervisor, Edward Cerullo, never investigated Jett's trading strategy, despite exhortations to do so from suspicious co-workers. Perhaps Cerullo chose not to investigate Jett because both he and Jett received large bonuses in the wake of Jett's impressive trading success. Independent investigators later determined that Jett's profits were produced by the accidental or intentional exploitation of a glitch in the firm's trading software. And some of the investigators maintained that Curullo knew that Jett's trading profits were fictitious, or at the very least should have suspected as much. Thus they concluded that Curullo was either explicitly or implicitly complicit in Jett's fraud. Kidder Peabody's top management apparently agreed. A sizeable portion of Curullo's bonus was reclaimed and he was fired after the fraud was exposed (Freedman and Burke 1998).

Second, and perhaps more vexing, due diligence in the hiring of employees, vigilant monitoring of employee behavior, and prompt and reliable administration of rewards and punishments raise costs in the form of increased managerial time and effort. Further, detailed elaboration of rules can raise costs in the form of reduced flexibility and efficiency. For these reasons, economists maintain that organizations should seek to hold wrongdoing to an optimal *non-zero* level, a level that balances the costs and benefits of suppressing wrongdoing (Becker 1968).

The limits to rational choice

Undoubtedly, much human behavior is guided by rational choice. But cognitive psychologists have conducted studies that suggest that rational choice sometimes is subject to error. These psychologists have examined how people frame decisions and make use of cognitive shortcuts when evaluating decision alternatives. And they have shown that the use of frames and heuristics can cause decision makers to choose options that contradict their self interest. The main thrust of cognitive psychology is signified by the title of a popular rendering of its findings, *Predictably Irrational* (Ariely 2008). Daniel Kahneman and Amos Tversky pioneered this line of inquiry (Tversky and Kahneman 1974; Kahneman, Slovic, and Tversky 1982). Max Bazerman was the first to introduce it into management scholarship (Bazerman 2006).

The work of cognitive psychologists is important because it suggests that people sometimes conduct faulty analyses of the costs and benefits likely to follow from wrongdoing. And when this occurs, they can embark on wrongdoing despite the fact that the costs outweigh the benefits. Below I briefly consider a few ways that decision frames and heuristics can lead to wrongdoing of this sort.

Decision frames

Cognitive psychologists have examined how decision frames influence decision-maker preferences, especially in contexts where decision options have uncertain pay-offs, that is, when the positive and negative outcomes to which options give rise cannot be predicted with certainty. Most famously, they have shown that people tend to pursue risky behavioral options (those that have high pay-offs, but that eventuate with less certainty), rather than safe options (those that have low pay-offs, but that eventuate with more certainty), when they frame decisions in terms of the losses that might be avoided, as opposed to the gains that might be obtained. For example, in one well-known laboratory study by Tversky and Kahneman (1981), two groups of subjects were asked to choose between alternative vaccines that could be administered in response to an impending flu: Program A and Program B. One group of subjects was presented with a gains framing. They were told that scientific evidence indicated that if the vaccines were administered to a group of 600 people, the first option (the certain option) would result in 200 lives being saved and the second option (the risky option) would result in a one-third chance that all 600 people would be saved. The other group was presented with a losses framing. They were told that the first option would result in 400 lives being lost and the second option would result in a one-third chance that none of the 600 people would die. The experimenters found that subjects preferred the second risky option when the two options were framed in terms of the deaths the vaccines could prevent (the losses framing), but preferred the safe option when the two options were framed in terms of the lives that could be saved (the gains framing).

The tendency of loss-focused decision makers to prefer risky options, known as the "risky shift," has implications for organizational participants who weight the costs and benefits of engaging in wrongdoing. In many cases, wrongful behaviors, when evaluated relative to their rightful alternatives, are risky options. For example, a manager with a performance-based compensation package who is presented with the options of misrepresenting or accurately reporting his firm's performance can be considered to face a choice between a risky and a safe option. The misrepresentation option presents the possibility of higher rewards, but risks detection and forfeiture of all compensation (as well as punishment). The accurate reporting option presents the certainty of receiving rewards commensurate with the firm's actual (lower than misrepresented) level of performance. The research on the risky shift suggests that the manager in the example above would be more likely to choose the first "manipulation" option if the manager approached the decision from a losses framing, that is, if the manager was preoccupied by a fear of failure as opposed to a desire for success (a prediction that, incidentally, runs counter to the popular belief that greed motivates wrongdoing).

Recently, Mattel Inc. and its Fisher-Price subsidiary paid a $2.3 million fine for selling toys covered with lead-based paint (The Associated Press 2009a). Managerial decisions conditioned by a loss framing might have contributed to this instance of wrongdoing. Mattel did not manufacture the toys itself, but rather purchased them from a Chinese supplier. The supplier's manager obtained the paint from a long-standing subcontractor, and then, in violation of prior agreements and policy, applied the paint to toys destined for Mattel without first testing it for lead content. The manager might have chosen to pursue this risky option (using the paint without first substantiating that it was lead-free) because the supplier was behind schedule in delivering toys to Mattel. While the firm had enjoyed considerable past success, it was at that moment overwhelmed with backlogged orders. And the manager likely worried that if he did not step up the delivery of toys or fell further behind schedule he might lose his lucrative contract with the U.S. toy company (Lacter 2008).

The impact of framing is sometimes difficult to separate from the impact of strain, discussed above. This is because experienced failure is one reason why decision makers might adopt a loss framing. For example, Joseph Jett's foray into wrongful behavior, attributed above to his blocked aspirations to succeed, might have resulted partly from the framing he used to evaluate decision options or, to put it more prosaically, his fear of failure rather than his desire for success (Freedman and Burke 1998). As indicated earlier, Jett earned undergraduate and graduate degrees from prestigious schools, but he was dismissed from his first two Wall Street jobs because of poor performance, and began his third job in a similarly inauspicious manner. With his past and imminent failures clearly in mind, and thus a loss framing likely guiding his decision making, Jett became involved in what later was determined to be the reporting of fictitious government scripts trading profits.

Decision heuristics

Cognitive psychologists also have examined how decision heuristics influence decision-maker preferences. The availability heuristic is among the most well-researched cognitive shortcuts. When people use the availability heuristic, they factor into their decisions those anticipated consequences that are, for one reason or another, easiest to envision. Temporal discounting is among the most well-researched form of the availability heuristic. When people engage in temporal discounting, they factor into their decisions those anticipated consequences that are most immediate in time.

Research on temporal discounting has implications for organizational participants who weigh the costs and benefits of engaging in wrongdoing. It is often the case that the potential benefits of wrongdoing promise to materialize in the short term, whereas the possible costs of wrongdoing only threaten to come about in the distant future. The availability heuristic suggests that people will be more influenced by the immediate rewards associated with wrongdoing than the more temporally distant punishments that might attend it, even if decision makers perceive the rewards and punishments to be equally likely to eventuate, and even if they consider the rewards and punishments to have equivalent (albeit opposite) valences.

Pyramid schemes provide persuasive testaments to the human capacity to focus on immediate pay-offs while discounting likely future detection and punishment. Pyramid schemes entail raising money from investors on false pretences and using that money to pay off other investors from whom money was raised earlier on similar false pretences. These schemes almost invariably have short lifespans because they create victims who quickly become aware of their losses and who unambiguously identify their victimizers, although there are a few notable long-lived exceptions, such as the scam orchestrated by Bernard Madoff (Gaviria and Smith 2009). The architects of pyramid schemes often start out as legitimate business persons who employ a pyramid system to close what they believe to be a temporary gap between their firm's operating costs and earnings. But as time goes on they make the raising of money on false premises their dominant business model, despite the fact that the fraudulent enterprise is destined to be uncovered in short order.

Barry Minkow's ZZZZ Best carpet-cleaning con would seem to be a good example of such a fraud (Domanick 1991). Minkow established a small carpet-cleaning business and, with the help of various scams, grew the company into a large publically traded building restoration enterprise. His most lucrative scams entailed raising money from investors, who ranged from private individuals to large financial institutions, on false premises, such as the funding of non-existent building restoration jobs. He then used the money to pay back investors who had invested in earlier phony projects. To keep the scheme going, to pay back previous investors and sustain ongoing operations, Minkow had to fabricate bigger and bigger restoration jobs. Ultimately, he created an audacious ruse to convince investors that his small carpet-cleaning business had won a contract to restore a large high-rise office building in downtown Sacramento, California. He told investors that the office building, which was under construction at the time, had experienced catastrophic water damage after a small fire set off the building's sprinkler system. Minkow and his co-conspirators entered the high-rise on a Sunday when work crews were off duty and surreptitiously placed ZZZZ Best paraphernalia, including company signs and t-shirts, throughout the building.

Then Minkow took the investors on a tour of the building to substantiate his contention that his small business had in fact won the large restoration contract. Minkow was arrested three years after embarking on his first fraudulent scheme and a year later was sentenced to twenty-five years in jail.

Assessment of the rational choice explanation

The rational choice explanation of wrongdoing assumes that people deliberate before embarking on wrongdoing, weighing the costs and benefits associated with possible alternative wrongful and rightful courses of action. Further, the core rational choice account assumes that people deliberate in a mindful and rational way. The rational choice explanation also largely assumes that people deliberate about the costs and benefits of alternative wrongful and rightful courses of action in a social vacuum. In this explanation, other people only enter the picture by affecting a potential wrongdoer's capacity to perpetrate the possible wrongdoing and to avoid detection and punishment. The rational choice explanation also implicitly assumes that people arrive at discrete decisions to either pursue or eschew wrongful behavior, insofar as it does not examine how wrongdoers' deliberations evolve over time. Finally, it explicitly assumes that if people decide to pursue wrongful behavior, they engage in wrongdoing because they are positively inclined (i.e. "motivated") to do so.

On balance, the rational choice explanation of organizational wrongdoing views wrongdoers as "bad" in one respect or another. It locates the causes of wrongdoing partly in the individual. People who conduct cost-benefit analyses that lead to wrongdoing have concluded that the rewards of engaging in wrongdoing outweigh the possible costs. And insofar as the negative cognitive and emotional states triggered by wrongdoing, such as the awareness of one's violation of societal norms and one's feelings of guilt, are costs of engaging in wrongdoing, people who decide to engage in wrongdoing can be considered *predisposed* to engage in such behavior (because they likely are not as deterred by these negative cognitive and emotional outcomes as they are attracted to wrongdoing's fruits). This is particularly clear in sociological and psychological theories that view wrongdoers as possessing low self-control and antisocial personalities.

The rational choice explanation also locates the causes of wrongdoing in the incentive structures in which individuals are embedded. For example, expectancy theory holds that the causes of wrongdoing rest in the effort–performance and performance–outcome expectancies associated with alternative wrongful and rightful courses of action. Thus the rational choice account partly absolves (here I am speaking in causal, rather than moral terms) wrongdoers of responsibility for their behavior. But as indicated above, the end result

63

of cost-benefit analyses that lead to wrongdoing are persons who are positively inclined or "motivated" to engage in wrongdoing. Thus, the rational choice account implicitly assumes that wrongdoers are "bad" from the start or "good people who have broken bad."

The rational choice explanation of organizational wrongdoing clearly has merit. People undoubtedly often mull over the costs and benefits of alternative courses of action before embarking on a particular line of behavior. And this mulling over of costs and benefits indubitably often influences the courses of action people ultimately pursue. Thus it seems reasonable to conclude that organizational participants frequently engage in cost-benefit calculations when confronted with the possibility of engaging in wrongdoing and that these calculations have a bearing on whether they move towards or away from wrongdoing. With this said, the rational choice explanation of wrongdoing is limited by the fundamental assumptions upon which it rests, which I believe are not universally valid.

I have indicated one way in which the rational choice account might be modified to relax one of the dominant assumptions on which it rests. I have shown how recent cognitive psychological research might be tapped to develop explanations of how rational choice cost-benefit calculations can go wrong in predictable ways, causing organizational participants to engage in wrongdoing that is not in their self-interest. As this book progresses, I will consider explanations of organizational wrongdoing that depart further from the assumptions that people deliberate before engaging in wrongdoing, that they reason in a mindful and rational way, that they ruminate in a social vacuum, that their deliberations result in discrete decisions, and that their decisions produce positive inclinations to engage in wrongdoing. In the process, I will move increasingly far from the view that bad things are the work of bad people, closer to a view that bad things are often done by good people, and thus closer to an explanation of how good people come to do bad things. But before I proceed with this endeavor, I want to briefly summarize what I have done in this chapter.

Conclusion

In this chapter I elaborated the first of eight explanations of organizational wrongdoing to be considered in this book. I briefly characterized the rational choice explanation, presented two specific theories that fall under the rubric of this account, and developed an overarching framework for elaborating this explanation. I also provided numerous illustrations of rational choice facilitated organizational wrongdoing, each of which constitutes an instance of wrongdoing that meets the definition delineated in the previous chapter, a definition that considers wrongdoing to be any behavior that social control agents label as such. Next, I turn to the second of the dominant explanations of organizational wrongdoing, the culture account.

5

Culture

Introduction

The cultural explanation is the second dominant account of organizational wrongdoing. It is rooted in a theoretical perspective that views organizations as communities, and organizational participants as normative appropriateness assessors. Organizations are populated by people who share the same ideas about the appropriate ways to think and act. People scrutinize alternative courses of action with an eye to determining whether they are in keeping with those ideas. In this view, organizational wrongdoing arises when an organization's culture becomes perverted and deems wrongdoing appropriate.

In this chapter I present the basic concepts of cultural analysis. I then elaborate the two ways that organizational cultures facilitate wrongdoing: by endorsing wrongdoing and by stipulating extenuating circumstances in which wrongdoing can be considered acceptable. I also describe how people come to embrace their organization's culture and delineate how cultures that facilitate wrongdoing arise and can be eradicated. I conclude by considering the relationship between the rational choice and culture explanations of organizational wrongdoing and by offering an overall assessment of the culture account.

The basic concepts of cultural analysis

Cultures have content and form. Cultural content consists of norms, values and beliefs, and assumptions that specify appropriate ways of thinking and acting in a social context. Assumptions are highly abstract notions about the way people actually think and act in the context. Values and beliefs are less abstract conceptions about the righteousness of alternative thoughts and actions that people exhibit in the context. Norms are more concrete understandings about what one should think and do in the context.

Cultural forms consist of artifacts and practices that convey cultural content. Artifacts are the smallest units through which cultural content is conveyed. They include tangible things such as the layout and furnishing of offices. They also include intangibles such as slang, slogans, and stories. Practices are behavioral patterns that include workgroup lunches, company picnics, industry conventions, and the like. Often artifacts are employed in practices, as is the case when a worker is awarded a certificate for team spirit (an artifact) at a company picnic (a practice).

People who are situated in a cultural context experience pressure to embrace the norms, values and beliefs, and assumptions of that context, that is, to exhibit attitudes and perform behaviors consistent with the cultural content of the context. But, people can be situated in and influenced by multiple cultural contexts, including occupational, professional, organizational, industrial, sectoral (e.g. for-profit, not-for-profit, and government), and even societal contexts. I will focus primarily on organizational contexts in this chapter, although I will refer to cultural content at other levels of analysis periodically to indicate the considerable scope of this approach. Further, each context's culture can vary in strength, depending on the extent to which their forms convey content in a consistent and redundant way, and the degree to which that content holds sway with employees (i.e. the extent to which employees align their thoughts and actions with that content). A strong culture has many forms that convey the same message or multiple interrelated messages to which employees adhere religiously. A weak culture has few forms that convey different and contradictory messages that employees freely ignore.

Thus, the cultural explanation assumes that people will engage in a wrongful course of action when they think that the wrongdoing is consistent with their organization's culture, that is, its norms, values and beliefs, and assumptions. But, the cultural account allows that people sometimes must take into account multiple cultural contexts that vary in salience when assessing the appropriateness of a particular wrongful course of action.

The two ways that cultures can facilitate wrongdoing

The endorsement of wrongdoing

A culture can give rise to wrongdoing in a straightforward manner when its content consists of norms, values and beliefs, and assumptions that endorse wrongful courses of action as rightful (Hochstetler and Copes 2001). In some cases, cultural content endorses specific types of wrongdoing. In other instances, it endorses wrongdoing more generally. I consider both types of endorsements below.

SPECIFIC ENDORSEMENT

Organizational cultures can endorse specific types of wrongdoing by containing artifacts and practices that convey the message that a behavior labeled as wrongful by social control agents is appropriate. Archer Daniel Midland's orchestration of price-fixing agreements in the market for lysine, an animal feed ingredient, illustrates well how cultural *assumptions* can foster wrongdoing. ADM's culture included the assumption that the firm's competitors were natural allies and its customers were inherent antagonists, reflected in managers' frequently voiced axiom "the competitors are our friends and the customers are our enemies" (Eichenwald 2000: 51). This assumption might have provided a rationale for the company's collusion with competitors at the expense of its customers.

Geis's (1995) study of the unlawful allocation of contracts among heavy electrical equipment manufacturers in the late 1950s illustrates how cultural *values and beliefs* can foster wrongdoing. It also illustrates how different levels of cultural content can reinforce one another. Bid rigging in the heavy electrical equipment industry in the late 1950s was extensive. And because it involved equipment used in the generation and transmission of electrical power, it affected federal, state, and municipal governments. Thus, its discovery resulted in public hearings at which industry participants were called to testify. Several of the salespersons who testified expressed the belief that allocating business among competitors in the industry was good, not just for the firms involved, but also for the industry and the economy as whole. These salespersons explained that by establishing agreements to determine which of the corporate co-conspirators would get particular contracts, they were smoothing out sales revenues among the firms in the industry, and thus reducing the negative externalities of destructive competition in the industry.

Geis's depiction of bid rigging in the heavy electrical equipment industry also illustrates how cultural *norms* can endorse specific forms of wrongdoing. Soon after salespersons in this industry were hired, they learned that meeting with representatives from other heavy electrical equipment producers, for the purpose of determining which company would win particular contracts, was a normal part of their job. Several salespersons testified that they agreed to participate in the meetings, because they thought others, most importantly their superiors, expected them to take part in the meetings. Further, they thought that if they did not agree to participate in the meetings, they would be replaced by other salespersons willing to take part in them.

In some instances, cultural endorsement of specific types of wrongdoing can be subtle. TAP Pharmaceuticals contained cultural artifacts that appear to have conveyed cultural content conducive to the adoption of illegal sales practices. TAP did not have an in-house legal counsel. According to one manager, "legal counsel was considered a sales-prevention department." When the company held a sales meeting to launch its ulcer drug Prevacid in 1995, it devoted little time to discussing scientific data testifying to the drug's efficacy. The meeting culminated with a party that featured "Tummy," a large mechanical stomach that belched fire (Haddad and Barrett 2002). These cultural artifacts might have conveyed the message that sales representatives need not formulate their sales pitches with legal concerns in mind. They also might have conveyed the message that sales representatives should not base their sales pitches on scientific evidence pertaining to a drug's therapeutic effectiveness. And together, these artifacts might have conveyed content that was consistent with the sales techniques employed by many of the company's representatives, including providing physicians with free and discounted samples of drugs and then encouraging them to bill insurers (including Medicare) for the retail price of the drugs, a subterfuge later judged to constitute an illegal kickback scheme.

GENERAL ENDORSEMENT

Organizational cultures also can endorse wrongdoing in a more general fashion by containing artifacts and practices that convey the message that engaging in behavior that is labeled as wrongful by social control agents is broadly acceptable and even appropriate. Most explicitly, a culture can contain practices that are wrongful, which conveys the message that other forms of wrongdoing also might be appropriate. While professional cycling's major races were honest competitions in the 1980s, the post-Tour de France criteriums typically were rigged. The senior most riders negotiated agreements in formal meetings the night before the race, or in a more ad hoc fashion on the morning of the race, in which the first several positions were allocated to the most popular non-local riders (bypassing top local riders to reduce the likelihood that their ruse would be uncovered). Paul Krimmage expressed no discomfort with this tradition. Like most riders, he apparently saw it as a way to capitalize on the Tour de France's buzz and expand the sport's footprint in the mind of the public. Indeed, he participated actively in the rigging of three 1987 post-Tour de France criteriums because his Irish compatriot Stephen Roche won that year's Tour. This illicit practice, which like the rigging of the 1950s quiz shows could be considered fraudulent, might have provided one precedent upon which the use of banned performance-enhancing substances could be based.

Similarly, some maintain that Enron was populated with executives who exhibited disrespect for the law, ethics, and social responsibility, and that these executives created a breeding ground for additional wrongdoing. Many journalists have cast Lou Pai, a top Enron trader, in this role. They have drawn attention to the fact that Pai frequented strip clubs, developed illicit sexual relationships with exotic dancers, and charged the costs of these activities to his Enron expense account (Bryce 2002; McLean and Elkind 2004; Eichenwald 2005). Of course, this explanation of the relationship between culture and wrongdoing raises the question of how wrongful organizational practices that elicit other wrongful behavior become entrenched in the first place.

Less explicitly, a culture can contain practices and artifacts that convey the message that wrongdoing is tolerated. MCI was a telecommunications company that became the site and perpetrator of a number of frauds in the late 1990s. A good number of MCI's customers were engaged in lines of business, such as dial-a-porn services, that its employees considered morally reprehensible. Further, many of its customers failed to pay their bills on time. A sizable portion of these delinquent customers withheld payment intentionally, sometimes making false representations, in an effort to force MCI to renegotiate their contracts. And some customers, referred to as "bust-out" artists, never paid a nickel of what they owed MCI, closing up shop and leaving town before the firm could collect what it was owed. In addition, some of MCI's customers used financing arrangements that pushed the outside of the usury-law envelope. Not surprisingly, some of MCI's customers were owned and led by people who previously had been indicted for fraud. Derogatory terms used to describe these customers, such as "dirtbags," "snake pit of thieves," and "scum of the earth," appeared to be part of MCI's lexicon, and conveyed the message that the firm was embedded in a network of unsavory associations. While members of the MCI unit tasked with collecting bills from customers, Carrier Finance, complained about the firm's marketing strategy, little was done to alter it. MCI had a unit dedicated to conducting due diligence on prospective customers, but its filter was porous. Thus the sales unit, supported by top management, continued to sign up questionable customers. Walter Pavlo, a member of MCI's Carrier Finance unit, co-authored a book about his experience at MCI upon which I will draw heavily in this chapter and Chapter 6. In the book, *Stolen Without a Gun,* Pavlo said that MCI employees interpreted the practices and artifacts described above as indicating that it was acceptable to engage in questionable business practices at the firm (Pavlo and Weinberg 2007).

Even less explicitly, a culture can contain practices and artifacts that convey acceptance and even appreciation of actions that break rules and violate norms, particularly actions that are considered risky or innovative. Enron's culture appeared to value behavior that pushed the envelope with respect to rules, as long as such behavior benefited the firm in some way. One former manager stated, "There were no rules for people, even in our personal lives. Everything was about the company and everything was supposed to be on the edge—sex, money, all of it . . . " (Boughton 2002). Another said, "it was all about creating an atmosphere of deliberately breaking the rules. For example, our official vacation policy was that you could take as much as you wanted whenever you wanted as long as you delivered results. It drove the human resource department crazy" (Bartlett and Glinska 2001). Sims and Brinkmann (2003) contend that Enron's culture also contained the value that cleverness was good and the assumption that the firm's employees were brilliant. If true, such cultural content might reinforce rule-breaking behavior. Managers who believed that cleverness was valued might feel authorized to break rules, and those who saw themselves as brilliant might think they could get away with it. There is an indication that MCI's culture included such a message as well. According to one observer, the firm's founder, Bill McGovern, voiced disdain for operating by the book, and once even threatened to fire anyone caught writing a systems or procedures handbook (Spurge 1998: 7).

Even less explicitly, a culture can contain artifacts and practices that focus members of a community on achieving ends while simultaneously conveying a lack of concern about the moral or legal character of the means by which ends are achieved. Enron's culture contained what Kulik (2005) characterizes as agency theory assumptions and beliefs. It was assumed that human behavior was predicated solely on self-interest, and it was believed that innovation and exceptional performance were maximized by unfettered competition. Enron's CEO Jeff Skilling promoted rivalry among his subordinates (McLean and Elkind 2004). Further, the company used a bi-annual performance evaluation system that guaranteed that only employees performing in the upper 85th percentile would be retained (Swartz and Watkins 2003). In this "anything goes" environment, the ends justified the means.

Least explicitly, a culture can contain artifacts and practices that focus members of a community on achieving ends without simultaneously providing guidance about the means with which ends should be achieved. Coleman (1987) contends that organizations in industrial societies generally exhibit this character. Industrial societies organize production for the market, generate an economic surplus, and use money to facilitate exchange. Coleman argues that such societies possess "culture(s) of competition" that in turn give rise to pervasive insecurity and fear of failure. Some maintain that capitalist societies exhibit an extreme form of this culture because the legal structures in these societies enforce the unrestrained pursuit of economic self-interest, a view portrayed graphically in the documentary *The Corporation* (Achbar and Abbott 2004). Others, though, maintain that the extent to which capitalist societies exhibit this cultural outlook varies, depending upon whether the dominant ideology is a "vulgar libertarian" type, which champions unfettered free markets, or a "republican" sort, which values citizenship and a commitment to social responsibility (Braithwaite 1988).

The stipulation of extenuating circumstances

Cultures also can give rise to organizational wrongdoing by containing artifacts and practices that convey assumptions, values and beliefs, and norms
that stipulate extenuating circumstances under which behavior understood to
be wrongful in general can be considered acceptable. Ashforth, Anand, and
Joshi (Ashforth and Anand 2003; Ashforth, Anand, and Joshi 2004) identify
six ways in which cultural content can stipulate conditions under which
wrongful behavior committed in and by organizations can be considered
acceptable. They refer to these six mechanisms as "techniques of neutralization," following nomenclature introduced by Sykes and Matza (1957) in their
path-breaking study of how street gang members understand their delinquent
behavior. Below I elaborate the six techniques of neutralization, drawing very
heavily on Ashforth, Anand, and Joshi's exposition.

Before describing the six techniques of neutralization, though, I need to
make two points. First, the six techniques of neutralization that I elaborate
below can operate in three different ways. All six techniques can be used by
wrongdoers as *after-the-fact* excuses for wrongdoing that protect them from
the consequences of their actions, both other's castigation and punishment
and their own feelings of guilt (Sonnenfeld 1981). In addition, as we will see in
Chapter 8, all six techniques can also be used by wrongdoers as *contemporaneous* justifications for their wrongdoing that help wrongdoers make sense of
their behavior and that blunt emerging feelings of guilt as they are making the
transition from right-doing to wrongdoing. This is the sense in which Anand,
Ashforth, and Joshi discuss techniques of neutralization. In this chapter,
though, I argue that techniques of neutralization serve a third function:
as *before-the-fact* causes of wrongdoing. Each of these "techniques of neutralization" can work on a cognitive level, by providing guidance on how to
conceptualize questionable behavior, or on an emotional level, by blocking
the emergence of feelings of guilt that would otherwise come to the surface
when people engage in wrongdoing. This third view is in keeping with Sykes
and Matza's original formulation, which held that techniques of neutralization free youth gang members from the general cultural (cognitive and emotional) constraints that would otherwise keep them from participating in
delinquent behavior.

Second, the six techniques of neutralization discussed in this chapter are
ubiquitous in American society, are likely prevalent in many Western societies, and might even be widespread in a good number of non-Western societies. Thus they are available to potential wrongdoers in all American
organizations and probably organizations in many other societies. However,
these six techniques of neutralization vary in the extent to which they are
available to members of different organizations. That is, any of the six

techniques might be considered acceptable justifications for wrongful behavior in some organizations, but unacceptable justifications in other organizations. An organizational participant will consider a technique of neutralization to be an acceptable justification for wrongdoing when others in the organization frequently use the technique. An organizational participant also will consider a technique of neutralization to be an acceptable justification for wrongdoing when the person's organizational context resembles the extenuating circumstances referenced by the technique. Of course, these two conditions tend to go hand in hand. The more frequently an organization's employees and managers find themselves in situations that resemble the extenuating circumstances referenced by a technique of neutralization, the more often they will invoke the technique of neutralization in question.

DENIAL OF RESPONSIBILITY

Some cultures contain content that conveys the message that it is acceptable for people to engage in wrongful behavior if conditions over which they have little or no control require them to do so. Conditions over which people have little or no control and that might render wrongdoing acceptable include coercive constraints, dire financial straits, and intense peer pressure. Wrongdoers who embrace this technique of neutralization do not regard themselves as wrongdoers. Rather they view themselves as right-doers, ethical, socially responsible, and law-abiding individuals, who are forced into wrongful acts.

In 1967, B.F. Goodrich perpetrated fraud against Ling-Tempco-Vaught Corporation (LTV) and the U.S. Navy in connection with the design and manufacture of a brake to be used for the Navy's new A7D attack fighter aircraft. It would appear that B.F. Goodrich's culture included the assumption that managers could not control the actions of employees outside their chain of command, and the related belief that it was not good for managers to assume responsibility for the actions of employees outside their chain of command, even if managers knew those actions were wrongful. Further, it would seem that this assumption and belief played a role in at least one manager's decision to tolerate wrongdoing perpetrated by design and test engineers involved in the development of the A7D brake (Vandivier 1972). The knowing acceptance of wrongdoing perpetrated by others is the most modest form of wrongdoing in which an organizational participant can engage.

Kermit Vandivier was a technical writer at B.F. Goodrich. When he learned that engineers and test specialists at the firm planned to produce a fraudulent qualification report for the A7D brake, he informed a superior, Russell Line, and pressed him to bring the information to the attention of his boss, Bud

Sunderman. But Line resisted saying, "Bud probably already knows about this thing anyway, and if he doesn't, I'm sure not going to be the one to tell him." When Vandivier asked Line why he would not advise Sunderman of the wrongdoing, the manager replied, "Because it's none of my business, and it's none of yours. I learned a long time ago not to worry about things over which I had no control. I have no control over this." When Vandivier asked Line whether his conscience would bother him if the wrongdoing led to a test pilot's injury or death, the exasperated manager replied, "I just told you I have no control over this. Why should my conscience bother me?"

DENIAL OF INJURY
Some cultures contain content that conveys that it is acceptable for people to engage in wrongful behavior if no one is harmed by the wrongdoing. Some cultures include the related message that it is acceptable for a person to engage in wrongful behavior if the harm it causes is small relative to the harm that would be caused by more extreme forms of wrongdoing that the person conceivably could commit. Wrongdoers who embrace this cultural content do not regard themselves as wrongdoers because they do not recognize their actions as producing actual or relatively significant harm.

Above I made reference to Walter Pavlo, who was a manager in MCI's Carrier Finance unit. Pavlo became involved in three different but related forms of wrongdoing about a year after he joined MCI. Here I focus on Pavlo's participation in a scheme conceived by Harold Mann, the owner of a dial-a-porn company with which MCI did business, to defraud MCI and its past-due customers. It would appear that Pavlo's involvement in this fraud was facilitated by his use of the denial of injury technique of neutralization.

Mann initiated the fraud by creating a dummy corporation named Orion. Then he, on behalf of Orion, offered to assume MCI customers' past due debt for an upfront fee and subsequent monthly payments. The customers were led to believe that Mann/Orion would negotiate with MCI to clear their debt by paying MCI a substantial part, if not the entire amount, of what the customers owed the telecommunications firm. And the customers expected that, with their debt presumably cleared, they would be allowed to remain on MCI's network. In fact, though, the money paid to Orion was divided among the co-conspirators. It was left to Pavlo to put the finishing touch on the scheme. He manipulated MCI's books so that his superiors and others at the firm believed that the customer's bills actually had been paid down, allowing the customer to regain its good standing with the firm.

Mann proposed the scheme to Pavlo in somewhat elliptical terms over lunch. As he elaborated the scheme, he offered Pavlo several techniques of neutralization that could be used to ward off feelings of guilt that Pavlo might otherwise experience from participating in the scheme, the first of which was the denial of injury. Mann began his exposition of the scheme by suggesting that Orion offer to assume the debt owed MCI by a company called TNI, run by Robert Hilby, which was to be the scheme's first victim. Trying to follow Mann's explanation, Pavlo asked him, "Lemme make sure I have this straight. Hilby pays you $300,000 up front. Then the monthly payments go to MCI." Mann responded, "I was figuring it'd be a wash for MCI." Still confused, Pavlo asked, "Meaning what?" Mann answered this inquiry with a rhetorical question of his own, "Is Hilby planning to pay MCI?" Pavlo responded, "He's better than most about paying something. But if you're asking whether we'll ever see the $2 million he's behind on, I doubt it." Mann followed Pavlo's response with the essence of the denial of injury technique, "Then, if we don't pay MCI, it's not really out anything. I mean you can't steal money MCI wasn't going to get anyway, right?" Their subsequent exchange suggests that Pavlo experienced guilt as he contemplated joining the scheme, guilt that might be neutralized by Mann's logical analysis. When Mann finished explaining the details of the scheme, Pavlo remained unconvinced of the scheme's merits, saying "It isn't that easy, Harold." Misunderstanding Pavlo's concern, Mann responded, "Hey you're a smart guy! You telling me you can't hide a $2 million needle in MCI's billion (dollar) haystack?" Pavlo replied, "That's the easy part. But what you are suggesting is . . . you know . . . wrong." (Pavlo and Weinberg 2007: 118–120).

DENIAL OF VICTIM

Some cultures include content that conveys the message that it is acceptable for a person to engage in wrongful behavior if the victim of their wrongdoing deserves to be wronged. Wrongdoers who embrace this technique of neutralization essentially deny that the people harmed by their wrongdoing are real victims. The categorization of some types of victims as authentic and others as inauthentic is called "moral exclusion" (Opotow 1990). This technique of neutralization has at least two forms.

First, wrongdoers can believe that the people they harm deserve their fate due to moral failings on their part. Harold Mann suggested this version of the denial of victim technique to Walter Pavlo, in addition to his submission of the denial of injury technique discussed above, when he pitched his scheme to defraud MCI and its past-due customers. In direct response to Pavlo's concern that his proposed scheme was "wrong," Mann said, "Spare me the sermon, Wally, Hilby and the rest of 'em are out-and-out deadbeats" (Pavlo and Weinberg 2007: 120). This denial of victim rationalization resonated with Pavlo because it accorded with reality, the views of his MCI co-workers, and his own experience.

As noted earlier, half of the Carrier Finance customers were 900 number companies, many of whom were "dial-a-porn" providers. The other half were discount carriers, who charged their customers switching fees for unilaterally changing their service without the customers' approval, a scam called "slamming." A good number of both types of customers never intended to pay their bills to MCI in full. Some feigned economic hardship and demanded discounts. Others, the "bust-outs," got access to the MCI network, sold a service or prepaid phone cards, and then skipped town without paying their bills. Finally, some of the customers had prior convictions for fraud. Carrier Finance employees referred to the unit's customers in derogatory terms. Further, Pavlo had spent the better part of the previous year struggling unsuccessfully to collect money owed MCI by the shadiest of these customers. For all of these reasons, the denial of injury technique of neutralization rang true to Pavlo. As he recalled, "Embezzlement was the legal term for Mann's proposal. But it wasn't like he was going to trick old ladies out of their savings or bash anyone over the head. It was *victimless* embezzlement (emphasis added)—unless you count hustlers as victims" (Pavlo and Weinberg 2007: 120).

Second, a wrongdoer can believe that those harmed by their wrongdoing deserve their fate due to their inferior status. In recent years, several investment banks have been successfully sued and/or prosecuted for providing investment advice that benefited themselves at the expense of their clients. For example, in 2002 Merrill Lynch paid $100 million to settle a suit brought by the New York Attorney General for inflating its stock rating of several Internet companies in which it had vested interest. Then in 2006, Merrill was fined another $50 million by the National Association of Securities Dealers for encouraging its employees to push its proprietary mutual fund products at the expense of other superior available financial products (Rauch 2006). Michael Lewis's (1990) portrayal of the Wall Street investment bank Salomon Brothers depicts cultural content that might reinforce such practices. In the Salomon Brothers' culture, customers were assumed to be stupid, an outlook reflected in the derisive idiom "you are proof that some people are born to be customers," which was directed at employees who demonstrated ignorance or incompetence of one kind or another (Lewis 1990: 171). Further, the Salomon Brothers' culture fostered the belief that stupid people deserve to be exploited. The views that customers are stupid and that stupid people deserve to be exploited might have provided investment bank employees with a rationale for pursuing their firms' best interest at the expense of their clients.

A similar constellation of beliefs appears to have been in place at Enron and might have facilitated the company's manipulation of California's electric power market, for which Enron was eventually fined millions of dollars. The company's culture contained the belief that the free market, rather than government regulation, was the appropriate way to organize economic activity in most industries, including the energy industry. It also contained the assumption that Enron's managers were smarter than most other corporate executives and certainly smarter than government officials (reflected in the title of the most well-known depiction of the Enron saga, *The Smartest Guys in the Room*). This belief and assumption shaped Enron managers' reaction to California's incomplete deregulation of its energy market. In McLean and Elkind's words, "Everyone at Enron was annoyed at the way California had put deregulation into effect; the state hadn't followed the company's long-held position that a completely free marketplace was the only thing that made sense. Having failed to listen to Enron, the state therefore deserved whatever it got." One senior executive summed up the prevailing attitude at the firm, "If they're going to put in place such a stupid system, it makes sense to try to game it" (2004: 267).

SOCIAL WEIGHTING

Social weighting, the fourth technique of neutralization, can take two forms. Some cultures contain content that conveys the message that it is acceptable for a person to engage in wrongful behavior if their wrongful behavior is no more severe or less severe than others' wrongful behavior. Wrongdoers who embrace this cultural content compare their behavior to the behavior of others, primarily focusing on behaviors that can be considered as bad or even worse than their own. This allows wrongdoers to believe that their behavior is not really wrongful when evaluated from a relativist standpoint.

Harold Mann offered this technique of neutralization to Walter Pavlo when pitching his scheme to defraud MCI and its past-due customers, in conjunction with the denial of victim and denial of harm techniques discussed above. Responding to Pavlo's reticence to participate in the scheme, Mann reminded him that MCI was itself guilty of serious transgressions. After characterizing MCI's customers as "out-and-out deadbeats," Mann went on to say, "You guys at MCI aren't any different. Just better dressers." Then he elaborated, "You guys're cookin' the books over there and you know it. Everybody cheats. That's the way the world works. Your problem, Wally, is that you haven't figured out how to make money at it."

This technique of neutralization, like the others offered by Mann, resonated with Pavlo because it was rooted in his practical knowledge and his co-workers' experience at MCI. As Pavlo recounted (in the third person) in his co-authored book, "The scheme Mann was describing...was no worse than what MCI's customers were doing to MCI, or what MCI was doing to its shareholders...Mann's twisted logic made perfect sense. Money, tons of it was being manipulated, lied about, misused, misplaced, stolen. By everybody.

Pavlo knew the whole world didn't work that way, but his did, from the corporate chiefs above to the scumbag customers below" (Pavlo and Weinberg 2007: 120). It was the correspondence of Mann's argument with MCI's reality that made the social-weighting technique of neutralization viable.

Alternatively, some cultures convey the message that it is acceptable for a person to engage in wrongful behavior if the legitimacy of the entity that labels their acts as wrongful is questionable. Wrongdoers who embrace this variant of the social-weighting technique implicitly embrace the sociological definition of wrongdoing that I employ in this book, namely, that behaviors are considered wrongful when social control agents classify them as such. But wrongdoers who embrace this technique also take a normative stand on the legitimacy of social control agents, social control agents' judgments, or both. For instance, wrongdoers may characterize social control agents as incompetent or self-interested and their judgments as capricious or malicious. James Stewart (1991) suggests that this technique of neutralization might have underpinned Wall Street arbitrager violations of Securities and Exchange Commission (SEC) margin requirements. According to Stewart, arbitragers had little respect for SEC examiners, whom they considered unintelligent (to which their relatively low pay was a testament). And they thought SEC margin requirements, which stipulated the amount of cash investors had to have on hand to cover their stock positions, were excessive. For this reason, they viewed violation of SEC margin requirements as acceptable and little cause for embarrassment.

APPEAL TO HIGHER LOYALTIES

Some cultures convey the message that it is acceptable for a person to engage in wrongful behavior if the wrongdoer, in the course of perpetuating wrongdoing, achieves a higher moral goal. Unlike the other techniques of neutralization, this technique may go beyond rendering wrongdoing acceptable to making it noble. Perhaps the most common higher moral goal is the defense of group interests. Wrongdoers are particularly likely to embrace this technique when they belong to a group that is highly cohesive, perhaps because it faces an external threat to its survival. This type of cultural content appeared to partially underpin Enron's manipulation of California's electric power market. Many Enron employees shared the belief that the firm was a uniquely innovative company at odds with the mainstream business world. The firm's employees believed that they had to remain focused on achieving its goals rather than worry about the interests of others affected by the firm's actions. This outlook is in keeping with the pursuit of trading strategies that benefited the firm at the expense of California. In the words of one Enron executive, "It was the traders' job to make money, not to benefit the people of California" (McLean and Elkind 2004: 268).

A less commonly invoked higher moral goal is the defense of sacred principles. This type of cultural content also appeared to support Enron's manipulation of California's electrical power market. As indicated above, Enron's culture included the belief that the free market was superior, both more economically efficient and more socially advantageous, to government regulation when it came to governing economic transactions. For this reason, Enron's top executives frequently proselytized the virtues of the free market, and the company spent millions of dollars lobbying for deregulation of the U.S. energy industry. As a result, behavior that was geared towards the pursuit of free market objectives, even if questionable on legal, ethical, or social responsibility grounds, was considered laudable. For example, in response to criticisms that Enron's aggressive pursuit of deregulation of the California energy market wreaked havoc on the state, the firm's CEO, Jeff Skilling, crowed, "We're on the side of angels (2004: 281)." And when McLean and Elkind described the architect of Enron's California strategy, Tim Belden, they wrote, "He was, as they liked to say at Enron, intellectually pure—a trader who believed in the beauty of free markets and had no scruples when it came to exploiting inefficiencies to make money" (2004: 264).

BALANCING THE LEDGER

Finally, some cultures contain content suggesting that it is acceptable for a person to engage in wrongful behavior if they have done, are doing, or plan to do other good deeds that offset the wrongful acts. Walter Pavlo appears to have used the balancing the ledger technique when contemplating whether to join Harold Mann in his scheme to defraud MCI and its customers. In his mind, he was providing MCI much more in services and sacrifice than the firm was providing him in compensation. Implicitly, the wrongdoing in which he engaged balanced this compensation shortfall. As he recounted in his book, "If MCI had been paying him what he was worth, treating him fairly, he reasoned, he'd have less to complain about. But he was getting screwed, too. Sixty-three thousand dollars a year (his salary at the time) to play nanny to two billion! MCI had driven him away from his family and into the arms of cigarettes and booze. 'They' were cooking the books and he was helping 'them' do it, while enjoying none of the benefit (Pavlo and Weinberg 2007: 120)." Importantly, Pavlo's complaints about his compensation were not unique. Other MCI employees shared his view of the firm's compensation system, which was structured such that long-standing employees were generally undercompensated relative to newcomers. Veteran employees were restricted by company policy in the frequency and magnitude of the pay raises they could obtain. In contrast, new employees were hired at the ever-increasing market wage.

How organizational participants come to embrace cultures that facilitate wrongdoing

The process by which people come to embrace an organization's cultural content, regardless of whether that content supports rightful or wrongful behavior, is called "organizational socialization." According to Schein (1961a, b), who presents a particularly accessible account, organizational socialization consists of three stages that in theory evolve sequentially but in practice often overlap.[1] In the first stage, which Schein calls "unfreezing," socialization targets abandon their old identity. This stage consists of three dynamics: humiliation of the old identity, isolation from supports for the old identity, and motivation of change away from the old identity.

In the second stage of the socialization process, which Schein calls "change," socialization targets embrace their new identity. This stage also consists of three dynamics: motivation of change to the new identity, identification with a role model who exemplifies the new identity, and internalization of the new identity. Socialization targets tend to choose as role models others who are similar to them but who have progressed further than they have in the socialization process. People only internalize cultural content, meaning they embrace it as their own point of view, after they have tailored the cultural content to fit their unique organizational situation and used the modified content successfully to cope with the problems they confront in their organizational life.

The third and final stage of the socialization process, which Schein calls "refreezing," reinforces socialization targets' new identity. When socialization takes place in a non-work context, such as a military academy, professional training program, or corporate retreat, this stage consists of transplanting the target from the socialization context to the work context in which the new norms, values and beliefs, and assumptions are operative. When socialization takes place "on the job," this stage consists of transporting the socialization target from an old milieu to a new work environment in which the new norms, values and beliefs, and assumptions are in force. When socialization takes place on the job and involves the reinforcement of attitudes that underpin wrongdoing, this stage can consist of transporting the socialization target from a rightful reference group to a wrongful one.

Michael Lewis' (1990) depiction of the training and development of new employees at Salomon Brothers provides evidence of the way in which an organizational socialization process can inculcate new employees into a culture that facilitates wrongdoing (Lewis 1990). More specifically, it suggests

---

[1] My analysis of the process by which people become socialized into organizational cultures that facilitate wrongdoing overlaps with John Darley's (1996) excellent prior analysis.

how new investment bank employees were socialized into a set of assumptions, values and beliefs, and norms that might have supported behavior geared to advance the welfare of their firms at the expense of their clients, behavior for which (as indicated above) several investment banks have been successfully sued and/or prosecuted.

New employees entered Salomon Brothers through its training program. The program served primarily to unfreeze the firm's recruits but also introduced them to the cultural content that they would be expected to embrace as employees of the firm. Trainees were humiliated in a variety of ways. Each day began with a series of lectures by Salomon executives, who showered the trainees with a constant stream of insults and peppered them with questions that they could not possibly answer. Each day ended with a field trip to the trading floor, where trainees were routinely ignored or treated with disdain. Lewis offered a colorful description of his experience as a trainee on the Salomon trading floor. "As a trainee, a plebe, a young man lying under all that whale shit, I did what every trainee did: I sidled up to some busy person without saying a word and became the Invisible Man. That it was perfectly humiliating was, of course, precisely the point. Sometimes I'd wait for an hour before my existence was formally acknowledged; other times, a few minutes. Even that seemed like forever. Who is watching me in my current debased condition? I'd wonder. Will I ever recover from such total neglect?" (51).

Trainees were somewhat isolated from others who might reinforce their old identities by the all-consuming nature of the training program, which began in the classroom early in the morning and sometimes ended at a social engagement late in the evening. More important, though, they were punished for signs that they retained previously acquired inappropriate assumptions, values and beliefs, and norms. And they were rewarded for signs that they abandoned their prior outmoded identities. For example, when trainees asked questions indicative of concerns that Salomon executives considered irrelevant, such as queries pertaining to ethics and social responsibility, the questions were summarily and hostilely dismissed. But all trainees knew that successful completion of the program, which required the jettisoning of old attitudes and behaviors, guaranteed them a job at the firm and progression up the hierarchy of statuses: from "trainee," to "geek," to "man," to "Big Swinging Dick." The cultural content that was imparted at this stage of the socialization process included a number of assumptions, values and beliefs, and norms. Trainees learned that at Salomon money was the most valued commodity. They also learned that Salomon employees should think of themselves as superior and should behave in an arrogant fashion. And most to the point, trainees learned that they worked for Salomon rather than their clients and that their clients were stupid (about as smart as trainees) and thus exploitable.

The socialization process continued when trainees graduated from the program and entered their first jobs, passing from "trainee" to "geek." There they were assigned a hierarchy of role models. Each new employee had a "rabbi," a manager to whom they were assigned, and a "jungle guide," a direct superior to whom they reported. In addition, new employees naturally found peers to look up to. Michael Lewis looked up to a fellow salesman named Dash and a junior trader named Alexander to obtain clues regarding how to think and act at the firm. Rewards played a larger role than punishments when it came to learning Salomon's cultural content. Among the biggest rewards was recognition by superiors and peers for adopting the Salomon way. And among the most potent forms of recognition was mention on the "hoot and holler," a public address system that announced salesperson and trader successes. It was through the hoot and holler that Lewis came to understand in a concrete way the priority of the firm's welfare over its customers' well-being. Lewis was manipulated by one of the firm's traders to sell a bundle of poorly performing Salomon-owned ATT bonds to an unsuspecting German banker, thus transferring a growing loss from Salomon's accounts to the German banker's books. When the sale of Salomon's ATT bonds was announced in glowing terms on the hoot and holler, Lewis simultaneously realized that he had inadvertently swindled a customer and that this was considered a noteworthy achievement by the firm.

While new Salomon employees observed role models and attended to rewards and punishments in their work environment, they had considerable leeway to develop their own unique adaptation to the Salomon culture. And this freedom to develop one's own approach facilitated trainees' internalization of the culture. Lewis noted that the many Salomon executives who were paraded before the trainees in his class exhibited a remarkable variety of character types. This led him to realize that, "More different types of people succeeded on the trading floor than I initially supposed." He went on to observe that, "The range of acceptable conduct within Salomon Brothers was wide indeed" (70). Once on the job, Lewis was allowed leeway to find his own way to success and, infuriatingly, failure as a salesperson. Dash, his immediate role model and growing friend, often let Lewis pursue courses of action that he knew were ill advised. But as Lewis increasingly found his own way to success on the trading floor, he came to be viewed differently by his co-workers. Ultimately, he made the transition from "geek" to "man." And this passage was signified by the fact that new employees now lined up next to his desk seeking his advice.

How perverse cultures develop and how they can be eradicated

Many believe that leaders play a crucial role in developing and disseminating organizational cultures. For example, the founders of Hewlett Packard Company are widely believed to have fostered a culture that put a premium on innovation and service, known as "The HP Way." In fact, Dave Packard wrote a book of this title about HP, which was given to all new employees to supplement their socialization into the Hewlett Packard culture. In Packard's words, the HP Way is a "core ideology . . . [which] . . . includes a deep respect for the individual, a dedication to affordable quality and reliability, a commitment to community responsibility, and a view that the company exists to make technical contributions for the advancement and welfare of humanity."

Schein (1985) contends that leaders propagate cultural content through five channels: 1) the things to which they pay attention, 2) the ways in which they respond to crises, 3) the behaviors they model, 4) the behaviors they reward and punish, and 5) the kinds of employees they hire and dismiss. Sims and Brinkmann (2003) contend that leaders use the same five conduits to propagate cultures that facilitate wrongdoing. They describe how Enron executives used these avenues to foster a culture that facilitated a variety of forms of wrongdoing. Enron CEO Jeff Skilling's tolerance of Lou Pai's questionable behavior, such as his violation of company policy in support of what many employees found distasteful behavior (his use of a corporate expense account to fund long lunches at strip clubs) falls under the heading of things to which leaders pay attention or behaviors that they reward or punish. A good number of co-workers complained about Pai's misuse of company funds and generally objectionable behavior. But Skilling failed to reprimand him, presumably because he valued above all else Pai's unparalleled trading acumen. As McLean and Elkind put it, "Pai served as the human template for the trading culture at Enron" (2004: 58).

The view that leaders disseminate cultures that foster wrongdoing suggests a relatively simple strategy for combating culture-facilitated wrongdoing: replacing top with managers who lead inappropriately with executives who attend to the proper things, respond to crises in the proper way, model the proper behaviors, reward and punish employees appropriately and hire and dismiss the right employees. Of course, replacing bad leaders with good ones cannot eradicate a corrupt culture immediately. Once socialized into a culture, employees internalize its norms, values and beliefs, and assumptions and evince attitudes and behaviors consistent with the cultural content, even in the absence of leader influence. Thus, lower-level employees who have been socialized into a corrupt culture must be re-socialized. And the re-socialization of employees requires extensive effort. But eradicating a culture that facilitates wrongdoing might require even more than this.

Structural functionalist anthropologists think that societies develop cultures that help them adapt to the environments in which they are situated (Radcliffe-Brown 1965). Following this line of thought, some organizational theorists maintain that organizations develop cultures that help them adapt to their environments (c.f., Schein 1995), which are characterized as having internal dimensions (dictated largely by an organization's size, technology, and structure) and external aspects (dictated primarily by an organization's strategy and the actions of other organizations upon which it depends for resources needed for survival). And consistent with this reasoning, some research shows that organizations with cultures that are well adapted to their environment have survival and performance advantages over those with cultures that are not well adapted to their surroundings (Carroll and Harrison 1998; Sorenson 2002).

Military organizations provide an extreme example of how cultures can facilitate organizational functioning. These organizations develop cultures that contain the assumption that their enemies are less than fully human, reflected in the jargon according to which their enemies are referred. In World War II, U.S. soldiers referred to German soldiers as "krauts." In the Vietnam War, they referred to North Vietnamese and Viet Cong soldiers as "gooks." And in the Iraq and Afghanistan conflicts, U.S. soldiers referred to enemy combatants (as well as civilians with whom they are often indistinguishable) as "towel heads." Such jargon provides the basis of the denial of victim technique of neutralization, which frees soldiers to engage in behaviors that they would otherwise consider wrongful, most importantly, killing.

The emergence of cultural content that helps organizations adapt to their environments, though, paradoxically also can give rise to wrongdoing. For example, some pharmaceutical company managers view the Food and Drug Administration (FDA) as an unscrupulous adversary. Pharmaceutical company employees work hard to develop drugs that can cure diseases and alleviate pain and suffering. But the FDA determines whether pharmaceutical companies can market their drugs to consumers. Viewing the FDA as an unscrupulous adversary can focus pharmaceutical employees' attention on a crucial gatekeeper, ensuring that it is adequately taken into account. But it also can support the denial of victim and social weighting techniques of neutralization that might free pharmaceutical company employees to engage in wrongful behaviors such as the falsification of test results that call into question the efficacy and safety of drugs. If one believes that the FDA is unfairly keeping useful drugs from the customers who need them, then the falsification of test results can be seen as harmless and as being no worse than the FDA's own behavior.

The view that organizations develop cultures that help them adapt to their environments suggests that simply replacing organizational leaders and even re-socializing employees will not eradicate corrupt cultures. It suggests that organizational cultures will be resistant to change and, if changed, subject to reversion, because cultures tend to be anchored in a number of stable internal and external structures. In other words, wrongdoing will sometimes be the *normal* consequence of a well-adjusted culture.

Integrating the rational choice and culture explanations

The rational choice and culture explanations of organizational wrongdoing offer very different portraits of the mechanisms and factors that cause people to become involved in wrongdoing. The rational choice explanation focuses on cost-benefit calculations regarding rewards and punishments. The culture account focuses on normative assessments regarding shared understandings of right and wrong. For this reason, the two approaches often are pitted against one another, as reflected in the title of an article on Enron referenced above, "Enron Ethics (Or: Culture Matters More than Codes)" (Sims and Brinkmann 2003). But the two perspectives are not incompatible. In fact, they dovetail with each other in at least four respects.

First, an organization's culture can shape its incentive structure, which in turn can facilitate organizational wrongdoing. When this is the case, organizational culture facilitates wrongdoing indirectly. For example, cultural content can underpin behavior that leads to losses that are difficult to recoup, which the rational choice explanation contends breeds wrongdoing. Enron's culture placed a high value on the consummation of deals: the arrangement of contracts with the energy suppliers and purchasers, the acquisition of independent energy production and distribution operations, and the building of new power plants. Enron's CEO, Jeff Skilling, telegraphed this value by giving Enron's deal-makers titles such as "managing director" that mimicked those used by Wall Street investment banks (McLean and Elkind 2004: 57). At the same time, Enron's culture placed a low value on deal implementation. This was particularly evident when the firm entered the retail sector and began negotiating contracts with businesses and government agencies to provide the full range of energy services (such as designing, installing, and maintaining heating and lighting equipment in facilities). Employees involved in the negotiation of contracts with large energy consuming customers such as Lockheed Martin and the University of California were loudly praised. But those involved in the development of resources (employees and equipment) needed to fulfill the contracts received little acclaim. In fact, the firms that Enron purchased to fulfill this role were referred to contemptuously as "butt-crack businesses" (Eichenwald 2005: 183). As a result, the company became burdened by a plethora of large contracts that generated losses rather than profits. Losses, of course, are not in themselves illegal, unethical, or socially irresponsible. However, as indicated in the previous chapter, Enron's losses provided the impetus for many questionable accounting practices, which ultimately were the target of government investigations.

Second, an organization's incentive structure can convey cultural content, which in turn can facilitate wrongdoing. When this is the case, an organization's incentive structure facilitates wrongdoing indirectly. Most organizational arrangements have both practical and symbolic significance. For example, a large mahogany desk provides an expansive surface on which a manager can work, but it also conveys the message that social status is valued in the organization. Analogously, incentive structures both reward and punish employees for specific behaviors and convey messages about the behaviors that are valued in the organization. Enron conducted semi-annual reviews in which employees were assigned scores from one to five that reflected top management perceptions of their performance, dictated the size of their bonuses, and influenced their promotion chances. Executives responsible for doing deals invariably fared better in the performance review process than executives assigned to other tasks (such as those delegated to risk analysis and management). This practice both rewarded dealmakers for their service to the firm and conveyed to all employees that deal-making was the firm's most important activity. The fact that rational choice and cultural factors often are intertwined sometimes makes it difficult to sort out the unique contribution of each to particular instances of wrongdoing.

Third, people are capable of engaging in both cost-benefit and normative appropriateness deliberations when considering the merits of engaging in a particular wrongful course of action. People can engage in cost-benefit calculations and normative appropriateness assessments sequentially. For example, Walter Pavlo appears to have gone back and forth between cost-benefit calculations and normative appropriateness assessments when deciding whether or not to cooperate with Harold Mann in his plan to defraud MCI and its customers. First, he contemplated the feasibility of the scheme, implicitly estimating the effort–performance expectancy associated with the plan, by asking Mann to describe in greater detail how he planned to pull off the scam. Then he considered the normative implications of participating in the scheme, contemplating the serviceability of the various techniques of neutralization that Mann offered up for consideration. Finally, he returned to contemplating the potential pay-off of the scheme, implicitly estimating the performance–outcome expectancy associated with the plan by calculating the number of clients available to be scammed.

People even can engage in cost-benefit calculations and normative appropriateness assessments at the same time. Donald Cressey (1972) developed a theory of embezzlement that explicitly incorporated the simultaneous consideration of blocked aspirations and techniques of neutralization. In his classic book *Other People's Money*, Cressey interviewed people who were incarcerated for embezzling funds from their employers or clients and concluded that people embezzle funds when they experience a performance shortfall that they cannot reveal *and* when they have access to techniques of neutralization that allow them to view embezzlement as acceptable under the circumstances—specifically, when they are employed in a line of work in which they take care of other people's money and thus can view their embezzlement as a form of borrowing.

Fourth, one can view the cultural explanation of organizational wrongdoing as one component of the rational choice account. If internalized assumptions, values and beliefs, and norms are considered elements of a person's preference structure, people can be viewed as varying in the valence they assign to the good feeling they obtain when their behavior is aligned with assumptions, values and beliefs, and norms current in their organization. And if this is done, normative appropriateness assessments can be considered one dimension of the larger cost-benefit analysis. In this light, Pavlo's equivocation in response to Mann's wrongdoing pitch, described above, can be viewed as a simultaneous mulling over of the potential economic and psychological consequences for him of participating in Mann's scheme.

Assessing the normative appropriateness approach

The cultural explanation, like the rational choice account, is based largely on the four assumptions that characterize the dominant approach to understanding organizational wrongdoing. It assumes that people deliberate before embarking on a wrongful course of action, assessing the degree to which a contemplated behavior is consistent with their internalized norms, values and beliefs, and assumptions. In addition, insofar as it does not explicitly consider ways in which normative appropriateness assessments can be compromised, the cultural account implicitly assumes that such deliberations are rational. Further, the cultural explanation of organizational wrongdoing assumes that if people decide to pursue a wrongful behavior, they do so because their decision results in a positive inclination to engage in the behavior—a state of mind rooted in the assessment that the wrongful behavior is in fact rightful, either in general or in light of specific circumstances.

The cultural explanation of organizational wrongdoing, like the rational choice account, also largely locates the causes of wrongdoing in the individual. The root cause of wrongdoing is the individual's possession of assumptions, values and beliefs, and norms that either endorse wrongdoing or stipulate extenuating circumstances under which wrongdoing is acceptable. The cultural account allows that organizational participants might not possess assumptions, values and beliefs, or norms that facilitate wrongdoing before they enter the organization that is the site of the wrongdoing in question. Indeed, it explains how external forces operating in the socialization processes can inject organizational participants with cultural content that facilitates wrongdoing. Nevertheless, the culture account assumes that at the time organizational participants engage in wrongdoing, the norms, values and beliefs, and assumptions they hold make them prone to engage in wrongful behavior. In a sense, the cultural explanation of organizational wrongdoing locates the cause of organizational wrongdoing in people who have been pickled in "bad barrels" and in the process become "bad apples."

But the cultural explanation of organizational wrongdoing departs from the dominant approach in two important respects. First, while for the most part it ignores situated social interaction and temporal dynamics, it takes both into account in the socialization process. The cultural account assumes that people are socialized in the course of interacting with others (most obviously, role models) and it characterizes the socialization process as progressing over time in three phases. Of course it assumes that once the socialization process is complete, situated social interaction merely reinforces internalized cultural content (in the refreezing process). Moreover, when people confront opportunities to engage in wrongdoing, they make discrete choices either to pursue or eschew the wrongful course of action, depending on their assessment of the behavior's appropriateness.

Second, while for the most part the cultural account assumes that people deliberate before embarking on a wrongful course of action, assessing the degree to which a contemplated behavior is consistent with their internalized norms, values and beliefs, and assumptions, many social psychologists believe that deliberations involving norms often are severely truncated. Norms are more specific than assumptions, values and beliefs, prescribing precisely how people should think and act in a particular social setting. As a result, they can give rise to attitudes and behaviors in a programmed automatic fashion.

Conclusion

I have now elaborated the second of eight explanations of organizational wrongdoing to be considered in this book. Like the rational choice account considered in the previous chapter, the culture explanation contributes much to the understanding of wrongdoing in and by organizations. Undoubtedly, people often engage in normative appropriateness assessments when confronted with the possibility of engaging in wrongdoing. And assuredly, the results of such assessments often have a bearing on whether people move towards or away from wrongdoing. With this said, the culture explanation of wrongdoing is limited by the extent to which it rests on the four assumptions of the dominant approach, assumptions that I contend are not invariably valid.

Chapters 6 through 11 will present explanations of wrongdoing that depart further from the dominant approach, increasingly embracing the view that people can become involved in wrongdoing in a mindless and boundedly rational way, influenced by their immediate social context, through a temporally building process, without ever developing a positive inclination to engage in wrongful behavior. The further we move towards developing such an understanding, the closer we will come to an explanation of how good people can come to do bad things. With this in mind, I turn next to an explanation of organizational wrongdoing that in its earliest formulations conformed closely to the dominant approach, but in its most recent expression represents a bridge to the alternative approach to explaining wrongdoing.

6

Ethical Decisions

Introduction

The ethical decision explanation of organizational wrongdoing is rooted in a theoretical perspective that views organizations as collections of people engaged in complementary tasks, and views organizational participants as decision makers. Organizations are populated by people who perform tasks that, when coordinated appropriately, achieve a collective goal. And people collect and process information in an effort to determine how best to complete their tasks so that their work is efficient, effective, and dovetails appropriately with the work of others in the organization.

The earliest work on ethical decision-making focused almost exclusively on how people *should* make ethical decisions. The classical philosophers, including Socrates and Aristotle, wrote extensively on ethics. More modern philosophers, such as Kant, also have made substantial contributions to this subject. Philosophers situated in management schools have drawn on this work to analyze business decisions in an attempt to distinguish ethical choices from unethical ones (Nielsen 1988). The vast majority of management school courses on ethics still use this normative approach. The typical course covers the main philosophical perspectives on ethics, engages students in discussions of the merits and drawbacks of the different approaches, and challenges students to apply the different approaches to managerial dilemmas, both real and fabricated. Further, much research on ethical decision-making continues to employ the normative approach. Nielsen's (2010) recent analysis of the 2008 mortgage meltdown, in which he identifies a number of behaviors that were prevalent in the financial system and contributing factors to the meltdown as unethical, provides an excellent illustration of this type of work.

Beginning in the latter part of the past century, though, psychologists began studying how people *actually* make ethical decisions. Over the past few decades, social scientists situated in management schools also have taken up this line of inquiry. The behavioral study of ethical decision-making is now a vibrant field. The ethical decision-making explanation of organizational wrongdoing represents a bridge between the dominant and alternative approaches to explaining organizational wrongdoing. The early ethical decision theorists largely embraced the four assumptions that characterize the dominant approach, that is, they tended to assume that people deliberate mindfully and rationally, in social isolation, make discrete decisions, and formulate positive inclinations, all before embarking on wrongdoing. But the more recent work in this tradition jettisons, in part or whole, some of these assumptions.

In the first part of this chapter, I briefly characterize early ethical decision theory and research. In the second part of the chapter, I briefly discuss recent theory and research and at length elaborate two ways in which I think this recent work can be usefully extended. At the end of each section, I assess the extent to which the work discussed adheres to or departs from the dominant approach to explaining organizational wrongdoing. My characterization of ethical decision theory and research, both early and recent, is not intended to be comprehensive. It is intended to be only thorough enough to convey the main currents of this approach so as to provide a foundation for my suggested extensions of this approach and to lay the groundwork for the alternative explanations of organizational wrongdoing considered in the chapters to come. Excellent comprehensive summaries of the early ethical decision-making literature and recent developments in this literature are available in O'Fallon and Butterfield (2005), Trevino, Weaver, and Reynolds (2006), Tenbrunsel and Smith-Crowe (2008) and Bazerman and Tenbrunsel (2011).

Before beginning my discussion of the ethical decision account, though, one caveat is in order. Ethical decision theorists' conception of unethical behavior does not correspond exactly to my definition of organizational wrongdoing. As a result, theory and research on ethical decision-making may not apply to organizational wrongdoing as defined here in a straightforward manner. For the most part, ethical decision theorists *conceptualize* the distinction between right and wrong in abstract philosophical terms. But ethical decision researchers generally *define* ethical behavior and its converse vaguely or not at all (Trevino, Weaver, and Reynolds 2006; Tenbrunsel and Smith-Crowe 2008). This is not surprising given that philosophers have debated the validity of alternative ethical frameworks for centuries without reaching consensus. Without a precise definition of unethical behavior to guide them, ethical decision researchers tend to focus on behaviors that the vast majority of people would agree are unethical, such as lying and cheating. In essence, they implicitly acknowledge that they cannot articulate a generally acceptable precise definition of unethical behavior, but assume that they can identify (a few) indisputable concrete instances of unethical behavior.

Although the definition of unethical behavior remains unclear, it seems reasonable to say that unethical behavior, as reflected in ethical decision theory and research, and wrongdoing, as defined in this book, are positively correlated. Most forms of organizational wrongdoing can be considered unethical. For example, financial fraud is illegal and can be considered unethical insofar as it denies stockholders their right to free consent. Thus, theory and research that helps us understand why people choose to engage in unethical behavior also should help us understand why people engage in wrongful behavior. However, many types of unethical behavior cannot be considered wrongdoing as defined in this book. For example, misrepresenting a colleague's contribution to group work in an effort to claim greater responsibility and reward for group success can be considered unethical, but it does not constitute wrongdoing as defined here. I proceed with my presentation of the ethical decision theory explanation of organizational wrongdoing with this caveat in mind.

Early ethical decision theory

Early ethical decision theory was based on the premise, most notably articulated by Rest (1986), that people proceed through a four-stage sequence when making ethical decisions. In the first stage, people become aware, or fail to become aware, that a decision requires the application of ethical criteria. If they become aware that a decision calls for the application of ethical criteria, they proceed with a "moral" decision, a decision that takes into account ethical considerations. If they fail to become aware that a decision calls for the application of ethical criteria, though, they proceed with an "amoral" decision, a decision that does not take into account ethical considerations and that thus resembles the cost-benefit decisions apprehended by the rational choice account.

If people become aware that a decision calls for the application of ethical criteria and thus embark on a moral decision, they proceed to the second and possibly third and fourth stages of the ethical decision-making process. In the second stage, people deliberate and identify (or fail to identify) the ethical course of action. In the third stage they develop (or fail to develop) an intention to act that is consistent with the judgment they arrived at in the second stage. Finally, in the fourth stage they act (or fail to act) in a fashion consistent with the intentions they developed in the third stage. Rest assumed that people use reason (that is, rational deliberation) to navigate the four analytically distinct stages of the ethical decision-making sequence.

Early research on ethical decision-making employed either experimental or survey research methods to explore three types of factors believed to influence a person's resolution of each of the four stages that comprise the ethical decision-making process. Some research focused on the characteristics of ethical dilemmas. Perhaps most representative of this research is work on moral intensity. It maintained that ethical decisions vary in their perceived moral significance, depending on the extent to which they possess the potential to create significant harm, the degree to which decision makers play an intentional and active role in producing potential significant harm, and a variety of other factors. Further, it showed that as the moral intensity of a decision increases, the likelihood that people will view the decision as an ethical problem and the likelihood that they will adjudicate it ethically also increase (Jones 1991).

Other research focused on the context within which people make ethical decisions. Research on context tended to focus on factors suggested by the previous two chapters. Some work focused on the impact of rewards and punishments. Other work focused on the impact of culture, sometimes differentiated from the related concept "organizational climate" and sometimes inferred from top management "leadership style." Not surprisingly, researchers generated a considerable amount of evidence indicating that people are more likely to become aware of ethical issues, make ethical judgments, develop ethical motivations, and behave ethically when rewards, punishments, and cultural elements reinforce ethicality. Much research in this area has concentrated on assessing the relative impact of incentive systems, characterized as formal mechanisms, and cultures, represented as informal mechanisms, on ethicality. Recent evidence suggests that formal mechanisms deter unethical behavior less well than informal mechanisms do (Tenbrunsel et al. 2010) and, as I will discuss below at some length, one study even suggests that formal mechanisms can suppress moral awareness (Tenbrunsel and Messick 1999).

Still other research focused on decision makers' individual attributes. Some of this research examined demographic characteristics, such as decision makers' age, gender, and organizational or professional tenure. Other research examined decision makers' state of mind, such as their moral development and ethical orientation. Not surprisingly, studies indicate that individual differences matter. For example, researchers found that, by and large, people for whom religious values are important exhibit greater moral awareness and are more likely to make ethical judgments, develop ethical intentions, and enact ethical behavior (Singhapakdi, Marta et al. 2000; Clark and Dawson 1996; Razzaque and Hwee 2002; Wagner and Sanders 2001; Wimalasiri et al. 1996; Kennedy and Lawton 1996, but see Hall, Matz, and Wood 2010). Finally, some research examined the interaction of individual attributes and issue characteristics. For example, as common sense would suggest, one study shows that individuals who embrace formalist ethical perspectives, philosophical outlooks focused on fundamental principles of rights and justice as opposed to some form of utilitarian calculus, tend to be more sensitive and more accurately apply ethical criteria to formalist decisions, dilemmas that involve options that potentially violate basic human rights and canons of justice (Schminke et al. 1997).

Thus, early ethical decision theory implied that people embark on unethical behavior, and by extension wrongdoing, when they 1) fail to recognize that a decision requires the consideration of ethical criteria, or 2) recognize that a decision requires the consideration of ethical criteria but fail to apply ethical criteria correctly, or 3) apply ethical criteria correctly but fail to develop the motivation to engage in ethical behavior, or 4) develop the motivation to engage in ethical behavior but fail to follow through on their intentions. Further, early ethical decision research identified a series of issue, individual, and contextual variables that affect how people progress through the four-stage ethical decision-making process and that thus influence the likelihood that people will engage in unethical behavior and, by extension, wrongdoing.

Early ethical decision theory dovetails with the explanations of wrongdoing presented in the previous two chapters in at least three ways. First, early ethical decision theory that analyzed the factors that influence whether an organizational participant will entertain non-ethical or ethical considerations when making a decision, for the most part equated non-ethical considerations with cost-benefit concerns and ethical considerations with normative concerns. Thus, early ethical decision theory implicitly helps us understand the factors that regulate whether a person is influenced by rational choice factors or cultural factors when choosing between alternative behaviors. Second, early ethical decision theory that analyzed how contextual factors influence the way people make ethical decisions largely conceptualized the decision-making context in rational choice and culture terms. Thus, early decision theory implicitly presents a more fine-grained analysis of how people conduct cost-benefit and normative assessments. Third, early ethical decision research indicated that a person's ethical outlook influences their sensitivity to different kinds of ethical issues and their adjudication of different kinds of ethical judgments. And the culture explanation of organizational wrongdoing identifies an important source of a person's ethical outlook, the norms, values, and beliefs current in the person's organization.

Assessing early ethical decision theory

For the most part, early ethical decision theory conforms to the dominant approach to explaining organizational wrongdoing. Rest's four-stage model of the ethical decision process, upon which most early work is based, explicitly assumes that people deliberate rationally when navigating the decision process. Further, Rest's model explicitly assumes that if people decide to engage in ethical behavior, they develop the intention to do so in the third stage of the decision process. Thus, Rest's model implicitly assumes that people develop the inclination to engage in wrongful behavior before engaging in wrongdoing (although wrongdoers may erroneously perceive their behavior to be ethical and thus rightful).

Further, early ethical decision theory implicitly assumed that people adjudicate ethical decisions in a situational vacuum. Early ethical decision theory did not consider the impact of the immediate situational context on decision makers. It did consider the impact of organizational culture and climate, as well as occupational and professional socialization, on ethical decision-making. But, as the cultural account of organizational wrongdoing does, early ethical decision theory implicitly assumed that these contextual factors produce semi-permanent changes in decision makers, which in turn directly affect their choices. The implicit assumption that a person's immediate context does not affect his or her ethical decision-making is reflected in early ethical decision research, which predominately employed survey and experimental methods that required human subjects to respond to questions administered by researchers individually and in artificial settings (i.e. outside of their regular work environments).

Early ethical decision theory, though, somewhat departed from the dominant assumption that people make discrete decisions to engage in wrongdoing. On the one hand, it explicitly assumed that people make a single decision to engage in ethical or unethical behavior. On the other hand, it assumed that people make ethical decisions in four stages. Further, insofar as it conceptualized the four-stage process as a sequence, it implicitly assumed that the four stages unfold over time. Finally, the first two stages of the decision process might be understood to constitute two separate decisions: the decision to consider the dilemma a moral one, and the decision to adjudicate the dilemma in an ethical fashion.

Insofar as early ethical decision theory embraced many of the same assumptions about the causes of organizational wrongdoing that the rational choice and culture accounts embraced, it is not surprising that early ethical decision theory, like the previously discussed accounts, also tended to view bad people as the source of bad behavior in organizations. The research on decision makers' individual traits assumed that some people (e.g. men rather than women) are more prone to engage in unethical behavior. The research on decision makers' contexts assumed that people situated in some contexts develop outlooks that make them prone to engage in unethical behavior. Thus, like the cultural explanation of organizational wrongdoing, the research on decision makers' context located the cause of organizational wrongdoing in people who had been pickled in "bad barrels" and in the process had become "bad apples."

Early ethical decision theory and research greatly improved our understanding of the process by which people make ethical decisions. It provided a framework within which to conceptualize ethical decisions and offered useful information on the factors that regulate ethical decision-making. But it also left many questions unanswered. Perhaps most vexing, the early research generated a sizable number of contradictory findings. For example, while some studies indicate that women are more likely than men to make ethical judgments, other studies show that men are more likely than women to make ethical judgments, and a good number of studies reveal no relationship between gender and ethical judgment (Tenbrunsel and Smith-Crowe 2008: 556–7, 566–7). While some ethical decision researchers continue to generate results that speak to the contradictions and other gaps in earlier findings, other researchers have begun to generate ideas and report results that call key elements of early ethical decision theory into question. Some of this work departs from the explicit assumption that people deliberate rationally before engaging in unethical behavior. Some of this work departs from the implicit assumption that people make discrete decisions before engaging in wrongdoing. It is to this theory and research that I now turn.

Recent ethical decision theory

The limitations of rationality

BOUNDED ETHICALITY

Early ethical decision theory assumed that people adjudicate ethical decisions rationally. But, as indicated in Chapter 4, cognitive psychologists have shown that human rationality is limited. Building on the work of these cognitive psychologists, David Messick, Max Bazerman, Ann Tenbrunsel and others have developed an impressive body of theory and research that explains how human beings' cognitive limitations influence their adjudication of ethical decisions (Messick and Bazerman 1996; Messick and Tenbrunsel 1996).

The first theory and research on the cognitive limits on ethical decision-making, referred to as "bounded ethicality" (Chugh, Banaji, and Bazerman 2005), focused on the unrealistic understandings that people tend to have about the world, others, and themselves. This work revealed, for example, that people tend to underestimate the range of potentially affected parties and disregard low probability consequences when contemplating ethical decision options. This work also demonstrated that people tend to view others as homogeneously inferior and themselves to be uniquely superior both intellectually and morally. One much cited study along these lines showed that people tend to underestimate the extent to which they are susceptible to conflicts of interest (Moore, Tetlock, Tanlu, and Bazerman 2006).

The most recent work on bounded ethicality has drawn on the research pertaining to the impact of decision frames and heuristics. This work reveals, for example, that the tendency to favor risky options when decisions are framed in terms of losses, and the propensity to discount temporally distant consequences of behavior when making cost-benefit calculations, discussed in the context of the rational choice account, also influence ethical decisions. One exemplary study demonstrates that decision makers are prone to pursue unethical courses of action when they frame decision options in terms of the avoidance of loss as opposed to the pursuit of gain, especially when decision makers are subject to time pressures (Kern and Chugh 2009).

A MORE PROBLEMATIC BOUNDED ETHICALITY

The work on bounded ethicality is extremely important, because it indicates that systematic errors in reasoning can cause otherwise ethical people to be insensitive to ethical issues, misapply ethical principles, fail to develop ethical motivations, and engage in unethical behavior. But I think the impact of this work can be enhanced if it is extended in two ways.

First, I think the concept of bounded ethicality can be expanded to encompass the more general constraints that human beings face when acquiring, storing, and processing information. March and Simon (1958) used the broader term bounded rationality to refer to human beings' natural limits with respect to the acquisition, storage, and processing of information. People cannot always collect and store information fully and accurately. They also cannot always thoroughly and flawlessly analyze the information that they are capable of acquiring and holding. These more general limits to human rationality cause people to make decisions based on partial and inaccurate information and on incomplete and flawed analyses. The impact of bounded rationality is greatest when people have to deal with large quantities of information and work within time constraints, which is typically the case in organizations. This suggests that people often will struggle to accumulate, store, and process information needed to make sound ethical decisions in organizations. As a result, they sometimes will engage in unethical behavior, and by extension wrongdoing, simply because they lose the struggle.

Second, I think theory on bounded ethicality can be broadened to take into account the immediate information context within which people conduct ethical decisions. Information contexts vary with respect to the amount and availability of information people must process to make a sound decision. The greater the amount of information that people must process and the more difficult it is for them to obtain that information, the more bounded rationality will influence their decision choices. Williamson (1983) identified several dimensions along which decision contexts vary with respect to the demand for, and the availability of information needed to make, sound decisions. The most important dimensions are complexity, uncertainty, and information impactedness.

Complexity pertains to the number of decision alternatives available to decision makers, the number of possible consequences that flow from these decision alternatives, and the number of pros and cons (both cost-benefit and normative) associated with those consequences. Complex decisions involve many options, each of which has numerous potential consequences, each of which has many pros and cons. Complexity overwhelms decision makers' cognitive capacities, such that even the most cognitively capable people are hampered in their ability to make sound decisions.

Uncertainty pertains to the extent to which decision makers can predict the consequences of decision alternatives as well as the pros and cons (both cost-benefit and normative) of those consequences. Uncertain decisions involve decision alternatives that have consequences, and pros and cons that cannot be predicted with certainty. Uncertainty limits a decision maker's ability to understand the implications of available decision alternatives, such that even the most cognitively capable people in simple decision contexts are hampered in their ability to make sound decisions.

Information impactedness, a technical economic term, pertains to the inaccessibility of information pertaining to the options, consequences, and the pros and cons discussed above. Information may be unavailable for a wide variety of reasons, ranging from the inherent characteristics of the decision context to the strategic action of others. Information impactedness causes decision makers to develop inaccurate understandings of the implications of alternative decision options, such that even the most cognitively capable people in simple and certain decision contexts are hampered in their ability to make sound decisions.

These ideas suggest that people will find it particularly hard to acquire, store, and process information needed to make sound ethical decisions when their decision context is fraught with complexity, uncertainty, and information impactedness. As a result, they will be particularly likely to engage in wrongdoing when their decision context exhibits these features.

DANIEL BAYLY, MERRILL LYNCH, AND THE ENRON NIGERIAN BARGE PARKING SCHEME

The case of Daniel Bayly, the head of investment banking at Merrill Lynch and one of four Merrill executives convicted of participating in an asset parking scheme with Andy Fastow, an officer of Enron, illustrates the impact that bounded rationality, complexity, uncertainty, and information impactedness can have on people confronting decisions that can lead to unethical and wrongful behavior (Eichenwald 2005; Thomas 2005). Bayly helped arrange a transaction in which Enron first sold three Nigerian power barges to Merrill and then later re-purchased the barges from Merrill within a period of six months. Enron's sale of the barges, which were floating power plants used to bring electricity to remote locations, enabled the firm to report a temporary $12 million in revenues and, in doing so, meet quarterly earnings targets. Merrill's purchase and subsequent resale of the barges allowed it to reap a 22 percent profit.

The sale and repurchase of assets can be considered unethical and fraudulent if the buyer purchases the assets with the understanding that the seller will repurchase them at a later date at a guaranteed higher price. When this is the case, the assets do not really leave the seller's books and the revenues from the sale do not really enter its books. Instead, the assets are just temporarily "parked" with the buyer and the revenues from the sale essentially are loaned to the seller (to be repaid to the buyer with interest). Such an arrangement misleads investors about the true financial status of the asset's buyer and seller. In this case, the prosecution claimed, and the jury agreed, that Bayly had an understanding with Fastow that Enron would repurchase the assets within six months. As a result, Bayly was convicted and sent to prison. But matters might have been more complicated than the prosecutor maintained and the jury concluded.

The Nigerian power barge fraud began in December 1999, when Jeff McMahon, Enron's treasurer, approached Robert Furst, a Merrill banker tasked with managing the bank's relationship with Enron, with a proposition. McMahon told Furst that Enron needed to unload the barges, and claimed that the firm had a buyer on the hook, but that the transaction was coming along too slowly. He asked Furst if Merrill could purchase and hold the barges for a short period of time while Enron found another long-term buyer for the power plants. Furst liked the idea, not only because it promised a high rate of return, but also because it provided him with an opportunity to demonstrate Merrill's loyalty to Enron and thus increase the bank's chances of getting a larger share of Enron's future investment banking business. So he presented the plan to Bayly.

Bayly was initially uneasy about buying the Nigerian barges because it was not the sort of investment with which he had previous experience. Further, while the investment promised to deliver a high rate of return, the magnitude of the promised profit was relatively small. The risk-reward ratio was not favorable. But over time, Bayly warmed to the idea, partly because it was in keeping with internal pressure to pursue more aggressive merchant banking business. So Bayly convened a meeting of other Merrill bankers and several of the firm's attorneys to vet the deal. One banker at the meeting, James Brown, opposed the deal because he thought it smacked of earnings management.

Further, he argued that if Enron ever ran into financial difficulties and the deal became public knowledge, Merrill would look bad. But the other bankers at the meeting argued that the deal did not constitute earnings management, partly because they believed the amount of money involved was not material, given Enron's presumed strong earnings (a belief that was ill-founded) and partly because they assumed that Enron's auditor Arthur Anderson had already looked at the deal and approved it (an assumption that proved false). Further, they argued that Enron was unlikely to run into financial trouble down the road, partly because they believed Enron was in fabulous financial shape at the time (an assessment that also proved erroneous).

Ultimately, the group gave Bayly the go-ahead to pursue the deal and Bayly's superior signed off on it, under the condition that Bayly speak with Fastow and get his assurance that Enron would find a buyer for the barges within six months. So Bayly called Fastow and, in a five-minute conversation, Fastow assured him (using vague language) that Enron would either find a buyer for the barges or repurchase the barges by June 30. As things turned out, Fastow could not find an independent buyer for the barges. So when Merrill executives pressured Enron to make good on its promise to take Merrill out of its investment, Fastow asked his subordinate, Michael Kopper, to repurchase the barges from Merrill using the Enron special purpose entity, LJM2, which he and Kopper controlled. And when Enron went bankrupt, as Brown feared, the deal came to light.

This evidence suggests that Daniel Bayly was boundedly rational in this decision context. His knowledge of the market for power barges, especially Nigerian ones, was limited. This evidence also suggests that the decision context was complex. A group of high-level bankers and lawyers scrutinized the deal at length and did not arrive at a unanimous assessment of its propriety. In addition, the evidence suggests that the decision context was fraught with uncertainty. Bayly could not forecast with accuracy the future state of the market for Nigerian power barges, and thus the likelihood that Enron would be able to find a third-party buyer for the barges. Further, Bayly and his colleagues could not forecast with accuracy Enron's financial future. In addition, it seems likely that Bayly was at least a little unsure about the terms of the deal to which he and Fastow agreed over the phone. Finally, the evidence suggests that information that might have increased Bayly's ability to navigate this complexity and reduce this uncertainty was impacted. In all likelihood, Enron knew it would have a hard time finding a third-party buyer for the barges, but it did not share this information with Merrill (in fact, it conveyed the opposite impression). Further, it was likely difficult for Merrill to check its presumption that Anderson had approved the deal and its assessment that Enron's financial situation was sound.

This bounded rationality, complexity, uncertainty, and information impactedness was likely consequential. If Bayly knew more about the market for power barges, if the issues surrounding the purchase were simpler, if the future state of the world related to the decision could be predicted with greater certainty, and if information possessed by Enron about these matters were made more available, Bayly might not have facilitated Merrill's purchase of the barges. In fact, I strongly suspect that if Bayly had known just three things: that there were few potential buyers of the barges, that Arthur Anderson had not looked over the deal, and that Enron was in shaky financial health, he would have summarily dismissed the idea of buying the barges.

None of this is to say, though, that Daniel Bayly should be held harmless for his decision to facilitate the Nigerian barge deal. I have tried to show that understanding of Daniel Bayly's route to participating in the purchase and resale of the Nigerian power barges can be enhanced by considering the boundedly rational character of his reasoning and the complexity, uncertainty, and information impactedness inherent in his decision context. I have not tried to argue that Daniel Bayly's behavior was ethical or legal. The question of Bayly's morality or legal culpability is a normative one. With this distinction in mind, it is worth noting that a judge recently overturned the convictions of Bayly and his fellow Merrill executives, ruling that the "honest services" theory used to prosecute them and several other recently convicted white-collar criminals was too broad. This judicial decision can be considered either sound or ill advised, depending on one's normative point of view. But from a social scientific standpoint, this decision can be considered further testament to the complexity of the decision context. Apparently, deciding whether a behavior is right or wrong can be more difficult than it sometimes, with the benefit of hindsight, appears.

BEYOND BOUNDED ETHICALITY: INTUITION AND EMOTION
Recently, some ethical decision theorists have begun to question the extent to which people deliberate, even in a bounded rational way, when confronted with a decision that has ethical implications. These theorists contend that decision makers often respond to ethical dilemmas in an automatic fashion, quickly arriving at ethical judgments and only later discovering or manufacturing, often with some difficulty, the rational basis for those judgments (Haidt 2001). Automaticity in ethical decision making is believed to be governed by deep-seated intuition (e.g. cognitive templates), perhaps underpinned by emotion (Damasio 1994). Most recently, decision theorists have begun to formulate a dual-process understanding of ethical decision making in which emotional states are not counterposed to cognitive processes, but rather are viewed as constitutive (i.e. key ingredients) of cognition. Consistent with this model, Green and Haidt (2002) found that people who have

sustained injuries to the part of the brain that regulates emotions exhibit diminished capacity for ethical reasoning.

Wrongdoers often report having intuitive understandings of right and wrong as well as emotional reactions to the idea of engaging in wrongdoing. Betty Vinson, a WorldCom accountant, was convicted of fraud for implementing a misleading accounting adjustment at the request of a superior. She initially refused to make the adjustment because she worried that it was improper, but she eventually gave into the request (for reasons that we will discuss in Chapter 9). Afterwards, though, Vinson "suffered pangs of guilt" and resolved to quit the firm. But, she reconsidered when her superior, the firm's highly respected CFO, Bill Sullivan, provided her with an authoritative justification for the accounting treatment (Pulliam 2003). Clearly, Vinson's first assessment and gut reaction were superior to Sullivan's extensive reasoning. As indicated in the introduction, Paul Krimmage experienced revulsion at the thought of injecting himself with performance-enhancing drugs because he associated the injection of any substance into his body with doping. And this revulsion was part of the reason that he resisted the temptation to use amphetamines for two years, before eventually succumbing at the first of the French Classic criteriums in 1987.

Although decision theorists focus on the role that intuition and emotion play when people contemplate engaging in wrongdoing, I suspect that both intuition and emotion continue to influence people even after they have embarked on wrongful courses of action. Martin Segal, a mergers and acquisitions partner at Kidder Peabody, provided inside information to Ivan Boesky in the early 1980s. Initially Segal provided the information in exchange for a share of Boesky's brokerage business, which the struggling Kidder Peabody sorely needed. After a while, though, Segal sought to reap personal gain from the arrangement. So he asked Boesky to provide him with monetary compensation, a "bonus" for his services. Boesky agreed and, in a scenario worthy of a spy novel, instructed a bag man to deliver the money to Segal using a briefcase swap in the lobby of the New York City Plaza hotel. After receiving the briefcase, Segal went straight to his Upper East Side apartment, opened the case, took in the sight of the $150,000 in crisp large denomination bills, and collapsed with his head in his hands, overcome with nausea (Stewart 1991). Similarly, Walter Pavlo reported that as his involvement in the Harold Mann scheme to defraud MCI and its customers deepened, he felt increasingly anxious and found it difficult to sleep, problems that he attempted to manage by medicating himself with excessive amounts of alcohol.

Ethical decision making as a temporal process

THE TEMPORAL DYNAMICS OF CONTEMPLATION,
ACTION, AND REFLECTION

Early ethical decision theory suggested that ethical decision making unfolds over time. As indicated above, it assumed that people make ethical decisions in a sequence of four chronologically ordered stages. And these four stages, especially the first two, could be considered separate decisions. For the most part, ethical decision theorists have not developed the suggestion that ethical decision making evolves over time. There are, though, two important exceptions.

First, Tenbrunsel and her colleagues (Tenbrunsel, Diekmann, Wade-Benzoni, and Bazerman 2010) suggest how individual ethical decisions develop over time. They maintain that people possess two selves, a "want" self (in my terminology, a rational choice self) and a "should" self (in my terminology, a normative assessment self). Further, they contend that these two selves do battle with each other when contemplating unethical courses of action, the "should" self dominating in advance of and after an ethical decision is translated into action, and the "want" self overriding the "should" self in the moment that a decision is enacted. According to Tenbrunsel and her colleagues, people tend to think abstractly when reflecting on future and past actions, but reason more concretely when in the moment of translating decisions into action. As a result, normative considerations loom large in advance of and after a decision, while potential rewards and punishments loom large in the moment. Tenbrunsel and her colleagues maintain that this is one reason that people often behave in ways that are inconsistent with their ethical beliefs.

Second, Murnighan and his colleagues (Zhong, Ku, Lount, and Murnighan 2009; Jordan, Mullen, and Murnighan 2011) suggest how multiple ethical decisions can interrelate with one another over time. They maintain that people seek to preserve ethical identities, which define their unique level of ethicality. When people make decisions that are less ethical than their ethical identities would prescribe, they compensate by making more ethical decisions in the future. When they make decisions that are more ethical than their ethical identities would prescribe, they compensate by make less ethical decisions in the future. In this way, a person can maintain a level of ethical behavior that vacillates around his or her identity's norm.

ETHICAL DECISION MAKING AS MULTIPLE SERIES OF LINKED
DECISIONS

I think the suggestions provided by early ethical decision theory and the recent analysis of Tenbrunsel, Munighan, and their colleagues can serve as the basis of a more temporally dynamic theorization of the ethical decision process. With this in mind, I suggest a rudimentary theoretical framework that is based on two fundamental assertions. First, I contend that the process through which people become involved in unethical behavior (and by extension wrongful behavior) often consists of a stream of linked decisions, with the early decisions in a decision stream being linked to subsequent decisions by the consequences that they produce. Initial decisions lay the foundation for subsequent decisions by creating decision opportunities, opening up and closing off decision options, and shaping the way in which decision makers evaluate those options.

Second, I maintain that people often simultaneously proceed through multiple interrelated decision streams, their progression through one decision stream influencing their progression through one or more other parallel decision streams. Decisions in one decision stream can lay the foundation for decisions in a second stream in the same way that early decisions in a decision stream can lay the foundation for later decisions in the stream: by creating decision opportunities, opening up and closing off decision options, and shaping the way in which decision makers evaluate those options.

To understand how a person's progression through a series of linked decisions can result in wrongdoing, one must identify the types of consequences that can flow from the decisions composing the series, and how those consequences shape the decisions faced, the options contemplated, and the choices made down the road (i.e. later in the decision stream). Many consequences can flow from decisions. Below I enumerate a handful of consequences suggested by the rational choice, culture, and decision-making explanations of wrongdoing considered so far in the book.

To state the obvious, people often make decisions about whether or not to engage in a particular behavior. Further, when people decide to engage in a behavior, they often embark on the chosen behavior (albeit, with uneven success). The behaviors to which decisions give rise can cause people to have experiences that they otherwise would not have had. And these experiences can alter people's perceptions of their ability to successfully engage in wrongdoing, as well as their ability to reap rewards from engaging in wrongdoing. They also can increase their appreciation for the rewards to which wrongdoing can give rise. In the terminology of expectancy theory considered in Chapter 4, decisions can alter a person's assessment of the effort–performance and performance–outcome expectancies associated with a course of action, as well as the valence that the person attaches to the rewards that can follow from the behavior. And as such, the experiences can alter a person's motivation to engage in wrongdoing.

The behaviors to which decisions give rise also can cause other persons in the decision maker's environment to act in ways that they might not act otherwise. And in the process, the decision maker may develop an increased appreciation of his or her organization's culture. Consistent with the discussion of organizational culture in Chapter 5, the decision maker can become aware of the extent to which his or her organization's culture endorses wrongdoing. The decision maker also can become aware of the extent to which his or her organization's culture supports techniques of neutralization that stipulate extenuating circumstances in which wrongdoing might be considered acceptable.

Finally, the behaviors to which decisions give rise can start decision makers on what is commonly called a slippery slope, which can increase their likelihood of engaging in wrongdoing. When people engage in behaviors that are questionable on ethical, social responsibility, or legal grounds, they can become habituated to the behavior, making it more likely that they will engage in the behavior in the future. In addition, people can become desensitized to the aversion that they feel in the wake of engaging in questionable behavior, making them more likely to engage in other questionable behaviors in the future (Ashforth and Kreiner 2002). In a sense, the perpetration of questionable acts loosens the emotional constraints that inhibit the perpetration of wrongdoing.

Further, when people engage in questionable behavior, they can move the normative yardstick that they use to assess prospective behavior closer to, and across, the line separating right from wrong. Cognitive psychologists have found that people frequently make use of available external standards when making judgments, anchoring on those standards and adjusting away from them as seems appropriate for their immediate circumstances (Bazerman 2006). Use of the anchoring and adjustment heuristic allows people to economize on decision-making effort, but it can lead to errors when the available external standards are inappropriate. When people consider the wisdom of a new behavior, whether with respect to cost-benefit or normative considerations, they often anchor on recent behavior because it is a readily available standard against which their prospective behavior can be evaluated. And if the prospective behavior does not differ much from recent behavior, people conclude that it is a sound course of action. Thus, recently enacted behaviors establish new benchmarks against which subsequent behaviors are evaluated. This manner of evaluating alternative courses of action can propel people into wrongful courses of behavior. Prospective *questionably wrongful* behavior can be considered rightful because it is not much different from previous behavior that was *entirely rightful*. And prospective *wrongful* behavior can be considered rightful, because it is not much different from previous behavior that was *questionably rightful*, but that was perceived as *entirely rightful*.

This extended characterization of the process through which people proceed when making ethical decisions has three implications. First, it raises the possibility that the adjudication of decisions that, considered in isolation, do not have ethical implications can shape the adjudication of other contemporaneous and subsequent decisions that do have ethical implications. Ethical decision theorists who embrace Rest's four-stage model assume that people first decide whether a decision requires the application of ethical criteria. And they maintain that if decision makers decide that a decision requires the application of ethical criteria, they proceed to the second stage of the ethical decision-making process, which entails deciding how to apply ethical criteria to the decision at hand. If people fail to recognize that the decision requires the application of ethical criteria, though, they engage in "non-ethical" decision making. Ethical decision theorists have focused exclusively on understanding the choices of people who conclude that a decision requires the application of ethical criteria. Thus, they implicitly assume that the choices of people who conclude that a decision does not require the application of ethical criteria are unrelated to the ethical decision-making process.

But if organizational participants become involved in unethical behavior as the result of their progression through multiple interrelated series of decisions, then it is possible that their handling of "non-ethical decisions" can influence their resolution of concurrent and future ethical decisions. For example, a socially minded MBA student might make the apparently non-ethical decisioin to accept a job at an investment bank. But the decision might cause the student to develop an enhanced taste for the considerable monetary rewards that the bank can provide and might cause the former student to embrace organization-centered (as opposed to client-centered) culture operative at the bank. And this might increase the likelihood that the former student will engage in wrongdoing in the future.

Second, this extended characterization of the ethical decision process, when considered in the context of bounded rationality, complexity, uncertainty, and information impactedness, suggests an additional way in which otherwise ethical people can come to engage in unethical behavior. Boundedly rational people in decision contexts characterized by complexity, uncertainty, and information impactedness find it hard to predict the consequences of their initial decisions and thus find it difficult to anticipate the trajectory of their subsequent decision making. Thus, they sometimes find themselves facing decisions, contemplating options, and choosing alternatives that they did not foresee when they embarked on the series of decisions. And this means that people can make decisions early in a decision stream that they might not have made had they realized the decisions would lead to wrongdoing. Had they known how their initial choices would play out, they might have adjudicated their earlier decisions in a different way. This might explain why people who have perpetrated organizational wrongdoing and attempted to retrospectively make sense of their journey into wrongdoing sometimes find it difficult to understand how they arrived at their destination.

Third, the extended characterization of the ethical decision process points to an important line of inquiry ignored by ethical decision theorists and researchers. Ethical decision theorists develop ideas about how people respond to ethical dilemmas. And ethical decision researchers who employ experimental methods formulate ethical dilemmas and expose subjects with predetermined attributes to those dilemmas. Ethical decision theorists and researchers have for the most part not investigated how people come to confront actual ethical dilemmas in real organizations. The extended characterization of the ethical decision process suggests that people engage in wrongdoing at least partly because their prior decisions led them to confront decisions that pose the possibility of engaging in wrongdoing. Conversely, the extended characterization suggests that people remain on the straight and narrow at least partly because their prior decisions did not lead them to confront decisions that pose the possibility of engaging in wrongdoing. Thus, developing an understanding of how people come to confront the ethical dilemmas they do is crucial to developing an understanding of how people come to make decisions that lead to wrongdoing.

WALTER PAVLO, MCI, AND THE CUSTOMER FACTORING SCAM

Walter Pavlo's participation in a scheme initiated by Harold Mann to defraud MCI and its past-due Carrier Finance customers, discussed briefly in Chapter 5, illustrates how people can become involved in organizational wrongdoing as the result of their progression through multiple decision streams (Pavlo and Weinberg 2007). It also provides a deeper illustration of how complexity, uncertainty, and information impactedness can lead people to engage in wrongdoing. For this reason I re-examine this case here in more depth.

As indicated earlier, Pavlo worked in MCI's Carrier Finance group, initially as a subordinate and later as the group's manager. Carrier Finance was responsible for collecting bills owed MCI by major resellers (firms that sold access to MCI's network at elevated per minute prices to customers who did not want or could not afford to enter a regular monthly contract with the phone company) and 900 phone number customers (firms that sold services over the phone, such as dial-a-porn providers). Mann was the CEO and owner of an MCI 900 number customer. According to the proposed plan, Pavlo would threaten to cut off service to past-due customers if they did not pay a sizeable portion of their delinquent bills. Then Mann, apparently independently, would approach the customers with an offer to assume their debt in return for a fixed fee and monthly installments, commonly referred to as a "factoring" arrangement. But Mann did not intend to pay off the customers' bills. Instead, he planned to share the customers' payments with Pavlo, who (with the help of two co-conspirators) would manipulate MCI's accounting books to create the appearance that the customers had fulfilled their obligation to the firm. Mann's proposed scheme was unethical on a number of grounds: it violated MCI's and its customers' property rights as well as the firm's investors' right to free consent. The scheme also was illegal, and Pavlo and Mann received prison terms for their part in it. Below I describe Pavlo's decision to join Mann in this scheme as a series of decisions. Then I describe two other series of decisions in which Pavlo engaged that conditioned his decision to join Mann in the scheme to defraud MCI and its customers. In the process, I highlight the ethical decision theory arguments made to this point.

The main series of decisions
Walter Pavlo's association with Harold Mann began long before Mann pitched the factoring scheme to him over lunch in 1996. Soon after Pavlo joined MCI in 1992, an MCI sales representative offered Pavlo two tickets to attend a professional golf tournament, one of which could be used by Pavlo's wife. Despite being wary of the sales representative's motives—in particular, the possibility that the sales representative had a quid pro quo in mind, Pavlo chose to accept the tickets. After Pavlo accepted the tickets, the sales representative informed him that Mann, whose company owed MCI a considerable amount of money in past-due bills, and Mann's wife, would accompany Pavlo and his wife at the tournament. In addition, she gave Pavlo a check from Mann for $25,000 as partial payment of his company's past-due bills.

Pavlo did not know that his acceptance of the tournament tickets would constitute an acceptance of an invitation to spend the weekend with Mann and his wife. He also did not know that his acceptance of the tickets would be followed by Mann's partial payment of his company's past-due bill. Information about these two consequences of his decision was impacted and could not be factored into his decision to accept the tickets. Pavlo might have accepted the tickets, despite concerns about the sales representative's motivations, because he underestimated his susceptibility to conflicts of interest (Moore et al. 2006). Even if Pavlo underestimated his susceptibility to conflicts of interest, he might not have accepted the tickets for the tournament if he had known that a decision to accept the tickets was a de facto decision to attend the tournament with Mann, and possibly a precondition for receiving partial payment of Mann's debt to MCI. If Pavlo had known these consequences of his decision, he would have seen more clearly that acceptance of the tickets exposed him to a conflict of interest, in which a business relationship with a client might get overlaid with a personal one. And that would have increased the chance that he would have judged the decision to accept the tickets to be unethical and decided to forgo the opportunity.

Regardless of why Pavlo elected to accept the tickets and despite the fact that he did not relish the idea of spending the weekend with Mann and his wife (because Pavlo considered MCI's delinquent customers to be unsavory characters), he and his wife attended the golf tournament and, much to his surprise, enjoyed the weekend. In the weeks that followed, Pavlo was presented with a series of small, undoubtedly seemingly inconsequential, decisions to go to lunch and speak by phone with Mann. On several of these occasions, he chose to dine or speak with him. Pavlo likely chose to meet or speak with Mann on the first such occasion because he enjoyed spending time with him at the golf tournament. Pavlo likely chose to meet or speak with Mann on later occasions partly because he learned from earlier lunches and phone conversations that Mann had much to offer him in terms of enjoyment, small gifts (Mann often paid for Pavlo's share of the lunches), and work-related information and expertise (Mann often imparted wisdom about the telecom wholesale business).

These early decisions laid the foundation for later decisions in the decision stream that led to Pavlo's participation in the fraudulent factoring scheme in several important respects. First, Pavlo would not have become acquainted with Mann had he not accepted the tickets to the golf tournament and subsequently accepted invitations to speak and meet with Mann. And Pavlo would not have considered participating in the fraudulent factoring scheme had he not become acquainted with Mann. The scheme was, after all, Mann's idea. Second, Pavlo would not have perceived proposals originating with Mann to have high effort–performance and performance–outcome expectancies had he not found his many interactions with Mann rewarding. And Pavlo would not have given the factoring scheme a second thought had he not perceived proposals originating with Mann to have high effort–performance and performance–outcome expectancies.

Mann presented Pavlo with the proposition to defraud MCI and its customers during one of their occasional lunches. Mann began by asking Pavlo how much a discount carrier named TNI owed MCI. Mann and Pavlo had spoken about TNI's CEO, Robert Hilby, on a previous occasion, because Hilby had offered Pavlo a job at one of his other ventures, Simple Access. When Pavlo told Mann that TNI owed MCI $2 million, Mann suggested that Pavlo "put the heat on him to come up with the whole $2 million fast." Pavlo dismissed the idea, saying that there was no way that Hilby could come up with such a large sum of money that quickly. To which Mann replied, "No, but he'll bust his ass to come up with enough to keep TNI alive. Then I'll be there for him." Going on, Mann said, "I'll tell Hilby I'll take over his $2 million debt to MCI. In exchange, he's got to give me an upfront fee for restructuring the deal and pay back the rest over time. Could you pressure him first?" Pavlo responded, "I could, but why should I? When Hilby pays you, are you gonna pay MCI?" "Not necessarily," replied Mann mysteriously. "Don't worry about that for now," he continued. "Just pressure Hilby. Do it for yourself. If he settles up with MCI, it means he's got a big stash somewhere and you should take that Simple Access job. If he doesn't, and I know he doesn't, then we have the makings of a lucrative new venture." Unbeknownst to Pavlo, Mann owed Hilby a considerable sum of money at the time, increasing the likelihood that Hilby would turn to Mann when squeezed by Pavlo, thus providing Mann with the opportunity to pitch the factoring proposition to Hilby without generating suspicion.

This description suggests that Pavlo faced uncertainty regarding the probable fallout of his decision to pressure Hilby to pay his MCI bill. If he decided to "put the screws on" Hilby, a number of possible outcomes might eventuate, the likelihoods of which he could only estimate imperfectly. Hilby might pay up, in which case MCI would receive the money it was owed and Pavlo would be praised by his bosses. And if this eventuated, his decision to put the screws on Hilby would be ethical, at least from a utilitarian standpoint, and entirely legal. If Hilby did not pay up, Hilby might or might not turn to Mann for help. If Hilby did not turn to Mann for help, MCI and Pavlo would be no better or worse off than was currently the case. If Hilby did turn to Mann, MCI might get some of the money TNI owed the firm. Mann had said that he would "not necessarily" pay off TNI's debt, which left open the possibility that Mann would relay at least some of the money TNI owed it. And if this eventuated, Pavlo's decision to put the screws on Hilby might be ethical and legal. But something more nefarious might happen. Mann had said that "we" would have "the makings of a lucrative new venture." This suggests that Pavlo and Mann might benefit in some as yet unspecified, possibly illicit, way. If this eventuated, Pavlo's decision might be unethical and even illegal, depending on what Mann did with the balance of the money Hilby paid him.

This description also indicates that information pertaining to the likelihood of these different eventualities was impacted. Pavlo did not know at the time that Mann owed Hilby a considerable sum of money, increasing the likelihood that Hilby would turn to Mann when squeezed by Pavlo, and thus increasing the likelihood that a decision to put the squeeze on Hilby might be considered unethical and illegal. Faced with this uncertain decision context, in which information was impacted, Pavlo decided to put the screws on Hilby and TNI, reasoning, "I guess there's no harm in putting the thumb screws to (Hilby and TNI) . . . I do it to dozens of others every month" (113). Had Pavlo faced less uncertainty and possessed more information, he might have chosen a different course of action.

Shortly after Pavlo delivered the ultimatum to Hilby to pay his past-due bill or get cut off by MCI, Hilby, as Harold Mann predicted, called Mann. Then Mann, as planned, offered to take over Hilby's debt to MCI in return for a one-time flat fee and additional monthly installments. And Hilby, as Mann predicted, accepted the deal. Mann then called Pavlo to pitch the rest of the scheme, suggesting that Mann and Pavlo (if he joined the conspiracy) pocket TNI's payments, and that Pavlo alter MCI's accounting records to make it appear as if TNI was paying its bills. It was only at this point that Pavlo understood the consequences of his decision to pressure Hilby to pay his past-due bills. By putting the heat on Hilby, he had set in motion a scheme to defraud TNI and MCI. In the process, Pavlo had generated evidence that the scheme was feasible. In the language of expectancy theory, he could see that the plan had a high effort–performance expectancy—at least with respect to the ability of Mann to convince MCI's past-due customers to subscribe to the factoring arrangement. He also likely realized that he exposed Mann, a friend, and himself to the possibility of significant punishment. If he did not go along with Mann's scheme, Mann's misrepresentation to Hilby would most certainly be discovered and this would subject Mann and perhaps himself to criminal prosecution.

Pavlo told Mann that he needed some time to consider his pitch. At the end of the day, he examined a spreadsheet of in-arrears accounts and determined that there were a sufficient number to support a lucrative fraudulent enterprise. In the language of expectancy theory, he determined that the scheme had a high performance–outcome expectancy. And based on his assessment that the scheme had both a high effort–performance and performance–outcome expectancy, and with the possible awareness that failure to go along with the scheme could hurt a friend and possibly even himself, Pavlo decided to accept Mann's invitation to join the scheme to defraud MCI and its customers. Had he not decided to put the squeeze on Hilby, Pavlo would not have had the information about the scheme's effort–performance expectancy, he would not have sought out the information about the scheme's performance–outcome expectancy, and he would not have placed himself in the position of possibly harming a friend and himself (which he might do, if he eschewed participation in the scheme). And without this information and in the absence of this predicament, he very well might have declined to join Mann in the scheme.

Pavlo subsequently decided to work with Mann to use the same basic scheme to defraud a number of other MCI customers and ultimately MCI as well. In all likelihood, the decision to defraud TNI and MCI laid the foundation for Pavlo's subsequent decisions to work with Mann to defraud other MCI customers (and, in the process, MCI). One might consider this a trivial point, if one views the decision to defraud TNI as equivalent in all respects to the subsequent decisions to defraud other MCI customers. But in all likelihood, the subsequent decisions were not the same as the initial one in several important respects.

First, each time Pavlo and Mann successfully defrauded an MCI customer, the effort–performance expectancy associated with the scheme likely increased. Second, each time Pavlo successfully plied the scheme, he received a pay-off. And with each pay-off he received, the valence he associated with the pay-offs seemed to increase. Indeed, as prosecutors zeroed in on the fraud and his arrest grew imminent, Pavlo took one last trip to the Cayman Islands, where his ill-gotten gains were sequestered, just to feel one last bundle of crisp large denomination bills in his hands. Both the increasing effort–performance expectancy and the increasing valence for the scheme's proceeds likely left Pavlo more inclined to defraud another customer.

Third, each time Pavlo successfully plied the fraudulent factoring scheme, the divergence between MCI's actual and reported financial situation grew. And the more MCI's actual and reported financial situation diverged, the harder it became for Pavlo to defect from the scheme without exposing himself to severe punishment. The dilemma Pavlo faced in this regard was colorfully characterized by another corporate fraudster, Ramalinga Raju. Raju founded Satyam, an Indian software services exporter, in 1987. The firm grew to become the country's fourth largest software services exporter but began to experience financial difficulties in the first years of the new century. In an attempt to forestall a decline in investor and creditor confidence, Raju began manipulating the firm's books at the same time that he worked feverishly to right the corporate ship. Ultimately, though, he found it impossible to dig his firm out of the deepening hole into which it had slipped. After turning himself in to the authorities, he told reporters that he had wanted desperately to unwind the scheme, but could not figure out how to do so without being apprehended. In his words, he felt as if he were "riding a tiger, not knowing how to get off without being eaten" (Reuters 2009).

Finally, Pavlo's identity evolved over the time he engaged in the wrongdoing. A year or more into the fraud, he had become, to a significant extent, a different person. He had come to interpret wrongdoers and wrongdoing in a positive light. He referred to Mann not as an abhorrent figure, but as an "evil genius." And he came to view himself as a daring and adventurous character. The transformation seemed to be nearly complete at the very moment he was anticipating being indicted for his crimes. Embracing the combat-pilot mantra to "shut up and die like an aviator," he purchased an oceangoing speedboat, which he brazenly christened "Miss Deeds."

Two concurrent series of decisions
As multifaceted as the above series of decisions was, it unfolded in the context of two other series of decisions. And Pavlo's progression through these two other series of decisions partly laid the foundation for his decision to conspire

with Mann to defraud MCI and its delinquent customers. For the sake of brevity, I will describe these two series of decisions in an abbreviated fashion.

After Walter Pavlo developed an association with Harold Mann, but before he decided to participate in Mann's scheme to defraud MCI and its customers, Pavlo participated in the manipulation of corporate records to disguise the proportion of MCI's past-due bills that likely were uncollectible, a behavior that abrogated the firm's investors' right to free consent and constituted accounting fraud. MCI top management placed a high priority on revenue growth because revenue growth elevated the firm's stock price. As the firm's stock price increased, the value of managers' stock options and the size of their annual bonuses grew. In addition, the company's ability to attract a merger partner was enhanced, which in turn increased the chance that MCI employees could cash out their investment in the firm at even higher levels.

MCI top management fostered revenue growth by providing strong incentives for MCI salespersons to sign up wholesale customers, who purchased a much larger number of minutes than retail customers, and by providing weak incentives and instituting few controls to insure that the customers were likely to pay their bills. As a result, Carrier Finance found itself with a growing number of questionable customers and an increasing volume of past-due and likely uncollectible bills. This was perceived as a problem by Carrier Finance. The more uncollectible bills on their books, the poorer their performance appeared. This was also perceived as a problem by MCI top management. The more uncollectible bills on the firm's books, the more incumbent it was on the firm to restate its earnings, an outcome that would certainly result in a market correction in the firm's stock price.

It was in this context that Pavlo embarked on a series of decisions that culminated in the manipulation of corporate records to disguise the volume of past-due and likely uncollectible bills. Initially, Pavlo, with the guidance of his superior Ralph McCumber and with the approval of MCI's top management, formulated a plan to offer past-due customers the opportunity to sign promissory notes that pledged eventual payment of their bills. This allowed MCI to remove a customer's debt from the past-due category and count it as revenue, while allowing the customer to remain delinquent. In the case of customers that MCI had reason to believe would in fact eventually pay their bills, this decision was consistent with generally accepted accounting principles and widely held ethical canons. But in the case of customers that MCI suspected might never be in a position to pay their bills, the decision was unethical and fraudulent. And Pavlo knew that many of the customers who signed the promissory notes were unlikely to pay all, or even a portion of their past-due bills.

Later, as the size of MCI's past-due and likely uncollectible bills grew, Pavlo and McCumber devised an innovative scheme to obtain alternative compensation from a hopelessly delinquent customer. Without the knowledge, let alone the approval, of their superiors, the two Carrier Finance executives accepted, on behalf of the firm, a substantial block of the customer's stock in lieu of payment of its past-due bill, thus increasing the chance that MCI would receive some compensation for the minutes it had sold the customer. When Pavlo and McCumber's superior learned of the deal, he severely reprimanded the pair. However, later, after the customer's stock price soared, all was forgiven.

These efforts, though, were insufficient to keep the volume of past-due and likely uncollectible bills within budgetary parameters. So, top management implicitly exhorted McCumber and Pavlo to adopt illegitimate means to resolve the problem, ordering the pair to reduce the amount of past-due bills by an amount that everyone knew was unrealistic. Still later, top management explicitly ordered McCumber and Pavlo to shuffle some of the current year's past-due and likely uncollectible bills into the subsequent year's budget. The two complied with the order, despite voicing opposition to it. This act intensified MCI's misrepresentation of the amount of revenue it actually had earned, and in the process moved the benchmark against which future behavior would be evaluated squarely into unethical and fraudulent territory. As time went on, MCI top management exhorted McCumber and Pavlo to make greater use of this and the other two subterfuges described above, eventually authorizing the annulment of two of the largest past-due accounts.

Pavlo's progression through this series of decisions influenced his progression through the series of decisions that led him to participate in the factoring fraud discussed above in two ways. First, it provided Pavlo with the opportunity to develop skills necessary to carry out the scheme to defraud MCI and its delinquent carrier finance customers. Most importantly, it provided Pavlo with an opportunity to become skilled at the fraudulent elimination of unpaid bills from MCI's books. Second, it taught Pavlo that management was willing to break the law to obtain valued outcomes. And this provided a basis for the development of a technique of neutralization that blunted the guilt that he felt when contemplating joining Mann's scheme to defraud MCI and its delinquent carrier finance customers. As described in Chapter 5, Mann explicitly contended, when pitching the plan to Pavlo, that MCI could not be considered a victim, as the firm itself had been deceiving investors on a regular basis for some time.

About the same time that MCI's top management team instructed Pavlo and McCumber to delay the writing off of past-due debt, Pavlo implemented a rogue financing program to accelerate the pace with which customers paid their MCI bills, a violation of company rules that abrogated the firm's property rights. MCI's customers often failed to pay their MCI bills on time partly because their customers' (MCI's customers' customers) failed to pay them

(MCI's customers) on time. Pavlo embarked on a series of decisions that led to the implementation of the financing program when Harold Mann introduced him to Mark Benveniste. Benveniste proposed a legitimate business endeavor that Mann encouraged Pavlo to accept, in which Benveniste's company, Manatee, would loan MCI's customers money in an amount equal to the sum they owed MCI and would then take over responsibility for collecting those billings. This would allow MCI's customers to pay MCI on time.

The program, later given the name Rapid Advance, made financial sense. MCI's customers would receive their revenues more promptly, MCI would receive its revenues more promptly, and Manatee would be paid for its service with interest. There was just one hitch. Manatee's financial backers, a Canadian bank, demanded that MCI guarantee to reimburse Manatee for any customer debt that proved uncollectible. Pavlo knew that MCI top management would not make such a guarantee. After all, top management knew just how hard it was to collect from its customers. Despite this fact, Pavlo agreed to meet with Benveniste over a period of weeks to work out the details of the proposed program, apparently hoping that as time went by he would figure out a way to deal with the Canadian bank's condition that MCI guarantee its customers' payments. Ultimately, the bank did not withdraw its condition, and Pavlo could not figure out a way to obtain MCI top management approval for the guarantee. Reluctant to forego the now almost done deal, Pavlo orchestrated a fraudulent phone conversation that led Manatee and its backers to believe that MCI top management was willing to guarantee its customers' payments.

Pavlo's progression through this third series of decisions, in conjunction with his progression through the second series of decisions described above, likely influenced his progression through the series of decisions that directly lead to his involvement in Mann's fraudulent factoring scheme. Pavlo's progression through the second and third decision streams likely altered the benchmark against which future behavior would be evaluated. Pavlo's progression through the decision stream that culminated in his manipulation of MCI's books (to disguise the firm's volume of past-due and likely uncollectible bills) led him to engage in wrongful behavior that was in the firm's interest and was endorsed by the firm's top management. That provided a foundation for Pavlo to progress through the decision stream that culminated in his creation of the Rapid Advance program, which was in the firm's interest but was not endorsed by top management. And this provided a foundation for Pavlo's progression through the third decision stream that culminated in his participation in Mann's fraudulent factoring scheme, which was not in the interest of the firm and was not endorsed by the firm's top management. In fact, Mann suggested this line of reasoning to Pavlo when he completed his pitch to defraud MCI and its customers. As noted in Chapter 5, when Pavlo expressed his reticence to participate in the scheme, saying it "was wrong," Mann pointed out that Pavlo had been engaging in similar practices on MCI's behalf for years. The only difference between Pavlo's past behavior and the proposed behavior was that Pavlo would now benefit from it.

Pavlo's progression through the second and third decision streams also likely activated a psychological process that desensitizes people to engaging in wrongdoing. As Pavlo moved from engaging in wrongdoing on behalf of the firm and endorsed by the firm's top management to engaging in wrongdoing on behalf of the firm but not endorsed by the firm's top management, he might have become desensitized to engaging in wrongdoing. And this might have made his involvement in Mann's scheme to defraud MCI and its customers more palatable (Bandura 1990, 1999; Bandura et al. 1996).

Summary

Walter Pavlo's experience at MCI illustrates the multidimensional character of some decision contexts. In addition to attending to the series of decisions that eventually led him to embark on the scheme to defraud MCI and its customers, Pavlo navigated two other series of decisions that laid the foundation for his participation in Mann's bogus factoring arrangement. His progression through the early stages of the decision to participate in the factoring fraud brought Pavlo into contact with the person who devised the plan and led him to view that person as an efficacious actor. His progression through the two contemporaneous series of decisions provided him with skills that were useful in perpetrating the fraud against MCI and its Carrier Finance customers, provided him with the raw material with which to fashion techniques of neutralization that could assuage the guilt of participating in the fraud, and ultimately served as a benchmark against which the fraud could be measured and found only marginally deviant.

Early decision theory would suggest that MCI's incentive structure and culture facilitated Walter Pavlo's decision to perpetrate the frauds described above. This is likely true (in fact, I say as much in Chapter 5). It also would suggest that Pavlo possessed attributes (e.g. demographic characteristics, an educational background, or a value orientation) that made him prone to engage in unethical behavior and hence wrongdoing. This also is likely true. After all, other MCI employees were exposed to the same incentive structure and culture yet did not engage in wrongdoing.

But, if my characterization of the decision process through which Pavlo came to engage in wrongdoing is correct, it suggests that Pavlo might not have made the decision to participate in the scheme to defraud MCI and its customers had he not made the many prior and contemporaneous decisions to which it was related, some of which had no apparent ethical implications. It also suggests that Pavlo might not have been fully cognizant of the implications of many of these decisions, and thus might not have been able to forecast his progression through this series of ethical and amoral decisions. As mentioned in connection with Daniel Bayly, though, this does not imply that Walter Pavlo was not culpable for his involvement in the scheme to defraud MCI and its customers. Pavlo's guilt or innocence is a normative question, to which a jury gave an unambiguous answer. Pavlo was sentenced to three years and five months in prison for various legal infractions.

ANOTHER POTENTIAL CONSEQUENCE OF DECISION-MAKER CHOICES: COGNITIVE DISSONANCE

A person's decisions can generate a plethora of consequences that prefigure his or her subsequent decisions. So far I have discussed only decision consequences suggested by the rational choice, culture, and evolving decision-making explanations of organizational wrongdoing. Before leaving this topic, I want to consider one additional consequence to which a person's decisions can give rise that is not suggested by the theories covered so far and that I believe is particularly important: the post-hoc interpretation of choices. This consequence is important in its own right. Theoretically, it links ideas about the limitations of rationality in decision making with ideas about the temporal dimension of decision making. Practically, it helps explain why people sometimes persist in wrongful courses of action despite the fact that they become aware that their behavior does not make sense from a cost-benefit or normative appropriateness standpoint. This consequence also is important, though, because it lays the foundation for an important situational social influence process discussed in Chapter 8: escalating commitment to a failing course of action.

Some psychologists believe that while people often embark on behavior without first engaging in thorough rational deliberation, they tend to account for their behavior after the fact as if it was the result of consummate rational forethought (Festinger 1957; Aronson 1973; Aronson 2007[1972]; Tavaris and Aronson 2007). In the words of Elliot Aronson, one of the pioneers of this perspective, while human beings are not rational animals, they are "rationalizing animals." Sometimes, though, the post-hoc accounts that people develop to explain their behavior conflict with their closely held conceptions of themselves. When this occurs, they experience "cognitive dissonance," a state in which people simultaneously understand themselves to be motivated by particular cost-benefit or normative considerations but to have behaved in a fashion that suggests they are motivated by contrary considerations. Aronson contends that people find cognitive dissonance emotionally unsettling and that they respond to this uneasiness in one of three ways: by adjusting their post-hoc explanations of their behavior so that they are consonant with their self concepts, by ignoring information that suggests their behavior is inconsistent with their identities, or by stewing in their dissonance.

Cognitive dissonance, the way in which people respond to it, and the ways in which those responses shape future behavior can cause boundedly rational people in decision contexts characterized by complexity, uncertainty, and information impactedness (hereafter simply boundedly rational decision makers in problematic decision contexts) to get locked into decision streams that lead to wrongdoing. Boundedly rational decision makers in problematic decision contexts who embark on wrongdoing often experience dissonance. Such wrongdoers can experience dissonance because they understand themselves to be generally "good" (i.e. law-abiding, ethical, and socially responsible), but recognize their behavior in a particular instance to have been "bad" (i.e. illegal, unethical, or socially irresponsible). Alternatively, they can experience cognitive dissonance because they believe themselves to be capable of pursuing behavior consistent with their self-interest, but recognize their wrongful behavior in a particular instance to have been contrary to their self interest (i.e. likely to lead to detection and punishment). Wrongdoers can reduce these kinds of dissonance by adjusting their post-hoc understandings of their behavior so as to render it sensible from a normative and/or self-interest standpoint. Alternatively, wrongdoers can avoid information about the extent to which their behavior lacked merit from a normative and/or self-interest vantage point, or they can simply stew in the recognition that they have done something that is counter-normative and/or self-destructive.

Dissonance reduction typically reinforces wrongdoers' involvement in wrongdoing because it provides a justification for their behavior. Dissonance avoidance and tolerance can have two contradictory effects. On the one hand, avoiding or living with dissonance provides wrongdoers with the opportunity to abandon their wrongdoing. As long as wrongdoers do not possess a rationalization for their wrongful course of action, their dedication to the course of action is incomplete. On the other hand, avoiding or living with dissonance can allow wrongdoers to continue their wrongful behavior. And the longer a wrongdoer continues a wrongful course of action, the more he or she invests (with respect to time, effort, and other resources) in the behavior. And, as I will discuss in considerable detail in Chapter 8, the more wrongdoers invest in a wrongful course of action, the more they become committed to the course of action.

When boundedly rational decision makers in problematic decision contexts embark on a wrongful course of action and experience dissonance between their understanding of themselves as generally good and their recognition of their behavior in a specific instance as bad, they can reduce their dissonance by employing one or more of the six techniques of neutralization discussed in connection with the cultural explanation of wrongdoing considered in

Chapter 5. The use of techniques of neutralization to reduce cognitive dissonance is, though, fundamentally different from the use of techniques of neutralization discussed in connection with the cultural account. According to the culture explanation of wrongdoing, the presence of techniques of neutralization in an organization's culture increases the likelihood that organizational participants will embark on a wrongful course of action. According to cognitive dissonance theory, the presence of techniques of neutralization in an organization's culture increases the likelihood that organizational participants will persist in a wrongful course of action upon which they have already embarked, because the techniques allow the person retrospectively to place their wrongdoing in a positive light. Techniques of neutralization when used in this way also have been called mechanisms of moral disengagement (Bandura, Barbaranelli, Caprara, and Pastorelli 1996; Bandura 1990, 1999). In Chapter 4 I briefly discussed Robert Wilkis's participation in an insider trading scheme organized by David Levine, noting that Wilkis found the intrigue exciting and that the exhilaration motivated him to remain in the scheme. Wilkis, though, also experienced pangs of guilt. But he assuaged those pangs of guilt by employing the denial of injury technique of neutralization, concluding that no one was being harmed by his sharing and trading on inside information about corporate acquisitions. The acquisitions in question went through, and the acquired firms' stockholders made substantial profits, despite the fact that Wilkis profited illegally from the deals.

When boundedly rational decision makers in problematic decision contexts experience cognitive dissonance between their understanding of themselves as generally capable of pursuing their self-interest, and their recognition of their behavior as ill-advised, they can reduce their dissonance by concluding that the likelihood of being detected and punished is actually low. For example, after David Levine began his foray into insider trading, he reassured himself and his co-conspirators that they would not get apprehended for their activities because SEC investigators were not as smart as he and his co-conspirators. If the SEC investigators were as smart as they were, he reasoned, the investigators would be working on Wall Street and pulling down large salaries and bonuses, rather than policing Wall Street and earning a relative pittance.

Wrongdoers can avoid dissonance associated with their wrongdoing in many ways. In the most extreme cases, wrongdoers simply do not talk (and thus perhaps do not even think) about the wrongdoing in which they are involved. One of the most striking aspects of the quiz show fraud of the 1950s discussed in Chapter 4 is that the producers and contestants seldom explicitly acknowledged that they were participating in the rigging of broadcast contests, even as they were working out the mechanics of the deceit. In many cases, producers provided contestants with questions and answers that were to be used in the broadcast contests in the course of pre-broadcast "warm-up" sessions, without explicitly acknowledging that they were doing so. Many contestants figured out that they had been given the questions and answers after the fact, in the course of participating in the broadcast contests. But typically they did not speak with the producers about the arrangement, even after they became aware that they were participating in a subterfuge.

Further, even in those cases when producers explicitly pitched the idea of the contest rigging to contestants, they frequently referred to the deceit in obscure ways. Albert Freeman, one of the producers of "Twenty-One," introduced Harold Craig, a contestant, to the plan to rig his first contest by saying, "We want to try something new. I think it will be a lot of fun, but you mustn't tell Mr. Enright or anyone else because that would spoil it (Stone and Yohn 1992: 100)." The only reason to hide the fraud from Mr. Enright, who was the head producer and one of the orchestrators of the fraud, was to keep Craig's acknowledgment of the fraud (to others and thus to himself) to a minimum. Indeed, when contestants left the show, they were sometimes sent off with an explicit verbal declaration that nothing deceitful actually had transpired. For example, Freeman told Craig after his final contest, "If anyone tells you I gave you the answers, they won't be telling the truth (Stone and Yohn 1992: 102)." And later when the producers and contestants came under investigation by the office of the district attorney of New York County and the United States Congress, the producers reassured the contestants that they had nothing to fear because they simply could tell the truth—that the contests were not rigged.

Typically, though, dissonance avoidance takes more subtle forms. Robert Wilkis appeared to engage in dissonance avoidance by failing to acknowledge or fully process information that David Levine revealed about his insider trading activities. In the months before Levine explicitly pitched the insider trading scheme to Wilkis, Levine dropped hints that he already had begun trading on inside information. With each hint, Levine was (perhaps intentionally) effectively involving Wilkis in his insider trading scheme. By knowing more and more about Levine's inside trading activity, but not notifying the authorities, Wilkis essentially was becoming complicit in Levine's scheme. But Wilkis did his best to ignore these "hints." For example, in the summer of 1979, Levine confided to Wilkis, "I'm playing with the big boys now." Wilkis responded, "What's that mean?" Levine responded, somewhat annoyed, "For a guy who went to Harvard, you're not very bright" (Stewart 1991: 63). Later in the conversation, Levine alluded to the fact that he had a Swiss bank account. Again, Wilkis seemed unable to comprehend the significance of this information, responding, "So what?" Levine, again somewhat exasperated, responded, "If you don't get it, I'm not going to spell it out" (Stewart 1991: 64). Later, when reflecting on these early conversations, Wilkis recalled "that on some level, (I) had known what was going on, but had preferred not to focus on it" (Stewart 1991: 66).

Boundedly rational decision makers in problematic decision contexts who embark on wrongdoing and who subsequently experience value-based cognitive dissonance, but who do not develop post-hoc rationalizations that cast their wrongdoing in a positive light, can also simply tolerate their dissonance. They simply can live with the simultaneous belief that they are generally good people engaged in a specific bad behavior—simmering, so to speak, in their dissonance.

Ralph Gretzinger and Kermit Vandivier were B.F. Goodrich employees who participated in the writing of a fraudulent qualification report for a brake to be used on the A7D fighter jet, under construction by Ling Tempco Vought (LTV) Corporation for the U.S. Navy in the late 1960s (Vandivier 1972). I mentioned the A7D brake case in Chapter 5 and will discuss it again in considerable detail in Chapter 8. Here I use it to illustrate how wrongdoers can stew in the dissonance created by their wrongdoing. In describing how he made sense of his participation in the writing of the report, Vandivier recalled thinking that, "It made no difference who would falsify which part of the report or whether the actual falsification would be by misleading numbers or misleading words . . . all of us who contributed to the fraud would be guilty." Gretzinger, after unsuccessfully attempting to reduce his dissonance with the post-hoc rationalization that he was just "drawing pictures," similarly concluded that his participation in the preparation of the report was fundamentally wrong. Speaking with Vandivier, he confessed, "We're going to screw LTV. And speaking of screwing, I know now exactly how a whore feels, because that's exactly what I've become, an engineering whore." Later, as the report neared completion, Vandivier and Gretzinger frankly compared their behavior with the behavior of Nazi concentration camp guards then on trial in Nuremburg, Germany.

Similarly, boundedly rational decision makers in problematic decision contexts who embark on wrongdoing and who subsequently experience self-interest-based cognitive dissonance, but who do not retrospectively cast their wrongdoing in a sensible light, also can merely tolerate their dissonance. They can live with the simultaneous belief that they are generally capable of pursuing their self-interest and that they are engaged in a behavior that is likely to result in detection and punishment. The producer of "Twenty-One," Daniel Enright, recalled that while he was rigging that show's contests, "There was always fear—there was always a fear lurking that somehow the story would be exposed, that we would be revealed and that kept gnawing at us" (Krainin Productions, Inc. and WGBH Educational Foundation 2000: 14). Of course, the more a wrongdoer stews in the dissonance associated with the risks of detection and punishment, the more he or she experiences pressures to reduce this dissonance. Thus, Enright also recalled, "But after a while, you rationalize that by thinking to yourself, 'What contestant would reveal that he played a part in rigging?" (2000: 14). The obvious answer to this rhetorical question is, of course, "the contestants who will lose money and social esteem when the program's script calls for their defeat." Eventually two such contestants blew the whistle on the fraud.

Assessing recent ethical decision theory

Recent ethical decision theory departs significantly from the dominant approach to explaining organizational wrongdoing. Most important, theory on bounded ethicality calls into question the dominant assumption that people deliberate rationally before embarking on a wrongful course of action. And my discussion of the complexity, uncertainty, and information impactedness inherent in many decision contexts pushes the decision-making account further from the dominant approach in this respect. Further, theory on automaticity calls into question the assumption that people deliberate at all, at least in a conscious way, before embarking on wrongdoing. In addition, Tenbrunsel et al.'s work on the temporally varying impact of the "should" and "want" selves calls into question the dominant assumption that people make discrete decisions to eschew or engage in wrongdoing. And Murnighan and colleagues' work on the interaction between successive ethical decisions points to how ethical behavior evolves over time. Finally, my suggested extensions of this work, which characterizes the decision process as a series of linked decisions that unfolds in the context of other related decision streams, push the decision-making explanation even further from the dominant approach in this regard.

Organizational wrongdoers sometimes find it hard to understand looking back how they became involved in misconduct. If the enhanced decision-making explanation of wrongdoing elaborated in this chapter is right, it is no wonder that this is the case. This account assumes that people sometimes cross the line separating right from wrong by engaging in a series of decisions. Further, the account suggests that people find it difficult to forecast their progression through such series of decisions. People make each decision in a series of decisions leading to wrongdoing without the benefit of thorough rational deliberation, and sometimes without the benefit of conscious deliberation at all. Further, their adjudication of each decision produces consequences that shape their future options and the way in which they evaluate those options in a manner that they, because they are boundedly rational, are ill equipped to comprehend in advance. People might pause periodically in their navigation of a decision stream leading to wrongdoing to evaluate their position relative to the line separating right from wrong. But when they do, they likely use their previous behavior as a benchmark against which to judge their current behavior. And because each decision in a decision stream leading to wrongdoing often leads to only small deviations from prior behavior, such evaluations are not likely to produce alarms.

This account of organizational wrongdoing departs considerably from the accounts of wrongdoing considered in previous chapters insofar as it implicitly views people as fundamentally good, albeit congenitally susceptible to unwittingly slipping into wrongdoing. There are no bad barrels or bad apples, pickled or otherwise, in the enhanced decision-making account of organizational wrongdoing. If one were to choose an apt metaphor to represent the enhanced decision-making account's understanding of organizational wrongdoing, it might be that of a visually impaired person negotiating a minefield.

With this said, even the most recent work on ethical decision-making (my suggested extensions included) conforms to the dominant approach to explaining wrongdoing in three respects. First, it tends to assume that people embark on wrongdoing in a mindful fashion. The work on bounded ethicality assumes that people deliberate (albeit in a boundedly rational way) before developing intentions to act. The work on automaticity assumes that people tap deep-seated intuition or emotion before developing intentions to act. And as indicated in Chapter 2, mindfulness is a state of mind in which people attentively process the unique aspects of the situations in which they find themselves on both a cognitive and emotional level. Second, the extended ethical decision account implicitly assumes that people formulate their behavior in a social vacuum. As one influential review of the field has noted, most recent work on ethical decision making has failed to explore the way in which social interaction influences decision makers' choices (Trevino, Weaver, and Reynolds 2006: 977), although the work of Murnighan and colleagues presents a promising exception (Cantelon, Elyashiv, and Murnighan 2001; Cohen, Gunia, Kim-Jun, and Murnighan 2009; Gunia, Wang, Huang, Wang, and Murnighan forthcoming). Third, the extended ethical decision account assumes that people develop positive inclinations to engage in wrongdoing before embarking on wrongful behavior. Even people who chose ethical or unethical courses of action by tapping intuition or by responding to emotions are assumed implicitly to develop positive inclinations to engage in behaviors consistent with their intuition or emotional states.

Conclusion

I have now elaborated three explanations of organizational wrongdoing: the rational choice, culture, and ethical decision accounts. Each of these explanations contributes to our understanding of the causes of wrongdoing in and of organizations. But each, like all theories, also is limited by the assumptions on which it is based.

I began my discussion of the ethical decision explanation of organizational wrongdoing by characterizing it as bridge between the dominant and alternative approaches. The early work in this tradition embraced the four assumptions underpinning the dominant approach. The more recent work jettisoned several of these assumptions, embracing the corresponding contrary presuppositions characteristic of the alternative approach. In the process, the ethical decision account became more comprehensive (e.g. allowing for both rational and boundedly rational deliberation), and thus expanded our understanding of the causes of organizational wrongdoing. Still, the ethical decision account, even in its most recent advanced form, remains limited by the assumptions upon which it is based. Interestingly, ethical decision researchers have generated evidence that implicitly attests to the limitations of this approach and points to other fruitful lines of inquiry, lines of inquiry to which we will turn next.

Ethical decision researchers have found that people are less likely to perceive a decision as requiring the invocation of ethical criteria if a sanctioning system is in place (i.e. if costs and benefits are associated with decision options), as is the case in most business contexts (Tenbrunsel and Messick 1999). They also have found that people are less likely to adjudicate decisions in an ethical manner when the decisions pertain to work-related matters as opposed to non-work-related issues (Weber 1990; Weber and Wasieleski 2001). Together these results suggest that people are less likely to view decisions as requiring the invocation of ethical criteria and less likely to employ ethical criteria consummately when situated in work organizations as opposed to other settings. To put it crudely, ethical decision researchers have generated evidence suggesting that the ethical decision literature might be more relevant to decision making in the laboratory than to decision making in work organizations.

Further, as indicated earlier, ethical decision theorists have argued that people vary in their moral development and in the corresponding tendency to engage in principled ethical reasoning when adjudicating ethical decisions. Kohlberg (1969, 1981) contends that only those who have reached the highest level of moral development engage in principled reasoning. Further, recent studies indicate that only about 20 percent of the population reasons at the highest level of moral development. Some of the remaining 80 percent of people make decisions by adhering to rational choice or cultural logics, in which self-interest and collective understandings of right and wrong dominate reasoning. The balance make decisions by attending to rules, peer pressure, authority, and fear of punishment (Rest et al. 1999). We turn to the subject of rules, peer pressure, authority, and fear of punishment, social forces that are omnipresent in work organizations, in the next three chapters. And in the process, we explore explanations of organizational wrongdoing that depart further from the assumptions that wrongdoers reason mindfully, make discrete decisions, operate in a social vacuum, and invariably develop positive inclinations to engage in wrongdoing.

7

Administrative Systems

Introduction

The rational choice account views the organization as a nexus of contracts between multiple stakeholders, each of whom agrees to contribute something to the organization for something else in return. Further, it portrays organizational participants as cost-benefit calculators, scrutinizing behaviors from the standpoint of the benefits they provide and the costs they incur. From this vantage point, wrongdoing arises when an organization's incentive structure is conducive to wrongdoing. The cultural explanation views the organization as a community whose members share the same norms, values and beliefs, and assumptions about the organizational world. Further, it portrays organizational participants as normative appropriateness assessors, scrutinizing behaviors from the standpoint of whether they are in keeping with their organization's culture. From this vantage point, wrongdoing arises when an organization's cultural content is conducive to wrongdoing. The ethical decision account essentially straddles the rational choice and cultural accounts. This account, especially in its early manifestation, assumes that people largely respond to the incentive or normative environments in which they are situated when navigating the four-stage process through which people are presumed to proceed when making ethical decisions. From this vantage point, wrongdoing arises when incentive systems and normative contexts cause decision makers to lack moral awareness, judgment, and intention, and thus lead them to engage in unethical behavior.

Granovetter (1985) has characterized rational choice and cultural arguments as undersocialized and oversocialized conceptions of human action, respectively. Rational choice arguments offer undersocialized conceptions of human behavior because they tend to ignore societal influences. Cultural arguments are considered oversocialized conceptions of human behavior because they tend to assume that human action is completely determined by societal influences. Granovetter points out, though, that despite the fact that rational choice and cultural arguments are polar opposites with respect to the importance that they attribute to society, they share a "common conception of action and decision carried out by atomized actors." Granovetter used the term "atomized actors" to signify people and organizations that were not linked to one another or to other people and organizations. In the rational choice view, "atomization results from narrow utilitarian pursuit of self interest." In the culture view, atomization results from "the fact that behavioral patterns have been internalized." Thus, in Granovetter's view, both types of explanation largely ignore human beings' "immediate social context" (1985: 485), and more specifically their "history of relations and their position with respect to other relations—what might be called the historical and structural embeddedness of relations" (1985: 486). In this and the following three chapters, I consider explanations of organizational wrongdoing that take the immediate social context, its history and structure, into account.

The basic administrative systems explanation

The administrative systems explanation of organizational wrongdoing is rooted in a broader theoretical perspective on organizations that views organizations as structures for coordinating people engaged in interdependent tasks, and depicts organizational participants as decision makers who operate within these structures to acquire and analyze information with an eye to performing their tasks in a way that optimizes efficiency, effectiveness, coordination, and ultimately organizational goal attainment. The earliest modern theorists of organizations as administrative systems characterized organizational task environments as complex, and organizational participants as "boundedly rational" (March and Simon 1958). In their view, organizational environments present organizational participants with a multitude of complicated decisions. And organizational participants are limited in their ability to accumulate and process information needed to make these many complicated decisions.

Administrative structures help organizational participants cope with this complex environment/bounded rationality dilemma. They reduce organizational participants' need to conduct mindful and thorough rational analyses of each situation before choosing a course of action by providing them with guidelines for action. By allowing organizational participants to act in a programmed fashion, they help organizations economize on the volume of resources that they must devote to decision making, making the organizations more efficient. Thus, the administrative systems explanation of organizational wrongdoing can be considered to take up where recent ethical decision theory left off. Like the most recent ethical decision theory, the administrative system account assumes that organizational participates are cognitively limited and situated in problematic decision contexts. But, unlike the ethical decision account, it adds that a variety of administrative structures dictate how organizational participants respond to their complex environment/bounded rationality dilemma.

Theorists have identified two broad classes of administrative structures (Perrow 1972). *Obtrusive controls* provide relatively explicit guidelines on how organizational participants should complete their tasks. They include rules and standard operating procedures, as well as the division of labor. *Unobtrusive controls* provide more implicit guidelines on how organizational participants should complete their tasks. They "limit information content and flow, thus controlling the premises available for decisions; they set up expectations so as to highlight some aspects of the situation and play down others; they limit the search for alternatives when problems are confronted, thus insuring more predictable and consistent solutions; they indicate the threshold levels as to when a danger signal is being emitted (thus reducing the occasions for decision-making and promoting satisficing rather than optimizing behavior); they achieve coordination of effort by selecting certain kinds of work techniques and schedules" (Perrow 1972: 156–7). Unobtrusive controls include occupational and professional norms, scripts and schemas, communication channels, and technologies.

In the administrative systems explanation, organizational wrongdoing arises when obtrusive and unobtrusive controls program wrongdoing. In some cases, these controls are designed to obtain the participation of others in wrongdoing. In other cases, they are designed to program rightful behavior, but inadvertently facilitate wrongdoing. In this chapter, I examine how obtrusive and unobtrusive controls can facilitate organizational wrongdoing, distinguishing between instances in which they do so inadvertently and occasions on which they do so by design. I also consider how multiple obtrusive and unobtrusive controls can operate in consort to facilitate wrongdoing. I conclude by offering an overall assessment of the administrative systems account.

Obtrusive controls

Rules and standard operating procedures

Rules instruct employees on how to complete tasks, partly by telling them how to respond to work-related contingencies (e.g. how to process inputs with varying attributes). Standard operating procedures are collections of rules related to the same task. Rules and standard operating procedures often are written down in company documents such as memos and policy statements. And when attended to in a mindless manner, they substitute for time-consuming mindful and rational cost-benefit calculations or normative assessments that employees might otherwise be required to conduct when faced with contingencies at work. For this reason, rules and standard operating procedures make organizations more efficient. But rules and standard operating procedures also can lead organizational participants to engage in wrongful courses of action in a mindless fashion because dutiful employees and managers typically do not question the wisdom (legal, ethical, or otherwise) of rules and standard operating procedures. They simply follow them. Of course, the extent to which rules and standard operating procedures are followed mindlessly varies from situation to situation. In many cases, employees likely engage in at least cursory, partly mindful and somewhat rational, cost-benefit calculations and normative appropriateness assessments to determine whether the rules and standard operating procedures they follow "make sense." I will take this nuance into account below.

WRONGDOING BY DESIGN

Rules can be designed by superiors with the intention of directing subordinates to participate in wrongful behaviors on which the higher-ups have mindfully and rationally embarked. In one 1950s quiz show, *For Love or Money*, a prize was displayed to the contestants and the audience, but its value, between $1 and $9999, was displayed on a screen visible only to the audience. Then as contestants were given a question to answer, a mechanical device caused a "dancing decimal point" on the screen to move sequentially through six decimal places (e.g. for a $50 dollar prize, the decimal point moved such that the displayed figure took on the value of five cents, 50 cents, $5, $50, $500, and $5,000). The audience was told that the mechanical device was set such that the decimal point would stop dancing as soon as one of the contestants got the correct answer, at which time the winner could chose to take either the prize or the amount of money displayed on the screen hidden from their view. And this was true, with one important exception. A backstage employee was assigned the job of controlling a switch on the mechanical device that could move the decimal point forward at any time. And the producers promulgated a rule, to which the employee dutifully adhered, stipulating that the employee "bump" the decimal point ahead if it looked like it was going to land in the $1,000 range (so that it landed in the one-cent range), thereby ensuring that no contestants had the opportunity to win a prize in the most expensive range (Stone and Yohn 1992: 229).

It is possible, though, that the *For Love or Money* decimal-point bumper contemplated and understood the wrongful character of his behavior, insofar as the wrongful character of his action was relatively transparent. If this was the case, the rule guiding his wrongful behavior did not generate wrongdoing in a fully mindless and incompletely rational manner. That is, it is possible that a cost-benefit calculation or a normative-appropriateness assessment partly underpinned the employee's decision to follow the decimal-point bump rule.

The manner in which Enron's senior energy traders disseminated market manipulation protocols to junior traders provides an illustration of how rules and standard operating procedures might work in a more thoroughly mindless fashion. After Enron's leading traders developed, partly through experimentation, strategies for manipulating the California energy market, they wrote protocols for implementing these strategies. These protocols initially were transmitted in e-mail messages. In one e-mail message, which bore the subject heading "The Final Procedures for Death Star," a trader provided detailed instructions on how to replicate a strategy that entailed creating congestion on some power lines in order to reap super profits by providing back-up power through alternative routes. In the message, the trader noted that "project Death Star has been successfully implemented to capture congestion relief across paths 26, 15, and COI" and concluded "Thanks and good luck" (McLean and Elkind 2004: 270). The trading protocols later were formalized in the Enron Services Handbook. This instruction manual, in McLean and Elkind's words, "contained a list of various market conditions that might arise, which of the '(trading) partners' to call, what steps to follow in order to take advantage of a particular situation, and an explanation of the profit-sharing arrangements" (2004: 271).

It seems likely that at least a few of the Enron employees who used the Services Handbook did not contemplate or understand the wrongful character of their behavior, because the wrongful behavior was anything but transparent. Indeed, when Enron's lead traders tried to explain their transaction protocols to the firm's lawyers, the details were in many cases too complex for them to understand. If it were not for the strategies' suspicious names (e.g. "Fat Boy," "Death Star," "Get Shorty," and "Ricochet"), the lawyers would not have fretted about their wrongful character. Thus, it is likely that at least some of the employees who used the handbook facilitated wrongdoing in a mindless and incompletely rational manner. Still, it is possible that the Enron employees who used the Services Handbook did, to some extent, contemplate or understand the wrongful character of their behavior. And to the extent that they did, their participation in the wrongdoing could not be considered completely mindless and boundedly rational.

The manner in which Arthur Anderson legal staff induced account executives to shred documents related to Enron's fraudulent accounting practices provides a still clearer illustration of how rules and standard operating procedures can facilitate wrongdoing in a mindless fashion. When Arthur

Anderson's senior accountants became aware that Enron had been using fraudulent accounting practices, they realized that they might be held responsible for their client's behavior. To reduce the likelihood that they would be held responsible for Enron's fraudulent accounting practices, they instructed their subordinates to destroy e-mail messages and documents that might provide evidence of their culpability. But they did not explicitly order their subordinates to destroy potentially embarrassing documents. Rather they reminded their subordinates of a corporate policy that required the destruction of records that weren't needed for finished audit files, a policy that was written down and available for inspection on the firm's website. One accountant, John Stewart, protested when told that he had to delete most of the e-mails and destroy most of the documents related to the work he performed for Enron. In response, an Anderson legal department official, Nancy Temple, told Stewart that he was required to delete the e-mails and destroy the documents. "Anderson has a policy," she said. "You should follow it" (Eichenwald 2005: 529).

This interchange between Temple and Stewart illustrates well the automatic manner in which rules and standard operating procedures guide behavior. Temple only had to invoke the existence of the policy—she did not have to explain and justify it—to obtain compliance. As Eichenwald points out, "few in the firm understood Anderson's retention policy" (2005: 529). It also illustrates well how rules and standard operating procedures can override subordinate predilections. Stewart, a day after his first encounter with Nancy Temple, complained, "I have to tell you, I am still very uncomfortable with deleting the e-mails and destroying the draft documents in the Enron situation" (2005: 529). Temple then offered a compromise. Stewart could set aside a restricted set of e-mail messages and documents that he did not want to destroy and she would hold them for him. Eichenwald writes, "Stewart wasn't happy about the idea. But he agreed."

INADVERTENT WRONGDOING

Of course, rules and standard operating procedures are generally designed by superiors with the intention of directing subordinates to perform ethical, legal, and/or socially responsible behavior. But rules and standard operating procedures are formulated to guide organizational participants' behavior under normal conditions or in the event of typical departures from normal conditions (e.g. in the event of foreseeable declines in input quality). Because organizational task environments are complex and those who design rules and standard operating procedures are boundedly rational, rules and standard operating procedures sometimes are ill suited for conditions that arise. When this occurs, rules and standard operating procedures can have unanticipated consequences; including the inadvertent facilitation of organizational wrongdoing.

As noted in Chapters 4 and 5, many believe that rational choice and culture factors caused Ford Motor Company to introduce the Pinto despite the fact that pre-production safety tests indicated that the car was prone to burst into flames when struck from behind at low speeds, because the car's gas tank was placed in a disadvantageous position with respect to its rear axle and bumper. But, rules also might have contributed to the decision to introduce the Pinto, despite the fact that company engineers knew of its design flaws. Ford's president, Lee Iacocca, stipulated that the Pinto be designed so that it weighed no more than 2,000 pounds and cost no more than $2,000, a requirement that became known within Ford as the "rule of 2,000." Adherence to this rule might have led engineers to forgo even modestly costly fixes to the gas tank position problem, some as inexpensive as $11 per car, because doing so would add weight and cost to the car, and thus risk violating the rule (Dowie 1977).

The division of labor

The division of labor is another pervasive element of organizational structure. Organizations that employ a division of labor allocate their complete set of tasks to subunits of employees, each of which specializes in a different subset of the organization's full complement of tasks, and each of which conforms to a subset of the organization's full body of rules and standard operating procedures. The division of labor reduces the amount of information organizational participants have to collect and process in the course of their jobs. As a result, it reduces the decision-making burden employees must carry. Most management theorists, following Adam Smith (1991), believe that the division of labor increases the efficiency with which an organization's goals are achieved. Others believe that the division of labor is a device to control employees, reducing their sphere of influence and reducing the organization's need for skilled employees (Braverman 1974; Edwards 1979; Clawson 1980).

Regardless of its principal function, though, the division of labor can facilitate collective wrongdoing in at least two ways. It can fragment information, such that participants in one part of an organization lack information available in another part of the organization that would otherwise cause them to eschew behavior that contributes to a wrongful course of action. It also can diffuse responsibility, such that participants in one part of an organization do not feel obligated to stop or expose (and might even feel forbidden from stopping or exposing) the wrongful behavior of employees in another part of the organization (Braithwaite 1989; Darley 1992).

WRONGDOING BY DESIGN

A division of labor can be created to facilitate wrongdoing. Equity Funding Corporation's sale of phony insurance policies to re-insurers in the late 1960s illustrates well the role that the division of labor can play in the facilitation of organizational wrongdoing (Soble and Dallas 1975). Initially, Equity Funding top managers wrote the phony policies themselves at periodic "policy parties." As the fraud expanded, though, the initiators established a separate unit (misleadingly named the "mass marketing division"), located it across town, staffed it with low-level data entry employees, and instructed the workers to manufacture fictitious insurance policies. The employees were not told the purpose to which the manufactured policies were to be put, and the available evidence suggests that the workers performed their jobs without feeling an obligation or inclination to determine the purpose. Indeed, even the head of the mass marketing unit apparently did not feel compelled to investigate the purpose of his division's work assignment. In his words, while he "knew something was wrong," he "didn't know the total picture of what was going on." Of course, the division of labor is generally developed so that everyone in an organization does not *need* to know the total picture.

An existing division of labor can be used to facilitate wrongdoing as well. Andy Fastow's infamous Cuiaba deal illustrates how a firm's existing division of labor can facilitate wrongdoing by fragmenting both information and responsibility. Enron owned a power plant in Cuiaba, Brazil, that had a lucrative gas production contract (with Enron itself) but suffered from construction delays and financial problems. An Enron manager, Kent Castelman, was tasked with selling the plant because selling the plant would generate earnings while removing debt from the firm's balance sheet. A member of Enron's special projects group, Ben Glissan, approached Castleman with a suggestion to sell the plant to a company called LJM. At the time, Castleman did not realize that LJM was in fact a special-purpose entity set up by Enron's CFO, Andy Fastow, and thus not an independent company. But he caught on later when he was told that he would have to negotiate with one of Fastow's lieutenants, Cheryl Lipshutz, to complete the sale. Still, he went through with the transaction. According to Kurt Eichenwald (2005: 262), who researched the deal, Castleman asked "You're negotiating for LJM?" "That's the assignment," responded Lipshutz. "Strange," thought Castleman. "An Enron executive was negotiating with an Enron executive—to sell something to Enron?" "Not his place to question, though," he concluded.

Finally, an existing division of labor can be used to thwart efforts to expose ongoing wrongdoing. Vince Kaminski was a risk manager at Enron who became worried about the cumulative effect of the firm's many complex financial arrangements. He believed that while the risks associated with the vast majority of individual deals might have been scrutinized adequately on a

133

case-by-case basis, the hazards associated with the entire system of deals were largely unexplored.

Kaminski received approval from a superior, Rick Buy, to conduct a company-wide study. But his efforts to collect data from specific units, such as Andy Fastow's Global Finance Group, were thwarted by these subunits' territoriality. Later, when Kaminski became suspicious about one of Fastow's questionable deals, he sent a memo to the firm's outside accountants, Arthur Anderson, requesting additional information. But he was chastised for doing so by one of the firm's internal accountants, Ryan Siurek. Siurek said that while he shared Kaminski's concerns, no one but the senior Enron accountant, Rick Causey, was authorized to communicate directly with the outside accounting firm. Despite Kaminski's determination to follow his suspicions, he quickly deferred to the organizational division of labor, saying "Okay, fine. If this is the procedure, I won't send any more messages to Anderson" (Eichenwald 2005: 526).

INADVERTENT WRONGDOING

Because organizational task environments are complex and those who design organizational divisions of labor are boundedly rational, the division of labor also can give rise to wrongdoing inadvertently. The Ford Pinto case illustrates well how organizational structures inadvertently can facilitate wrongdoing by *fragmenting information*. As described earlier, Ford Motor Company began selling the Pinto in the 1970s despite pre-production tests that revealed the car burst into flames when struck from behind at relatively low speeds. Ford declined to recall the Pinto after it went into production, even as evidence accumulated of its propensity to ignite in rear-end collisions. The division of labor at Ford might have been behind management's failure to recall the Pinto in a timely fashion. Ford's pre-production safety test unit and its recall unit were situated in different parts of the organizational hierarchy, and information about the gas tank's propensity to ignite upon rear-impact was not transmitted to the company's recall department. Thus, Ford's field recall coordinator, Denis Gioia, could not use this information to help interpret the evidence of Pinto fires that slowly trickled in during the car's first years on the market (Gioia 1992).

Events surrounding the marketing of Fen-Phen, an appetite suppressant drug cocktail that gave rise to serious, and in many cases fatal, side effects appear to illustrate how the division of labor can inadvertently facilitate the initiation of wrongdoing by *diffusing responsibility* (Mundy 2001). A safety officer at Wyeth-Ayers, maker of fenfluramine (one of Fen-Phen's two components), became aware of a growing number of instances in which the drug was associated with negative side effects, known as adverse drug events, or ADEs. The safety officer, Amy Myers, recommended to her superior, Dr. Fred

Wilson, that the growing number of ADEs be acknowledged on the drug's label. Dr. Wilson in turn drafted an updated version of the label and passed it up the chain of command for final approval. Shortly thereafter, though, Wilson retired and no one was hired to take his place. And the departed manager's boss declined to implement the change, possibly because he thought that doing so would hinder the firm's ongoing efforts to get a related drug (dexfenfluramine) approved by the Food and Drug Administration (FDA). Amy Myers who initially recommended the label change, did not press for the label change to be implemented. While we cannot say for sure why this was the case, it seems possible that once she voiced her concern about the rising number of ADEs associated with fenfluramine and the new label was drafted, she believed that her job was done and that it was someone else's responsibility to implement the change. The fact that an intermediate level of the organizational hierarchy was left unoccupied made this even more likely, as there was a gap in the chain of command. An employee is likely to feel some obligation to remind her superior to follow through on a piece of work. But she is less likely to feel obligated to remind her superior's boss to do so.

Unobtrusive controls

Occupational and professional roles

While employees obtain specific guidance about how to act from rules, standard operating procedures, and the division of labor, they also learn more general principles about how to perform their jobs from superiors, peers, and even their subordinates. These more general principles consist of mutually agreed upon understandings about the way employees in their position are expected to perform their jobs in different circumstances. Social psychologists refer to an employee's position in the organization as their "role", and the mutually agreed upon understandings associated with their role as "norms." These role-specific norms, which stipulate how organizational participants should perform position-related tasks, are distinct from the organizational norms discussed in Chapter 5, which dictate how employees should think and behave with respect to attitudes and behavior more generally.

Rules and standard operating procedures are extremely effective in providing guidance to employees faced with foreseeable specific circumstances. But it is difficult to develop rules and standard operating procedures for every circumstance an employee might confront, partly because the number of such circumstances is large, and partly because some circumstances are difficult to foresee. Role-specific norms provide employees with more flexible guidelines on how others in their organization expect them to deal with a wide range of sometimes difficult-to-anticipate situations.

People who occupy roles are obligated to adhere to the norms associated with them, without engaging in mindful and rational cost-benefit calculations or normative assessments regarding the merits of the norms, and sometimes even if they disapprove of them. Occupational and professional norms are among the most important role-specific norms in organizations, providing guidance for people in occupations and professions for which specific rules and standard operating procedures cannot be written. Typically these norms delineate acceptable behavior, but, like more specific rules and standard operating procedures, they also can give rise to wrongful behavior.

WRONGDOING BY DESIGN

A number of ethical and legal questions arose in connection with the prescription of Fen-Phen's two main components, fenfluramine and phentermine, which had been independently approved by the FDA for the treatment of obesity. One question pertained to the propriety of prescribing the drugs for cosmetic weight loss. Carrie Cox, a vice president of women's healthcare at Wyeth-Ayers, the maker of fenfluramine, became concerned about the prescription of Fen-Phen for cosmetic weight loss, and sought approval from her superior, a medical doctor himself, to write a "dear doctor" letter reminding physicians of the drugs' approved uses. Her superior, though, nixed the idea, saying that "it was not the company's place to tell physicians how to prescribe drugs or how to do their jobs" (Mundy 2001: 261). Cox relented, even though at the time she felt uncomfortable about doing so. Presumably Cox failed to warn the physicians about the inappropriate prescription of the company's drug, because she was reminded that it was not her role to do so, even though she was well positioned to make a judgment on the issue.

INADVERTENT WRONGDOING

The mortgage meltdown and subsequent financial crisis that spanned the final years of the new century's first decade provides much raw material for students of wrongdoing. Beginning in 2006, housing prices began to plateau and then decline. This caused homeowners with variable-rate balloon mortgages to default on their loans, which in turn eroded the value of securities backed by the mortgages. In the two years that followed, the declining value of mortgage-backed securities reverberated through the financial system, eroding the value of other financial derivatives, and ultimately undermining the viability of the world's largest financial institutions and the global economy. In the wake of the financial crisis, which we will discuss in much more depth in Chapter 10, investigative reporters and law-enforcement officials scoured the business landscape in search of wrongdoing and wrongdoers who could be held accountable for the calamity. Some reporters and investigators zeroed in on mortgage brokers, whom they charged sometimes unethically and perhaps illegally facilitated loans to homebuyers who they knew were likely to default on their obligations. But mortgage brokers are essentially salespersons, and their behavior in this instance appears to conform to the norms of their occupation. As one mortgage broker said, "In any sales position, you don't turn away a client." The president of the National Association of Mortgage Brokers characterized this norm as an obligation, saying, "If they meet the criteria, you have to write the loan" (Spivak and Bice 2008).

Communication channels

Despite the fact that organizational participants have rules, standard operating procedures, the division of labor, and norms to guide them in their daily work, they often have to make decisions about how to complete their tasks by collecting and processing information about the decision context. Communication channels shape the amount and type of information organizational participants have at their disposal when making decisions and thus shape their choices. Communication channels can facilitate organizational functioning by increasing the likelihood that organizational participants make decisions on the basis of the most relevant information and on the basis of the most reasonable interpretation of that information. But they also can facilitate wrongdoing by increasing the chance that organizational participants will make decisions on the basis of incorrect information or distorted interpretations.

WRONGDOING BY DESIGN

Middle managers at Prudential Bache Securities began marketing shares in limited partnerships in the late 1970s. These partnerships were billed as safe investments that both served as tax shelters and possessed high growth potential. But over time, an increasing number resembled risky and fraudulent investments. The Pru-Bache brokers who sold the partnerships to clients, though, knew little about their true character. Their understanding of the partnerships was based on documents provided by their superiors, that misrepresented the partnerships' real nature. Eichenwald (1996), who chronicled the Prudential Bache Securities fraud, described the experience of one Pru-Bache broker in this way. "Piscitelli never reviewed the dense, legalistic documents each partnership filed with the Securities and Exchange Commission—he had neither the time nor the desire. . . . Instead, like most stockbrokers, he examined the sales material provided by the firm. That was supposed to summarize, in simple English, what the filings said. Then he passed that information on to his clients" (1996: 5). Piscitelli only learned of the partnerships' questionable, and in some cases fraudulent, character when his clients, many of whom were friends, began losing money. And when he became aware of his unwitting promulgation of the fraud, he became so distraught that he seriously contemplated suicide.

INADVERTENT WRONGDOING

The Enron debacle provides numerous opportunities to explore alternative explanations of organizational wrongdoing. In Chapter 4, I discussed wrong-doing at Enron in connection with the rational choice explanation (in regards to unrealistically high performance expectations). In Chapter 5, I discussed wrongdoing at Enron in connection with the culture account (in regards to normative content that promoted rule-breaking). Then earlier in this chapter, I discussed wrongdoing at Enron in connection with the administrative struc-ture explanation—in regard to standard operating procedures for manipulat-ing California's energy market.

Some wrongdoing at Enron also apparently was facilitated by the structure of its communication channels. The most straightforward way that commu-nication channels can facilitate wrongdoing is by structuring the flow of information such that organizational participants are denied access to infor-mation that they need to make rightful decisions. Enron, like many modern corporations, maintained an ongoing working relationship with both an outside accounting firm, Arthur Anderson, and an independent law firm, Vinson & Elkins. But these professional service firms were not linked by formal communication channels. As a result, information possessed by one of these firms and needed by the other did not always find its way to the second firm, sometimes causing the second firm to make decisions that facilitated wrongdoing.

In one instance, a lawyer at Vinson & Elkins became concerned that the design of a prospective special purpose entity, LJM, was problematic from an accounting standpoint. The lawyer, Ronald Astin, voiced his concern to Enron's treasurer. But the treasurer, Ben Glissan, dismissed the concern with what Astin believed was a semantic argument. As recounted by Kurt Eichen-wald in his book about the Enron debacle, "Astin wasn't convinced. Glissan's word game just sounded too cute. Still, the lawyers had time to mull it over, maybe talk it through with Anderson. After all, they were the accountants. Not Vinson & Elkins" (2005: 213). Astin did not, though, ever talk it over with anyone at Anderson, even though he remained troubled about the deal's accounting propriety. In all likelihood, he would have had to make a special effort (i.e. he would have had to circumvent normal channels of communica-tion) to bring his concerns to Anderson's attention. And he did not make such an effort. As a result, Anderson ruled favorably on LJM, only to find out later that the special purpose entity violated generally accepted accounting principles (GAAP) in several crucial respects.

Technology

Organizations use technologies to process inputs and generate outputs. In some cases the inputs are material and the outputs are products. In others, the inputs are human beings and the outputs are services. The first scholars to examine organizational technologies considered them, along with size, to be a primary determinant of administrative structure (Woodward 1965; Perrow 1967). These scholars distinguished between certain and uncertain technologies. Further, they maintained that organizations with certain technologies perform best when they use mechanistic structures typified by centralization of decision-making, while those with uncertain technologies perform best when they adopt organic structures typified by decentralization. Subsequent scholars have conceptualized organizational technologies as forms of behavioral control in their own right that determine the kinds of decisions that organizational participants can make, and the premises upon which they can make them (Braverman 1974; Edwards 1979; Clawson 1980). Regardless, insofar as technologies provide organizations with the means to generate products and perform services, they are indispensable to organizational survival. But technologies also can give rise to organizational wrongdoing.

WRONGDOING BY DESIGN

Organizational technologies can be used intentionally to encode behavior that is wrongful. As described above, Prudential Bache began selling deceptively risky, and in some cases fraudulent, limited partnerships in the late 1970s. By the mid 1990s, the practice had become so integrated into the firm's routines, that an internal sales force was constituted to market the partnerships to Pru-Bache brokers. Further, computer programs that brokers used to develop judiciously diversified portfolios for their clients included them on the list of possible portfolio components. And, as Kurt Eichenwald wrote, "The computer almost always said that a chunk of the client's money should go into Pru-Bache partnerships" (1996: 5).

INADVERTENT WRONGDOING

Organizational technologies also can unintentionally encode behavior that is wrongful. The computer program used by Joseph Jett to trade government scripts at Kidder Peabody clearly played a role in his venture into wrongdoing at the firm (Freedman and Burke 1998). As described in Chapter 4, Jett was responsible for initiating trades with the Federal Reserve Bank, a type of trading that typically generates only modest returns. Jett's trades with the

139

Fed, though, were fantastically profitable and he was rewarded handsomely with extravagant bonuses and a significant promotion. Eventually it became known that the majority of Jett's profits were fictitious—the result of an error in the computer software that registered gains from trades that in fact produced no real profit.

Disagreement exists among Jett, his co-workers, independent investigators, and other experts regarding Jett's responsibility for the fraud. Many thought Jett knew all along that the trades produced fictitious profits. Some, though, thought that Jett did not realize that his trades produced fictitious profits at first, but became aware of this fact and exploited the serendipitous program glitch to his advantage as time went on. A few even thought that Jett was unaware of the fictitious nature of his earnings. Roy C. Smith, a professor of finance at New York University, gave voice to both of the last two assessments. He mused, "I think [Jett] stumbled upon a way to make money on the firm's computers, and probably thought (at least at first) that the money was real.... It is telling, I think, that $8 million of the $9 million paid to Jett was still in his brokerage account when the dam broke. If he was trying to cheat Kidder, why leave the money where it could be frozen?" (Freedman and Burke 1998: 13). Martin Mayer, a visiting scholar at the Brookings Institute went even further. During a *Sixty Minutes* television broadcast devoted to the fraud titled "Did He or Didn't He," Mayer stated, "I don't think to this day [Jett] is entirely conscious of the extent to which his profits were the reflection of a faulty computer program" (CBS News, February 19, 1995). Regardless, all agree that the fraud was made possible by the computer software's glitch.

Schemas and scripts

Sometimes rules, standard operating procedures, norms, and the other administrative structures described above do not provide employees with sufficient guidance on how to do their jobs because their jobs require knowledge and understandings that only those tasked with performing them can acquire through on-the-job experience. As a result, employees sometimes have to figure out on their own how to respond to particular contingencies. When they are successful, workers tend to incorporate what they have learned about how to handle those contingencies in what social psychologists call "schemas" and "scripts." Schemas dictate how organizational participants process information and assimilate emotions when confronted with particular work-related contingencies. Scripts dictate how organizational participants perform tasks when faced with particular work-related contingencies, which are interpreted by organizational participants according to the schemas they employ. As such, like the other administrative structures considered so far, schemas and scripts substitute for more time-consuming mindful and rational cost-benefit or normative deliberations. And as such, they tend to make organizations more efficient. Also like the other administrative structures discussed so far, though, schemas and scripts can facilitate wrongdoing. But because employees create scripts and schemas primarily to improve their efficiency, these administrative structures only facilitate wrongdoing inadvertently.

INADVERTENT WRONGDOING

Earlier in this chapter, I argued that the division of labor at Ford Motor Company might have contributed to the firm's failure to recall the Pinto despite mounting evidence that it was prone to bursting into flames when struck from behind at low speeds. Scripts and schemas also might have contributed to Ford's failure to recall the Pinto. Dennis Gioia, Ford's field recall coordinator, recalls that he did not view early evidence of rear-impact-induced Pinto gas tank fires as indicative of a problem that required a recall because this evidence did not contain cues that he used in his job to identify problems that should trigger recalls (Gioia 1992 and personal communication). Gioia suggests that the schemas he used to identify problems that mandated recalls focused on the categorization and frequency of incidents, with frequent problems of the same type triggering recalls, and occasional problems of different types not triggering recalls. Incidents were categorized as being of the same type partly on the basis of whether or not they appeared to be the result of the same underlying cause. In this case, as noted above, Gioia did not have information at his disposal to suggest that the fires might be the result of a common cause (e.g. the placement of the gas tank in close proximity to the rear bumper and rear axle). And the number of rear-end-collision induced fires was relatively small.

Gioia also suggests that the schemas he used to identify problems that should trigger recalls focused on *mechanical failures* (e.g. cracked axles) that might *cause* accidents and thus injury. But the Pinto gas tank fires were not mechanical failures that caused accidents. They were the result of accidents (e.g. the failure of drivers to leave sufficient following distances between themselves and the cars in front of them). Finally, Gioia hints that the schema he used to identify problems that might trigger recalls blocked or blunted emotional reactions to incoming reports. In the course of performing his job, he learned to tune out the sometimes-gruesome character of accident reports so that he could process reports objectively. Thus, he tuned out the horrifying nature of the early Pinto gas tank fire reports (even though the gruesomeness of the reports later played a major role in labeling Ford's behavior in connection with the Pinto as unethical).

Thus Gioia did not discount the importance of the early reports of rear-collision-induced Pinto gas tank fires because of a mindful and rational cost-benefit calculation or normative assessment. Instead, he discounted the reports because, given the administrative structures in which he was situated, the reports did not fit the profile of a problem that should trigger recalls. As a result, Gioia did not recommend the Pinto be recalled, and his decision to leave the car in service seemed completely ethical to him at the time. Years later, though, when he learned of the Pinto's gas tank flaws and contemplated the schemas he used in his daily work, he concluded that the decision to leave the car in service was unethical (Gioia 1992).

Structural redundancy

I have discussed a number of structural elements that can facilitate organizational wrongdoing: rules, standard operating procedures, the division of labor, occupational and professional roles, communication channels, organizational technologies, and schemas and scripts. While I have considered each structural element separately, it is important to recognize that several structural elements can operate in tandem to facilitate the same wrongful behavior. For example, I suggested that marketing brochures at Prudential Bache Securities, a communication channel, caused brokers to recommend risky and sometimes fraudulent limited partnerships to their retired fixed-income clients who were looking for safe and solid investments. But I also suggested that a computer program, an organizational technology, also facilitated this wrongful behavior. Further, other elements of Prudential Bache Securities' administrative system might have contributed to this wrongdoing, as well. Importantly, the division of labor at Prudential Bache reduced the likelihood that brokers suspicious of the limited partnerships' integrity would raise questions about the partnerships. When recounting one Pru-Bache broker's unquestioning use of the information in the marketing brochures, Eichenwald notes that the broker did not second guess the information partly because it was "not his job" to do so (Eichenwald 1996: 5).

Assessing the administrative systems explanation

The administrative systems explanation of organizational wrongdoing departs from the dominant approach to explaining organizational wrongdoing in several respects. First, it allows that much behavior in organizations is mindless. Most obviously, organizational participants often follow rules and standard operating procedures in an automatic fashion, without deliberating about the merits of the course of action the rules and operating procedures encode. Second, the administrative systems explanation allows that much organizational behavior that is mindful is boundedly rational. The division of labor limits the amount of information available to organizational participants. And schemas and scripts cause organizational participants to process available information in restricted ways. Third, the administrative systems explanation takes into account the immediate situational context, which is conceptualized in terms of administrative structures. Finally, the administrative systems account allows that when organizational participants respond to organizational structures in a mindless way, they do not develop positive inclinations to engage in the behavior the structures prescribe. Again, when administrative structures give rise to mindless action, people respond to them in an automatic fashion, without forming inclinations to act, at least without forming the sort of inclinations that we usually associate with the concept of intent.

Nevertheless, the administrative systems explanation of wrongdoing retains some elements of the dominant approach. First, it does not consider how organizational participants' behavior is shaped by social interaction. For the most part, organizational participants are viewed as responding to organizational structures. While it is true that some of these structures have been explicitly designed by others, the interaction between structure-followers and structure-designers is at best indirect (i.e. mediated by the structures). The organizational structure explanation does incorporate the impact of professional and occupational norms. But once organizational participants are socialized into the roles and norms associated with their profession or occupation, these structural elements become internalized constraints. Others in an organizational participant's environment are important only insofar as they remind the individual of the expected roles and norms.

Second, the administrative systems explanation implicitly assumes that people make discrete decisions to engage in wrongdoing and thus does not take into account how wrongdoing can develop over time. Organizational participants are portrayed as coping with work-related contingencies by making reference to organizational guidelines or making use of information shaped by organizational arrangements and then embarking on behavior consistent with those guidelines and shaped information. And their response is not conceptualized as having a temporal dimension. Finally, the organizational structure explanation implicitly assumes that when people make decisions mindfully, on the basis of structurally conditioned information, they develop positive inclinations to engage in the behavior in question.

Conclusion

The administrative systems explanation of organizational wrongdoing, like the most recent and enhanced version of the ethical decision account, allows that people sometimes embark on wrongdoing in a mindless or boundedly rational way. Thus, like that version of the ethical decision explanation, it also allows that people sometimes embark on wrongdoing without developing a positive inclination to do so. But the administrative systems account goes beyond the most recent and enhanced version of the ethical decision explanation by explicitly considering the immediate situational context in which people are embedded. It views people as organizational participants, rather than as atomized decision makers. Still, the administrative systems account clings to some of the assumptions associated with the dominant approach to analyzing organizational wrongdoing. In the next chapter, we will explore another explanation of wrongdoing that departs even further from the dominant approach.

8

Situational Social Influence

Introduction

The situational social influence explanation of organizational wrongdoing is rooted in a theoretical perspective that views organizations as systems of localized social interaction and views organizational participants as by nature or necessity attentive to the attitudes and behaviors of those in their immediate environment. Organizations are populated by people who are linked to each other by social relationships based on their proximity in physical space and the division of labor. People appraise alternative ways of thinking and behaving with an eye to determining whether they are in line with the expectations of those with whom they interact.

Importantly, proponents of the situational social influence perspective believe that people focus on the expectations of others proximate to them because the situations in which they find themselves often are ambiguous and thus not amenable to thorough cost-benefit calculations or normative assessments. Further, proponents of this perspective consider some of the situational social influence processes that shape behavior to be substantially mindless. Indicative of this, Cialdini (2001) characterizes the operation of these processes by the term "click-whir," where "click" refers to the occurrence of a stimulus and "whir" refers to a mechanism that is set in motion by the stimulus. Thus the situational social influence perspective implicitly assumes that organizational participants are at best boundedly rational deliberators, and in many cases mindless actors.

Early management theorists considered situational social influence detrimental to organizations, causing employees to deviate from administrative structures that specify appropriate behavior. But later theorists came to view situational social influence as beneficial to organizations, furnishing employees with guidance that could not be provided by more formal structures and even motivating employees to work hard and well at assigned tasks (Perrow 1972).

Social psychologists have demonstrated how an understanding of situational social influence can be used strategically to shape the behavior of others (Cialdini 2001). I adopt the outlook of management theorists and draw on the insights of social psychologists to explain how a variety of forms of situational social influence can facilitate organizational wrongdoing.

I begin with three forms of situational social influence that build on ideas presented in previous chapters: social information processing, groupthink, and definition of the situation. I then move on to additional forms of situational influence, ending with a discussion of commitment to a failing course of action (a form of social influence that my case study reading suggests deserves extended attention). Situational social influence can cause organizational participants inadvertently to slip into wrongdoing. It can also be used by mindful and rational wrongdoers intentionally to recruit other organizational participants to join their planned or ongoing wrongdoing. I present illustrations of both the inadvertent and intentional effects of situational social influence below, although for reasons of parsimony I do not present illustrations of both types of effects for each form of situational social influence.[1] I conclude by offering an overall assessment of the situational social influence account.

Social information processing

The expectancy theory of worker motivation, discussed in connection with the rational choice account of organizational wrongdoing elaborated in Chapter 4, assumes that people evaluate the potential costs and benefits of alternative courses of action in a social vacuum. Salancik and Pfeffer (1978) have offered a situational social influence extension of expectancy theory, which has far-reaching implications for understanding motivation in organizations. Their social information processing theory of motivation holds that a person's appraisal of the rewards and punishments associated with a course of action as well as that person's estimation of the effort–performance and performance–outcome expectancies related to the course of action are influenced by the explicit perceptions of other workers in the environment as well as the implicit perceptions of other workers, as reflected in their behavior. An employee's desire for a particular reward or aversion for a particular punishment will tend to align with the desires and aversions of others in the social environment. Similarly, an employee's assessment of the effort–performance

---

[1] I presented illustrations of both inadvertent and intentional effects of each administrative structure considered in the previous chapter. I think presenting a similarly detailed exposition in connection with situational social influence would be unnecessarily tedious.

and performance–outcome expectancies associated with a course of action will tend to align with the assessments of others in the environment.

The social information processing theory of motivation suggests that the other people in a person's environment can have a profound impact on a person's motivation to engage in tasks. Not only can other people influence a person's capacity to perform a task and be rewarded (or avoid punishment) for task completion, other people can influence how much a person values rewards or eschews punishments, and can influence a person's estimation of the chances of completing a task and being rewarded or punished for task completion. Social information processing can be beneficial to organizations. It causes employee evaluations of rewards, punishments, and expectations of the links between effort and performance and between performance and outcomes to converge. And when employee perceptions of their task environments converge, organizations can develop standardized motivation schemes (which are less costly to design and implement than multiple schemes tailored to employees' divergent perceptions). But social information processing can also facilitate wrongdoing.

The insider trading scandals of the 1980s, as described by James Stewart in his book *Den of Thieves* (1991), provide ample evidence that social information processing can shape wrongdoers' perceptions of the rewards and punishments associated with a wrongful course of action, as well as the expectancies associated with the course of action. I have already discussed the relationship between David Levine, the organizer of one of the biggest insider trading schemes of the 1980s, and Robert Wilkis, one of Levine's recruits. In Chapter 6 I contended that Wilkis experienced cognitive dissonance when he first learned of Levine's clandestine activities, and employed techniques of neutralization to assuage his guilt after he became involved in them. In Chapter 4 I maintained that Wilkis derived excitement from his participation in the scheme and that this reward likely fueled his motivation to continue with it. But Wilkis's decision to join Levine's clandestine enterprise is best explained by the social information processing theory of motivation.

Levine and Wilkis began exchanging insider information in the early 1980s, when Wilkis was an investment banker at Lazard Freres and Levine was a investment banker at Smith Barney. Levine asked Wilkis to provide him with information about mergers and acquisitions pending at Lazard so that Levine could trade on the basis of it. And Levine promised to provide Wilkis with information he gleaned from Smith Barney so that Wilkis could, in turn, trade on it. It is well established that the targets of merger and acquisition bids tend to increase in value in the course of acquirer bidding. Traders with advance knowledge of bids can purchase stock in target firms before the bids are announced and then sell at a considerable profit after the bids are made public. After a day's contemplation, Wilkis agreed to Levine's proposal and the two embarked on a prolonged insider trading relationship.

Wilkis appeared to embark on the insider trading scheme because he thought that the rewards associated with the scheme outweighed the risks. According to Stewart, Wilkis did not feel fulfilled by the rewards available in his job. Wilkis held liberal political beliefs and sought work that meshed with those values. He left his first job at Citibank for a post at Blyth Eastman Dillon because Blyth was starting a new international merchant bank business that would finance development projects in the Third World. When those plans fell through, he left Blyth for Lazard Freres' international department. But the Lazard position also failed to provide an outlet for his progressive aspirations. Levine took note of Wilkis's dissatisfaction when pitching the insider trading scheme to him, describing the enterprise as freeing him up to do the good deeds that he sought to perform. "You could get rich, get out of Wall Street," Levine suggested. "You could go to Nepal, become a Buddhist monk. Isn't that what you want?" Over time, Wilkis warmed to the idea. As Stewart (1991: 66) put it, "The germ of an idea had taken hold in Wilkis's mind. He didn't like his work at Lazard any better than he had at Blyth or Citibank. Maybe he could get rich, as his friend was suggesting—and get out of Wall Street for good."

Further, it would appear that Wilkis's motivation to participate in the insider trading scheme hinged partly on his effort–performance expectancy. Levine taught Wilkis how to conduct illegal trades. He explained how to open an offshore Cayman Islands bank account through which to trade and in which to store his ill-gotten profits. He instructed him to make multiple small trades so that his trading would not attract the attention of Securities and Exchange Commission (SEC) investigators. But more germane, in addition to offering Wilkis this technical information and training, Levine repeatedly offered his assessment that the system was foolproof. Further, he flaunted his insider trading successes, which appeared to substantiate his assessment.

Finally, there is evidence that Wilkis's participation in the scheme vacillated in direct proportion to the apparent performance–outcome expectancy associated with the enterprise. Wilkis's enthusiasm waxed with each completed deal, but waned with news of investigations, firings, and indictments of insider traders at his own and other firms. But more to the point, Levine did not leave Wilkis to interpret these developments on his own. Instead, he repeatedly offered his assessment that the trading system he had engineered was invulnerable to detection. Further, he exuded a supreme confidence, which appeared to substantiate his assessment.

Groupthink

The early ethical decision theory discussed in Chapter 6 assumed that people engage in wrongdoing when they fail to successfully negotiate the four stages believed to constitute the ethical decision process. More recent ethical decision theory, also discussed in Chapter 6, explores how bounded rationality causes people to fail in their negotiation of the four stages of the ethical decision process. But all of the decision theory and research that I have discussed so far focuses on individual decision making. And many decisions are made in groups. Trevino, Weaver, and Reynolds (2006) have noted that research on ethical decision making has for the most part ignored how groups make ethical decisions. But there is theory on group decision making more generally that has obvious implications for ethical decision making in groups, the theory on "groupthink."

Irving Janis proposed that when groups are highly cohesive, members have a tendency to censor their own and fellow group members' contributions to collective decisions as an act of loyalty to the group (i.e. in the interest of preserving group unity), especially when the group is under stress (Janis 1971, 1972). Pressures to censor one's own and fellow group members' contributions to group decisions can sometimes redound to a group's benefit, by inhibit the rehashing of dissenting points of view that are unlikely to improve the quality of the group's decisions. But in the extreme, such pressures can cause groups to converge too quickly on a preferred decision option. Specifically, they can cause groups to eschew the thorough and realistic examination of the preferred option and its alternatives. Further, it can cause groups to focus on information that confirms the wisdom of their initial preference, and forego the search for potentially disconfirming information. Janis asserted that groupthink causes decision-making errors in both practical matters and "moral judgments." He maintained that cohesive groups under stress typically hold an inflated sense of members' moral and intellectual superiority and also tend to view outsiders as inferior and to treat them harshly.

Janis identified a rather long list of symptoms that groups exhibit when they suffer from groupthink, including a belief in the group's invulnerability and moral superiority, the characterization of outsiders in stereotypical ways, and an unusually high level of unanimity. He provided detailed analyses of several well-known group decision-making fiascos that he believed were caused by groupthink, including the Kennedy administration's invasion of the Bay of Pigs and the Johnson administration's pursuit of the Vietnam War, uncovering evidence of both the underlying mechanisms and symptoms of groupthink.

Two management scholars have used theory about groupthink to analyze organizational wrongdoing. Sims (1992) offered a groupthink analysis of three famous cases of organizational wrongdoing: Beech-Nut's "phony" apple juice gambit, E.F. Hutton's check kiting fraud, and Salomon Brothers' Treasury auction scam. Scharff (2005) offered a groupthink analysis of World-com's accounting fraud. While the Sims and Scharff analyses are convincing, both focus exclusively on the presence of groupthink symptoms as opposed to the underlying groupthink mechanisms. This is understandable, given that the mechanisms that give rise to groupthink are typically hidden from view. But it is a problem, because most of the symptoms of groupthink can be symptoms of other organizational maladies.

The Dow Corning breast implant controversy illustrates how the social psychological mechanisms theorized to generate groupthink might contribute to wrongdoing. Dow Corning manufactured breast implants that many believe caused a host of severely debilitating autoimmune-related medical conditions in the women who received them. As a result, the firm was the target of substantial negative media attention, numerous civil law suits, and eventually a Justice Department criminal investigation. Critics charged that Dow Corning failed to ensure that their implants were produced to high quality standards, neglected to conduct thorough testing of the implants' performance and safety, and knew of the implants' possible defects and hazards but failed to share this information with both potential implant recipients and regulatory bodies—all at the same time that it aggressively marketed the product to the public. Ultimately, while the Justice Department dropped its criminal charges against the firm for lack of evidence, Dow Corning was ordered to remove its breast implants from the market by the FDA and forced to pay billions of dollars in compensation to recipients, developments that led to the firm's bankruptcy.

John Byrne has written one of several detailed accounts of the Dow Corning breast implant tragedy. His book, *Informed Consent* (1996), is unique in that it draws heavily from information provided by John Swanson, a Dow Corning employee who served on the firm's Business Conduct Committee, the group that was tasked with overseeing the firm's ethics program and that ultimately played a key role in the firm's defense of its breast implant business. Swanson is a crucial source of information about the crisis, not just because he occupied an unparalleled vantage point over Dow Chemical's ethics program and its handling of the breast implant controversy, but also because his wife, Colleen, was a recipient of Dow Corning implants and subsequently experienced serious autoimmune-related conditions that Swanson and his wife attributed to the implants. Thus, he was able to lend insight into both Dow Corning's decision processes and the way in which a dissenting member of Dow Corning's management was treated and comported himself.

Byrne presents evidence suggesting that Dow Corning suffered from the type of decision-making flaws that Janis contends stem from groupthink. Dow Chemical's top executives unquestioningly held to their initial belief that silicone was biologically inert, despite mounting anecdotal evidence of the association between surgical insertion of its breast implants and the subsequent emergence of autoimmune-related diseases. In addition, the firm's executives never wavered from their initial strategy to refute critical evidence, fight or settle out of court civil suits, and continue marketing the devices, despite the overwhelming costs of pursuing this strategy. In fact, Dow Corning executives were so strong in their beliefs about silicone and were so confident in the wisdom of their strategy that Byrne reports they were "shocked" when juries and judges ruled in favor of plaintiffs. Finally, throughout the crisis and to John Swanson's dismay, Dow Corning's executives exhibited little compassion for the women who clearly suffered greatly from what they believed were implant-related autoimmune conditions, some of whom were so physically compromised that they struggled to participate in court proceedings.

Importantly, neither Byrne nor Swanson expressed the belief that the Dow Corning executives were unethical individuals. Further, throughout the breast implant crisis, Dow Corning's executives believed themselves to occupy the moral high ground. As legal fees and court judgments swelled and bad press accumulated, the firm briefly contemplated getting out of the implant business and cutting their losses. But the firm concluded that it had a moral obligation to stay in the business because there was a sizable group of women who depended on them to provide their valuable product. Indeed, the Dow Corning executives tended to view those who were attacking the firm, the contingency fee lawyers and investigative reporters, as self-interested and unethical.

Byrne also presents evidence suggesting that decision making at Dow Corning was hampered by the social mechanisms that lead to groupthink. Dow Corning executives were homogeneous and socially isolated. They were almost exclusively white, born and raised in the Midwest, and trained as engineers. Further, because Dow Corning was a private subsidiary of two large public companies (Dow Chemical and Corning Glass), its executives were not subject to the input of stockholders. And because the firm was headquartered in a remote small town that it dominated, Midland, Michigan, its executives were not subject to much public scrutiny. Such social similarity and isolation served to increase group cohesion. Perhaps for these reasons, overt conflict and even public disagreement among Dow Corning executives was frowned upon and rare.

It is possible that the outward harmony among Dow Corning executives was the product partly of the underlining alignment of corporate executives' individual outlooks. When Colleen Swanson began experiencing serious auto-immune related symptoms (such as pain and a rash across her chest), neither John Swanson nor his wife considered the possibility that the breast implants might be to blame, despite the fact that John was well aware of public concern and mounting law suits related to the implants. Further, when Colleen confided to John that she had become convinced that the breast implants were the cause of her health problems, John was dumbfounded. Apparently both Colleen and John were so immersed in the Dow Corning culture that they were slow to connect the dots.

But John and Colleen Swanson's other experiences suggests that self-censorship of the sort that Janis believes gives rise to groupthink also played a role. Presumably out of fear of censorship, both Colleen and John Swanson kept information about Colleen's health problems to themselves. Indeed, John did not even tell his best friends, one of whom, Dan Hayes, was the chief operating officer of the unit that manufactured the implants, about Colleen's condition. Further, when Colleen, with John's blessing, decided to pursue the option of having the implants removed, the two sought medical help outside of Midland. Both Colleen and John feared that news of Colleen's illness, assessment, and intended course of action would get back to Dow Corning's executives and leak to the closed community, making their continued association with the firm and life in the community untenable. This fear was apparently well-founded. When John Swanson eventually told his friend Dan Hayes about Colleen's health problems and the suspected cause, Hayes increasingly distanced himself from the Swansons.

In addition, in an explicit act of self-censorship, John Swanson elected not to become an active critic of Dow Corning's policy with respect to breast implants, but instead requested that he be excused from involvement in the breast implant crisis management process, even as Colleen's health deteriorated to the point of near death. Ultimately, Colleen had the implants removed and experienced some improvement. And John left Dow Corning as soon as he could retire with full benefits. His last assignment was to review the firm's ethics program, and his report did identify a number of serious weaknesses with the program. But when he presented his report to a group of senior executives on the eve of his retirement, he did not mention explicitly what by then must have been the obvious link between the ethics program's weaknesses and the company's breast implant crisis, which by that time had nearly totally consumed the firm. Amazingly, Swanson explained that he did not mention the breast implant debacle in his critique of the firm's ethics program because he feared that doing so might provoke a critical response among the managers, which he feared would distract them from his report's message.

When dealing with human tragedy at a distance, as I am doing here, it is easy to coldly dissect human behavior, infer causes, and in the process over-look and thus implicitly undervalue the humanity of the people involved. I hope I have not done that here. I think Colleen and John Swanson's handling of their private tragedy was honorable, and in many ways heroic. But I also think there is reason to believe that it reflects the constraining effects that social pressures associated with cohesive groups can have on decision making. And if these effects were manifested in the lives of other Dow Corn-ing executives, it seems possible that they might have given rise to groupthink that might have contributed to Dow Corning's fateful handling of the crisis. Interestingly, John Byrne concludes his book about the Dow Corning breast implant controversy by describing John Swanson's experience presenting the case to MBA students at the University of St. Thomas in Minneapolis, Minne-sota. Some of the students wondered why it took so long for Swanson to act decisively and leave the company. Byrne answered this question by explain-ing, "John Swanson was one of the most loyal people I have ever known in terms of giving the company the benefit of the doubt" (Byrne 1996: 245).

Definition of the situation

In the previous chapter, I discussed occupational and professional roles and norms that constitute one component of an organization's administrative system. There I maintained that conformity to norms is substantially mindless and automatic. But before people can conform to norms, even if their confor-mity is mindless, they must recognize the roles they are being asked to play in the situations in which they find themselves, and they must recall or quickly learn the norms that are associated with those roles. People identify their roles and the norms associated with them in two ways: they observe cues in their environment that indicate the roles and norms called for in the situation, and they scrutinize others in their environment who convey expectations about the roles they should play and the norms they should exhibit. Others convey expectations by manipulating subtle rewards and punishments in response to the attitudes and behaviors a person exhibits. They also convey expectations by modeling the appropriate attitudes and behaviors. Together these cues, subtle rewards and punishments, and modeled attitudes and behaviors "define the situation." Thus, an employee who enters a room and finds a male boss dressed in a suit and tie seated at the head of the table with co-workers seated in a circle around the boss and everyone exhibiting proper posture and silently reading a document placed in front of them might reason-ably conclude that the gathering is a formal business meeting. And if the employee greeted the superior with a casual, "Hi Rick," the greeting might be met with disapproving stares from both the superior and co-workers.

Managers can define situations in ways that redound to the benefit of their organizations. For example, if the male boss described above thought his group would perform more effectively if it conducted its business in a more informal fashion (perhaps inviting the participation of low-level employees), he might take off his suit jacket, loosen his tie, lean back in his chair, and interrupt the silence by asking one of the subordinates a non-work related question. Joan Emerson (1970) presents an insightful analysis of how gynecologists, nurses, and even patients work to define a gynecological examination as a "medical situation" as opposed to "a party, sexual assault, psychological experiment, or anything else." This ensures that the examination, which can produce disruptive anxiety for both patients and medical professionals, can be conducted in an efficient and effective way. But people also can define situations in ways that cause others to join wrongful courses of action that they wish to carry out.

The rigging of TV quiz show contests in the 1950s illustrates how wrongdoers can define a situation such that others are likely to join their wrongful enterprise (Stone and Yohn 1992). When Daniel Enright, the producer of "Twenty One," approached Herbert Stempel, a prospective contestant, with the opportunity to participate in rigged contests for the top-rated quiz show, he defined the situation not as a competition but rather as a theatrical production. Further, he comported himself as if the rigging of contests was an acceptable component of such productions. He began by asked Stempel in vague terms whether he wanted to participate in the rigging. But before Stempel could provide a definitive answer, Enright proceeded as if Stempel had already accepted the proposition and went on to outline what might be considered the casting and script of the upcoming show. In Stone and Yohn's (1992: 29) words, Enright indicated that Stempel "would be a contestant on 'Twenty-One' the following night; on the broadcast he would request a nine-point question in the first round of the game and a nine-point question in the second round, and he would win." Then, without waiting for Stempel to express a willingness to go along with the plan, he asked to see Stempel's wardrobe. On seeing an old, shiny and shabby, blue double-breasted suit, he said, "You'll wear this." Then he selected a blue and white striped shirt with a frayed collar saying, "It's blue. That's what you wear on television." Stempel, in testimony to the senior district attorney of New York County investigating the fraud, indicated that he was "overwhelmed" and "immediately took it for granted that being given the number of points to ask for, being rehearsed with the questions and answers, being told what to wear, was how a quiz show was run" (1992: 29).

The norm of reciprocity

In the previous chapter I discussed occupational and professional roles and norms that regulate behavior in organizations, and above I described how people come to learn such specialized roles and norms. But there also are more generalized roles and norms that govern behavior in organizations. The most fundamental role that organizational participants can play is that of a fellow human being, and the most basic norm associated with that role is the norm of reciprocity. The norm of reciprocity is the obligation to return favors to others in rough equivalence to others' previously provided favors, even if others' prior favors were unsolicited or even unwelcome. The more intimately related two people are, the more loosely the "rough equivalence" constraint is enforced. Indeed, among close friends, even loose enforcement of the rough equivalence constraint can be considered counter-normative. For example, if a person restricted her generosity towards a close friend so that it was in precise proportion to the generosity that the friend had shown her in the past, it would be considered calculating and instrumental—a violation of the norms of friendship. A corollary of the generalized norm of reciprocity and its specific friendship extension is the felt obligation to compensate people, especially friends, for injuries inflicted on them.

The norm of reciprocity is engrained deeply in the human psyche, either programmed at birth or learned in early life. People conform to the norm in a seemingly automatic fashion when it is invoked by a gift. For example, Cialdini (2001) found that people were more likely to donate money to a solicitor if they were first given a flower by the supplicant, even though many of those who received the flower and donated money almost immediately thereafter disposed of the flower. This suggests that it was the invocation of the norm of reciprocity, rather than the inherent lure of a flower, that provoked the donation. The norm of reciprocity may be a fundamental building block of society (Becker 1956; Gouldner 1960; Baker and Levine 2010). And the performance of favors for others, either to reciprocate prior favors or to lay the foundation for future favors, might be one of the most important bases of effective social interaction within organizations (Hargadon and Sutton 1997). The norm of reciprocity, though, also can facilitate organizational wrongdoing.

Above, I described how David Levine recruited Robert Wilkis to join him in an insider trading scheme, apparently employing the social information processing theory of worker motivation to recruit his co-conspirator. Levine also recruited a number of other accomplices to join the scheme. In some of these instances he employed the norm of reciprocity to entrap his conscript. This was evident in his recruitment of Ilan Reich, an attorney at Wachtell, Lipton, a law firm that specialized in corporate mergers and acquisitions. In March 1980, in only their second face-to-face meeting, Levine asked Reich to join the conspiracy. Reich replied that he needed to think about the offer before giving an answer either way. Two months later, Reich phoned Levine to volunteer information on a still secret Elf Aquitaine bid to take over Kerr-McGee Corporation that was percolating at Wachtell, Lipton. Soon Reich became one of Levine's best sources of inside information.

Reich might have embarked on the insider trading scheme partly because he estimated that the rewards associated with the scheme outweighed the risks. Reich, like Robert Wilkis, joined the conspiracy at a time when he felt dissatisfied with his work situation. (He eventually dropped out of the conspiracy when it became clear that he would make partner at the law firm, a development that brought him job security, additional monetary rewards, and the acceptance of his co-workers, which he valued above all else.) But this likely is not the only reason why Reich joined Levine in the conspiracy. When pitching the scheme to Reich, Levine offered to set up a bank account that Reich could use to trade on inside information that he obtained from Levine. And Reich might have viewed this offer as a gift that he was obligated to reciprocate by providing inside information.

But although Reich provided Levine with information, he refused to trade in the account Levine opened for him. So Levine began trading in the account for Reich (based on information that Reich and others provided him) and periodically reported back to him news of the earnings that he, Levine, accrued on Reich's behalf. Reich might have considered Levine's trading on his behalf an additional gift that he was obligated to reciprocate by providing more inside information, even though Reich never withdrew money from the account. As noted above, a corollary of the generalized norm of reciprocity is the felt obligation to compensate people for injuries inflicted on them. Reich's first tip to Levine, the above-mentioned forecast of an Elf Aquitaine bid for Kerr McGee, proved erroneous, and Levine lost money trading on it. James Stewart spoke with Reich about the bad Elf Aquitaine tip. In Stewart's words, Reich "felt he had to make it up to Levine." And his eagerness "to rehabilitate himself with Levine" led him to provide a second tip that did pan out (1991: 72–3). The words "had to" suggest the sense of obligation that is associated with norms. And the word "rehabilitate" suggests the restoration of equilibrium that is associated with the norm of reciprocity.

It is important to distinguish the norm of reciprocity from tit-for-tat arrangements, which have a mindful and rational cost-benefit character (Axelrod 1984). The norm of reciprocity obligates people to treat others in ways commensurate with the ways that others have treated them in the past, *regardless of whether* people expect to obtain favorable treatment in the future as a result. Tit-for-tat relationships are maintained *because* people expect favorable treatment in return in the future. In practice it can be hard to distinguish between favor-giving that is an expression of the norm of reciprocity and exchanges that are part and parcel of a tit-for-tat relationship. The evidence related to Reich's compliance with Levine's requests for insider information, though, appears to be more consistent with a norm of reciprocity interpretation than a tit-for-tat construal.

First, Reich never profited from his participation in the arrangement, as he never cashed out Levine's trades on his behalf. Second, Reich extricated himself from the scheme after he was made partner at his law firm in a way that suggests that his participation in the scheme was at least partly driven by a feeling of obligation. Reich did not inform Levine directly of his desire to stop providing him with inside information, as he might if his relationship with Levine was ruled by tit-for-tat logic. Instead, he began avoiding Levine. Initially, he stopped calling Levine. Then, when Levine called him, he pretended to be out of the office and neglected to return Levine's calls. Later, he actively cultivated the impression that he had nothing of value to offer Levine. Then he began intentionally providing Levine with incorrect or misleading information. Finally, in phone conversations, he began hinting to Levine that he wanted "out." When Levine tried to persuade Reich to continue in the conspiracy by emphasizing the risk-free nature of the scheme, Reich drew attention to the disutility of the information he had recently provided replying, "Yeah, lately it's been reward-free too." Explaining his behavior after the fact, Reich confessed to Stewart that he was afraid to tell Levine directly that he wanted to cease providing information because he did not want to face Levine's "emotional blackmail."

Group dynamics

In the previous chapter I discussed specialized roles and norms that dictate how people in particular occupations and professions should think and act. In the previous section of this chapter I discussed the generalized norm of reciprocity that prescribes how all human beings should treat one another. The first major revolution in management theory grew out of the discovery of yet another level of roles and norms that guide behavior in organizations, a level situated between the specialized and generalized extremes referred to above. The new theory, referred to as group dynamics, holds that employees maintain memberships in informal groups and that these informal groups' roles and norms shape employee behavior (Barnard 1938; Roethlisberger and Dickson 1947).

Proponents of group dynamics theory characterize informal groups as "emergent phenomena," by which they mean two things. First, informal groups form and sometimes evolve rudimentary structures on their own, without managerial direction. Organizational participants form groups to meet the basic human need for affiliation, to obtain rewards that the organization cannot otherwise provide (such as the satisfaction people obtain from associating with others whom they find attractive and with whom they share similar goals and outlook), and to learn and accomplish tasks that the organization's formal structure cannot program. Further, group members sometimes differentiate themselves into leaders and followers.

Second, informal groups tend to develop norms that dictate how members should think and act. All group members exemplify and enforce these norms. But leaders, when they emerge, are particularly likely to exemplify and enforce group norms. The principal reward for conformity to group norms is acceptance, and the principal punishment is exclusion. The earliest group dynamics research focused on group norms that specify how fast and well workers should perform their jobs (Roethlisberger and Dickson 1947). It also focused on the way in which group membership enhanced job satisfaction (Roy 1959). Thus the earliest theory on informal groups viewed membership in small groups as providing organizational participants with guidance about how to do their jobs and motivation to work hard and well. But membership in small groups also can facilitate wrongdoing.

The conspiracy to fix the 1919 Baseball World Series illustrates how group dynamics can facilitate organizational wrongdoing. Eight members of the Chicago White Sox baseball team were indicted for conspiring to lose several games in the sport's championship series intentionally, although available evidence suggests that only seven of the eight were actually involved in the scheme. The players conspired to "throw" the games in return for pay-offs provided by two separate groups of gamblers who planned to use their advance knowledge of the games' outcomes to place sure bets on the White Sox opponent, the Cincinnati Reds. Although the eight players, today known as the Black Sox, were not convicted of conspiracy in a court of law, they were banned from the sport for life by the newly appointed baseball commissioner, Judge Kenesaw Landis.

The White Sox appeared to consist of two informal groups, the first of which was the players, who set themselves apart from management and the coaches, and the second of which was a smaller clique of seven players, who set themselves apart from the balance of the team. And the seven-player clique appeared to have two leaders, Arnold "Chic" Gandil and Charles "Swede" Risberg. The conspiracy to fix the series was perpetrated by the seven clique members, and the fix was initiated and guided through several unexpected twists and turns by the clique's leaders, Gandil and Risberg.

Two informal group norms appear to have played an important part in facilitating the conspiracy. The first, most obviously, was the clique norm to follow the clique leaders' initiative and the clique members' growing involvement in the fix. There is some evidence that the fear of disapproval and exclusion might have caused some clique members to remain in the conspiracy, even when they sought to extricate themselves from it. The White Sox left fielder "Shoeless" Joe Jackson was insecure in his membership in the seven-player clique because he was relatively uneducated compared to his peers (he could neither read nor write). Although Jackson apparently joined the conspiracy willingly, he began to change his mind shortly before the first game of the series. But he did not convey his desire to drop out of the fix directly to his teammates as he might have done if his initial decision was based on a straightforward cost-benefit calculation or normative assessment. Instead, as the other players warmed up for the game, Jackson retreated to the team's dugout and informed the coach that he did not feel well and added, "I don't wanna play." When the startled coach inquired further, Jackson continued, "I said I don't wanna play. You can tell the boss, too!" (Asinof 1987: 59). It seems likely that Shoeless Joe was reluctant to confront his teammates with his decision to defect from the scheme because he feared their disapproval. So he chose a more indirect way to drop out of the fix, to feign illness (a tactic that ultimately failed).

There is very little hard evidence pertaining to the way in which White Sox clique members were recruited into the conspiracy.[2] But the drive for acceptance in sports teams and the role that it can play in pushing athletes towards wrongdoing is evident in Paul Krimmage's and Frankie Andreu's descriptions of their introduction to the use of banned performance-enhancing substances in professional cycling. Paul Krimmage said that his desire to be "one of the boys" factored into his decision to use amphetamines in the post-Tour de France French Classic criteriums. Frankie Andreu, who rode for the United States Postal Service when Lance Armstrong captained the team, said similarly that "to be accepted, you had to use doping products... There was very high pressure to be one of the cool kids" (Macur 2006).

The second norm that played an important part in facilitating the Black Sox conspiracy was the player norm to stick up for one's teammates. It might come as no surprise that the seven White Sox teammates who played an active role in the conspiracy did not "roll over" on their co-conspirators. But even the eighth wrongly indicted player, third baseman George "Buck" Weaver, refused to finger his fellow teammates. On his way to testify before the grand jury

---

[2] John Sayles' movie *Eight Men Out*, based on the Asinof book of the same title, includes several scenes that depict the recruitment of key players, including Shoeless Joe Jackson, into the conspiracy. While these scenes, which Sayles considered crucial to the movie (Sayles and Smith 1998), provide ample opportunity to illustrate the role that the desire for acceptance played in bringing clique members into the conspiracy, I do not discuss them here because I have been unable to substantiate their authenticity.

investigating the fix, he was asked by a reporter whether he would provide a particular piece of evidence that might incriminate a teammate. He responded, "I'm a long way from being a squealer." When he pleaded with Judge Landis for reinstatement after the eight players were banished from the game, he said that he had been invited to join the conspiracy by Chic Gandil, but declined to participate. Landis was unmoved, contending that if Weaver knew of the conspiracy, he should have done something to stop it. But Weaver said he could not have turned the conspirators in because they were his friends. And perhaps having second thoughts about his earlier revelation, he added that, besides, he never knew if they actually went through with it (Asinof 1987: 279–80). Indeed, even the other White Sox players whose hopes for a World Series title had been dashed by the conspirators' scheme refused to turn on them, remaining silent—at least as far as the press, the courts, and the baseball commissioner were concerned. Both the team's coach, William "Kid" Gleason, and its catcher, Raymond William "Cracker" Schalk, had physical confrontations with members of the conspiracy, and Gleason brought his suspicions to the attention of the team's manager, Charles Comiskey—all in the hopes that they might derail the conspiracy. But neither Gleason nor Schalk came forward to denounce the conspirators publicly before or after the conspiracy was unearthed.

Social comparison and liking-based compliance

I have discussed three types of roles and norms that shape attitudes and behavior in organizations, specialized ones that regulate how people in particular occupations and professions should think and act, generalized ones that prescribe how all people treat one another, and intermediate ones that dictate how members of informal groups should relate to one another. But there are situational social influence processes that do not operate through roles and norms. I end the chapter by discussing three such processes, the first two of which are referred to as social comparison and liking-based compliance.

Social comparison, also called social proof, refers to the use of others' behavior, attitudes, and emotions as a guide for our own behaviors, attitudes, and emotions. Liking-based compliance refers to the tendency to comply with the requests of others whom we like. Social comparison and liking-based compliance, while analytically distinct, sometimes are difficult to disentangle in practice because they can operate in tandem. First, social comparison processes can generate liking. We tend to like others who we think like us. Second, social comparison and liking have a common determinant—similarity. We tend to model and like others who are similar to us (Cialdini 2001). Social comparison and liking-based compliance, rooted in perceived similarity, can provide satisfactory guides on how to think, feel, and act when confronted with complex or unfamiliar organizational contingencies. Further, because they short-circuit decision making, social comparison and liking-based compliance economize on information search and analysis costs. These processes, though, also can facilitate wrongdoing.

Above I described how David Levine used both social information processing and the norm of reciprocity to recruit Robert Wilkis to join his group of inside traders in 1979. But Levine forged his relationship with Wilkis two years before he pitched the idea of joining his insider trading conspiracy, back when they both worked at Citibank (Stewart 1991). Levine laid the foundation for his relationship with Wilkis by establishing their similarity. In most respects, the two investment bankers could not have been more different from one another, exemplified by the fact that Levine was a graduate of City University of New York, while Wilkis was a graduate of Harvard College and the Stanford Graduate School of Business. But even the most dissimilar people have commonalities. Whenever Levine and Wilkis spent time together, Levine played up their commonalities, in particular, their shared Jewish heritage and their mutual dissatisfaction with their jobs and marriages.

To the extent that Wilkis saw himself as similar to Levine, one would expect Wilkis to use him as a model and see him as likable. And to the extent that Wilkis used Levine as a model and saw him as likable, one would expect Wilkis to adopt Levine's behavior, thoughts, and emotions, and to comply with his requests. Levine might have exploited the social comparison process to invoke liking-based compliance. Levine treated Wilkis as if he liked him, offering frequent effusive praise for his deal-making acumen. And he treated Wilkis as if he were a friend, sharing his most personal hopes and fears (Stewart 1991: 61). As time went on, Levine enlisted Wilkis in two small, but increasingly significant transgressions: first encouraging Wilkis to skip out of work early with him and then persuading Wilkis to obtain a counterfeit Citibank executive dining-room pass for him. Eventually, after Levine moved to Smith Barney and Wilkis moved to Lazard Freres, Levine pitched the inside trading scheme to Wilkis. And within a day, Wilkis came on board.[3]

---

[3] Liking-based compliance, as well as the norm of reciprocity, provided the foundation for a more recent insider trading conspiracy. Raj Rajaratnam, founder of the Galleon Group hedge fund and one of the world's wealthiest men, was convicted in 2011 for assembling a network of contacts at large US corporations that provided him with proprietary information that he used to make lucrative investments. Many of these contacts, a good number of whom have now pleaded guilty for their part in the conspiracy, were long standing friends of Rajaratnam and had received favors from him over the years. One contact, a former Intel executive named Raj Goel, had been friends with Rajaratnam since they met at the University of Pennsylvania's Wharton School of Business 25 years earlier. According to one report, "While they lived on different coasts, the men kept in touch regularly and their families vacationed together." During this time, "Mr. Rajaratnam twice gave Mr. Goel money for personal financial reasons." When he pled guilty for his role in the conspiracy,

Commitment

I complete my presentation of the situational social influence account of organizational wrongdoing with an extended discussion of commitment. Social psychologists characterize commitment as the process by which people act in a mindless or boundedly rational manner, retrospectively account for their acts, experience cognitive dissonance, alter their cognitions to reduce dissonance, and as a result, become more wedded to their course of action. Organization theorists have devoted considerable attention to commitment because it can support behavior that is both necessary for effective organizational functioning and cannot be sustained by other means. Among other things, commitment can help organizations extract supreme effort from their employees even when they are not in a position to provide their employees with valued rewards, such as during economic downturns (Salancik 1977). Organization theorists also are interested in commitment, though, because it can sustain failing courses of action, behavior detrimental to those who perpetrate it and by extension the organization more generally (Staw 1976). Wrongdoing is among the most important types of failing courses of action to which commitment can give rise.

The generic process

Social psychologists think that commitment to a failing course of action tends to begin with small, incremental steps, that is, with acts that differ little in normative character and cost-benefit consequence from previously chosen viable courses of actions. Because such small steps do not differ much from previously chosen viable courses of action, people do not feel compelled to engage in mindful and thoroughly rational deliberation before embarking on them. With each successive small step, though, people move farther from their original viable behavioral state and closer to, and eventually cross over into, a failing course of action. Importantly, people do not make a single discrete decision to pursue the failing course of action. Rather, they take a series of steps over a period of time. Each of these steps is taken in a substantially mindless and boundedly rational fashion. The evolution of an illegal stock-parking arrangement between Ivan Boesky and John Mulheren in the 1980s illustrates well how a succession of small steps, taken over time in a somewhat mindlessly and boundedly rationally fashion, can evolve into wrongdoing.

Mr. Goel said, "I gave Rajaratnam the information because of my friendship for him" (Kouwe 2010).

162

IVAN BOESKY, JOHN MULHEREN, AND STOCK PARKING IN THE 1980S

John Mulheren and Ivan Boesky were independent arbitragers. Arbitragers buy and sell large blocks of stock on the basis of quasi-public information in the hopes of making large aggregate profits, often on only small per-share price increases. Beginning in July 1985, Boesky asked Mulheren to purchase several blocks of stock from him. Boesky had embarked on an ambitious stock-buying spree and become in danger of falling short of Securities and Exchange Commission (SEC) margin requirements, which stipulate how much cash arbitragers must have on hand to cover stock purchased on credit. To avoid falling short of margin requirements, Boesky asked Mulheren to purchase, hold, and then sell back to him substantial blocks of his stakes in several firms, including Unocal Corporation, Storer Communications, Boise Cascade, and Warner Communications. A crucial condition of Boesky's request was that Mulheren resell the stock to him at a future date at the same price for which Mulheren purchased it. The SEC considers such transactions, known as "stock-parking" agreements, illegal because they are an artificial way to circumvent SEC margin requirements. Under such arrangements, for all intents and purposes, the stock never leaves the hands of the seller. Despite the SEC interpretation of such transactions, though, Mulheren essentially complied with Boesky's request.

It is possible that Mulherin made a single discrete mindful and rational decision to park stock for Boesky. Mulheren might have complied with Boesky's request as the result of a cost-benefit calculation in order to maintain an on-going beneficial tit-for-tat relationship. It is well-known that arbitragers frequently provide information and/or services to one another, with the expectation that other information and/or services will be returned in kind. Stewart writes that Mulheren believed that "Wall Street was one big network of interlocking favors" (Stewart 1991: 177). When one of Mulheren's subordinates questioned him about his newly purchased stake in Unocal, the value of which was sagging, Mulheren reportedly replied, "It's a favor for Ivan, don't worry about it" (Stewart 1991: 177). Mulheren also might have complied with Boesky's request as the result of a normative assessment, in accordance with his beliefs about the legitimacy of SEC margin requirements. According to Stewart, most arbitragers viewed SEC margin requirements "with thinly veiled contempt" (Stewart 1991: 177) because they considered the requirements excessively restrictive.

A more detailed reading of the evidence, though, suggests that Mulheren entered the illegal-parking arrangement incrementally and in an incompletely mindful and rational way. Boesky first contacted Mulheren regarding a block of stock he owned in Unocal Corporation. He asked Mulheren to purchase the stock, explaining simply that he was "raising cash" (Stewart 1991: 177). He made this request without indicating that he wanted Mulheren to resell the stock to him at a later date. Mulheren immediately agreed to this request. However, when Michael Davidoff, Boesky's assistant, contacted Mulheren to consummate the sale, Davidoff indicated that Boesky might want to repurchase the stock from Mulheren at a later date and implied that when he did, he would want to repurchase the stock at the same price for which Mulheren purchased it. As Davidoff put it, "I'm going to sell it to you and I might want to buy it back. And you'll be held harmless. You won't lose any money" (Stewart 1991: 177). According to Stewart, Mulheren immediately and definitively rejected this condition, saying, "You can stop right there. I don't do those trades. If I'm not at risk of the market, I will not do the trade." Boesky, perhaps because he was desperate to raise cash, agreed to Mulheren's alternative conditions. With this alternative understanding, the trade went through.

Shortly thereafter, Davidoff called Mulheren again to ask that he purchase Boesky's holdings in Warner Communications and a few other companies and indicated that Boesky would want to repurchase the stock at a later time and would "take the risk." Once more, Mulheren resisted the offer as stipulated, reportedly saying, "I told you before, I don't do those kinds of transactions. I'm a big boy and I take the risk *because it's not legal if you do it that way*" (emphasis added). Davidoff again relented and the trade went through on Mulheren's terms. In both instances, Mulheren clearly rejected the request to engage in an illegal market transaction and then concluded the transaction on completely legal terms.

The stock transactions only took on the character of an illegal "parking" arrangement many months later, when Davidoff called to request that Mulheren resell the block of Warner Communications stock to Boesky. The Warner stock had appreciated substantially in value, and Mulheren resold it to Boesky for a $1.7 million profit. Davidoff made it clear that he thought Mulheren owed Boesky something in return. Davidoff reportedly asked plaintively, "You're not going to do anything for us on this?" Mulheren reportedly responded, "I didn't say that, I'm just telling you whose positions they are and I decide what happens here." Later, after Mulheren resold Boesky some of the other blocks of stock for a considerable profit, Boesky himself pressed the issue with Mulheren, reportedly asking him "Don't you think you owe us something?" Mulheren again responded in a noncommittal fashion, saying, "I don't know." Boesky pressed him harder, "Well, would you write me a check." Mulheren reportedly shot back, "Under no circumstances. And I won't give you any money. I won't give you cash."

It was at this juncture that Mulheren took a fateful step. In response to further exhortations from Boesky, he agreed to compensate Boesky for the profit he earned as the result of holding his stock. Mulheren said, "I'll do other things for you. I'll give you ideas. I'll do more brokerage for you. I'll do all kinds of soft things, normal return-of-favor things." Over the ensuing months, when Mulheren received brokerage bills from Boesky, he paid him in excess of the amount that the brokerage services normally would justify. Eventually, the excess payments stopped, presumably when both parties judged that the compensation was adequate.

This sequence of events is consistent with the basic tenets of commitment theory outlined above. First, Mulheren did not make a single discrete decision to park stock for Boesky. Instead, he took a series of small steps that approached, and eventually crossed, the line between right and wrong. He first agreed to purchase the Unocal stock with no strings attached; he then purchased the stock after being warned that some strings might later be attached to the purchase; he then agreed to purchase the Warner stock after again being warned that some strings might later be attached to the purchase; and he then eventually agreed to return value to Boesky (again, in an incremental manner).

Second, each small step Mulheren took was made in a boundedly rational way. Each decision had consequences that were difficult for Mulheren to foresee and that shaped his subsequent decisions. Mulheren could not be sure that the Unocal, Warner, or other stock he purchased from Boesky would appreciate in value between the time he purchased it and the time he sold it back to Boesky. If the Warner and other blocks of stock had not appreciated in value in this period of time, Boesky in all likelihood would not have pressed Mulheren so vigorously to resell the stock to him at the original purchase price.

Third, it would appear that Mulheren had cultural understandings at his disposal that he could draw on to formulate a post-hoc rationalization to support his incremental involvement in the parking arrangement with Boesky. As noted above, Wall Street arbitragers believed that SEC margin requirements were excessive. Mulheren's likely disdain for SEC margin requirements clearly did not cause him to jump at the chance to construct a parking arrangement with Boesky. Mulheren repeatedly resisted Boesky's overtures to establish a parking relationship. But Mulheren's likely contempt for SEC margin requirements might have formed the basis of post-hoc cognitions that justified his increasingly questionable association with Boesky.

But this raises another question. Why did Mulheren take the series of small steps towards establishing a parking arrangement with Boesky? It might be true that small steps, by definition, do not provoke actors to engage in rational cost-benefit analyses or normative assessments. However, this does not explain why Mulheren took the steps in the absence of a thorough rational cost-benefit analysis or normative assessment. Another social influence process, the norm of reciprocity, might have led Mulheren to take these small steps.

As noted above, the generalized norm of reciprocity obligates people to treat others in ways commensurate with the ways others have treated them in the past. Mulherin and Boesky had been doing favors for one another in the normal course of business for more than ten years before the parking arrangement was proposed by Boesky. Mulheren provided Boesky with information and expertise (Stewart 1991: 85–6). Boesky provided Mulheren with brokerage business. The more specific norm of reciprocity that regulates behavior among friends dictates that people provide favors to their friends in ways that exceed the generosity that their friends have shown them in the past. Mulherin and Boesky had socialized frequently with one another for many years. Boesky had attended Mulheren's wedding. Mulheren had attended Boesky's daughters' bat mitzvahs. Indeed, Mulheren was co-trustee of Boesky's daughters' trust funds. Stewart remarks that Mulheren looked up to Boesky and was eager to be liked by him.

By the early 1980s, Boesky and Mulheren spoke daily. Mulheren might have purchased Boesky's shares in Unocal, Warner, and the other companies in reciprocation of past favors performed by Boesky on his behalf. There is reason to believe that Mulheren had done more favors for Boesky in the past than Boesky had performed for him. Mulheren had come to Boesky's rescue on several previous occasions, most notably when Boesky was at risk of losing his considerable fortune on the purchase of a very large block of Gulf Oil stock. And Mulheren had stepped in to organize an honorary dinner on behalf of Boesky when no one else would. But because Mulheren considered Boesky a friend, he might not have asked himself whether he owed Boesky the additional favors that his purchase of Boesky's Unocal and Warner stock constituted.

As pointed out above, the norm of reciprocity, both the general norm and the specific norm regulating friendships, is analytically different from a tit-for-tat relationship, which has a rational cost-benefit character. The norm of reciprocity, general and specific, obligates people to treat others in ways commensurate with the ways that others have treated them in the past, *regardless of whether* people expect to obtain favorable treatment in the future as a result. Tit-for-tat relationships are maintained *because* people expect favorable treatment in the future in return. Also as noted above, it can be hard to distinguish between favor giving that is an expression of the norm of reciprocity and favor giving that is part and parcel of a tit-for-tat relationship. In this case, though, the evidence appears to be more consistent with a norm of reciprocity than a tit-for-tat interpretation of Mulheren's behavior. Mulheren resisted Boesky's advances to the very end and even then complied with his supplications only reluctantly. In short, the evidence suggests that Mulheren felt obligated to return past favors, rather than felt desirous of maintaining an ongoing strategic agreement.

The factors that regulate commitment

Social psychologists think that people differ in their propensity to experience cognitive dissonance after engaging in a behavior that they retrospectively conclude lacks cost-benefit or normative merit. Persons whose identities are bound up with the notion that they are rigorous cost-benefit calculators and/ or good normative assessors are most likely to experience dissonance.

Social psychologists also think that situations differ in the extent to which they cause people who experience cognitive dissonance (after engaging in a behavior that they retrospectively conclude lacks cost-benefit or normative merit) to develop post-hoc rationalizations that cast their dissonance-producing behavior in a positive light and thus to continue their behavior. The more *responsible* people feel for their actions, the more *irreversible* they perceive their actions to be (the more time and effort they invest in the course of action), and the more *visible* their actions are to others, the more likely it is that people will embrace favorable post-hoc rationalizations of their behavior and continue their failing course of action (Staw 1976, Cialdini 2001).

Insofar as wrongful courses of action are one type of failing course of action, responsibility, visibility, and irreversibility should regulate the likelihood that wrongdoers will develop post-hoc rationalizations that cast their wrongful behavior in a positive light and thus the likelihood that they will continue their wrongful behavior. Conversely, the more absent these three conditions, the less likely wrongdoers will develop post-hoc rationalizations for their wrongdoing and the more likely they will defect. Thus, when people engage in wrongdoing via a commitment process, they not only do so in a mindless and/or boundedly rational way and slip into it over time, but they do so in a social context. Two illustrations follow of the roles that volition, visibility, and irreversibility play in regulating commitment to a wrongful course of action. The first is short and provides a succinct, barebones illustration of the operation of volition, visibility, and irreversibility. The second illustration is long and provides a more in-depth picture of the operation of volition, visibility, and irreversibility, as well as the other facets of escalating commitment to a failing course of action.

THE DALKON SHIELD

American Home Products (AHP) engaged in a number of unethical and legally questionable behaviors in the marketing of their intrauterine birth control device (IUD) known as the Dalkon Shield. They disseminated misleading information about the appliance's effectiveness, and they withheld accurate information about the device's dangers. Top managers at AHP purchased the Dalkon Shield from its inventors without full knowledge of its limitations, partly because they lacked the expertise to evaluate the IUD, partly because they had little time to make their decision (because another firm was already negotiating with the inventors to buy the device), and partly because the inventors withheld information from them (about the device's ineffectiveness and dangers). After AHP executives launched the Shield, they became increasingly committed to the product. They had purchased the IUD of their own volition (in competition with another drug company), they had initiated a highly visible marketing campaign (the product was purchased more for its symbolic than its profit-generating value), and they made a substantial investment in the IUD that could not be recouped (more than $1 million). Thus, as evidence of the device's ineffectiveness and dangers mounted, AHP top managers defended the product with increasing conviction, eventually incurring large legal costs and damage to the company's reputation (Perry and Dawson 1985).

B.F. GOODRICH A7D BRAKE CASE[4]

I used the B.F. Goodrich A7D jet brake case in Chapter 5 to illustrate the denial of responsibility technique of neutralization. I used it again in Chapter 6 to illustrate how people can experience cognitive dissonance, without successfully avoiding or reducing it. Here I use the Goodrich case to illustrate how commitment processes can facilitate wrongdoing. In the process I will connect to my earlier discussions of the case. The saga began when Goodrich's top management team submitted a bid for the brake to the A7D's general contractor, LTV Corporation (Vandivier 1972). The bid was based on a preliminary design that offered light weight and high performance, prepared by the firm's most senior and well-respected engineer, John Warren. Goodrich won the contract and Warren finalized the brake's design.

After Warren prepared the final design, he passed it off to his subordinate, Searle Lawson, with instructions to build and test a prototype. But when Lawson built the prototype and began testing, he found that it did not perform up to design specifications. The course of action pursued by Goodrich's top management and senior engineer was clearly boundedly rational. Further, the brake's unanticipated poor performance appeared to generate dissonance for Warren and his superiors. When Lawson passed on word of the brake's poor performance to his superior, Warren defended the brake's design and ordered him to test the prototype again with new lining materials.

Lawson tested the prototype with a variety of new linings but experienced the same disappointing results and began to suspect that the brake's design was flawed. So he reported his experience and assessment to Warren's superior, Robert Sink. But Sink, like Warren before him, assured Lawson that the

---

[4] John Darley (1996) also has analyzed this case in considerable depth and some of his analytic points overlap with mine.

brake's design was sound and ordered him to test the prototype again with additional new linings. Lawson tested the prototype with more new lining materials but experienced further disappointing results and became convinced that the brake's design was flawed. Lawson again reported to his superiors that the brake could not meet the promised performance standards. In response, they ordered Lawson to test the brake one more time and make sure that it passed so that a "qualification report" (which confirmed that the brake met contract specifications) could be written.

The decision to order the preparation of a fraudulent qualification report clearly represented increased dedication to producing the brake as designed. This decision can be analyzed in two ways. It is possible that Lawson's superiors became committed to a new course of action, the writing of what they knew was a misleading qualification report and the delivery of what they knew was a defective brake. The post-hoc "denial of responsibility" rationalizations that some of Lawson's superiors applied to their behavior, which indicate that the superiors understood that they were doing something that could be considered wrong, are consistent with this analysis. For example, Warren reasoned, "Well—technically I don't think what we're doing can be called fraud. I'll admit it's not right, but it's just one of those things. We're just kind of caught in the middle." And as noted in Chapter 5, Russell Line, who oversaw the unit that generated the fraudulent report, accounted for his behavior by saying, "I just do what I'm told...It's none of my business...I learned a long time ago not to worry about things over which I have no control. I have no control over this."

Alternatively, it is possible that Lawson's superiors just intensified their commitment to an ongoing behavior, believing (despite the mounting evidence to the contrary) that the brake's design was in fact technically adequate, and that writing an irregular qualification report was simply a necessary expedient for getting the fundamentally sound brake to LTV. If this was the case, the B.F. Goodrich managers and engineers were intensifying their commitment to delivering what they believed was a good brake. The denials of wrongdoing that some of the principals in the case voiced are consistent with this analysis. For example, Warren's immediate superior, Robert Sink, reasoned, "We're just exercising engineering license." And he continued, "It's not a matter of lying. We've just interpreted the information the way we felt it should be." Similarly, the plant's manager, Bud Sunderman, contended, "There's nothing wrong with anything we've done here."

It is tempting to rule out this alternative analysis as logically implausible. It is hard to imagine that a large group of high-level executives and well-trained engineers at an established firm could believe that the brake's design was sound, given the volume of evidence to the contrary. But there is one additional piece of information that supports this alternative account. After the brake was delivered to the general contractor, top management anxiously monitored the test flights to see if the brake would in fact perform poorly in operation. This suggests that top management, despite ample evidence to the contrary, held out hope that the brake actually would perform adequately, even to the very end. Perhaps they could hold out such hope because they were not directly involved in the laboratory testing of the brake, and thus could consider reports of the failed tests inconclusive.

After Lawson conducted the fraudulent brake test ordered by his superiors, the data were forwarded to Ralph Gretzinger and his subordinate, Kermit Vandivier, who were assigned the task of preparing the final qualification report. Gretzinger and Vandivier had gotten wind of the unusual circumstances surrounding the final brake test and were resolved to not participate in the preparation of a fraudulent report. But Gretzinger and Vandivier, when pressured by their superiors, reluctantly agreed to prepare fraudulent tables and diagrams to be used in the report. After they completed those tables and diagrams, under increased pressure from their superiors, they reluctantly agreed to write the fraudulent report. Shortly after the brake (almost catastrophically) failed its first flight test, though, first Vandivier and then Gretzinger contacted the FBI to blow the whistle on the fraud.

It would appear that Gretzinger and Vandivier were subject to commitment pressures similar to those that influenced their superiors, insofar as they took small steps and became increasingly involved in the fraud over time. Indeed, it is even possible that their superiors used commitment theory to entrap them in the scheme, insofar as they first asked Vandivier and Gretzinger to produce just the tables and figures for the report, and then later ordered them to write the entire report. But Vandivier's and Gretzinger's commitment to the fraud clearly was less intense than their superiors' commitment. And the relative amount of volition, visibility, and irreversibility that these two groups of actors experienced might explain their differential commitment to the scheme.

As described above, the brake's designer, John Warren, and his superiors, Sink, Sunderman, and Line, developed post-hoc "denial of responsibility" and what might be called "denial of wrongdoing" rationalizations of their behavior. This fact accords with these executives' high level of responsibility, visibility, and irreversibility in connection with the brake. Warren designed the brake. He was well known among B.F. Goodrich employees for his engineering expertise. Further, he was said to have a large ego that might make it difficult for him to admit that he had formulated a flawed design. Sink assigned the job of designing the brake to Warren. He personally had assured LTV that the brake prototype was working well and that its development was on schedule. And he had ordered sub-assemblies for the brake that had begun to arrive at the plant. Line and Sunderman occupied positions high in Goodrich's chain of command. Top managers tend to be considered responsible for their firm's actions. And they tend to be well known to members of their organization and to representatives of other organizations situated in their firm's environment. Finally, as time went by and the deadline for delivering the brake to LTV drew near, all of these executives' association with the brake must have felt increasingly difficult to reverse. If they were to admit that the brake was flawed, there would be no way to provide an adequate brake within the contract-stipulated time frame. And failure to deliver the brake on time would have serious consequences for B.F. Goodrich's defense contractor business. It had failed famously in a previous contract. If it failed again, it was likely that its defense contracting days would be over.

However, as noted in Chapter 6, Gretzinger and Vandivier, the test laboratory employees who actually prepared the fraudulent qualification report, never developed rationalizations in support of their involvement in the affair. Gretzinger experimented with the "denial of responsibility" rationalization when contemplating the implications of their preparation of exhibits for the fraudulent report, saying, "We're just drawing some curves and what happens to them after they leave here, well, we're not responsible." But according to Vandivier, neither Gretzinger nor he embraced this post-hoc account. In Vandivier's words, "He didn't believe what he was saying and he knew I didn't believe it either. It was an embarrassing and shameful moment for both of us."

Later, when it came to actually writing the fraudulent report, Vandivier remarked, "I made no attempt to *rationalize* what I had been asked to do (emphasis added)." This fact accords with these employees' level of responsibility, visibility, and irreversibility in connection with the brake. Gretzinger and Vandivier had no hand in designing the brake or appointing or supervising the person who designed it. Indeed, they had no role in testing the brake. Gretzinger and Vandivier did write the fraudulent report. Importantly, though, they did not volunteer to prepare the report. They merely obeyed orders to do so (I will discuss obedience to authority in the next chapter). Gretzinger and Vandivier also were low in the organizational hierarchy, presumably known to few other B.F. Goodrich employees and unknown to high-level LTV and government personnel. It is important to emphasize that Gretzinger's and Vandivier's failure to employ techniques of neutralization likely was not due to their failure to experience cognitive dissonance in connection with their participation in the fraud. At one point, Gretzinger remarked, "It's all I can do to look at myself in the mirror when I shave. I make myself sick."

Assessing the situational social influence explanation

The situational social influence explanation of wrongdoing departs substantially from the dominant approach to explaining wrongdoing in organizations. First and most obviously, it explicitly takes into account social interaction between wrongdoers and others in their immediate environment. Second, many of the situational social influence mechanisms considered in this chapter give rise to mindless behavior. Most obviously, when organizational participants respond to the norm of reciprocity, they do so in an automatic fashion. Further, some of the situational social influence mechanisms give rise to boundedly rational behavior. For example, when organizational participants engage in social comparison, they sometimes deliberate about the relative appropriateness of alternative courses of action, one of which is modeled by the object of social comparison. But this deliberation is short-circuited when people quickly lock on the modeled behavior.

Third, some of the situational social influence mechanisms evolve over time. Most obviously, commitment develops through a series of small steps. Further, each step provokes dissonance and a search for rationalizations that takes some time (consider Vandivier and Gretzinger's search for rationalizations as they prepared the fraudulent qualification report). Finally, when situational social influence gives rise to behavior in a mindless way, organizational participants fail to develop positive inclinations to engage in the behavior in question. Instead, they act in an automatic fashion. And when norms are involved, they can give rise to behavior even in the presence of negative inclinations to engage in the behavior. This is evident in John Mulheren's grudging decision to park stock for Ivan Boesky. Mulheren resisted Boesky's requests to park stock for him on at least two occasions. He subsequently resisted Boesky's requests to make cash payments to him that would transform the legal market transactions into illegal parking arrangements. It took several months and substantial cajoling before Mulheren agreed to return value to Boesky in an amount that could transform the legal market transactions, retrospectively, into an exchange that SEC investigators concluded constituted an illegal parking arrangement.[5]

With this said, the situational social influence explanation retains one element of the dominant approach. When situational social influence operates in the presence of mindful, albeit boundedly rational, deliberation, people can be thought to develop a positive disposition to engage in the wrongful behavior. This is particularly evident in the case of escalating commitment to a failing course of action. People may embark on the failing course of action

---

[5] Mulheren's conviction for stock parking was overturned on appeal.

mindlessly. But after they experience cognitive dissonance, stemming from their post-hoc assessment that the behavior lacks cost-benefit and/or normative merit, they actively search for post-hoc rationalizations for their behavior. And when this search is successful, they become increasingly resolved to continue the behavior into the future. In the next chapter, I examine an explanation of organizational wrongdoing that departs significantly from this assumption; indeed, that allows that people can engage in wrongdoing even when they are disinclined to do so.

Conclusion

I have now presented five different explanations of organizational wrongdoing, for the most part treating each account as distinct from the others. But many who study the causes of organizational wrongdoing offer analyses that integrate elements from several of these explanations. Most integrate elements of the rational choice and cultural accounts. But two offer more comprehensive integrations. Brief, Bertram, and Dukerich (2001) and Ashforth and Anand (2003) tap ideas from each of the explanations considered so far, as well as ideas from explanations to be considered in the next chapter, to develop an explanation of how wrongdoing can permeate an organization, rendering it "corrupt." These two syntheses, which are similar enough to present as a single integration, provide a useful way both to summarize my analysis so far and to lay a foundation for my analyses to come.

Brief and his associates and Ashforth and Anand implicitly elaborate a four-stage model of how wrongdoing spreads throughout an organization. In the *initiation stage*, top managers engage in mindful and rational cost-benefit calculations and/or normative assessments and, on the basis of these deliberations, decide to authorize wrongdoing. In the *proliferation stage*, top managers explicitly or implicitly direct employees further down the hierarchy to implement the wrongdoing. The most important mechanism through which top managers direct subordinates to implement wrongdoing is formal authority, which I will discuss in the next chapter. Ashforth and Anand (2003) add that commitment processes cement subordinates' compliance to top managers' directives by providing them with a rationale for doing so.

In the *institutionalization stage*, wrongdoing is embedded in organizational structures and cultures. In the *socialization stage*, new organizational participants are exposed to the techniques and attitudes that support the wrongful course of behavior. Organizational structures establish incentives and thus set the parameters of cost-benefit analyses. Organizational cultures (and subcultures) consist of norms, values, and beliefs, and thus set the parameters of normative assessments. And socialization processes inculcate people into organizational cultures. However, behavior in organizations also is regulated by the division of labor and routines that guide task performance. These structural elements deflect employee attention away from cost-benefit analyses and normative assessments and thus delimit rationality.

The syntheses presented by Brief and his associates and by Ashforth and Anand are extremely important. They draw attention to the subject of organizational corruption and have stimulated other work on the factors that lead wrongdoing to proliferate and become entrenched in organizations (Ashforth, Gioia, Robinson, and Trevino 2008; Lange 2008; Misangyi, Weaver, and Elms 2008; Pinto, Leana, and Pil 2008; Pfarrer, Decelles, Smith, and Taylor 2008). Further, they suggest how analyses of organizational corruption can go beyond the rational choice and culture accounts to consider the roles that administrative structure and situational social influence play in the diffusion and entrenchment of wrongdoing. In addition, they explicitly theorize the effects of rational choice, culture, administrative structure, and situational social influence as unfolding over time. In these regards, the integrations presented by Brief and his associates and by Ashforth and Anand were path-breaking. Nevertheless, their syntheses embrace three assumptions that can be disputed (Palmer 2008).

First, Brief et al. and Ashforth and Anand explicitly assume that organizational wrongdoing spreads from top to bottom in organizations, beginning with the organization's leaders and trickling down to its rank and file. But as many of the illustrations presented in this book indicate, wrongdoing often begins at lower levels of the organization. Further, when wrongdoing emerges at lower levels of the organization, it can both trickle down and percolate up the hierarchy. The A7D brake fraud began in B.F. Goodrich's engineering and test divisions. But it trickled down to the firm's technical writing department and percolated up to the plant's senior managers.

Second, Brief et al. and Ashforth and Anand also explicitly assume that organizational leaders initiate wrongdoing on the basis of mindful, rational cost-benefit calculations or normative assessments. But as the most recent work on ethical decision making suggests, there are many barriers to mindful and rational deliberation. People often respond to ethical dilemmas in an instinctive and emotional manner. Further, when they do deliberate about ethical issues, they do so in a boundedly rational way, subject to a wide variety of framing effects and cognitive biases.

Third, Brief et al. and Ashforth and Anand implicitly assume that the process by which wrongdoing proliferates through the organization is inexorable. Their model explains how once initiated at the top, wrongdoing proliferates throughout the organization, becoming institutionalized in administrative structures and cultural content. And it explains how new employees are trained to operate in these structures and socialized into these cultures. Ashforth and Anand (2003) acknowledge that the structures and processes through which top manager-initiated wrongdoing can diffuse throughout the organization sometimes are incompletely effective. However, neither Brief et al. (2000) nor Ashforth and Anand (2003) systematically examine the factors that might cause or allow lower-level organizational participants to resist these structures and processes. Thus, Brief et al. and Ashforth and Anand implicitly assume that once wrongdoing proliferates and is institutionalized, and after employees are socialized to follow the corrupt arrangements, opposition to wrongdoing ceases. Indicative of this, Brief et al. (2000) label the employees whose behavior has been shaped by these structures and processes "amoral automatons."

This last implicit assumption is incompatible with evidence that organizational participants sometime resist the spread of wrongdoing, in the most dramatic cases becoming whistleblowers who bring wrongdoing to the attention of authorities within and outside of the organization. In the next chapter I consider an explanation of wrongdoing that explicitly questions this assumption, an account that focuses on the role that power plays in the facilitation of wrongdoing.

9

The Power Structure

Introduction

The power structure explanation of organizational wrongdoing is rooted in a theoretical perspective that views organizations as arenas of conflict and views organizational participants as combatants. Organizations consist of people who possess divergent interests and different capacities to pursue their interests. The more powerful organizational participants pursue courses of action that serve their interests, while the less powerful pursue courses of actions imposed upon them by powerful others (Pfeffer 1981).

Popular thinking on the link between power and wrongdoing is well represented by the famous Lord Acton quote, "Power tends to corrupt and absolute power corrupts absolutely." It is even better represented by the less famous but more precise William Pitt quote, "Unlimited power is apt to corrupt the minds of those who possess it." These quotations suggest that the possession of power changes people in ways that make them more prone to pursue wrongdoing. But Lord Acton followed his famous remark with another more general but less well-known observation, "Great men are almost always bad men." This statement, if taken at face value, leaves open the possibility that the relationship between power and wrongdoing is more complex. People who are prone to engage in wrongdoing might also be prone to acquire power, either because the pursuit of wrongdoing requires the accumulation of power or because a common third human characteristic, such as greed or the "need for power" (McClelland and Burnham, 1976), gives rise to the pursuit of both power and wrongdoing. Alternatively, there might be something about acquiring power, as opposed to possessing it, that makes a person prone to engage in wrongdoing.

Social science research, though, largely has ignored the impact that power has on those who possess it. Instead, it has focused on the impact that power has on those subject to it. And most of this work is based on the postulate that people who possess formal authority can cause subordinate others to engage in behaviors that they are not inclined to enact. In this chapter, I consider how formal authority and a second type of power, informal power, can cause both the powerless and the powerful to engage in wrongful behavior. Before I do, though, I need to introduce a few definitions and distinctions.

The nature of power

The definition of power

Power has been defined in a variety of ways. I follow Max Weber's definition, which stipulates that power is the capacity to get what one wants over the resistance of others (Weber 1978). This definition has four elements. First, power is a capacity. It need not be exercised (i.e. translated into influence) in order to impact the behavior of others. Second, it pertains to particular interests. A person might possess power in one domain (i.e. with respect to one objective) but little power in another. Third, power is a relationship between a person and specific others. It is not an abstract attribute of the power holder. Fourth, power is something that operates by overcoming the resistance of others. It is not something that operates by changing the views of others. This definition circumscribes my analysis of power in ways that will make it narrower than other potential analyses.

The different types of power

Social scientists have identified several different types of power. French and Raven (1959) advanced arguably the most famous classification scheme, distinguishing six types of power: reward, coercive, legitimate, expert, referent, and information power. French and Raven's typology has been refined over the years so as to recognize variants of several of the six types of power, for example to distinguish between personal and impersonal reward power (Raven 2001). I think that some of these types of power are better treated as situational social influence, and accordingly I discussed them earlier in that context. For example, referent power resembles social comparison pressures, which I discussed in Chapter 8. I think that the remaining types of power can be grouped into two broad categories relevant to organizations. The first has been referred to as formal authority, formal power, or hierarchal power. This type of power is derived from one's position in the organization's hierarchy or chain of command. The second type of power has been referred to as informal power or resource dependence-based power. This type of power is derived from one's position in the organization's network of resource exchange relationships. Most social science research on organizational wrongdoing has focused on the former type of power. But both types can facilitate wrongdoing.

FORMAL AUTHORITY

Formal authority is a role relationship between superiors and subordinates, governed by the norm of obedience to authority. The norm of obedience dictates that subordinates comply with their superiors' commands, regardless of whether they agree with their orders. Stanley Milgram's pioneering experiments graphically illustrated the norm of obedience to authority (1963, 1974). In the Milgram studies, an experimenter asked subjects to teach another person a list of word association pairs. The experimenter briefly lectured the subject-teacher on the importance of education in society and told him or her that the experiment was designed to investigate the effectiveness of alternative education methods. The method the subject-teacher was asked to use consisted of administering increasingly severe electrical shocks to the person tasked with learning the word association pairs, called the learner, each time he or she erred. The teacher thought that the learner also was a subject in the experiment, but the learner was actually a confederate of the experimenter. Further, the teacher thought the electric shocks ranged from mild to severe (and even life threatening), but they were in fact bogus. The experiment was designed to determine whether (and the extent to which) subjects would comply with an experimenter's instructions to administer increasingly powerful electrical shocks to another person, despite the fact that the person had done nothing sufficient to warrant the pain-inducing stimuli.

Milgram conducted many variations of this experiment, and an army of psychologists has since conducted a bewildering array of additional variations. But Milgram's basic study design, described above, produced the most memorable result of the series, perhaps the most memorable result of all experimental social psychology. The vast majority of the subject-teachers in Milgram's experiments administered the bogus electric shocks to the learners. Further, most administered very high voltage shocks, including shocks labeled in ways that clearly telegraphed their presumed severe pain-inducing character (the highest voltage level in some experimental trials was two levels higher than the level labeled "Danger—Severe Shock"). Many teachers complied with the experimenter without voicing objections. Some, though, expressed reservations about the instructions. Of these, a few refused to follow the experimenter's instructions. Most, though, complied with the experimenter's commands after he issued bland programmed statements indicating that they were required to continue. Importantly, in debriefing sessions after the experiment, many of the subject-teachers who complied with the experimenter told interviewers that they thought it was wrong to shock the learners.

It is tempting to disregard the importance of the Milgram experiments because they were conducted in the 1970s. Perhaps modern society is different in ways that make the norm of obedience to authority less potent. It is not possible to precisely replicate the Milgram experiments today. Some of the subject-teachers who administered to the learners what they believed were dangerous shocks experienced psychological problems after participating in the study. In the wake of the experiments, universities created human subjects committees that prohibit researchers from conducting studies that possess the potential to harm subjects in similar ways. But Burger (2009) has replicated the Milgram study up to the point just before subjects were asked to administer presumably dangerous shocks. And he observed levels of compliance comparable to those Milgram observed up to those same levels. In addition, Arthur Brief et al. (2000) conducted an experiment that resembles the Milgram experiment in key respects. They simulated a business environment and examined the impact that a superior's instructions to discriminate against black job candidates had on subjects' propensity to discriminate. They found that a superior's instructions to discriminate significantly increased a subject's propensity to discriminate, even among subjects who did not hold biased views towards blacks.

The amount of formal authority that people possess depends most fundamentally on their position in the chain of command. All things being equal, the higher people rise in the chain of command, the more formal authority they acquire. The amount of formal authority that people can derive from their position in the chain of command, though, depends on the strength of the norm of obedience to authority in the organization, and the extent to which their subordinates consider them to be a legitimate authority, someone worthy of their obedience.

Milgram (1965) conducted variants of his basic experiment in which the strength of the norm of obedience to authority and the legitimacy of the experimenter were manipulated. He found, as expected, that compliance declined when the norm of obedience to authority was weak and the experimenter lacked legitimacy. Further, Brief et al. (2000), whose study of authority was situated in a simulated modern business context, conducted supplemental experimental trials in which superiors' legitimacy was manipulated. They found that subjects were less likely to comply with a superior's instructions to discriminate against black job applicants when they were informed that their superior had been involved in improprieties and was soon to be dismissed.

We can speculate about how the norm of obedience to authority might vary across organizational contexts. Experience suggests that the norm of obedience to authority is very strong in military organizations, weaker in private-sector firms, and even weaker in not-for-profit institutions. Soldiers generally obey their superior officers without question. In contrast, employees in private-sector firms generally obey their superiors more conditionally, following most orders but ignoring directives with which they seriously disagree. Volunteers in not-for-profit organizations obey their superiors even more conditionally, following only those orders with which they agree. Within the private sector, the norm of obedience to authority is stronger in manufacturing companies than in high tech firms.

Weber (1978/1992) wrote extensively on the question of legitimacy. He maintained that superiors possess legitimacy (i.e. are worthy of being followed) to the extent that they articulate a sound basis for their authority and act in accordance with that rationale. Weber identified three bases for legitimacy in organizations: religious, charismatic, and rational/legal (listed in the order that they appeared historically). The rational/legal rationale is the main basis for authority in contemporary business organizations. The primary legal basis of legitimacy is ownership. The principal rational basis is competence. Thus, formal authorities in modern business organizations tend to be considered legitimate by subordinates when they are owners of the firm and/or are effective leaders. But Weber also argued that a superior's legitimacy rests in the last resort on his or her ability to materially alter subordinates' life situations and chances. Thus, formal authorities in modern business organizations also tend to be considered legitimate by subordinates when they can effectively allocate rewards and dispense punishments, conditional on obedience.

Systems of formal authority can enhance an organization's efficiency and effectiveness. They reduce the total amount of decision making that must take place in an organization by restricting decision making to a small number of individuals at the top of the organizational hierarchy. And if people are allocated to the top positions on the basis of their competence, as Weber contended is the case in the ideal-typical bureaucracy, they restrict decision making to the most qualified people. Of course, the centralization of decision making at the top is not always beneficial. It can lead to poor choices when decisions require a diversity of competencies possessed by people at lower levels of the organization. Further, more relevant to the issue at hand, it can cause subordinates to engage in wrongdoing. But before I turn to that subject, I consider the second main type of power found in organizations.

INFORMAL POWER

David Mechanic (1962) was among the first management theorists to discuss informal power. He maintained that people possess this type of power to the extent that they control resources that are needed by others and that are not available from third parties. Mechanic grouped resources into three categories: information, people, and instrumentalities. Information includes data as well as the knowledge to process data (i.e. expertise). People include potential supporters as well as individuals who constitute resources (e.g. by virtue of their capabilities) or have access to other resources (e.g. by virtue of their position in the organization's division of labor or its social network). And instrumentalities represent a catch-all category that includes everything else a person might need, both tangible (e.g. money) and intangible (e.g. ego gratification). When a person is highly dependent on another person, he or she tends to comply with the other person's demands.

Pfeffer and Salancik extended Mechanic's analysis of power (Salancik and Pfeffer 1977; Pfeffer and Salancik 1978). They showed that informal power tends to flow to those organizational participants who control resources needed to cope with the organization's critical contingencies, the most dangerous threats to the organization's existence, or the most promising opportunities for its future success. Most organizational participants favor organizational survival and success, although they may differ substantially with respect to their specific interests. Thus, they are dependent on those individuals who possess the resources needed by the organization to ensure survival and achieve success.

Resource dependence-based power explanations of behavior sometimes are equated with rational choice explanations because the powerful actors in resource dependence-based power relationships presumably provoke their relatively powerless counterparts to engage in cost-benefit calculations about the pros and cons of complying with their demands (Milgrom and Roberts 1988). But while the relatively powerless actors in resource dependence-based power relationships might engage in cost-benefit calculations about the merits of compliance, the nature of such calculations differ from classic rational choice related cost-benefit calculations in at least three respects. First, the benefits motivating a relatively powerless actor's compliance consist primarily of the push of negative consequences rather than the pull of positive ones. To put it in plain language, resource dependence-based power motivates by the fear of punishment rather than by the promise of reward. Second, to the extent that relatively powerless actors engage in cost-benefit calculations, they face highly constrained sets of options and thus experience the decision as forced. Third, as a consequence, when relatively powerless actors elect to comply with the demands of more powerful others, they do so reluctantly, often begrudgingly or hostilely, and sometimes resolving to reverse the course of action in the future.

Pfeffer has articulated a variety of means by which people can build resource dependence-based power in organizations (Pfeffer 1992, 2010). People can acquire resource dependence-based power by receiving training and experience that is valued and scarce in their organization. They also can acquire resource dependence-based power by obtaining positions in the division of labor that afford them control of resources that are valued by the firm and specific co-workers (subordinates, peers, and, especially, superiors), and that are difficult to obtain from other sources. Of course, a person's ability to obtain such positions is at least partly a function of previous training and experience. People can also acquire resource dependence-based power by improving their location in the organization's communication and friendship networks, gaining more and more relevant allies and, in the process, gaining indirect control over additional resources. Because valued resources are only sources of power if they are scarce, people also can increase their resource dependence-based power by reducing others' control of valued resources. Finally, people can acquire resource dependence-based power in a comprehensive way by redesigning the firm's division of labor (its task interdependencies, rules, routines, and programs) and reporting relationships. This is one reason why major reorganizations often are resisted.

All of the above strategies entail altering organizational realities. But people also can alter others' perceptions of organizational realities. They can champion particular analyses of their firm's critical contingencies. They can foster particular assessments of the resources needed to cope with those contingencies. And they can offer arguments that attest to their monopoly over those resources. In short, they can work to make sure that regardless of what critical contingencies the firm actually faces, what resources the organization actually needs, and how much control they actually have over those resources (relative to competitors), others believe that they control scarce resources needed to cope with the firm's critical contingencies. As in many areas of life, though, the proof of the pudding is in the eating. Thus, among the most important perceptions people can cultivate is the perception that they are powerful. For this reason, periodically engaging in conflict and winning is necessary to enhance others' perception that one controls scarce and valued resources.

Because resource dependence-based power typically is equated with a contest between organizational actors, practitioners usually consider it detrimental to organizational functioning. The earliest academics to study this form of power, though, considered it beneficial to organizations. Mechanic argued that resource dependence-based power complements formal authority as a mechanism for specifying how things should get done in organizations because it can regulate relationships between organizational participants not linked by the official chain of command. Pfeffer and Salanck argued that resource dependence-based power helps organizations adjust to change because it tends to flow to those units and individuals best able to take advantage of the organization's most promising emerging opportunities or cope with its most pressing problems. In a sense, both Mechanic and Pfeffer and Salancik consider formal authority relations to be skeletal and rigid, and resource dependence-based power to be more pervasive and adaptive. But both also recognize that resource dependence-based power can be used to pursue parochial interests that run counter to the organization's interests. And the pursuit of parochial interests can sometimes lead to wrongdoing.

The impact that power has on those subject to it

Formal authority

The Milgram experiments demonstrate that formal authority can short circuit or circumvent deliberative processes and override the disinclination to follow orders, even when used in conjunction with apparently consequential commands—commands that if followed could produce significant harm to others. Thus, it is easy to see how formal authority can be used to elicit wrongdoing of the sort found in many organizations. A superior can use formal authority to compel a subordinate to engage in wrongdoing explicitly by issuing an order to engage in wrongful behavior. In some cases, a superior's order to engage in wrongdoing can produce unquestioning compliance of the sort exhibited by many of the subjects in the Milgram experiments. This is particularly likely to occur in organizations where the norm of obedience to authority is strong, such as in military organizations.

Pat Tillman, a charismatic U.S. professional football player, suspended his career to join the U.S. Army in the wake of the September 11, 2001 terrorist attack on the World Trade Center. He was killed by friendly fire two years later while serving in Afghanistan. Officials high in the U.S. Defense Department and the Army sought to cover up the true cause of Tillman's death, presumably to protect the military's image, and perhaps to reap public relations benefits. So soldiers, both low and high in the chain of command, were ordered to withhold the truth surrounding Tillman's death. General Philip Kensinger, the U.S. Army officer who took the fall for the misrepresentations (and was officially sanctioned), explained his role in the cover-up in this way. "I've been doing it (serving as a soldier), since (I was) seventeen. And when somebody tells me something, tells me to go do something, ya say in the army, you salute and about face and go get it done." Pat Tillman's brother Kevin served in the same platoon as Pat, but he was not present when Pat was killed. PFC Russell Baer, a fellow solider and good friend of the Tillman brothers, was asked to escort Kevin with Pat's remains back to the U.S. But he was told by his superior officer, "It is not your place to freakin' tell the family anything you know. You need to keep your mouth shut about it. You need to not cause any type of turmoil." And as Baer recalled, "I, you know, I said OK" (Bar-Lev 2010). PFC O'Neil, another friend of Pat and Kevin's, was both ordered to keep the truth from Kevin and reminded of the consequences if he failed to do so. "I was told by Col. Baley to not tell him that Pat was killed by friendly, you know, your career is on the line. Do not tell Kevin exactly what happened" (Bar-Lev 2010).

But formal authority can produce unquestioning compliance to orders to engage in wrongdoing even in organizations where the norm of obedience to authority is more moderate in strength, such as in private-sector firms. Amy Myers was a Safety Surveillance Officer at Wyeth-Ayers, responsible for maintaining the pharmaceutical company's Adverse Drug Event (ADE) database. When reports detailing adverse side effects associated with Wyeth-Ayers drugs were reported to the firm, she was required by company policy and FDA regulations to enter them in the company's ADE file for subsequent transmission to the FDA. In March 1997, reports of thirteen cases of heart valve disease related to fenfluramine, the company's appetite suppressant drug commonly known as Pondimin, were relayed to her from Fargo, North Dakota, via the Mayo Clinic. At the time, Pondimen was prescribed with another drug, phentermine, as part of a popular drug cocktail known as Fen-Phen. It would later be determined that the joint prescription of the two drugs led not just to heart valve disease, an often fatal condition, but also to primary pulmonary hypertension (PPH), a condition in which fluid accumulates in a person's lungs and is almost invariably fatal. Myers dutifully entered the reports of Pondimen-related heart valve disease in the company's database. But soon thereafter, in contradiction to company policy and FDA rules, she removed the reports from the file. Then, several weeks later, she re-entered the reports into the record. A senior Wyeth official who left the firm about the time of the incident confirmed that the removal of reports from the ADE database was a serious breach of company policy. Attorneys working on behalf of plaintiffs who used Pondimin and developed heart valve disease made the deletion of the reports the centerpiece of their successful civil suits against the firm.

The attorneys working on behalf of the Pondimin victims contended that Wyeth-Ayers removed the reports from the database because they feared that news of the drug's serious negative side effects might jeopardize the firm's effort to obtain FDA approval for another closely related drug, dexfenfluramine, commonly known as Redux. They argued that the company reentered the reports weeks later because they learned that an article slated to appear in *The New England Journal of Medicine* would soon make the drug's negative side effects public anyway. But was this shifting strategic intent foremost in the mind of Amy Meyers, the middle-level employee who removed the reports from the database? Court depositions given by Myers and summarized by Alicia Mundy (2001) indicate that Myers was ordered to remove the reports from the database in subtle ways that resemble those used by the experimenter in the Milgram experiments. Myers said that her immediate supervisor "questioned the necessity of entering those Fargo reports so quickly into the ADE database." She went on to say that her boss asked if she "was certain the Fargo patients had really taken" Wyeth's diet drugs and suggested that "if she wasn't 100 percent sure.... it was 'premature' to record them" (Mundy 2001: 182).

Further, she added that the firm's chief safety executive also approved deletion of the records using similarly subtle language. As she recalled, this high level executive posed the question, "'Couldn't the reports be canceled?'" (Mundy 2001: 264).

With this said, I suspect that a superior's order to engage in wrongdoing produces unquestioning compliance in organizations where the norm of obedience to authority is only moderately strong, primarily when subordinates are not fully aware of the wrongful nature of the requested actions. Two Credit Suisse personal bankers, Eric Butler and Julian Tzolov, were indicted in September 2008 on multiple charges related to securities fraud. Butler and Tzolov's clients asked them to invest their savings in safe government-backed student loans. But the personal bankers invested the money in higher commission high-risk mortgage backed assets known as collateralized debt obligations (CDOs), hiding this fact by providing doctored documentation about the investments. Like most managers, though, Butler and Tzolov did not personally provide their clients with this information. Instead they directed their sales assistants to provide the clients with this information, in some cases instructing them to forward e-mails about the investments in which references to "mortgage" and "CDO" were deleted. In all likelihood, the assistants followed their superiors' instructions without giving them much thought (Anderson 2008).

I think that when subordinates in organizations where the norm of obedience to authority is moderately strong are aware of the wrongful nature of requested actions, explicit orders to engage in wrongdoing only produce grudging acquiescence of the sort exhibited by the reluctantly compliant subjects in the Milgram experiments. For example, MCI's top management team ordered the head of the firm's Carrier Finance unit, Ralph McCumber, to delay writing off known bad debt until the following fiscal year. McCumber complied, but only after voicing serious objection. Then McCumber relayed this order to his subordinate, Walter Pavlo, for implementation. Pavlo complied, but only after he too voiced serious objection. Later, after Pavlo was assigned to run the Carrier Finance unit, MCI's top management directly ordered him to delay other write-offs. Again Pavlo complied, despite harboring serious disagreement with the policy (Pavlo and Weinberg 2007).

Each of the above examples illustrates how superiors can use formal authority to facilitate wrongdoing explicitly by ordering subordinates to engage in wrongful conduct. But superiors also can facilitate wrongdoing obliquely by ordering subordinates to pursue goals that can be attained only if they employ wrongful means. For example, MCI's top management knowingly established unrealistic targets for the amount of outstanding bills its Carrier Finance unit had to collect each year. And McCumber and Pavlo, who were tasked with hitting those targets, understood that top management knew those performance goals could not be met unless they employed one or more of a variety of illegal accounting maneuvers (Pavlo and Weinberg 2007). Similarly, top management at the gargantuan U.S. retailer Wal-Mart ordered its store managers to keep labor costs low, threatening them with curtailed compensation, demotion, and even dismissal if they failed to comply, in order to establish the firm as the industry's lowest price leader. And this caused managers to turn to a range of illegal practices, from forcing employees to work off the clock to shaving time off employee's payroll records. As one manager put it, "I screwed plenty of people in my career there. Honestly, you have to. It's either you do it, or there's the door. They told us in meetings, 'I can go hire anyone off the street and pay them fifty thousand dollars to run a store'" (Greenhouse 2008).

Finally, a superior can use formal authority to facilitate wrongdoing even more obliquely, by ordering subordinates to withhold opposition to another person's wrongdoing. In Alicia Mundy's book on the Fen-Phen debacle (2001), Doctor Leo Lutwak was portrayed as a hero. Lutwak was an accomplished researcher who joined the FDA after a distinguished academic career as a professor of pharmacology at Cornell University. Lutwak recognized Fen-Phen's dangers early and worked tirelessly to oppose the drug cocktail's chemical constituents, especially Pondimen and Pondimen's intended upgrade, Redux. But he found himself stymied at every turn in his efforts to expose the drugs' dangers, perhaps most often, by his superiors. Mundy recounts Lutwak's participation in a key hearing to evaluate Pondimen and Redux, in which he refrained from vigorously questioning the drugs' safety largely because his immediate superior, Jim Bilstad, instructed him to moderate his criticisms of the drugs. Mundy writes that Lutwak felt obligated to assume a passive posture at the beginning of the meeting.

> Leo sat next to Dr. Jim Bilstad, a director of the FDA office supervising endocrine and metabolic drugs. Leo was already on notice from Bilstad that he must not advocate approval or disapproval in his testimony or when answering questions. Bilstad had snapped at Leo after one session with Wyeth and Interneuron reps, "You cannot take sides, that's not our role!" "If our role isn't to take sides on whether a drug is safe or not, what is our role?" he had snapped back. "We cannot speak so bluntly to the industry," Bilstad told him, echoing the FDA line. "They are our customers. And you are rude to them," added Bilstad, warning Leo, "They've complained about you." With that earlier exchange in mind, Leo sat still and listened (Mundy 2001: 64–5).

As the meeting progressed, Lutwak found it impossible to resist raising implicit questions about Pondimin's safety, in particular, in regard to its association with primary pulmonary hypertension (PPH). But Lutwak still refrained from coming forward with all that he knew and believed about the drug's dangers.

The PPH issue had Leo fidgeting in his chair, worried that if he jumped in, Bilstad would shoot him down. At one point, he tried to lure Wyeth into admitting what he already knew—that there was a tidal wave of PPH cases being reported in conjunction with Pondimin, the sister drug of Redux. Leo told the meeting that he'd recently seen a report showing 101 PPH cases tied to the drugs. He linked the number 101 with numerous side effects, such as "shortness of breath.... that at least raise suspicion of possible early pulmonary hypertension." Ironically, Leo had accidentally hit on a warning signal of the crisis that would come later, but his remark passed into the ether. Then, he said pointedly that the official drug company reports he'd seen only confirmed seven cases of PPH associated with Pondimin, and waited—but the company didn't take the bait. "I couldn't just call them liars," he explained. "I was being subtle. I thought if I said there were seven reported cases, Wyeth would have to stop me and correct the figure and admit to everyone there were already dozens with Pondimin. But they didn't do that, and I didn't think Bilstad would let me force that point in public," he said dejectedly (Mundy 2001: 66–7).

Informal power

Informal power can facilitate wrongdoing in the same ways that formal authority can. It can facilitate wrongdoing explicitly by causing those subject to it to comply with demands to engage in specific wrongful acts. And when it does, it can lead to unquestioning or grudging compliance. Resource dependence-based power is most likely to lead to unquestioning compliance when those subject to it see themselves as powerless, typically because past experience suggests that resistance is futile (Gaventa 1982). Resource dependence-based power is most likely to lead to grudging compliance when those subject to it retain a powerful self-concept, typically because they have yet to experience long periods of uninterrupted domination—either because the resource dependence-based power to which they are subject is weak or because it only recently has been developed or exercised.

The 1950s quiz show fraud illustrates how resource dependence-based power can produce unquestioning compliance. The quiz show producers began the subtle rigging of broadcast contests using questions tailored to contestants' expertise because it was believed that "controls" of some sort were necessary. As one producer put it, "you cannot ask random questions of people and have a show. You simply have failure, failure, failure, and that does not make entertainment (Stone and Yohn 1992: 119)." However, the producers graduated to more overt rigging, retaining popular contestants and dispatching unpopular ones, partly in response to sponsor pressure. According to the producer of "The $64,000 Question," Merton Koplin, "We'd sit in the sponsor's meetings and they would say, 'Well, that one—that one's got to go on to $64,000' or 'I don't like that one, let's get rid of him'" (Krainin

Productions, Inc. 2000: 5). This influence and the resource dependence-based power upon which it was predicated were evident in the case of Revlon's sponsorship of "The $64,000 Challenge," a spin-off of "The $64,000 Question." According to Stone and Yohn (1992), when ratings for the program slipped, Revlon increased the pressure on the producers. "Expressing dissatisfaction at contestants, categories, and even the questions, they played on the inherent fear of the producers that Revlon might not exercise its options to renew the shows when the time came." The fact that sponsors had power to make the producers and even the networks comply with their demands is indicated by the fact that Revlon was able to "'steal' broadcast time to lengthen commercials beyond what CBS guidelines permitted" (1992: 147). But, the quiz show producers never openly resisted the sponsors' demands, perhaps partly because they thought they had little choice in the matter.

Colonial Pipeline Company's secret payments to Woodbridge, New Jersey public officials in return for political favors illustrate how resource dependence-based power can produce grudging compliance. When Colonial sought to obtain building permits and right of way access from the City of Woodbridge to build petroleum storage tanks on city property in 1963, the mayor and city council president made it clear that approval hinged on the company's provision of under-the-table payments (Mintz 1972). Colonial executives at first declined to comply with the public officials' demands and continued to pursue the required approvals through legitimate channels. But eventually, after failing to make progress, the executives capitulated and arranged a series of complex difficult-to-trace transactions that resulted in the transfer of money from Colonial to the city officials. When the scheme was uncovered and the case went to trial, Colonial Pipeline executives hinged their defense on the claim that the mayor and council president had extorted the payments from them. While the jury did not concur and found both company and city officials guilty of collusion, it seems clear that the company executives did not voluntarily initiate the bribery scheme. Instead, they reluctantly provided the payments because they depended on the mayor and city council president to provide the building permit and right-of-way easement.

But resource dependence-based power also can operate obliquely. It can cause those subject to it to pursue goals that can be attained only if pursued in a wrongful manner. It also can cause those subject to it to withhold opposition to wrongdoing. Bernard Madoff implemented his elaborate Ponzi scheme by building a network of well-remunerated associates who in turn recruited clients to invest in his funds. As time went on, some associates and clients became suspicious of the Madoff funds' integrity, largely because the funds were not well documented and generated curiously consistent, unusually high returns. Nevertheless, his associates largely withheld their reservations and used a variety of subterfuges to squelch their clients' concerns, because they feared that if they questioned Madoff's probity or allowed their clients' concerns to surface, he would expel them from his network—a fear bolstered by Madoff's periodic threats to this effect (Gaviria and Smith 2009).

As noted in the introduction, power is a capacity that need not be translated into influence to impact the behavior of others. Often people conform to the preferences of others who have power over them, even when the others do not issue explicit or even implicit orders of the sort described in the previous section, or make explicit or even implicit threats of the sort described above. In Chapter 6 I described Betty Vinson's decision to implement improper accounting adjustments requested by her superiors at WorldCom (Pulliam 2003). I noted that, while her intuition and emotional reaction to implementing the adjustments told her that they were wrong, she followed through with the alterations because WorldCom's chief financial officer provided an authoritative justification for them. But she also followed through with the alterations because she was her family's principal breadwinner and there were few other jobs in WorldCom's small headquarters town of Jackson, Mississippi that could provide an equivalent salary. Thus Vinson was dependent on her superiors to provide a resource that was both important to her and scarce. And her resource dependence on her superiors contributed to her decision to go along with their request to implement the accounting adjustments, even though her superiors never drew attention to the dependence in any way. Paul Krimmage intimated that many of his fellow professional cyclists elected to use banned performance-enhancing substances for similar reasons.

So far, I have focused on resource dependence-based power predicated on the control of resources needed by specific others. Resource dependence-based power predicated on the capacity to cope with an organization's critical contingencies merits separate attention for two reasons. First, it tends to facilitate wrongdoing in an indirect way. It causes those most interested in dealing successfully with the critical contingencies, the organization's leaders, to exert influence over others on behalf of those capable of coping with the key contingencies. Thus, people capable of coping with an organization's critical contingencies can enlist the assistance of those most concerned about addressing the contingencies, typically their superiors, to defeat their opponents. Second, resource dependence-based power rooted in the capacity to cope with critical contingencies tends to operate in an oblique fashion. That is, it places people in positions in which it is hard to achieve organizational goals without engaging in wrongdoing, or inhibits their ability to oppose others' wrongdoing, causing them to become complicit with others' wrongdoing.

The perpetration of accounting improprieties by MCI's Carrier Finance unit illustrates how resource dependence-based power predicated on the capacity to cope with critical contingencies can facilitate wrongdoing in an indirect fashion and can have an oblique effect. I have already described how Carrier Finance executives Ralph McCumber and Walter Pavlo manipulated their unit's books to disguise the extent to which they were unable to collect past-due bills. And I have said that McCumber and Pavlo engaged in this wrongdoing partly because their superiors established unrealistically high targets with respect to the collection of past-due bills, and partly because their superiors issued direct orders to manipulate the books. But Carrier Finance executives found themselves in the position of having to collect a large volume of delinquent bills (and needing to employ questionable practices to collect them) because MCI's sales representatives signed up a large number of customers who they knew were unlikely to pay their bills. The sales representatives signed up this motley crew of shady customers because the more customers they signed up, the more they earned on commission, regardless of whether the customers followed through on their obligations to the firm. Carrier Finance complained bitterly to top management about the sales divisions' practices as well as the failure of the firm's due diligence unit to reign in their excesses. But MCI's top management invariably sided with the sales division because they depended on it to generate a large volume of orders so as to maintain the appearance of sustained growth that was needed to attract a corporate suitor (Pavlo and Weinberg 2007).

The failed attempt of Enron lawyers to stop the firm's trading operation from manipulating the California energy market illustrates well how resource dependence-based power predicated on the capacity to cope with critical contingencies can facilitate wrongdoing in an indirect manner and have an even more oblique effect. While California's energy crisis deepened in 2000, with public utility companies losing vast sums of money and consumers experiencing brownouts and blackouts, Enron's trading profits soared, quadrupling in a single year. This juxtaposition of energy market failure and Enron success led several utility companies and municipalities to file complaints against the firm with the Federal Energy Regulatory Commission (FERC). These complaints spurred Enron's legal counsel to conduct internal investigations of the firm's trading operation in California. Over the following year, it became increasingly obvious to Enron's legal counsel that the firm's California traders were employing strategies that were possibly criminal and certainly sufficiently questionable to provoke government and consumer group civil suits. So the legal team pressed Enron's top managers to prevail on the traders to suspend their questionable trading practices. But Enron's senior managers never asked the traders to stop. McLean and Elkind (2004) contend that this was because the California traders were generating huge profits and because the firm's other units primarily were consuming capital rather than generating it. As a result, Enron's top managers were intensely dependent on the California traders for a crucial resource—cash.

The impact that power has on those who possess it

As noted in the introduction, popular thinking on the relationship between power and wrongdoing has long assumed that the possession of power increases the likelihood that people will engage in wrongdoing. But social scientists have only relatively recently begun to explore this relationship. The Stanford prison experiment was among the first and remains the most well-known study to examine the relationship between the possession of power and the perpetration of wrongdoing (Haney, Banks, Zimbardo 1973; Zimbardo 2007). It dramatically demonstrated that simply assigning subjects to a high power position could provoke them to treat those subject to their power in harsh and even brutal ways. In fact, the behavior that the possession of power provoked in the prison experiment subjects was so extreme that the study's principal investigator, Philip Zimbardo, was forced to suspend the study before it ran its intended course.[1] Below I consider four ways in which power can cause those who possess it to engage in wrongful behavior, organizing the discussion according to the type of power in question.

Both types of power

POWER AS OPPORTUNITY CREATOR AND MOTIVATOR

Sociologists, criminologists, and criminal justice professionals have long contended that the opportunity to engage in wrongdoing increases the likelihood that people will engage in wrongdoing, whether it be juvenile delinquency (Cloward and Ohlin 1960), routine crime (Cohen and Felson 1979), or organizational misconduct (Baker and Faulkner 1993). Power, by definition, provides those who possess it with the capacity to pursue their interests over the resistance of others. Thus both formal authority and resource dependence-based power should increase the likelihood that people predisposed to engage in wrongful behaviors actually will perpetrate those behaviors. Recently, social psychologists have conducted laboratory experiments that sharpen and extend this basic idea.

Several studies show that the possession of power is associated with the proclivity to view and treat women as sex objects, but this effect is strongest among men with pre-existing tendencies to engage in sexual harassment. Other studies show that the possession of power triggers socially irresponsible behavior, such as shirking responsibility for a communal burden, but only when power-holders are "exchange oriented," prone to see their relationships

---

[1] The Zimbardo prison experiment also provided evidence of other social psychological processes, including obedience to authority discussed above in connection with the Milgram experiments.

to others in instrumental terms. The possession of power actually triggers socially responsible behavior, such as shouldering a larger part of a communal burden, when power-holders are "communally oriented," prone to see their relationship to others in terms of their mutual responsibility to adhere to societal norms (Lee-Chai, Chen, and Chartrand 2001).

Some believe these results reflect the impact that power has on a person's unconscious goals (Bargh and Alvarez 2001). When a person's unconscious goals are "selfish," the possession of power stimulates malevolent behavior, such as sexual harassment or socially irresponsible choices. When a person's unconscious goals are "pro-social," the possession of power stimulates benevolent behavior. Proponents of this goal activation perspective believe that the possession of power activates unconscious goals primarily when the possession of power and the pursuit of the unconscious goals were associated with one another in the past (e.g. if a person's acquisition of power and harassment of women were linked in the past).

The notion that power creates opportunities dovetails with the idea, discussed in Chapter 4 in connection with expectancy theory, that human motivation is influenced, not just by internal states, but also by external contingencies. It is undoubtedly true that individuals' preferences and value structures differ in ways that cause them to pursue different objectives. But expectancy theorists show that the extent to which people expect that they can successfully perform a behavior (i.e. the extent to which they possess a high effort–performance expectancy) and the extent to which they expect that they will receive positive and/or negative outcomes from performing a behavior (i.e. the extent to which they possess a high performance–outcome expectancy) also influence their motivation to engage in the behavior.

Power, by definition, increases a person's capacity to accomplish tasks. Thus, the more formal authority and resource dependence-based power organizational participants possess, the more confidant they should be in their ability to successfully perform wrongful acts (e.g. to obtain insider information from knowledgeable informants) and, hence, the more motivated they should be to perform such acts. Power, by extension, also increases a person's capacity to extract favorable outcomes from accomplishing tasks. Thus, the more formal authority and resource dependence-based power organizational participants possess, the more confident they should be in their ability to extract favorable outcomes from wrongful acts (e.g. to make money trading inside information and avoid detection and punishment) and, hence, the more motivated they should be to perform such acts.

The possession of power also appears to alter a person's weighting of rewards and punishments that might be associated with wrongdoing. When people accumulate power, they come to value power as a thing in itself. As a consequence, they become more likely to pursue power as an end rather than as a means to an end (Kipnis 1972). More germane, as people accumulate power, they come to devalue the approval of others (Keltner, Young, Heerey, Oemig, and Monarch 1998). As a consequence, they become more likely to pursue courses of action that might meet with social disapproval. One clever laboratory study manipulated the amount of power experimental subjects believed they had over fellow subjects. At the conclusion of the study, the experimenters offered all the subjects complementary cookies and tracked the number of cookies subjects took and the way in which they ate them. They found that the subjects assigned to the high power condition took more cookies and ate them in a more socially unacceptable fashion (e.g. chewing with their mouths open and dropping a larger quantity of crumbs) than those assigned to the low power condition (Keltner, Gruenfeld, and Anderson 2003).

Steve Raucci's tyrannical reign in the Schenectady, New York, school district illustrates how the acquisition of power can increase opportunities and motivation to engage in wrongdoing. As head of the school district's maintenance department, Raucci exhibited a propensity to play nasty practical jokes on fellow employees. But when he began to build power beyond the department, his practical jokes evolved into harassment and more extreme illegal behavior. Raucci used his formal authority as maintenance department supervisor, bolstered by the threat of transfer, and even dismissal, to force his subordinates to do his bidding, which included volunteering for union official and board of education member re-election campaigns. These services in turn helped Raucci get elected president of the maintenance department's union, placed in charge of the school district's building and grounds department, and assigned to head the district's energy conservation program. Raucci then used these positions to solve problems for top union officials, high-level school district administrators, and ultimately members of the district's board of education, building dependencies that further enhanced his power.

As Raucci worked his way up the formal and informal power structure, his practical jokes became increasingly offensive. Many subordinates were repulsed by his behavior. But, Raucci appeared to delight in their discomfort. A few employees openly opposed his iron-fisted rule and appealed to higher authorities for relief. In those cases, Raucci increased the intensity of his harassment, eventually placing bombs in opponents' homes. For this he was convicted and sentenced to twenty-three years in prison. In surreptitiously taped conversations with undercover policemen Raucci portrayed himself as exercising power in the name of good, in particular, exacting justice for friends who had been unjustly harmed. If this self-assessment was honest, his malicious intentions can be considered to have been latent (Glass 2010).

POWER AS COGNITIVE ORIENTATION SHIFTER

Social psychologists have begun to examine how the possession and use of power affects the way people see themselves and others. Their research indicates that the possession of power increases the likelihood that people process information selectively and use cognitive shortcuts when choosing among alternative courses of action. Powerful people tend to overlook the distinctive features of those over whom they have power, increasing their propensity to stereotype and discriminate against them. They also tend to ignore the needs, emotions, and aspirations of those subject to their power, increasing their willingness to harm them (Anderson, Keltner, and John 2003; Bartky 1990; Fiske 1993; Frederickson and Roberts 1997; Galinksy Magee, Inesi, and Gruenfeld 2006; Goodwin, Gubin, Fiske, and Yzerbyt 2000; Gruenfeld, Inesi, Magee, and Galinksy 2008; Henley 1977; Keltner, Gruenfeld, and Anderson 2003; Nussbaum 1999; Vankleef, De Dreu, Pietroni, and Manstead 2006).

Researchers also have found that the use of power alters how people see themselves in relation to others. Most notably, Kipnis (2001) discovered that people who use "strong influence techniques," such as direct commands, rather than "weak influence techniques," such as rational argument, tend to see themselves as responsible for others' behavior and view those they control as not responsible for their own behavior. This produces a range of changes in the controlling person's views of themselves and others. On the one hand, when people successfully use strong techniques to control others' behavior, they come to see themselves as superior and responsible for the behavior of those they control. As a result, they view themselves as more deserving of ethical considerations and hence resources, freedoms, and rights. On the other hand, they come to view those they control as less competent and less responsible for their own behavior. Instead of seeing those they control as fully human, they regard them as their instruments and, ultimately, less worthy of ethical treatment. Such views of self and others provide the rationale for wrongdoing on the part of controllers at the expense of those whom they control. People who possess formal authority and resource dependence-based power are better positioned to use "strong influence attempts," such as direct commands. As such, this research provides support for a modification of the accepted wisdom that "power corrupts," suggesting instead that "*the use of* power corrupts."

There are numerous public officials who appear to have been virtuous public servants early in their careers when they possessed little power, but who perpetrated wrongdoing towards the ends of their careers after acquiring substantial power and a sense of entitlement. Darleen Druyun began her career as a civilian contracting intern for the U.S. Air Force in 1970. As she moved up the bureaucratic hierarchy over the course of her 32-year career, she earned a reputation for being a dedicated, hardworking, innovative, no-non-sense administrator who rescued important projects from abandonment, pushed through important new weapon systems, and ultimately saved the Air Force over $20 billion in procurement costs. But during her last years in the job, she, at her own admission, steered billions of dollars of contracts to Boeing Co., in appreciation for Boeing job offers to her daughter, future son-in-law, and ultimately herself (Cahlink 2004; Pasztor and Karp 2004).

An informal power greased slippery slope

The accumulation and use of informal power has been viewed as inherently problematic from an ethical standpoint (Cavanagh, Moberg, and Velasquez 1981). While it is possible to accumulate and use this kind of power in an ethical way, some strategies for accumulating and using resource dependence-based power are facilitated by the violation of basic human rights, societal norms of justice, and the utilitarian principle. For example, the shaping of others' perceptions of the organization's critical contingencies requires the selective withholding of information. As a result, the accumulation of power can violate others' right to free consent (i.e. their right to have full access to available information relevant to their well-being). Further, the accumulation of allies often requires the allocation of resources, the distribution of punishments, and the enforcement of rules in a particularistic fashion. As a result, the accumulation of power also often violates norms of distributive, compensatory, administrative justice. And, of course, the accumulation of power can advance the interests of the power-holder at the expense of the common good, thus violating utilitarian precepts that dictate people act in ways that generate the greatest good for the greatest number.

If the accumulation or use of resource dependence-based power is problematic from an ethical standpoint, it can lay the foundation for additional unethical and increasingly wrongful behavior in the future. When the accumulation or use of power requires perpetration of unethical behavior, it tends to desensitize people to engaging in unethical behavior. And as indicated in Chapter 6, as people become desensitized to engaging in unethical behavior, they become more prone to commit such behavior in the future (Ashforth and Kreiner 2002). Further, when the accumulation or use of power requires the perpetration of unethical behavior, it tends to move the benchmark against which people evaluate their behavior closer to the line separating right from wrong. And as indicated in Chapter 6, as the benchmark against which people evaluate their behavior moves closer to the line separating right from wrong, they become more prone to cross the line in the future.

Robert Moses was a New York State public official from the 1920s until the late 1960s who engineered the construction of massive public works projects, beginning with parks and highways, and moving on to bridges, tunnels, and large public real estate development projects. Although he was not an elected official, shortly after his appointment to public office he proposed changes in New York state law that gave the state's park commissioner the right to seize private land to constitute parks under two conditions: 1) attempts to negotiate in good faith with the land's owners failed to produce a sales agreement and 2) the state had in its coffers sufficient money to purchase the contested property at full market value. Moses won state legislator approval of these changes largely because the reform bill was written using arcane language and was introduced in the waning moments of the 1924 legislative session, in effect denying the state's legislators their right to free consent. Then, after becoming state parks commissioner, Moses began seizing land without first negotiating in good faith with landowners, denying them the right to due process. With these two apparently unethical pursuits behind him, Moses took the further step of seizing a large tract of land on the south shore of Long Island, known as the Taylor Estate, without negotiating in good faith with its owners and despite the fact that the parks commission lacked the funds to pay for the estate at current market rates. For this last transgression, Moses was indicted, prosecuted, and ultimately found guilty, although only assigned a miniscule fine (Caro 1974).[2]

The temporal dynamics of formal authority, informal power, and wrongdoing

Although formal authority, informal power, and wrongdoing are distinct phenomena, they tend to develop interdependently over time. A person's position in the chain of command determines the resources over which he or she exercises control, not the least of which are subordinates who may control yet other resources. Thus, advancement up the chain of command typically improves a person's access to valued resources and increases his or her informal power. The more resource dependence-based power people acquire, the better able they are to lobby for definitions of the organization's

---

[2] I think the accumulation of formal authority might also increase a person's propensity to engage in wrongdoing in a unique way. Most previous work on the relationship between formal authority and wrongdoing has focused on the obligations that subordinates have to superiors and the way in which those obligations can cause subordinates to engage in wrongdoing. But Raven (2001) has identified what might be called the flip side of the norm of obedience to authority, the obligation to "provide for" one's subordinates. I think superiors might be constrained by additional obligations and that these obligations can, on occasion, cause them to engage in wrongdoing. For example, I suspect that formal authorities feel obligated to trust their subordinates and to stand up for them when others question their behavior. And, I think the obligation superiors feel to trust and support their subordinates sometimes can be used by subordinates to gain their superiors' complicity to wrongdoing.

critical contingencies and distributions of its resources that enhance their control of resources perceived to be important and scarce. At the same time, the more informal power people have, the better able they are to manipulate rewards and punishments salient to subordinates and to attain goals associated with their position in the chain of command. Thus, resource dependence-based power can enhance managers' legitimacy in the eyes of their subordinates. Finally, to the extent that informal power can increase a person's capacity to accomplish the goals valued by their superiors, it can increase his or her chances of promotion.

As elaborated in detail above, power can allow those who possess it to cause other people to perpetrate, support, or tolerate wrongdoing despite their disinclination to do so. Power also can cause those who possess it to become more prone to engage in wrongdoing; altering their motivations, cognitive orientations, and position on the slippery slope to wrongdoing. But, power also can allow those who possess it to set the stage for political conflict that later culminates in wrongdoing. Powerful people are the principal architects of the power structure, by which I mean the formal hierarchy and the resource topography, as well as the allocation of people to positions in those structures. By contributing to the design of reporting relationships and task interdependencies, by favoring the appointment of some potential position holders over others, and by affecting the dismissal of select position incumbents, powerful organizational participants can reduce their need to translate their power into influence so as to enact wrongdoing at a later time.

At the same time, the pursuit of wrongdoing can enhance an organizational participant's power. As people become immersed in wrongdoing, they can increase their control over rewards and punishments that when manipulated skillfully can increase their legitimacy as formal authorities. More important, they can develop access to resources that others need, most importantly resources that cope with the organization's critical contingencies. As they develop access to resources that others need, they develop informal power over these others. And the discussion above suggests that as they develop formal authority and informal power over others, they become even more likely to engage in wrongdoing. In this way, the acquisition of power and involvement in wrongdoing can accelerate over time in conjunction with one another.

Andy Fastow's illegal special purpose entities at Enron

I conclude this chapter with a description of the role that power played in the creation of illegal special purpose entities (SPEs) at Enron. My description focuses on Andy Fastow, the principal architect of the SPEs, and is primarily derived from Eichenwald's account of the Enron debacle *Conspiracy of Fools* (Eichenwald 2005). It will illustrate the ideas advanced in this chapter, especially ideas about how power and wrongdoing can co-evolve over time. In the process, it also will provide a corrective to existing analyses of the Enron debacle that focus on the role that incentives and culture played in facilitating wrongdoing at the firm.

The nature of Fastow's illegal SPEs

Special purpose entities are freestanding enterprises created by parent corporations and owned jointly by them and other investors. They are similar to partly owned subsidiaries in that they are independent of the parent firm from an accounting standpoint, maintaining their own balance sheets that itemize their separate assets and liabilities. They differ from subsidiaries in that they typically are created to carry out highly specialized businesses for a limited time. Formally speaking, Generally Accepted Accounting Principles require that at least 3 percent of an SPE's capitalization come from outside investors. Andy Fastow wanted to participate as an outside investor in the SPEs that he created for Enron so that he could benefit from their construction. But Enron's in-house lawyers ruled that this would compromise the SPEs' legal independence. With his aspirations blocked, Fastow used third parties, most importantly a co-conspirator named Michael Kopper, to surreptitiously invest in a number of Enron's SPEs. Fastow's involvement in Enron's SPEs became more problematic from an ethical and legal standpoint over time. SPEs are required to be functionally independent of their creators so as to effect an actual transference of risk. But Fastow was actively involved in, and received compensation for, management of several of the SPEs he created. Further, more generally speaking, corporate executives are expected to perform their duties in ways that advance the interests of their firms' stockholders. But on a number of occasions, Fastow managed the SPEs in which he had an ownership, management, and compensation interest in ways that provided him with personal benefits at the expense of both Enron and the SPEs' stockholders.

Fastow needed the approval, cooperation, and acquiescence of a large number of people and organizations to construct his illegal SPEs. He needed the authorization of his superiors to charter the entities. He needed the endorsement of gatekeepers within the firm, such as Enron's risk assessment professionals, who ruled on the soundness of the enterprises. He also needed the assent of his peers, whose objectives sometimes conflicted with his. In addition, Fastow needed the compliance of his direct and indirect subordinates, who were responsible for carrying out his directives. Fastow also needed capital to constitute the SPEs. As indicated above, 3 percent of the capital had to come from outside investors, which typically comprised financial institutions. But the bulk of the capital for Fastow's SPEs came from Enron itself in the form of the firm's stock. The value of Enron's stock as a source of SPE capital hinged on its price, and its price hinged substantially on investment bank stock analyst reports. Thus, Fastow also needed the participation of banks and the positive evaluation of their analysts to constitute his SPEs. Finally, Fastow needed the endorsement of outside gatekeepers, such as the firm's auditors who ruled on the accounting propriety of the SPEs. Below I indicate how Fastow used formal authority and informal power to secure the support or overcome the resistance of all of these actors—at least for a time.

How Fastow used power to construct illegal SPEs at Enron

FORMAL AUTHORITY

Fastow possessed formal authority by virtue of his position in Enron's organizational hierarchy. He entered the firm at a relatively high level, as an executive in the firm's finance division. In short order, he was promoted to head up the firm's retail unit. After a lackluster performance in retail, he was reassigned to his former position in finance. Then, only eight years after joining the firm, he was promoted to Chief Financial Officer (CFO). Ultimately he was assigned responsibility for all deal development at the firm.

Fastow used the formal authority associated with these positions to obtain the compliance of those beneath him in the chain of command. For example, when Fastow was CFO, the second of the three treasurers to serve under him, Jeff McMahon, assigned a subordinate, Bill Brown, to negotiate a deal in which Enron would purchase an investment held by one of its SPEs. The SPE, named Chewco, was officially managed by Michael Kopper and surreptitiously owned by Kopper and Fastow. The negotiations stalled on the profit to be earned by Chewco and thus Kopper and Fastow. Kopper sought a $10 million profit. But the subordinate Brown, backed by McMahon, thought this amount was overly generous. Eventually Fastow leaned on Brown to complete the negotiations quickly and in accordance with Kopper's conditions, which he did. Eichenwald (2005: 158) characterized Brown's response to Fastow's final exhortation to wrap up the negotiations in this way, "He couldn't shake the feeling that he had just been warned by Fastow to back off—a warning he figured he probably better keep in mind."

Fastow also used his formal authority to staff his chain of command with subordinates who were likely to support his wrongful activities, thus reducing the need to translate his formal authority into influence to overcome resistance to his directives. For example, he invited a skilled lawyer, Kristina Morduant, to join his special projects group partly because he knew her to be willing and able to "work in the grey areas." He also bypassed people whom he thought were unlikely to support his wrongful activities. For example, he contemplated promoting a skilled executive, Ray Bowen, to a higher position within finance. But after Fastow learned that Bowen was reluctant to take advantage of his position for personal gain, he deferred Bowen's promotion and eventually transferred him to another unit. Finally, he dismissed people he knew were disinclined to support his activities. For example, he fired one treasurer, Bill Gathman, after Gathman supplied Moody's Investors Services with unvarnished accounting numbers that nearly provoked it to downgrade Enron's bond rating. Then he pressured Gathman's successor, Jeff McMahon, to resign when he opposed him on Chewco and a variety of other matters. Fastow replaced McMahon with Ben Glissan, who previously had proved himself a faithful subordinate. Glissan, finally, did not disappoint.

INFORMAL POWER
Capacity to cope with critical contingencies
In addition to possessing formal authority, Fastow developed the capacity to cope with Enron's critical contingencies. And he used the informal power to which this capacity gave rise to enlist the support of his superiors in the war he waged against those who opposed his illegal SPEs. Enron's top management was preoccupied with doing deals (e.g. to build electric generating plants, to buy and sell natural gas, and even to develop water distribution networks) because doing deals helped the firm meet earnings targets set by Wall Street analysts. Top management was focused on meeting Wall Street earnings targets because failure to meet these targets threatened to undermine the firm's stock price. And the firm's stock price underpinned its capacity to raise capital in the form of bank loans, institutional and private investor stock purchases, and special project investments, which in turn supported the firm's deal-making activity. Top management's preoccupation with doing deals had some adverse side effects, though, with which the firm's top management had to cope. It led the firm to incur debt that threatened to slow the firm's deal making. It also resulted in the pursuit of questionable investments and business enterprises that sullied the firm's balance sheet, scaring off potential investors. Finally, Enron unlike most other non-financial firms, used mark-to-market accounting to value its assets. In mark-to-market accounting, assets are valued according to the price they would fetch if put up for sale. Thus, Enron's financial health depended considerably on the market value of its assets. And the market value of assets could change as a function of developments in the market for the assets, even if the assets themselves remain unchanged. Thus Enron was also preoccupied with finding ways to hedge the value of its assets.

Fastow helped Enron cope with all of these critical contingencies. He arranged deals like the Nigerian Barge sale discussed in Chapter 6, thus helping the firm meet earnings targets and sustain its stock price. More important, Fastow perfected a process called securitization in which debt is bundled into income-producing investments that can be sold to independent investors, thereby removing debt from Enron's balance sheet and generating cash that could be used for the firm's future deal-making. Further, even more importantly, Fastow implemented securitization in conjunction with the creation of special purpose entities. Fastow used SPEs to purchase the firm's securitized debt. He also used them to purchase questionable and depreciating assets, removing them from Enron's balance sheet so as to prevent them from undermining its attempt to raise yet more capital. Finally, Fastow used SPEs to attract outside capital to fuel the firm's ongoing deal-making and to hedge its assets.

Fastow's ability to cope with Enron's critical contingencies caused those who had a vested interest in addressing the contingencies, especially Enron's chief executive officer, Jeff Skilling, to become dependent upon him. Skilling was the mastermind of Enron's new business model, which combined investments in the production of energy (and increasingly other resources such as water), the trading of energy resources (and increasingly other resources such as Internet bandwidth), and securitization. He developed the basic concept while a McKinsey consultant working for Enron and implemented the first prototype, dubbed the "gas bank," after joining the firm as head of Enron's finance division. As the business model flourished, Skilling was promoted first to chief operating officer and then CEO.

Skilling recognized his dependence on Fastow and bowed to his preferences. At one point an associate, Rebecca Mark, advised Skilling to be wary of his three most senior managers, of whom Fastow was one. Skilling brushed the warning aside, saying, "Well, those are the people I depend on. Those are the people who got me where I am" (Eichenwald 2005: 185). Other Enron executives also recognized Fastow's importance to Skilling. When a senior executive wondered out loud why Skilling put so much trust in Fastow, Enron accountant Cliff Baxter answered, "Skilling sees Andy as a problem solver" (Eichenwald 2005: 235). Thus it should come as no surprise that Skilling typically approved Fastow's propositions and went to bat for Fastow when he met opposition. One instance stands out.

Vince Kaminski was a member of Enron's risk assessment group, responsible for conducting due diligence on the firm's proposed deals. Kaminski was called in to examine one of Fastow's earliest illegal SPEs, Swap Sub, and quickly concluded that the proposed entity was flawed. Kaminski brought the problem to Fastow's attention and suggested a solution, but was brusquely rebuffed. Unbeknownst to him, the proposed fix interfered with Fastow's plans to use the SPE illegally for personal gain. So Kaminski then brought his concerns about Swap Sub to the head of Risk Assessment, Rick Buy. Buy instructed him to prepare a more detailed analysis of the SPE and promised to oppose the deal if the additional scrutiny confirmed Kaminski's initial assessment. But before Kaminski could complete his analysis, Fastow gained approval for the deal from Enron's board. And Buy was unable to convince the board to revisit its decision, even after Kaminsky submitted his detailed analysis that showed the deal was not only flawed, but contained conflicts of interest and a payout structure disadvantageous to Enron shareholders. Shortly thereafter, Jeff Skilling phoned Kaminski to tell him that he was being transferred out of risk assessment into the firm's research unit, an Enron backwater. In an elliptical explanation for the transfer, Skilling said, "There have been some complaints, Vince, that you're not helping people to do transactions. Instead, you're spending all your time acting like cops. We don't need cops, Vince" (Eichenwald 2005: 250).

Control of resources needed by others
Fastow also developed control of resources that were scarce and important to others. And he used the informal power to which this resource control gave rise to obtain support for, and overcome opposition to, his illegal SPEs. Compensation was among the most valued resources inside Enron. And compensation hinged substantially on yearly bonuses, which were based on evaluations conducted by the firm's Performance Review Committee (PRC). Fastow was a member of the PRC and exerted considerable influence over the committee's evaluations, partly because of his elevated position in the chain of command, and partly because of his capacity to cope with the firm's critical contingencies. And he used this disproportionate influence to ensure that those who could and did support his endeavors received the highest ratings and the biggest bonuses, and that those who opposed his activities received low ratings and bonuses.

For example, Fastow used his influence in the PRC to reward Michael Kopper, his main co-conspirator, and to punish Kevin Kendall, who was a member of a risk assessment task force that uncovered problems with his cornucopia of questionable deals. Once Fastow developed a track record for using the PRC to reward supporters and punish opponents, he was able to use the threat of retaliation to gain the compliance of potential opponents. For example, Amanda Martin and Cliff Baxter successfully opposed Fastow's first illegal SPE, an entity designed to purchase an Enron-owned wind power generating facility called Calpine. In response, Fastow let it be known that he planned to punish Martin and Baxter's subordinates when they came before the PRC. This struck sufficient fear in Martin and Baxter that they backed off when Fastow presented his second, and first successful, illegal special purpose entity, RADR, which was created to purchase another Enron-owned wind power generation facility.

Fastow also developed informal power over organizations and individuals outside of Enron. As the firm grew, it became a source of lucrative business opportunities for other firms in its environment. Fastow used his control of these business opportunities to build informal power over the firms seeking to take advantage of these opportunities. It is widely known how Fastow used his control over lucrative auditing and business consulting contracts to build resource dependence-based power over Arthur Anderson, and then used this power to pressure the accounting firm to rule favorably on some of his questionable SPEs (Toffler and Reingold 2003). Less well known, Fastow used his control over lucrative investment and commercial banking business opportunities to build resource dependence-based power over the banks seeking these opportunities. Fastow kept a list on which banks were ordered according to their willingness to participate in Enron-related endeavors, and he allocated business to banks depending on their position on this list, reminding banks that he could alter their position on the list if they failed to bend to his requests.

Fastow used his informal power over investment and commercial banks to obtain their participation as outside investors in special purpose entities that they otherwise would not be inclined to support. For example, Fastow used this technique to win the participation of Credit Suisse First Boston in Swap Sub. He also used it to obtain commercial and investment bank participation in his most ambitious enterprise, LJM2. In addition, Fastow used his resource dependence-based power over investment banks to pressure them to compel their stock analysts to broadcast favorable assessments of Enron stock. Fastow denied Merrill Lynch a major role in a public offering of Enron stock, letting it be known that he was unhappy with the stock recommendations of a very highly regarded Merrill analyst, John Olson. After some back and forth with Fastow on the subject, Merrill transferred and eventually fired Olson. Fastow also denied Salomon Smith Barney a significant role in the Azurix offering, letting it be known that he was unhappy with the recommendations of its well-respected analyst Don Dufresne. Salomon soon dismissed Dufresne. In both cases the firms found enthusiastic cheerleaders for Enron stock to replace the dismissed analysts. Eichenwald writes that other investment banks "got the message" (Eichenwald 2005: 220).

How Fastow's power might have increased his propensity to create illegal SPEs at Enron

Fastow's propensity to create illegal SPEs at Enron increased over time. Fastow's first attempt to invest in an SPE, the entity intended to purchase

Calpine, was entirely above board. Fastow justified his plan to invest in the SPE by arguing that Enron resembled an investment bank, where similar arrangements were common. It was only after the firm's accountants blocked this above-board aspiration that Fastow, as strain theory would predict, arranged to invest in the SPE surreptitiously. As noted above, though, Amanda Martin and Cliff Baxter foiled this plan. Fastow's second attempt to invest in a special purpose entity, RADR, was also above board. But Enron's accountants blocked this plan as well, prompting Fastow to again pursue a surreptitious illegal arrangement. As noted above, this deal went through. Thus, initially Fastow appeared disinclined to pursue wrongful courses of action, employing illegal surreptitious means to invest in the SPEs he created only when his above-board attempts were blocked. As time went on, though, Fastow increasingly turned to illegal means of investing in and constructing his SPEs without first exploring alternative legal means to do so.

Any attempt to determine why Fastow became increasingly prone to create SPEs that were wrongful in character must be extremely speculative, because any such attempt requires one to draw conclusions about what was going through Fastow's mind at the time. Still, it seems possible that Fastow's accumulation of power increased his propensity to create illegal SPEs at Enron. First, Fastow's accumulation of power might have increased his motivation to construct illegal SPEs at Enron. His accumulation of power might have activated latent goals consistent with wrongdoing. Several of Fastow's colleagues, most obviously Vince Kaminski, found him sleazy from the start. More concretely, Fastow's accumulation of power might have increased the effort–performance and performance–outcome expectancies associated with the construction of illegal SPEs. After all, Fastow's power increased his ability to assemble illegal SPEs and enhanced his capacity to avoid detection. Second, Fastow's acquisition of resource dependence-based power might have placed him on a slippery slope to wrongdoing. His creation of SPEs required him to engage in behaviors that some of his subordinates and peers considered unethical. For example, Fastow threatened to withhold future business from Enron's banks to obtain their assistance in capitalizing his second equity fund, LJM2, a tactic that the then treasurer, Jeff McMahon, considered unethical and feared might poison Enron's other relationships with the banks and tarnish the firm's reputation more generally.

How Fastow's formal authority, informal power, and wrongdoing co-evolved over time

Andy Fastow's acquisition of power and his pursuit of wrongdoing co-evolved over time. Fastow's acquisition of formal authority was interrelated with his development of resource dependence-based power, the two types of power augmenting one another as time went on. When Fastow returned to the finance unit after his brief unimpressive stint in retail, he resolved to make himself an indispensable part of Enron's future. He began by assembling a team of highly talented individuals, named the special projects group, which was capable of coping with the firm's critical contingencies. Fastow then used his growing capacity to cope with Enron's critical contingencies to pressure Jeff Skilling to make two significant changes to the firm's organizational structure, over the opposition of several other high-ranking Enron executives. First, he requested that Skilling place a finance representative in each of the firm's major deal-making units and require those units to consult with the representative when arranging financing for their deals. This both increased the number of people reporting to Fastow and increased other units' dependence on his expertise. Second, he asked Skilling to designate finance as a profit center. This institutionalized the perception that Fastow was in charge of a unit that was critical to Enron's success.

In relatively short order, these increases in Fastow's resource dependence-based power were translated into even greater formal authority. First, Skilling promoted Fastow to the position of chief financial officer. Soon thereafter, he assigned Fastow the additional responsibility of supervising all deal-making at the firm. Both promotions went through, despite opposition from other high-level executives at the firm. Fastow then used his elevated formal authority to further enhance his capacity to cope with the firm's critical contingencies. Most importantly, he established the equity fund LJM, which provided easier access to capital needed to construct his SPEs. Fastow also used his elevated position in Enron's chain of command to advertise his capacity to cope with the firm's critical contingencies to those in even greater positions of formal authority, most importantly, the board of directors. For example, at Enron's final board meeting of 1999, the then treasurer, Jeff McMahon, reported that the firm had invested $4 billion more than budgeted in a wide variety of projects. Fastow immediately chimed in, "Anything we did that was in excess of the approved plan required my group to find additional financing" (Eichenwald 2005: 288).

In addition, Fastow's development of power was interrelated with his pursuit of wrongdoing, the two augmenting one another over time. I have already described how Fastow's formal authority and informal power facilitated his construction of illegal SPEs at Enron and might have motivated him to construct the devices at an elevated rate over time. But Fastow's construction of illegal SPEs in turn helped increase his formal power. For example, after Fastow developed special purpose entities in which he invested and from which he profited, he provided subordinates with opportunities to co-invest in and profit from them as well. Most notoriously, he invited three subordinates, Ben Glissan, Anne Yeager, and Kristina Morduant, to invest in the

Southampton deal, which netted the trio $1 million each. Such a reward to faithful subordinates likely reinforced Fastow's legitimacy as a formal authority in their eyes, worthy of being obeyed.

Fastow's construction of illegal SPEs also bolstered his informal power. As indicated above, Fastow's SPEs solved key problems for Enron. Further, his illegal SPEs tended to solve particularly sticky problems, dilemmas that could not be solved through legal means. For example, Fastow obtained the necessary outside capital for his Southhampton deal from Barclays Bank and Greenwich NatWest partly by guaranteeing the financial institutions a profit on their investments, transforming the investments into loans in violation of accounting rules. Similarly, as detailed above, Fastow arranged for Merrill Lynch to buy two Nigerian power barges it owned just before the end of the quarter and then arranged for his LJM equity fund to repurchase the barges six months later. This maneuver temporarily added $50 million to Enron's balance sheet, so that the firm could meet its earnings target. Had Fastow not controlled LJM through Kopper, this deal almost certainly would not have gone through.

Famously, in some cases Fastow's SPEs only appeared to benefit Enron. For example, Fastow created a number of special purpose entities that he pitched as hedges to lock in the market value of highly valued assets. But some of the hedges that Fastow created, such as Swap Sub, which was designed to hedge the firm's investment in Rhythms NetConnections, were flawed devices. The fact that they were flawed did not, though, undermine their utility as a source of Fastow's power. As long as his superiors thought the vehicles solved Enron's problems, they believed that they were dependent upon Fastow for the vehicle's construction. Indeed, insofar as the vehicles' flaws owed their existence to the difficulty, or even impossibility, of creating functional structures, the vehicles appeared particularly ingenious, and made Fastow appear all the more valuable. There was a perverse synergy at work here. Fastow could not have created many of the hedges legally, because they were flawed constructions, and knowledgeable outsiders would never invest in them. They could be constructed only if Fastow invested in them himself and/or if he guaranteed lenders a return on their investments. But by creating the flawed hedges, Fastow enhanced his power. Of course, by creating illegal special purpose entities that coped with Enron's critical contingencies and thus that enhanced his resource dependence-based power, Fastow became even more capable of engaging in wrongdoing.

Assessing the power structure explanation

The power structure explanation of organizational wrongdoing departs in important ways from the assumptions shared by the dominant explanations of wrongdoing. As defined here, power is a social relationship between powerful people and those who are subordinate to or dependent upon them. Thus, the impact of power on those who possess it and those who are subject to it is shaped by social interaction. Further, formal authority and informal power develop in tandem over time. And both types of power co-evolve with wrongdoing. Thus, the relationship between power and wrongdoing exhibits a crescive character.

In addition, as theorized here, the impact that power has on those subject to it departs from the other two assumptions shared by the dominant explanations of organizational wrongdoing. People who are subject to formal authority often respond to it without deliberating; that is, they respond in a mindless way. People who are subject to resource dependence-based power presumably deliberate before responding to it, but their deliberations are highly constrained. And, importantly, when people engage in a behavior as the result of their subjugation to formal authority or resource dependence-based power, they do so even though they might be disinclined to engage in the behavior.

Finally, as theorized here, the impact that power has on those who possess it departs from the dominant assumption that people deliberate mindfully and rationally before engaging in wrongdoing. The idea that the possession of power activates unconscious goals, suggests that powerful people embark on wrongdoing in a less than mindful fashion. The ideas that the acquisition of power changes the way people think about themselves and about those over whom they have power (e.g. causing them to use cognitive shortcuts) and alters the benchmark against which they evaluate future behavior (i.e. moving it closer to the line separating right from wrong) suggests that powerful people embark on wrongdoing in a less than fully rational manner.

But theory that focuses on the way power increases people's opportunities to engage in wrongdoing falls squarely within the dominant approach to understanding organizational wrongdoing. The idea that power creates opportunities to engage in wrongdoing, and in so doing increases motivation to engage in wrongdoing, assumes that people at least tacitly calculate effort–performance and performance–outcome expectancies. Further, the resource dependence-based power greased slippery slope argument is partly consistent with the dominant approach to understanding organizational wrongdoing. The idea that the acquisition of resource dependence-based power requires the pursuit of unethical behavior leaves open the possibility that people engage in a mindful and rational deliberation before deciding to employ specific strategies in their pursuit of power.

Conclusion

Since the first complex organizations were formed, managers have sought to increase the compliance of those subject to their control. Thus, from the dawn of organization theory, hierarchy and organization were considered synonymous, and hierarchical power was considered necessary to achieve coordination in organizations. As a result, organization theorists have sought to provide insights that managers can use to acquire and wield formal authority. More recently, organization theorists have recognized that resource dependence-based power is a pervasive force in organizations, and have even come to see it as necessary for healthy organizational functioning. As a result, organization theorists have sought to provide insights that managers can use to acquire and wield informal power. Hence, today most graduate schools of business include courses on power and influence in their curriculum. This makes it extremely important to understand the role power plays in organizational wrongdoing. With managers seeking to bolster their power and academics working hard on their behalf, we should remain mindful of the possible dark side of the enterprise.

Social science research has focused primarily on the ways that power can cause the relatively powerless to engage in wrongdoing. Most of this research has concentrated on one form of power: formal authority. People who are subject to formal authority embark on wrongdoing as the result of a social relationship they maintain with their superiors, a role relationship that dictates that subordinates comply with their superiors' commands. But another form of power prevalent in organizations, informal power, also can cause the relatively powerless to engage in wrongdoing. People who are subject to informal power also embark on wrongdoing as the result of a social relationship, an exchange relationship that causes people to be dependent upon those who control scarce valued resources.

Conventional wisdom on the dangers of power focuses on the way that the acquisition, possession, and use of power can cause powerful people to engage in wrongdoing. Recent social science research suggests that the use of power can produce motivational and cognitive changes in the powerful that lead them to treat those over whom they exercise influence in ways that are unethical, socially irresponsible, and even illegal. Further, I have suggested that the acquisition of resource dependence-based power can require people to engage in behaviors that are of questionable ethical character, and the perpetration of such behaviors can cause people to shift their reference points closer and over the line separating right from wrong. It is often said that the acquisition of power is both a blessing and a burden because the increased capacity to accomplish goals creates both the potential to do great good and the capacity to do great harm. But the theory presented in this chapter suggests that the acquisition, possession, and use of power does not only create the potential to do harm: it increases the likelihood that one will do harm.

Formal authority and especially informal power suppress opposition to engage in wrongdoing, but they do not eliminate it. This means that the maintenance of wrongdoing held together by power relationships is always problematic. People opposed to the wrongdoing held together by power, whether fully cognizant of that wrongdoing or unaware of its existence, are always a threat to its continuance. As such, they are quite different from the "amoral automatons" that Brief et al. (2000) and Ashforth and Anand (2003) assume are the perpetuators of organizational corruption. Thus, while power might be considered a dark force behind wrongdoing, the fact that it is needed means that the seeds of its destruction frequently are present. A sophisticated understanding of how power is accumulated can be used to defeat those who seek to use it for wrongful purposes.

Vince Kaminski's final effort to oppose Andy Fastow's special purpose entities at Enron illustrates how power can be used to combat wrongdoing. When the Raptors, a pair of highly complex SPEs designed to hedge several important Enron investments, began to unwind as the result of developments that Kaminski had earlier forecast, Fastow asked him to help repair the investment vehicle. In the process of his repair work, Kaminski discovered that the Raptors contained ethically and legally questionable provisions and, thus, that he, in pricing the deal at the beginning and devising temporary fixes over time, had unwittingly participated in wrongful behavior. This realization led Kaminski to conclude that his career at Enron was over, perhaps because he decided that he no longer wanted to remain with the firm, or perhaps because he thought he might become the subject of future criminal prosecution.

The failure of the Raptors and Kaminski's effective dissociation from the firm dramatically altered Kaminski's power relative to Fastow, to Fastow's co-conspirators such as Kopper, and to Enron's senior management more generally. On the one hand, Fastow, his associates, and Enron top management now depended on Kaminski to solve a growing crisis. On the other hand, Kaminski now was less dependent on Enron for future employment. Hence, rather than succumb to Fastow's power as he did on Swap Sub, Kaminski delivered an ultimatum to Rick Buy and refused to cooperate with Fastow's finance unit in any way. Further, he ordered his subordinates to do the same and (due to his formal power and perhaps enhanced legitimacy) they complied. Finally, Kaminski publically confronted Ken Lay when he attempted to put a positive spin on the firm's crisis as the firm came under attack from investors, stockholders, the media, and federal authorities. These efforts on Kaminski's part increased the speed with which the wrongdoing at Enron was uncovered and hastened the time when Fastow was removed from office. Unfortunately, it did not come quickly enough to save the firm and the many who suffered as a consequence of its demise.

10

Accidental Wrongdoing

Introduction

Most of the explanations of organizational wrongdoing considered under the umbrella of "the alternative approach" rest on the assumptions that organizational environments are complex and that people are boundedly rational. My extension of recent ethical decision theory, the administrative systems explanation, and the situational social influence account all are based on the assumptions that information required to conduct thorough analyses of alternative courses of action often is voluminous and/or incompletely available, and that people are limited in their ability to conduct thorough analyses of alternative courses of action even when the information needed to conduct a thorough analysis is modest and fully available. Because organizational environments are complex and organizational participants are boundedly rational, people typically face an information-processing deficit when evaluating alternative courses of action. And if people typically face an information-processing deficit when evaluating alternative courses of action, it stands to reason that they will sometimes make mistakes when choosing which course of action to follow. Because mistakes are blind with respect to the line separating right from wrong, logic suggests that some of their mistakes will lead to wrongdoing.

Information-processing deficits can lead to wrongdoing in two ways, which are distinct in theory but are difficult to disentangle in practice. First, organizational participants can *lack the information* needed to understand the wrongful character of the courses of action in which they are involved. Organizational participants can lack the information needed to make decisions for many reasons, most obviously because others intentionally withhold the information. As discussed in several of the previous chapters, in the 1950s a number of television producers conspired to rig game show contests so as to increase audience interest and respond to advertiser demands. Several of the crooked producers used a technique called "playback," in which they interviewed and pre-tested potential contestants to determine their intellectual strengths and formulate questions either to match or mismatch their expertise (depending on whether they wanted the contestant to win or lose the contest). In most cases, the contestants did not realize that the producers were tailoring the questions in this way and thus participated in the fraud unwittingly (Stone and Yohn 1992).

Second, organizational participants can *lack the capacity to process available information* that attests to the wrongful character of the course of action in which they are involved. As discussed in Chapter 7, in the late 1970s middle managers at Prudential-Bache Securities began marketing shares in limited partnerships that were billed as tax shelters with high growth potential. In increasing numbers, though, these partnerships were questionable constructions that at best were bad investments and at worst failed to meet Securities and Exchange Commission standards. All securities firms have due diligence departments charged with evaluating the soundness of the investment opportunities they market. But the Prudential-Bache due diligence department failed to discern the flimsy character of their limited partnerships, in part because the department was staffed with employees who had little prior experience in due diligence work (Eichenwald 1996).

Diane Vaughan (1999) was the first to recognize that accidents can lead to wrongdoing, although her conception of wrongdoing is broader than my definition of it, including any behavior that "deviates from both formal design goals and normative standards or expectations (1999: 273)." Vaughan identifies two types of accidents that can lead to this kind of wrongdoing, which she refers to as "organizational deviance." These two types of accidents, like the two fundamental causes of wrongdoing, are analytically distinct in theory, but can be difficult to disentangle in practice.

First, an individual (or organization) can attempt to achieve a rightful behavioral objective, but inadvertently achieve a different wrongful one. The Exxon Valdez oil spill illustrates well this type of accident. The Valdez's captain and first officer intended to steer the ship through the middle of the Prince William Sound because they understood that failure to do so might cause the ship to run aground. The ship's officers undoubtedly understood that running aground could result in damage to the ship and the loss of its cargo. They even likely realized that it could cause damage to the waterway's ecosystem and compromise the neighboring human communities' economic viability. Despite their best intentions, though, the captain and first officer failed to achieve their behavioral objective, and the feared consequences, as well as criminal indictments and civil suits, ensued (Lev 1990).

Second, an individual (or organization) can attempt to achieve a behavioral objective with the intent of producing a particular set of rightful consequences, achieve that behavioral objective, but produce unintended wrongful consequences. Bear Stearn's association with a fraudulent stock brokerage firm appears to illustrate this second type of misconduct. Bear Stearns effectively served as A.R. Baron and Company's clearing agent, but in doing so it unintentionally (or so it claimed) facilitated Baron's use of illegal boiler-room practices to pressure investors to buy stock in business ventures of dubious potential. The SEC considered Bear Stearns' involvement with Baron wrongful and sued the bank for a considerable sum, ultimately negotiating a $25 million settlement (Cohan 2009: 239).

In this chapter, I examine the factors that can give rise to accidents that constitute wrongdoing. My introductory remarks imply a two-by-two classification scheme in which accidents can be categorized according to fundamental cause (a lack of information or a lack of information processing capacity) and type (a failure to achieve behavior objectives or a failure to predict consequences of achieving behavioral objectives). I do not employ this scheme in this chapter, though, because as indicated above most accidents cannot be uniquely assigned to one of these four implied quadrants. Instead I will follow the literature on accidents and analyze them as the product of system failures at four levels of social organization: the individual, the small informal group, the formal organization, and the organizational field. And I will distinguish between two types of causal factors: faulty system design or operation and unavoidable system complexity and tight coupling.

Faulty system design or operation

Most accident researchers implicitly assume that accidents are attributable to aspects of a system's design or operation that can be altered so as to prevent system failure. Below I indicate how faulty system design and operation can lead to accidents at the individual, small informal group, formal organization, and field levels. I also consider a process through which design faults can develop at all four levels of social organization. Before beginning, though, one caveat is in order. The notion that accidents can be the result of faulty system design or operation immediately calls to mind the possibility that system designers or operators are "responsible for" accidents. And if system designers and operators are responsible for accidents, this raises the question of whether the events in question really are accidents. I consider this issue in the next to last section of the chapter.

The individual level

Individuals are the smallest integral components of social organization. Even the most capable individuals working in the simplest environments can be expected to make mistakes from time to time, because even the most capable individuals are boundedly rational, and even the simplest organizational environments exhibit some complexity. For this reason, accidents, and by extension instances of accidental wrongdoing, are endemic to organizational life. But individuals are most likely to make mistakes when their task environments are unnecessarily complex, needlessly increasing information collection and processing demands, and when conditions prohibit them from making full use of their cognitive facilities.

Task environments can be unnecessarily complex in myriad ways, too numerous and idiosyncratic to enumerate. The collision of two 747 jumbo jets on a runway at the Tenerife airport in the Canary Islands on March 27, 1977, illustrates how unnecessary task complexity on multiple dimensions can contribute to an accident. Karl Weick (1990) has conducted a penetrating analysis of this accident, upon which I draw heavily, albeit unevenly, below. The two jets collided partly because one of the jets, a Pan American Airways Boeing 747, was taking longer than expected to exit the runway on which a KLM 747 was taking off. The Pan Am jet was taking longer than expected to exit the runway for several reasons. After some difficulty (which I will discuss soon), the Pan Am crew determined that the Tenerife tower controller wished them to leave the runway using the third of its four exits. But as the crew taxied down the runway they became skeptical of the controller's exit assignment or their interpretation of it because they judged (correctly) that the third exit's configuration was extremely difficult to navigate (given the exit's tight turns and their 747's large turning radius). Thus, the Pan Am crew decided to proceed to the fourth exit. But they experienced difficulty orienting themselves to the runway's four exits because an intense fog engulfed the airport, the runway center lights were not illuminated, and the exits were not numbered. Had the task environment been simpler, the Pan Am jet might have exited the runway by the time the KLM jet began its take-off sequence (Roitsch, Babcock, and Edmunds 1979). The resulting collision resulted in the deaths of 583 passengers and crew, making it the worst disaster in aviation history to this day.

Organizational participants' cognitive capacities can be unnecessarily compromised in many ways as well. Perhaps the most obvious way is the presence of distractions. Darley and Batson (1973) were the first to demonstrate that distractions can facilitate wrongdoing. They conducted an experiment which showed that seminary students walking from one college campus building to another to deliver a short lecture were more likely to pass a person in apparent distress without offering assistance if they were distracted by the fact that they were late for the lecture. Interestingly, the seminary students were no less likely to pass the person in apparent distress when they believed that they had been assigned to deliver a lecture on the parable of the Good Samaritan, which extols the virtue of helping fellow human beings in need, as opposed to a presentation on career opportunities available to seminary graduates. That is, the hurried seminary students were likely to neglect a person in need of assistance, even when prompted to recall and contemplate a religious conviction that called for them to provide such assistance.

The role that distractions can play in the perpetration of organizational wrongdoing is illustrated by a second way in which producers rigged TV quiz shows in the 1950s. Above I indicated that producers often used the "playback" technique to tailor questions to contestants' intellectual strengths or weaknesses. In many cases producers also "warmed up" contestants before they went on the air by priming them with the same questions they were to be asked in the broadcast contests. However, the contestants did not realize that they were party to this subterfuge until they went on "the air." Once on air, the contestants' ability to incorporate this information in a cost-benefit analysis, normative appropriateness assessment, or ethical decision-making process and defect from the fraud was hampered by the distraction of competing in a contest in front of a live studio audience and, via the TV cameras, a live national audience. As a result, some contestants participated in the fraud, despite the fact that they found it abhorrent, because they were unable to engage in a thorough processing of the available information. One contestant, a minister named Reverend Charles Jackson, explained how he experienced this dilemma. "My first reaction was to say, 'No,—yes, I know this answer but I got it on a screening,' and I could see visions not only of six cases of apoplexy there, but I could see my bullet-riddled body as I passed an alley somewhere. I decided against that plan and when I got out off the stage, I even considered in my mind saying, 'Well, I don't think I ought to take this check'" (Stone and Yohn 1992: 253). Jackson refused to participate in future contests. After exploring and rejecting the possibility of returning his winnings to the producers (because he learned that he would have to pay taxes on the winnings regardless), he sent a portion of his winnings to the losing contestant.

Stress, which manifests itself when a person judges that environmental or internal demands threaten to exceed his or her resources for managing them, is one of the most frequent sources of distraction. Stress has a number of effects that can facilitate accidents. Most importantly, it can cause people to focus on the possibility of failure to meet environmental or internal demands and the likely consequences of failure, to the exclusion of attending to important aspects of the situation that influence the probability of success. Stress and its effects might have impeded the pilots of the ill-fated planes that collided on Tenerife from making full use of their cognitive capacities.

The pilot of the KLM jet was worried about further delays in his departure from Tenerife. He also worried about obstacles to the plane's expeditious trip to Amsterdam once airborne (in particular, possible flight controller delays due to heavy air traffic and air traffic controller labor actions). Moreover, the pilot worried about the consequences of those delays, most importantly, the possibility that additional delays might cause him to return to his airline's home base in Amsterdam too late to avoid exceeding flight time restrictions, which could lead to non-trivial legal penalties. The pilot also worried about the more remote possibility that the plane might be prohibited from taking off altogether, and about the potential consequences of getting stuck on Tenerife (in particular, the cost and availability of hotel accommodations for stranded passengers). The fact that the KLM pilot was a senior official at the airline, its head of pilot training, might have made him even more concerned about these possibilities. As a result, he appeared absent-minded as his plane taxied down the runway. He had to ask his first officer several times to repeat the controller's taxiing instructions, indicating that he had not taken in the instructions when the controller first issued them. He eventually took off without receiving take-off clearance.

The small informal group level

Organizational participants, of course, often work in small informal groups. And this means that accidents can stem, not just from the deficiencies of individuals, but also from the deficiencies of the small groups of which they are members. The smallest group consists of two interacting individuals. The most common cause of accidents involving two interacting individuals is miscommunication. In my first discussion of the Tenerife airport disaster, I made reference to the Pan Am crew's difficulty in making sense of the tower's runway exit instructions. Accident investigators determined that the Pan Am crew found it difficult to decipher the tower's instructions because the controller's command of the English language was poor and his accent strong. Accident investigators also determined that the KLM crew's decision to take off before the Pan Am plane exited the runway was partly due to communication problems: the result of non-standard and ambiguous language used by both the KLM pilots and the air traffic controller. The KLM first officer requested both take-off and air traffic clearance from the Tenerife controller as the plane sat at the end of the runway. The controller responded by granting the KLM plane only air traffic clearance, saying that it was "cleared to the Papa beacon", adding that it should make a "right turn after takeoff." But the KLM pilot, who overheard the controller's response to the first officer, apparently heard the words "cleared" and "takeoff" and concluded that he had been granted take-off clearance. It did not help that the first officer responded to the controller saying, "We are at takeoff" or "We are, uh, takin' off" (the black box recordings were inconclusive in this regard), which could have meant that the KLM crew either was in the take-off position or were actually taking off. The controller, perhaps unsure as to what the first officer meant, responded by saying "OK," but then paused, after which he added, "stand by for takeoff . . . I will call you." It is thought that the pilot and first officer only heard the word "OK" and interpreted it as approval to continue the take-off sequence (Roitsch, Babcock, and Edmunds 1979).

Miscommunications are consequential not only in technical environments. A miscommunication also appears to have been responsible for an accounting treatment at Enron Corporation that resulted in a material misrepresentation of the firm's assets and violated generally accepted accounting principles (GAAP). One of Enron's special purpose entities, the Raptors, was obligated to pay Enron Corporation $1.2 million. Ryan Siurek, an Enron accountant, was inclined to report the obligation under the category of "notes receivable." But before he went with his inclination, he e-mailed an Arthur Anderson accountant, Patricia Grutzmacher, to ask if she had any qualms about the proposed accounting treatment. When he did not hear back from Grutzmacher, Siurek assumed that she approved of the entry. But, in fact, Grutzmacher never opened his e-mail message.

Of course, informal groups often consist of larger numbers of individuals. And the larger a group, the more ways it can go wrong. Perhaps most notably, as groups grow in size, they tend to become differentiated with respect to roles, and they tend to evolve integrative mechanisms that allow for the coordination of the differentiated roles. While differentiation and integration generally is thought to facilitate group functioning, it sometimes can give rise to errors. Analyses of commercial airplane crashes suggest that the status hierarchy in cockpit crews sometimes shapes interaction in ways that impede the ability of crews to cope with crises. This problem also appears to have contributed to the disaster on Tenerife. The KLM first officer was relatively young and had only a few years' flying experience at the carrier. The KLM pilot was older, he was the airline's most senior pilot and its head of training, and he recently had qualified the first officer to fly 747s. This status difference between first officer and pilot appears to have influenced their interaction on the flight deck.

Immediately after maneuvering the plane into take-off position the KLM pilot began the take-off sequence, revving the engines to take-off speed. The first officer quickly bucked the status hierarchy, reminding the pilot that they had not yet received take-off clearance. Perhaps embarrassed, the pilot snapped, "I know that. Go ahead, ask." When the pilot began the take-off sequence again (because he misinterpreted the controller's response to the first officer's request for clearance), the first officer hesitated to correct his superior a second time. Although he clearly understood that they had *not* been cleared for take-off (he is heard on the black box recording re-reading the tower's message that awarded the plane only air traffic control clearance) and although he likely recognized that the Pan Am plane might still be on the runway, the first officer failed to intervene decisively—presumably fearing further admonishment from his superior. Instead he announced to the controller (and the Pan Am crew, which was listening in), "We are at takeoff" or "We are, uh, takin' off," perhaps attempting to alert all who were listening that they were in fact beginning to race down the runway.

The formal organization level

Small informal groups, of course, typically are situated in larger formal organizations. This means that accidents can stem from deficiencies, not just in individuals and small informal groups, but also from deficiencies in the formal organizations in which both are situated. Theory that explains the ways that formal organizations can fail focuses on organizational technologies and administrative structures. Most of this theory parallels the work on small groups, analyzing how faulty technological and administrative designs give rise to accidents.

TECHNOLOGICAL SYSTEMS

Technological systems sometimes are designed in ways that do not sufficiently take into account known natural scientific principles, which may lead them to fail in ways that can constitute wrongdoing. This appears to have been the case in the Vaiont Dam failure near Venice, Italy. The engineers who designed the dam were aware of the possibility that once the reservoir behind the dam was filled, its walls would be subjected to forces that might cause them to collapse. They also understood that if the reservoir's walls collapsed, a large volume of dirt, rocks, and trees would fall into the reservoir and displace an equally large volume of water that could overspill the dam. The engineers conducted pre-design analyses of the river bank's integrity. And they took corrective action in reaction to small slides that occurred after the dam began to fill and reached full capacity. But they did not forecast and plan for a slide of the magnitude that occurred on October 9, 1963. On that day, the reservoir's walls collapsed with such ferocity that 50 million cubic meters of water overspilled the dam and flooded the valley below, killing over 2,000 people (Paolini and Vacis 2000).

ADMINISTRATIVE SYSTEMS

Administrative systems also can be designed in ways that do not sufficiently take into account known scientific principles. And when this is the case, they are prone to fail in ways that can constitute wrongdoing. While the social science principles that govern administrative structures are much less well developed than the natural science principles that govern technological systems, those that do exist need to be reckoned with. For example, social scientists have conducted extensive research on the appropriate relationships between an organization's structure, technology, and external environment. Any organizational structure, technology, and environment configuration that does not conform to the social scientific principles identified by these researchers is prone to dysfunction and thus accidents.

Diane Vaughan (1996) made use of this insight in her highly influential analysis of the Space Shuttle Challenger disaster, which meets her definition of organizational deviance but not my definition of wrongdoing. It is axiomatic in organization theory that non-routine technologies (those that employ uncertain knowledge to process variable inputs) should be controlled by decentralized structures. Uncertain technologies give rise to many exceptions that can be addressed only by coordinating the behavior of organizational participants not directly linked in the chain of command. Exceptions are processed slowly and ineffectively by hierarchical structures because these structures kick them up the hierarchy until they reach a superior to whom all the affected organizational participants report. The referral process takes time. Moreover, the superior charged with resolving the exception typically lacks first-hand knowledge of the problem (Galbraith 1973).

Morton Thiokol engineers responsible for the field joints connecting sections of the solid rocket booster used to propel the Space Shuttle into orbit routinely conducted post-launch inspections of the spent boosters to check for signs of failure that might require correction. Early in the space-shuttle program, engineers noticed that sometimes the seals that were integral parts of the field joints failed to seat, eroded, and allowed hot gases to vent against the shuttle's center fuel tank. Recognizing that the venting of hot gases against the fuel tank threatened to ignite the tank, they referred the problem up the hierarchy, requesting time and resources to investigate and solve the problem. But the hierarchy was slow to react, to the considerable alarm of the engineers (Boisjoli 1987). Eventually, the engineers received some resources and time to study the problem and collected preliminary data that suggested that seal failure and hot gas blow-by increased at lower temperatures. But they could not complete their analysis and institute corrective action before the cold morning of January 28, 1986, when the Challenger was scheduled to fly its tenth mission. On that day, lacking what they thought was conclusive data indicating that the launch was ill-advised, Morton

Thiokol upper-level managers authorized launch of the shuttle, resulting in the loss of the craft and crew.

Boston's Big Dig ceiling collapse appears to provide a good illustration of how a faulty organizational structure can give rise to an accident that constitutes wrongdoing as defined in this book (Vennochi 2007). The Big Dig re-routed Boston's main traffic artery through a tunnel beneath the city's downtown area. Shortly after its completion, a concrete tile dislodged from the tunnel's ceiling and fell on a passing car, killing one of its passengers. Several subcontractors directly involved in the ceiling design and installation were fined for behaviors judged to have led to the ceiling collapse. Most germane, the project's general contractors, Bechtel Corporation and Parsons Brinckerhoff, were forced to pay fines in the hundreds of millions of dollars for failing to provide adequate coordination of the project's several ceiling subcontractors. I will return to this accident and its aftermath in the next chapter.

The field level

Organizations, of course, typically are situated in larger social aggregates, such as industries, fields of interacting organizations that might span several industries, and even societies. This means that accidents can stem from deficiencies, not just in individuals, small informal groups, and formal organizations, but also from deficiencies in the larger aggregates in which individuals, groups, and organizations are situated. To the best of my knowledge, there is no explicit theory on the way in which faulty design and operation can lead to accidents that unfold at the industry, field, or societal level, let alone the causes of accidents that unfold at these levels and constitute wrongdoing. But many analyses of debacles that unfold at the industry, field, or societal levels and that are associated with wrongdoing implicitly view the debacles as accidents. The recent mortgage meltdown in the United States and subsequent global financial crisis is among the most prominent debacles associated with wrongdoing that have been analyzed implicitly as an accident.

The mortgage meltdown consisted of a series of developments that some believe began unfolding as early as 2005. It originated in the U.S. housing market, when homeowners began defaulting on their mortgages in large numbers. The meltdown extended into the financial system when a range of financial derivatives composed of mortgages, known as mortgage-backed assets, dropped significantly in value. The investors who held these assets, most importantly investment banks and hedge funds, experienced large losses. As these investors collapsed, the pain spread to the commercial banks to which these investors were indebted. And as commercial bank losses grew, their capacity to loan money to any business, financial or non-financial, declined. In common parlance, the crisis on Wall Street spread to Main Street. Because the modern economy is global, these problems in the United States spread to Europe, Asia, the Middle East, and beyond. In the end, financial institutions and non-financial firms went bankrupt or were acquired, surviving businesses languished, and large numbers of people lost their jobs, homes, and savings. In the wake of the meltdown, an innumerable number of civil suits were filed, criminal indictments were handed down, and an impressive and still growing volume of fines and a few prison sentences were meted out.

A large number of scholars, journalists, and business executives have written about the cause of the mortgage meltdown. A handful of these commentators maintain that the meltdown was the work of individuals or organizations that intended to inflict catastrophic damage on the U.S. and world economies in order to reap financial or other gain. Taibbi (2009) has offered the purest form of this kind of analysis. He argues that Goldman Sachs intentionally engineered the meltdown so as to profit from it, as it did in a number of other previous financial debacles. Charles Perrow (2010) offers a more nuanced form of this type of analysis. He maintains that several organizations and individuals pursued courses of action that they knew could hurt investors and throw the economy into serious disarray (insofar as they had been warned by others to this effect), because they stood to gain from those behaviors. Politicians received campaign contributions for supporting legislation that gave financial institutions wide berth. Appointed officials received significant remuneration from financial institutions with which they had employment and ownership ties before and after their public service for promoting policies that granted these institutions unrestricted fields of operation. And banks marketed financial products that they knew were bad investments and then bet against them, earning profit both from their sale and from their subsequent demise (Morgenson and Story 2009).

With this said, the vast majority of analyses of the mortgage meltdown implicitly characterize the debacle as an accident, a catastrophe that resulted from ill-advised actions taken by individuals and organizations that did not intend to bring down the mortgage sector and the global financial system. The vast majority of these analyses focus on the financial equivalents of faulty system design and operator error. Those who focus on faulty system design concentrate on the regulatory system covering the U.S. financial sector, which allowed financial institutions of all stripes to escape close scrutiny and effective control. They also point to deregulation that preceded the meltdown, most notably the passage of the Commodity Futures Modernization Act and the repeal of the Glass-Steagall Act, which made the regulatory system even more porous. Finally, they expose the ineffectiveness of specific gatekeepers, such as the Office of Thrift Supervision (Glass 2009). Those who focus on operator error concentrate on apparently inept and negligent top management behavior. Indicative of this view of the crisis, the most popular book on the demise of Lehman Brothers is titled *A Colossal Failure of Common Sense* (McDonald and Robinson 2009). The most well-known book on the fall of Bear Stearns, *House of Cards* (Cohan 2009), describes in considerable detail the failure of the firm's CEO to take the firm's crisis seriously, remaining at a professional bridge tournament as the firm descended into a financial abyss. Some, though, focus on the incompetence of officials in private and public watchdog agencies, such as Moody's Investor Services (Glass 2009).

The process by which faulty system design and operation accidents unfold

Dianne Vaughan, who demonstrated how faulty administrative system designs can give rise to accidents, also has laid out the process through which accidents tend to evolve. She pointed out that many, if not most, accidents have their origins in mistakes that represent only small deviations from intended behavior or that produce consequences that differ only slightly from those anticipated. Such small deviations in behavior and consequences generally do not produce substantial negative outcomes. As a result, the perpetrators of such mistakes learn from them in a perverse way; namely, they learn that the mistakes can be tolerated. And as a result, mistakes are repeated and the procedures that generate them are embedded in organizational routines (both written and unwritten); to use Vaughan's term, they are "normalized."

The normalization of deviance is problematic for two reasons. First, it can institutionalize behaviors that organizational participants believe are safe, but that actually increase the likelihood of accidents in the future. Departures from good practice do not always lead to accidents. But if repeated enough times, they frequently do. Second, the normalization of deviance can result in behaviors that further elevate the likelihood of an accident. Deviations from good practice that do not lead to accidents and that thus are tolerated often escalate over time. In essence, people reason that if the deviations of a particular magnitude can be tolerated, then deviations of slightly greater magnitude also can be tolerated.

Vaughan (1996) uses this basic framework to explain why NASA and its subcontractors authorized the launch of the Space Shuttle Challenger despite the fact that they knew that the seals on the solid rocket booster used to propel the craft into orbit were prone to failure. As described above, engineers at Morton Thiokol, the firm responsible for manufacturing the solid rocket boosters, routinely checked the boosters after each launch. And from the earliest flights, they noticed that the seals designed to prevent leakage of hot gases where the vertical segments of the booster were joined showed signs of incomplete closure, precipitating what they called "hot gas blow-by" and creating the possibility of an explosion that could devastate the shuttle. But the engineers were unable to convince their bosses to address the problem expeditiously and were unable to convince NASA officials to postpone launches in acknowledgment of these problems. One reason why the engineers were unable to convince their bosses and NASA managers to address the problem or postpone flights in recognition of it was that the launches after which investigators found "hot gas blow-by" were successful, that is, they did not end in an explosion of the shuttle's main fuel tank. And with every successful launch that produced hot gas blow-by, the Morton Thiokol and NASA senior officials appeared to become more complacent. A similar process appears to have caused NASA officials to react slowly to evidence of a defect in the Space Shuttle Columbia's external fuel tank, which ultimately led to the craft's disintegration on re-entry to the Earth's atmosphere in 2003. NASA officials were aware that pieces of foam that covered the shuttle's external tank sometimes broke off during launch and that when the dislodged foam struck the craft, it inflicted damage to the vehicle. Officials even were aware that on what proved to be the Columbia's final launch, a piece of foam broke free from the fuel tank and struck the shuttle's wing. But they failed to act on this information, either to implement corrective action in preparation for the flight or to address the problem in flight. As William Langewiesche (2003) writes,

> Over the years strikes had come to be seen within NASA as an "in-family" problem, so familiar that even the most serious episodes seemed unthreatening and mundane. Douglas Osheroff, a normally good-humored Stanford physicist and Nobel laureate who joined the CAIB (the Columbia Accident Investigation Board) late, went around for months in a state of incredulity and dismay at what he was learning about NASA's operational logic. He told me that the shuttle managers acted as if they thought the frequency of the foam strikes had somehow reduced the danger that the impacts posed.

The Union Carbide chemical plant disaster that occurred in Bhopal, India on the evening of December 2–3, 1984, provides a good illustration of how the normalization of deviance can facilitate accidental wrongdoing (Shrivastava 1991; Steiner and Steiner 1994). On that night, contrary to protocol, a large volume of water flowed into a tank containing methyl isocyanate (MIC), a precursor to the active ingredient in the pesticide Sevin. When the water mixed with the MIC, the two substances reacted to produce highly toxic MIC vapor that escaped the containment vessel and spread to the surrounding community. The diffusing vapor caused over 3,000 deaths and many more serious injuries. In the wake of the accident, an arrest warrant was issued for Union Carbide's CEO, and indictments were handed down for several Bhopal plant managers. In addition, numerous government and private civil suits were filed. While the U.S. government refused to extradite Union Carbide's

CEO to stand trial in India, the plant managers were tried, convicted, and sentenced to prison, and Union Carbide agreed to pay $470 million in compensation.

Post-accident investigations revealed that the plant had sequentially placed a number of safety devices off-line in the months preceding the accident, devices that if in place might have prevented the accident or at least reduced the severity of its consequences. One device, a refrigeration unit that could have kept the water-MIC mixture from vaporizing, was disabled to save money. Two devices, a scrubber that could have chemically degraded the toxic MIC vapor and a flare tower that could have incinerated it, were placed off-line to facilitate maintenance. Post-accident investigations also revealed that economic pressures had led managers to reduce staffing levels at the plant in the months leading up to the accident. Most notably, management left unfilled a maintenance position responsible for the installation of a "slip blind" which, if properly installed, could have prevented water from mixing with the MIC and setting off the catastrophic chemical reaction. In each case, the shutdown of safety devices and reduction in staffing levels was not promptly followed by negative consequences. As a result, the successive disabling of safety devices and reductions in staffing levels likely lulled the plant's operators into believing that the devices and additional staff were not really necessary.

The role of incentives and culture in "avoidable" accidents

Accidents can have their origin in perverse incentive structures. Sometimes organizational participants are rewarded for pushing ahead without checking their work to make sure it is error-free. Occasionally they are punished for going slowly and checking their work. Prudential-Bache marketing reps were encouraged to sell limited partnerships at an accelerating pace to shore up the firm's weak financial position. Those who were successful at doing so were rewarded handsomely with large bonuses, even when they sold partnerships at suspiciously high rates; rates that suggested they were not checking to make sure that the investments served their clients' best interests. Those who asked questions about the integrity of the partnerships were passed over for promotions and, in some cases, were given less lucrative assignments (Eichenwald 1996).

Accidents also can have their origin in malformed cultures. Sometimes cultural norms, values and beliefs, and assumptions discount safety concerns. Enron's culture appeared to include the assumption that its managers were infallible, an assumption reflected in the title of the most well-known book on the firm's demise, *The Smartest Guys in the Room* (McLean and Elkind 2004). In keeping with this assumption, Enron top managers implicitly considered the due diligence unit, which was tasked with double-checking the wisdom of the firm's dealmakers' transactions, to be superfluous and treated it as such. Of course, incentive structures and cultural content tend to go hand in hand, partly because incentive structures can have both practical and symbolic impact. Thus, at Enron, employees were rewarded handsomely for each deal they closed. But employees were not rewarded for identifying problems with proposed deals. In fact, quite the contrary, as described in Chapter 9, employees such as Vince Kaminski were punished for finding problems with deals.

Nevertheless, I suspect that we overestimate the extent to which accidents are the product of incentive structures and cultures. As indicated in Chapter 2, we tend to assume that most wrongdoing has its origins in economic and cultural structures. Thus, some have maintained that the horrendous accident that unfolded in the Union Carbide plant in Bhopal had its origin in a perverse incentive structure and malformed culture. Post-accident investigators focused on the relative lack of attention that local managers paid to maintaining safety devices and attributed that inattention to economic pressures and a corresponding unrealistic faith in the plant's technology. Further, Union Carbide officials argued and OSHA investigators agreed that differences in the incentive structures and cultures at comparable MIC plants in the United States made it unlikely that a similar accident would take place elsewhere. But less than a year later, a similar accident did occur in the United States, suggesting that while a misaligned incentive structure and perverse culture might have played a role in the Bhopal accident, incentives and cultural content were not the sole causes of the accident (Perrow 1999).

Unavoidably complex and tightly coupled systems

Most researchers assume that accidents are the product of faulty system design or operation, aspects of a system's design or operation that can be altered in ways that will prevent system failure in the future. Thus, all of the accidents described above were followed by corrective action of some sort. For example, in the wake of the Tenerife airport disaster, regulations mandating the use of standard language in communications between air traffic controllers and airplane crews were passed. Further, guidelines calling for reduced emphasis on hierarchical relations among cockpit crew and increased use of team decision making were promulgated. But Charles Perrow (1999, 2007) has argued that many accidents are not the result of faulty design or operation that can be corrected by design modification and increased training. He maintains that some systems are prone to accidents, and that attempts to redesign them not only will fail, but often will make matters worse. Perrow developed his framework at the organizational level of analysis and focused on technological systems. I will elaborate his highly influential approach. Then I will indicate how it has been extended to the field level of analysis.

The organizational level

Perrow contends that technological systems are prone to accidents when they are inherently complex and tightly coupled. He calls the accidents produced by complexity and tight coupling "system accidents" or "normal accidents," the former indicating the systemic character of the accidents and the latter indicating their inevitability. In Perrow's framework, technological systems are subdivided into component parts, many of which are systems themselves (that is, subsystems). Systems are complex when they include many complex interactions. Complex interactions are unanticipated interrelationships between a system's components. Interactions may be unanticipated because they are not designed into the system or because they, although designed into the system, occur infrequently. Complex interactions also are unmanageable. Interactions may be unmanageable because they are not readily visible or because they, although visible, are difficult to comprehend. Thus, in complex systems, relationships appear where none are expected. And when they appear, they are overlooked or misinterpreted.

Technological systems are tightly coupled when the interacting components of which they are composed are related in a "direct" fashion. Perrow considers two components to be related in a direct fashion when a change in one produces an immediate and invariant change in the other. A change in one component produces an immediate change in another when a change in the first component precipitates a change in the second that follows in very short order. A change in one component produces an invariant change in another when a change in the first component precipitates a change in the second component that occurs with certainty and completeness (e.g. when A occurs, B—and not ½ B or ¼ B—always follows). Thus, to use Perrow's term, there is not much "give" in tightly coupled systems. If A is present (or if A is present in conjunction with B), C eventuates with certainty, immediacy, and in totality. There is little that anyone can do to slow down or divert the process.

Perrow examines a variety of complex tightly coupled systems, including petrochemical refineries, nuclear power plants, commercial airliners, and ocean-going ships. He demonstrates that each of these systems is prone to system or normal accidents. Typically the accidents in these systems begin with a routine inevitable failure in one component, such as the wearing out of a part, that could not be avoided indefinitely and that precipitates subsequent unanticipated and unmanageable changes in one or more other subsystems. Sometimes interactions between subsystems are unanticipated because they coincide with unique, but inevitable, conditions. Some unique inevitable conditions stem from developments in the environment of the system (e.g. an unusually high or low temperature). Some stem from developments in the system (e.g. a component failure that produces an unexpectedly high level of a chemical reagent).

Perrow notes that much effort has been devoted to reducing the likelihood of accidents in each of the systems he studied and acknowledges that some of this effort has been to good effect. But he points out that many of these efforts entail the creation of new subsystems. And these new safety subsystems, like all subsystems, are themselves susceptible to failure. Moreover, they often interact in complex ways with the larger systems of which they are a part. In most cases, safety subsystems monitor the performance of the systems they are designed to safeguard (setting off alarms when performance degrades). In many cases, though, safety subsystems also control other subsystems of the larger system (automatically correcting or shutting down subsystems or the entire system when performance degrades). As a result, they typically increase the system's coupling and complexity because they automate and obscure the interactions they control. Thus, ironically, the addition of safety subsystems can increase a system's propensity to fail in unexpected and unmanageable ways. Indeed, many of the accidents Perrow documents contain an interaction in which a safety subsystem fails, or include an interaction in which a failing subsystem and the safety subsystem interrelate in unexpected ways, exacerbating the accident.

I think the Union Carbide pesticide plant accident in Bhopal, India provides a good example of how complexity and tight coupling can facilitate accidental wrongdoing (Shrivastava 1991; Steiner and Steiner 1994). The pesticide plant, like most chemical plants, consisted of an extensive network of pipes, storage tanks, and reaction vessels, whose interconnections were regulated by a large number of control and safety valves. Designers both articulated the possible connections among pipes, tanks, and vessels, and elaborated a protocol for activating valves so as to establish specific connections and set in motion or stop particular chemical reactions. But despite the designers' efforts, the system still contained some mystery. The number of possible connections was very large. Further, the actual connections were not completely dictated by the designer's protocols. This is partly because physical events, such as clogs and leaks, sometimes obstruct or divert flows in unexpected directions.

On the night of December 2–3, 1984, a supervisor at the plant ordered a subordinate to flush with water pipes in the vicinity of three MIC tanks, a routine procedure employed to prevent residue build-up in the pipes. But a clog in one of the pipes blocked the water from flowing in the intended direction and caused it instead to flow back into a series of pipes that led to one of the MIC tanks, where it reacted with the MIC liquid and produced the toxic MIC vapor that escaped from the tank and reeked havoc on the surrounding community. The operator could readily see that the water was not flowing in the intended direction as it did not exit the system of pipes as expected. But he (and his superiors) could not see that the water was flowing back toward the MIC tank. Further, there are reasons why the operator and his supervisors would not expect the water to flow back towards the MIC tank.

The system of pipes that connected back to the MIC tank had only been installed in the past year to facilitate maintenance of the system. Further, a control valve that typically closed off the route to the MIC tank was left open, probably because the valve was used to control flows *out* of the MIC tank into a reaction vessel (not *back* into the MIC tank) and the tank was not currently in use. Finally, a "slip blind" used to close off the MIC tank from the rest of the plant was not inserted, perhaps because the employee responsible for inserting the slip blind recently had departed the firm and his position had been left vacant. Because the operator and his supervisors were not aware of the unique confluence of clog, control valve setting, and slip blind omission (and likely could not have predicted the consequences of this unique combination of conditions were they aware of it), they did not react promptly to evidence of the pipe clog. They continued the flushing operation for a considerable period of time, even after they became aware of the clog. Further, after suspending the flushing procedure, they postponed addressing the clog and its possible consequences to allow for a tea break.

When the control-room operators finally became aware of a problem in the MIC tank, it was too late to avoid its consequences (especially in light of the fact that, as discussed above, several safety devices had been deactivated). They struggled to diagnose and correct the problem because they could not directly observe the chemical reactions taking place in the tank and could not keep pace with the velocity of the reactions. They examined pressure and temperature gauges, which they saw were generating rapidly climbing readings. Presumably because these devices are subject to failure, they also listened to and felt the MIC tank, which they found to be hissing and hot to the touch. By the time the operators were convinced that something was seriously wrong, MIC vapor had begun to escape the tank and diffuse to the surrounding community.

The field level

While Perrow formulated normal accident theory at the organizational level of analysis, it has been used at the field level of analysis. Most notably, Mezias (1994) used normal accident theory to analyze the U.S. Savings and Loan Crisis of the 1980s, which I discussed in Chapter 4 in connection with the rational choice account. He contends that the S&L crisis was the product of increasing complexity and tight coupling in the industry. Over the decades leading up to the crisis, financial markets became global, trading became continuous (round the clock), new technologies were instituted, the pace of transactions accelerated, new sophisticated financial instruments were created, and a bewildering array of government regulations were promulgated, all of which increased the number of unexpected and unmanageable interactions.

I think normal accident theory also can be used to analyze the recent mortgage meltdown and subsequent financial crisis of 2008. I present a detailed normal accident analysis of the mortgage meltdown to illustrate the impressive topical flexibility of this theory and to provide an empirical foundation for the final two issues to be addressed in this chapter: the relationship between the two types of accidents considered here and modes of analysis that focus on intentional behavior, and the multidimensional character of the relationship between accidents and wrongdoing. To analyze the mortgage meltdown as a normal accident, one must establish that the financial system, especially that part of the system that processed home mortgages, was complex and tightly coupled before the meltdown. One also needs to demonstrate that the meltdown unfolded as the result of complex and tightly coupled interactions. My analysis of the meltdown proceeds with these two objectives in mind.[1]

THE FINANCIAL SYSTEM AS A COMPLEX AND TIGHTLY COUPLED SYSTEM

The financial system, especially that part of the system that processed mortgages, became increasing complex in the years leading up to the mortgage meltdown, that is, it became characterized by an increasing number of relationships that were both difficult to anticipate and hard to manage. Until about 1970, buyers entered the housing market, and lenders (mostly savings and loan institutions) wrote mortgages to facilitate buyers' home purchases, typically holding the mortgages as investments.

In the late 1970s, financial innovators began securitizing mortgage debt, which transformed the simple mortgage transaction stream into an extensive network of branching relationships. Mortgage holders, either the lenders that wrote the mortgages (such as Countrywide Financial) or diversified financial

---

[1] The following discussion borrows heavily from two articles co-authored with Michael Maher: "A Normal Accident Analysis of The Mortgage Meltdown," which appeared in *Research in the Sociology of Organizations* (2010) and "The Mortgage Meltdown as Normal Accidental Wrongdoing," which appeared in *Strategic Organization* (2010). It also dovetails with other normal accident analyses of the global financial crisis formulated by Cebon (2009), Guillen and Suarez (2010), and Van der Heijden, Ramirez, Selsky, and Wilkinson, (2011).

institutions that purchased them from lenders (such as Lehman Brothers), began bundling the mortgages into multi-tiered bonds called collateralized debt obligations (CDOs), which were then sold to investors, many of which were diversified financial institutions (such as Bear Stearns) or independent hedge funds (such as Peloton Partners). Often the diversified financial institutions that purchased the CDOs re-combined their component tiers into second order bonds (CDO^{2}s) that they then sold to still other investors.

In 2000, David Li developed a mathematical formula that enhanced the securitization process by facilitating the bundling of subprime mortgages, which promised high rates of return but were at significant risk of default, such that the bundled mortgages' default risks counterbalanced each other. The resulting derivatives were exceptionally popular with investors because they promised high rates of return and relative safety. The enhanced securitization process had two important features from the standpoint of normal accident theory. First, it was difficult to comprehend. It produced derivatives that had multiple moving parts (mortgages and tranches of mortgages) that related to one another in complicated ways. Further, each derivative was somewhat unique, being created with a different mix of mortgages, having a particular tranche structure, and linking the underlying mortgages to the CDO holder in a wide variety of ways (Bookstaber 2007). Second, the new securitization process created mortgage-backed securities that were very difficult to value because each CDO was composed of a large number of individual mortgages, the values of which were interdependent. As a result, different firms and even different units of the same firm often developed very different valuations of the same assets (Story 2008).

Several aspects of the way investment banks and hedge funds made investments, both in mortgage-backed securities and other securities, added to the complexity of the mortgage field. Most importantly, investment banks and hedge funds tended to engage in arbitrage, which entails making relatively sure bets for relatively small gains. In order to make a substantial profit on arbitrage, banks and funds had to wager large sums of money. They did this by taking on very large loans from multiple commercial banks. Thus, each investment bank tended to be interconnected with a number of commercial banks whose fates hinged on its success.

Tight coupling
The financial system, especially that part of the system that processed mortgages, also was tightly coupled in the years leading up to the mortgage meltdown. The financial system became increasingly tightly coupled as the result of deregulatory reforms such as the Commodity Futures Modernization Act. As a result of these reforms, market actions and reactions for the most part played out without government intervention that might slow the pace or alter

the trajectory of market interactions. In addition, technological advances and market developments shortened the period of time between the occurrence of financially relevant events, the dissemination of information about those events, and the trading of securities on the basis of those events, all on a global scale. Management information systems circulated financial information immediately, and computer programs produced trading responses to that information instantaneously. Both this information and the responses to this information were transmitted around-the-clock and worldwide (Bookstaber 2007).

Further, the lending arrangements linking investment banks and hedge funds to commercial banks contained little "give." First, most investment banks and hedge funds borrowed on margin. When they borrowed from commercial banks, they were required by their lenders to set aside a pool of assets or collateral that the lenders could seize if pre-specified triggers indicative of the bank's or fund's inability to repay their loans were reached. Further, lenders in turn were required by banking regulations to set aside cash reserves to cover the loans they made. These margin and cash reserve requirements were intended to protect borrowers and lenders from financial events that might precipitate a crisis. But like safety devices in chemical plants, they increased coupling. Investment banks, hedge funds, and commercial banks had few alternatives when their financial health and loan portfolios deteriorated to the pre-specified levels: when triggers were reached, they had to sell assets to generate cash.

Second, most investment banks and hedge funds borrowed on a short-term basis, even though the borrowed money was used to make long-term investments. In fact, much of the short-term financing was obtained on a daily basis. If banks or hedge funds had long-term financing, they could survive short-term declines in their financial health because they had substantial time to obtain new loans, during which they could work to re-establish their financial health. But banks or hedge funds that have short-term financing cannot survive short-term declines in their financial heath because they have relatively little time (in some cases, no more than twenty-four hours) to improve their financial health before they have to obtain new loans.

Mark-to-market and mark-to-model accounting

Two accounting methods used to value assets were particularly important sources of complexity and tight coupling in the pre-meltdown financial system and for this reason deserve separate treatment.[2] The mark-to-*market*

---

[2] A unique form of financial derivative that was developed to insure mortgage-backed assets in the years leading up to the meltdown, the credit default swap, was also an important source of complexity and tight coupling in the financial system. I do not discuss this "safety device" here, though, because doing so would not add additional theoretical insights.

method valued assets and liabilities according to their market worth. This method was used to price liquid assets and liabilities that were traded in active secondary markets, where prices were publicly posted. The mark-to-*model* method valued assets and liabilities using forecasting models. This method was used to price illiquid assets and liabilities that were not actively traded on a secondary market and for which posted prices were not available. In some cases, mark-to-market and mark-to-model accounting provided the foundation for negotiated agreements between transaction partners who were required to arrive at compatible valuations of the assets they exchanged.

Mark-to-*market* accounting added complexity to the financial system, by tying the asset values of one firm to the asset values of other firms in ways that created an extensive network of relationships. Under this method, when a firm alters its asset values, other firms with similar assets are required to modify their asset values. And when these other firms alter their asset values, the alterations can provoke further changes in still other firms' asset values. Mark-to-market accounting also gives rise to difficult-to-predict relationships. Firms must re-value their assets when other firms sell similar assets, taking into account those assets' selling price, even if they did not intend to sell their own assets. But they cannot anticipate when other firms will sell identical or similar assets. Mark-to-*model* accounting contributed additional complexity to the financial system. This method often entails the use of sophisticated mathematical models that are difficult to comprehend by all but the highly specialized econometricians who design them. Further, they are relatively opaque from the standpoint of outsiders, insofar as they measure the current market value of assets according to proprietary algorithms.

Mark-to-*market* accounting also tightened coupling in the financial system. Regulators articulate strict rules for marking assets that are traded on a limited basis but for which there are not quoted prices. Most importantly, they establish procedures that firms must follow when counterparties value the same assets differently. Mark-to-*model* accounting, though, loosened coupling somewhat. Firms have discretion regarding when to employ the mark-to-model method and how to implement it (Story 2008). But this discretion added an important final dimension of complexity, unpredictability, to the system. Firms cannot predict when and how other firms will use mark-to-model to value their assets and thus cannot predict when and how they will have to revalue their own identical or similar assets.

THE MORTGAGE MELTDOWN AS A NORMAL ACCIDENT

A number of conditions set the stage for the mortgage meltdown. Most importantly, federal legislation such as the Community Reinvestment Act of 1977 and U.S. Department of Housing and Urban Development policies in the 1980s motivated, and in some cases required, lenders to loosen lending criteria so as to increase the number of mortgages written for low-income homebuyers, increasing the supply of subprime mortgages. At the same time, the Federal Reserve Bank lowered interest rates, causing investors to seek new higher-return investment vehicles, increasing the demand for subprime mortgages.[3]

From the standpoint of normal accident theory, each mortgage can be considered a part in the mortgage subsystem, each default can be considered a part failure, and unexpectedly high default rates can be considered an unexpectedly high part failure rate. Mortgage default rates began to increase in 2006. The most frequently cited cause of rising default rates was the increasing number of low quality (i.e. default-prone) subprime mortgages entering the system. Most financial industry participants expected a good number of mortgages, especially subprime mortgages, to default. But they believed that the securities backed by these mortgages, assembled using sophisticated mathematical algorithms designed to balance the underlying mortgage risks, were constructed in a way that could tolerate a good number of failures. But, the number of defaults that eventuated in 2007 overwhelmed the technology. This set in motion developments that at the time were experienced as unexpected and baffling. As the default rate increased, the value of the securities based on those mortgages declined. But the financial institutions that held the sophisticated mortgage-backed assets, as well as their counterparties, lenders, and investors, found it difficult to estimate the precise effects of the defaults on the value of the assets. Some institutions sensibly, but somewhat arbitrarily, reduced valuation of their assets. Others holding similar assets, bound by mark-to-market accounting requirements, were forced to do the same. This led to a downward spiral of asset valuations.

The downward spiral in asset valuations caused lenders to make margin calls, and this caused investment banks such as Bear Stearns and Lehman Brothers to liquidate their positions. Further, banking regulations required lenders to increase their cash reserves by liquidating their positions. As investment houses and lenders sought to liquidate their positions, the value of their assets declined. As the value of their assets declined, volatility in their markets increased, causing other market participants to cease trading, which precipitated a liquidity crisis, which further depressed asset prices (as desperate sellers could not find buyers for their assets). Of course, as asset prices declined further, new triggers were hit, prompting additional liquidations. Seemingly overnight, famously profitable financial institutions such as Bear Stearns and Lehman Brothers were driven to the brink of bankruptcy and dissolved into other financial entities.

---

[3] These twin developments set in motion a feedback process commonly referred to as the "housing bubble," which amplified the dynamics described here.

Importantly, many of the assets liquidated by banks were in non-mortgage-related and even non-U.S. markets because these were the most liquid assets at the time. Thus, the crisis in mortgage-related assets appeared to jump from one market to another. These jumps were almost completely unexpected because they were not driven by observable economic trends. Instead, the pattern of impacts depended on the identity of the banks experiencing trouble and the portfolios of those banks, both of which could not be predicted ahead of time because bank portfolios were largely unknown to customers and competitors. This caused the financial institutions' counterparties, lenders, and investors to withdraw from the market, precipitating the credit crunch in the domestic economy, which had repercussions on a global scale (Guillen and Suarez 2010).

Mark-to-market and mark-to-model accounting
Mark-to-market and mark-to-model accounting played a particularly important role in the mortgage meltdown. This role is illustrated well by two examples. The first pertains to a short chain of events that began at the end of April 2007, when Goldman Sachs, a counterparty of Bear Stearns' Enhanced Leverage Fund, issued an unexpectedly low valuation of some of the fund's mortgage backed assets. The chain of events is graphically chronicled in an interview given by an anonymous Enhanced Leverage Fund executive:

> They (Goldman Sachs) give us these 50 and 60 prices. What we got from the other counterparties is 98. The SEC rules say that when you do this, you either have to average them—they're meant to be averaging 97s and 98s, not 50s and 98s—or you can go ask if those are the correct marks. But you can't ask the low mark. You've got to go back and ask the high mark. Everybody knows the procedure. So we got to go ask the high mark. We ask the 98 guy—another major Wall Street firm—and you know what he says? Remember, he knows he's high now. He goes, 'You're right. We were wrong. It's 95.'... Now we got nothing we can do but take the 50 and 95 and average them. We have to repost our NAV (net asset value). And now we go from minus 6 to minus 19—minus 18.97 to be exact—and that is game fucking over (Cohan 2009: 337).

The second example pertains to a longer chain of events that began on February 14, 2008, when UBS wrote off $13.7 billion of investments in U.S. mortgage loans. UBS described this write-off as follows:

> The markets for many of these financial instruments continue to be illiquid. In the absence of an active market for similar instruments, or other observable market data, we are required to value these instruments using models.... We began using these models in third quarter 2007 and have since then continuously reviewed their assumptions and recalibrated them in the light of new market information

(UBS AG. U.S. Securities and Exchange Commission, Form 6-K, Report of Foreign Issuer. February 14, 2008, p. 2).

Because of the UBS write-downs, the hedge fund Peloton Partners was forced to write down its similar mortgage assets. This write-down provoked Peleton's creditors to demand payments that the hedge fund could not meet. Peleton's collapse in turn created problems for other financial institutions. Paul Friedman, Bear Stearns' chief operating officer of the fixed income division stated, "February 29 (2008) was the day Peloton blew up, and so you had a huge liquidation, us and others, of really high-quality stuff that went at really distressed prices . . . It was sort of the beginning of the end" (Cohan 2009: 7).

The practical implications of normal accident analysis

The normal accident approach represents a major breakthrough in our understanding of unintended and sometimes catastrophic events at the organizational and field level. It is both intuitively appealing and topically flexible, making possible eminently plausible explanations of widely divergent phenomena, from petrochemical plant explosions to financial system crises. Further, it raises fundamental questions about prevalent strategies for preventing accidents. Normal accident theory contends that standard fixes, such as the addition of safety subsystems that monitor and control the larger systems of which they are a part, will be ineffective, and might even increase the likelihood of accidents. Further, it maintains that attempts to reduce a system's susceptibility to failure should concentrate on reducing its complexity and coupling. In keeping with this general prescription, some have argued that attempts to reduce the global financial system's vulnerability to crises should focus on reducing its complexity and coupling (Schneiberg and Bartley 2010). Proponents of the normal accident theory recognize, though, that it is often not feasible to reduce a system's complexity and coupling. Thus, many normal accident theorists recommend, when possible, that complex and tightly coupled systems be replaced with alternative less complex and tightly coupled systems. For example, most advocate that complex tightly coupled technologies such as nuclear power be abandoned in favor of less complex and tightly coupled solar and wind power systems.

The relationship between types of accident analyses

Many who study accidents believe that catastrophic events of the sort analyzed here should be characterized as falling into one or the other of these three categories: as a normal accident, a faulty system design or operation accident, or an event that is the result of self-interested behavior, sometimes referred to as "agency." But attempts to categorize events into just one category typically end in controversy. For example, in apparent contradiction to my exposition, Perrow has categorized the Bhopal tragedy as the product of faulty system design and operation: in his terms, a "prosaic accident" (1999). And he has categorized the mortgage meltdown as the result of agency: caused by individuals and firms in pursuit of financial gain with at best a callous disregard for the harm they might inflict on others (2010). I think this approach has merit, because it focuses attention on the most salient causes of accidents and the most effective types of remedial action. Thus, categorizing the Bhopal tragedy as a prosaic accident appropriately draws attention to the many features of the plant's design that were ill-conceived or abrogated and points to design and operation changes that are likely to reduce the incidence and human consequences of similar accidents in the future.

With this said, I think this approach also has drawbacks. Methodological problems make it difficult to categorize events into unique categories. It is impossible to definitively determine whether an event is a normal accident rather than a non-normal one (an accident due to faulty system design and operation), because no one has offered a way to quantify either complexity or tight coupling. Further, even if someone develops a way to operationalize these two determinants of normal accidents, no one has identified the levels of complexity and coupling necessary to produce normal accidents. Further, it is hard to precisely determine the extent to which an event is the product of agency as opposed to faulty system design or operation on the one hand or complexity and coupling on the other. All human endeavors involve agency. Finally, categorizing events into unique categories inhibits a comprehensive understanding of events, ruling out consideration of causal factors that, while secondary or even tertiary, are still important. This last drawback is particularly salient in the case of multifaceted events such as the mortgage meltdown. I think the mortgage meltdown can only be understood fully if one considers complexity and coupling, faulty system design and operation, and self-interested actors.

The relationship between accidents and wrongdoing

Undoubtedly, some will question the premise underlying this chapter, that accidents, normal or otherwise, can constitute wrongdoing. Those who believe accidents are the result of faulty system design or operation typically distinguish between two kinds of unintentional calamities. The first consists of mishaps that stem from negligence on the part of designers or operators. They are not considered real accidents because negligence is considered tacitly willful, at best an absence of good intent and at worst a callous disregard for the likely consequences of one's actions. Instead they are analyzed as wrongdoing. The second kind of calamity consists of mishaps that eventuate despite the best efforts of designers and operators. They are considered true accidents and not analyzed as wrongdoing. Those who embrace the normal accidents framework also implicitly believe that normal accidents and wrongdoing are mutually exclusive. Perrow even employs a special label, "executive failure," to denote events that appear to be accidents but are the consequence of negligence in system design or operation at the highest levels (Perrow 2007). Mezias, who used normal accident theory to analyze the savings and loan crisis of the 1980s, contrasts his normal accident explanation of the crisis with a wrongdoing account, contending that the evidence fits the normal accident explanation better than the wrongdoing one (Mezias 1994).[4]

I think attempts to distinguish between inauthentic accidents that are the result of negligence on the part of system designers and operators, and genuine accidents that occur despite the best intentions of system designers and operators has merit. They draw attention to instances in which the identification and punishment of individuals considered responsible for an event that causes harm is appropriate, either to uphold norms of social justice or to reduce the incidence of future similar calamities. Thus, Perrow analyzes the mortgage meltdown as not only the result of agency but as an instance of executive failure. And in doing so, he adds impetus to the effort to identify those who bear responsibility for the crisis, so that they might be held responsible, and so that behavior such as theirs might be curbed in the future.

But I also think that this approach has drawbacks. Insofar as it is motivated by concerns of social justice, it confounds normative considerations (which pertain to the assignment of responsibility for the purpose of allocating blame) with social science considerations (which relate to the identification of the causes of phenomena). Insofar as it is motivated by a deterrence objective, it implicitly assumes that malicious intent (in this case, a lack of concern with the interests of others) is a necessary precursor to wrongdoing. I have argued that malicious intent is not a necessary precondition for wrongdoing. Moreover, conceptualizing accidents and wrongdoing as mutually exclusive by definition prohibits empirical examination of the relationship between accidents and wrongdoing.

The definition of wrongdoing that I employ in this book, which assumes that any behavior that social control agents designate as wrongful is wrongful,

---

[4] Mezias (1994) does not, though, maintain that the savings and loan crisis was solely the result of normal accident processes. He contends that the crisis was largely the product of increasing complexity and tight coupling in the industry. But he also holds that intentional malfeasance played a role in the unfolding of the debacle.

allows for an essentially unrestricted analysis of the relationship between accidents and wrongdoing. Most obviously, as I have argued in this chapter, it allows that accidents can constitute wrongdoing. The Tenerife airport accident can be considered an instance of wrongdoing because one of the parties involved, KLM airlines, was forced to pay restitution to victims of the KLM-Pan Am jet collisions. The Union Carbide Bhopal pesticide plant accident can be considered an instance of wrongdoing because the Union Carbide CEO was indicted and seven Indian executives were fined and sentenced to prison terms for safety violations.

But the definition of wrongdoing employed in this book allows that accidents can be related to wrongdoing in other ways as well. Below I explore four other ways in which accidents can be related to wrongdoing in the context of the mortgage meltdown. The meltdown constitutes wrongdoing insofar as a number of mortgage industry participants have been sued and successfully litigated, or have been indicted and successfully prosecuted for a variety of offenses related to the meltdown. But the notion that the mortgage meltdown constitutes wrongdoing can be unpacked to reveal a more fine-grained understanding of how accidents can be related to wrongdoing.

First, *wrongdoing can facilitate accidents*. Wrongdoing typically alters the state of systems, degrading inputs or processes, in ways that increase their susceptibility to failure. Several forms of wrongdoing appear to have contributed to the mortgage meltdown. In addition to the wrongdoing enumerated in my initial discussion of the meltdown above, some mortgage brokers falsified documentation attesting to homebuyers' eligibility for loans (Temple-Raston 2008). This fraudulent behavior injected additional questionably credit-worthy homebuyers into the system, supplementing the impact of federal legislation and policies that increased the supply of default-prone subprime mortgages.

Second, *accidents can facilitate wrongdoing*. Accidents often create incentives and opportunities to engage in wrongdoing. The mortgage meltdown appears to have stimulated several types of wrongdoing. It provided a variety of mortgage industry participants with an incentive to engage in wrongful behaviors in an attempt to avert the meltdown, avoid blame for the meltdown, or escape harm from the meltdown. For example, Angelo Mozilo, the founder and CEO of Countrywide Financial, is believed to have known that Countrywide was about to experience heavy losses as a result of the downturn in the housing market. But he continued to project a positive picture of the firm's and the mortgage sector's future, perhaps to shore up investor confidence in Countrywide and the industry. At the same time, he sold much of his own stock in the firm, presumably to avoid personal losses. After two years of public scrutiny and criticism, Mozilo was indicted for fraud and insider trading (Scannell and Emshwiller 2009). The mortgage meltdown also provided victims with an incentive to engage in wrongful behaviors in an attempt to escape harm. For example, homeowners and other borrowers in deteriorating financial condition have engaged in insurance fraud, such as setting their homes and cars on fire in an attempt to obtain payouts to avert the financial consequences of their impending defaults and repossessions (Tom 2009).

The mortgage meltdown also created opportunities for mortgage industry participants to engage in wrongdoing. In the wake of the mortgage meltdown, the market for mortgage modifications grew dramatically. Existing lenders altered their business models and new firms emerged to buy defaulted loans from the government at bargain basement prices and then negotiate interest rate reductions with mortgage holders, earning considerable profit while allowing borrowers to remain in their homes. Most of these entrepreneurs operated in an entirely rightful fashion, although some who previously sold subprime mortgages that helped precipitate the mortgage crisis have been criticized for benefiting from conditions that they helped to create (Lipton 2009). But some fraudulent firms have emerged in the shadow of the legitimate ones to prey on unsuspecting borrowers, falsely representing themselves as associated with government programs, negotiating new mortgage terms that leave the borrowers in worse shape than before and pocketing a profit for their bogus service. (Federal Trade Commission 2009).

Third, *accidents can lead to the detection of unrelated wrongdoing*. When accidents occur, circumstances change in ways that cause victims of unrelated wrongdoing to become aware of their injury. The mortgage meltdown appears to have led to the detection of several instances of wrongdoing that were not causally related to the meltdown. For example, Bernard Madoff and Allen Stanford orchestrated elaborate Ponzi schemes that stole hundreds of millions of dollars from investors in the years leading up to the mortgage meltdown (Gaviria and Smith 2009; Creswell and Krauss 2009). As the meltdown unfolded, investors sought to liquidate their Madoff and Stanford holdings so as to place them in safer investment havens. When they did, the investors found that Madoff and Stanford could not meet their liquidation requests because the two fund managers had spent their money rather than investing it.

In addition, when accidents occur, social control agents swing into action in search of wrongdoing and wrongdoers ostensibly to serve justice (i.e. to punish those responsible and extract compensation for those victimized) and to reduce the likelihood of future accidents. And when social control agents swing into action, they frequently cast a wide net. In some cases they apprehend actors who clearly are engaged in wrongdoing related to the accident. But in other cases they snag actors engaged in wrongdoing that is largely unrelated to the accident. For example, the FBI had hundreds of mortgage fraud cases under way at the onset of the mortgage meltdown. In the immediate wake of the meltdown, it organized its mortgage fraud investigation activities into a high-profile program that it dubbed "Operation Malicious Mortgage" (Burns 2008). This program and related efforts drew considerable attention and raised the prospect of adding staff to the division of the agency tasked with investigating fraud, staff that it had lost to counterterrorism efforts in the wake of the September 11 attacks (Barrett 2009). Similarly, fair housing activists and the NAACP had for years been assailing mortgage lenders for discriminating practices, such as red-lining—denying or increasing the costs of mortgages to areas that were predominately populated by people of color. In the immediate aftermath of the mortgage meltdown, their attention turned to subprime loans (Tedeschi 2007; Appel 2009). While it is likely that some of the fraudulent and discriminatory lending that was the target of the FBI and the NAACP contributed to the mortgage meltdown, much of it was probably tangential to the meltdown. Indeed, two of the three main types of wrongdoing targeted by the FBI's Operation Malicious Mortgage pertained to offenses made possible by the meltdown: foreclosure rescue scams and mortgage-related bankruptcy schemes (Federal Bureau of Investigation 2008). And one of the biggest cases pursued in the post-meltdown period involved a garden-variety fraud that entailed the overvaluation of properties in exclusive California enclaves to obtain larger than necessary loans, which were then used to fuel other investments (Schmitt, Christensen, and Reckard 2008).

In fact, in some instances, social control agents focus on wrongdoing that is unambiguously tangential to the accident that gave rise to the enforcement effort. For example, as the mortgage meltdown unfolded, information emerged indicating that two U.S. senators obtained special reduced-interest rate loans from Countrywide Financial. In a much-publicized effort, several of their senatorial colleagues pushed for an investigation of the two senators, one of whom was Connecticut Senator Christopher Dodd (Herszenhorn 2008). While the investigation ended in only a mild rebuke of the senators, it figured in Dodd's decision to forgo running for re-election in 2010 (Nagourney 2010). Of course, the two senators' Countrywide loans in no way contributed to the mortgage meltdown.

Fourth, *accidents can lead to broader definitions of wrongdoing, which create the possibility of new forms of wrongdoing in the future.* As just indicated, when accidents occur, social control agents swing into action in an attempt to identify wrongdoing and wrongdoers. But social control agents often are hampered in their effort to identify wrongdoing and wrongdoers by current interpretations of existing codes and by the codes themselves. Accidents, especially normal accidents, are often the product of behaviors that typically do not give rise to calamities. That is why they are called accidents! As a result, the behaviors that cause accidents tend not to violate existing interpretations or definitions of wrongdoing.

The problems faced by social control agents in this regard are illustrated well by the Federal Bureau of Investigation's effort to prosecute the managers of two failed hedge funds that were heavily invested in mortgage backed assets—the Bear Stearns-affiliated High Grade and Enhanced Leverage funds. According to the FBI, the funds' managers, Matthew Tannin and Ralph Cioffi, told investors that the funds were in sound condition and that they were maintaining (and even contemplating increasing) their own stakes in the funds. But in fact, the funds were deteriorating in value and the fund managers were reducing their investments in them. The FBI indicted the two executives for fraud and insider trading, contending that their behavior, like Angelo Mozilo's conduct described above, was motivated by the desire to maintain investor confidence in the funds (and to thus stave off collapse of the funds) and to preserve their careers and wealth (Chittum 2008). However, when brought to trial, Tannin and Cioffi were acquitted of all charges. The defense argued persuasively that the hedge fund managers' behavior, which in hindsight (i.e. in light of the funds' eventual demise) appeared suspicious, was at the time entirely within the bounds of accepted practice and the law (Kouwe and Slater 2010).

The opportunity to offer new interpretations of existing codes is greatest in the area of civil law, especially tort law, where underlying principles are broad. Thus, a number of civil suits have been filed against subprime lenders that characterize their practices as predatory, taking advantage of borrowers' economic weaknesses and relative ignorance (Appel 2009). Eleven states reached a $8.4 billion agreement with Countrywide Financial, now owned by Bank of America, to renegotiate the unfair terms of mortgages sold by the lender at the height of the housing boom (Morgenson 2008). The State of Massachusetts negotiated a $10 million settlement with subprime lender Fremont Investment and Loan for what it contended were unfair lending practices. More recently, Massachusetts reached a $60 million settlement with Goldman Sachs for its role in the securitization of questionable subprime mortgages. Middle-class victims of predatory refinancing schemes, as well as non-profit legal service agencies (and entrepreneurial lawyers willing to defer compensation until settlement) acting on behalf of lower-class victims, also have filed suits against lenders. But these less well-endowed and less politically powerful victims are not likely to have much success in their cases, which are very expensive and time consuming to prosecute (Luhby 2009).

Assessment and conclusion

The accidental behavior explanation of wrongdoing departs from the dominant approach to explaining wrongdoing more than the other alternative explanations considered so far. The perpetrators of accidental wrongdoing, by definition, do not engage in mindful and fully rational deliberation before embarking on their wrongdoing. Further, again by definition, they do not develop a positive inclination to engage in the wrongdoing in question. Instead, their mindlessness and boundedly rationality lead to behaviors that they are not inclined to perpetrate and/or consequences that they are not inclined to produce. The notion that many accidents are produced over time through the normalization of deviance explicitly takes temporal dynamics into account. Further, most theories of accidents take into account social interaction, either explicitly, as is the case with theories that focus on small group interaction, or implicitly, as is the case with theories that focus on organizational and field-level technologies and administrative structures.

Some think that accidents and wrongdoing are mutually exclusive because they believe that a behavior can only qualify as wrongdoing if its perpetrators possessed at least a minimal level of malevolent intent, that is, if they possessed at least a reckless disregard for the welfare of others. But because I define wrongdoing as any behavior that social control agents define as wrongdoing and thus conceptualize wrongdoing independent of perpetrators' intent, I argue that accidents can constitute wrongdoing. Further, with this broad outlook in mind, I identify four more fine-grained ways in which accidents and wrongdoing can be related to each other. The last of the four ways, in which accidents lead to new definitions of wrongdoing, which in turn make possible new forms of wrongdoing in the future, lays the foundation for this book's final substantive chapter. If accidents lead to new definitions of wrongdoing, which in turn make possible new forms of wrongdoing in the future, then it stands to reason that social control agents who draw the new lines separating right from wrong share in the production of wrongdoing. Further, if social control agents share in the production of wrongdoing, it stands to reason that we need to analyze the determinants of social control agent behavior in order to develop a complete understanding of the causes of wrongdoing. It is this final matter to which I now turn.

11

The Social Control of Organizational Wrongdoing

Introduction

The social control explanation of organizational wrongdoing is the final account of wrongdoing that I will consider in this book. It follows from the normal organizational wrongdoing perspective presented in Chapter 2, which views wrongdoing as a ubiquitous phenomenon produced by social control agents in the course of stipulating rightful behavior. It also builds on the sociological definition of wrongdoing elaborated in Chapter 3, which defines wrongdoing as any behavior labeled as wrongful by social control agents. The normal organizational wrongdoing perspective and my definition of organizational wrongdoing imply that social control agents create wrongdoing, albeit in a much different way than the perpetrators of wrongdoing do. Thus, if one wants to develop a comprehensive understanding of the causes of organizational wrongdoing, one must study the role that social control agents play in creating wrongdoing. But organization studies scholars interested in wrongdoing, whether they embrace the dominant approach or the alternative view, have for the most part ignored this topic.

This chapter examines the role that social control agents play in creating organizational wrongdoing. I focus primarily on the state, because in Chapter 3 I identified it as the most salient social control agent for organizational participants, and the principal determiner of whether behavior is considered wrongful for the purposes of this book. But I also consider other social control agents because they sometimes influence the state's behavior. First, I describe two ways that the state creates wrongdoing. Then, I elaborate the factors that determine where the state draws the line separating right from wrong, which ultimately dictate the kinds of wrongdoing that the state creates. Both discussions are based substantially, but loosely, on two sociological theories of deviance, labeling theory (Lemert 1951; Becker 1963; Schur 1971) and conflict theory (Coser 1967; Collins 1975). After each discussion, I draw inferences about the impact of social control agent behavior on organizational participants, the potential perpetrators of wrongdoing. And I conclude the chapter by considering the overarching implications of these inferences. The arguments in these sections of the chapter are highly speculative, being largely based on my experience teaching and speaking with business executives over the last thirty years.

The idea that social control agents create wrongdoing is sometimes characterized as a "social constructionist" perspective because it assumes that social dynamics determine what is right and wrong in a particular time and place. It also is sometimes characterized as a "relativist" perspective because it suggests that the location of the line separating right from wrong varies from time to time and from place to place because social control agent behavior varies over time and space. Many dislike social constructionist and relativist perspectives on wrongdoing because they assume that wrongdoing is a subjective phenomenon, without a base in practical necessity or philosophical and/or religious absolutes. I understand the appeal of definitions of wrongdoing that are rooted in necessity and absolutes. They provide a comfortable sense of orderliness and stability to our experience. Further, there are some social scientific reasons for preferring objective definitions of wrongdoing.

Still, I have embraced a social constructionist or relativist definition of wrongdoing because I think the social scientific advantages of this definition outweigh those of alternative objective definitions. I have reviewed the pros and cons of my approach in Chapter 3, so I will not reiterate them here. I will only add that I think the social constructionist and relativist definition of wrongdoing that I adopt here has the additional advantage of capturing the very real disorderly and dynamic experience of organizational participants. To emphasize this point, I interrupt the exposition that follows in two places to describe in more detail cases that both illustrate the arguments advanced so far and demonstrate the subjective character of an actual definition of wrongdoing in use. The first case represents an instance in which a behavior that many people would consider rightful on an absolute basis is, in practice, labeled wrongful. The second represents an instance in which a behavior that many would consider wrongful on an absolute basis is, in practice, labeled rightful.

How social control agents create wrongdoing

Drawing the line separating right from wrong

Social control agents can create wrongdoing, most obviously, by drawing or repositioning (hereafter, for the sake of brevity, simply "drawing") a line separating right from wrong. Organizational behavior varies along many dimensions. When social control agents draw a line separating right from wrong along any of these dimensions, they create or reconstitute two classes of behaviors, a rightful one and a wrongful one. They also create or reconstitute two classes of organizations or organizational participants; one composed of right-doers and the other composed of wrongdoers.

Social control agents can draw the line separating right from wrong by instituting new rules. For example, the passage of the Cellar-Kefauver Act in 1950 strengthened the Clayton Antitrust Act of 1914 such that many types of vertical and horizontal acquisitions were rendered illegal in the United States. As a result, firms that engaged in vertical and horizontal acquisitions legally before the act was passed found themselves in violation of U.S. antitrust laws when they pursued the same types of acquisitions after the legislation was passed. Social control agents also can draw the line separating right from wrong by altering the enforcement of existing rules. Social control agents can alter the enforcement of existing rules in a direct fashion, by increasing their resolve. For example, although the Cellar-Kefauver Act was passed in 1950, the Federal Trade Commission (FTC) and the Justice Department only began policing the law vigorously in the early 1960s. Thus, many firms became the subject of FTC and the Justice Department investigations for pursuing acquisitions in the mid 1960s that were identical to ones they pursued in the 1950s without prompting FTC and Justice Department actions.

Social control agents also can alter the enforcement of existing rules in an indirect fashion by employing tactics that increase the propensity of third parties to come forward with evidence of an organization's or organizational participant's (hereafter, reflecting my focus on the individual level of analysis simply "organizational participant's") wrongdoing. Social control agents often do this on a case-by-case basis by offering immunity or reduced penalties to wrongdoers for providing information on other presumably more culpable wrongdoers. For example, prosecutors offered leniency to UBS AG investment banker Nicos Stephanou for providing information on the insider trading of four colleagues that allowed the prosecutors to put at least one of the men behind bars (Glovin 2011).

Social control agents also can alter the enforcement of existing rules in an indirect fashion by instituting new rules that increase the propensity of third parties to come forward with evidence of an organizational participant's wrongdoing. *Qui tam* laws allow private citizens to file civil suit against companies on behalf of the federal government. The first U.S. qui tam law, the False Claims Act, was passed during the American Civil War to encourage whistle blowers to finger companies making false claims about the products they sold to the union forces (most importantly, dud gun powder). The False Claims Act was modified in 1986 to motivate employees of government contractors with knowledge of organizational wrongdoing to bring that wrongdoing to the attention of the federal government. The modification increased a private citizen's cut of any financial judgment against a defendant from 10 percent to 30 percent, and reduced the threshold of guilt to include "deliberate ignorance" or "reckless disregard" of regulations.

The amended False Claims Act likely played a role in the successful prosecution of TAP Pharmaceuticals for Medicare and Medicaid fraud. In 1996, TAP Pharmaceutical's marketing director, Douglas Durand, became uncomfortable with the company's sales practices in connection with its prostate cancer drug Lupron (Rogers and Weinstein 2002; Haddad and Barrett 2002; Japsen 2004; Weinberg 2005). He subsequently left and filed suit against the company contending that TAP offered gifts to physicians to entice them to, and reward them for, prescribing Lupron for their patients, provided free samples of Lupron to physicians, without keeping a record of such exchanges, and encouraged them to bill the Medicare and Medicaid administrations for these samples, and posted high prices for Lupron, while charging physicians lower prices, allowing physicians to reap extra profit from the use of Lupron. Durand's suit prompted the federal government to file its own civil suit and criminal charges against the company. After prolonged legal maneuvering, TAP agreed to pay $885 million in fines. Under the amended False Claims Act, Durand's cut of the settlement was $126 million. Durand likely would not have endured the seven years of investigation and court proceedings needed to complete the case against TAP had he not been able to look forward to such a substantial payday.

Influencing the behavior of organizational participants

Social control agents are linked to organizational participants through a social relationship in which each influences the other. Social control agents strive to detect and punish organizational participants who cross the line separating right from wrong. At the same time, organizational participants strive to avoid social control agent scrutiny and punishment. Organizational participants can avoid detection and punishment simply by engaging in behaviors that clearly are on the right side and far from the line separating right from wrong. But competitive pressures often compel organizational participants to engage in behaviors that are located close to the line separating right from wrong because to do otherwise surrenders advantages to competitors willing to operate in the vicinity of the line. As a result, organizational participants often are required to walk a tightrope, operating close to the line separating right from wrong without crossing the line. For example, salespersons cannot eschew well-established manipulative sales techniques because to eschew these techniques risks losing customers to other salespersons willing to use those techniques. At the same time, they must refrain from using variants of those techniques that cause them to run afoul of the law.

The relationship between social control agents and organizational participants leads social control agents to behave in ways that increase the likelihood that organizational participants will cross the line separating right from wrong. This dynamic is particularly impactful in the case of organizational participants who are forced by competitive pressures to operate close to the line separating right from wrong, who I will refer to as potential wrongdoers. And it creates two kinds of wrongdoing, which I describe below.

THE CREATION OF FIRST ORDER WRONGDOING

As indicated above, social control agents exist to apprehend wrongdoers. Moreover, the constituencies on whose behalf social control agents act and upon whom social control agents rely for legitimacy evaluate them on the basis of their success at apprehending wrongdoers. Thus, social control agents have an incentive to increase the likelihood that organizational participants end up on the wrong side of the line separating right from wrong. By doing so, they increase their opportunity to apprehend wrongdoers and thus their opportunity to reap the rewards for a job well done. When social control agents increase the likelihood that organizational participants end up on the wrong side of the line separating right from wrong, they create what I call "first order wrongdoing." I briefly describe two ways in which social control agents can create first order wrongdoing.

First, social control agents can make it difficult for organizational participants to remain on the right side of the line separating right from wrong. Most simply, social control agents can promulgate rules that are difficult to interpret or enforce laws in ways that are hard to fathom. Under such circumstances, potential wrongdoers inadvertently can stumble across the line separating right from wrong. Social control agents can promulgate complex rules and police them in ways that are hard to fathom without intending to trip up organizational wrongdoings. Or they can do so with the intent to trip up wrongdoers. Regardless, the effect is the same. For example, the FTC and the Justice Department, which began enforcing the Cellar-Kefauver Act in the 1960s, each policed the act in different ways. The former prosecuted acquisitions that had been completed in the ten years since the legislation was passed. The latter prosecuted only acquisitions that were under way at the time. Further, the two agencies used different and somewhat inconsistent criteria for identifying acquisitions that violated the new law. The FTC primarily pursued acquisitions that provoked complaints among an acquirer's competitors. The Justice Department pursued acquisitions that it deemed questionable and that it thought were vulnerable to prosecution. As a result, corporate executives at the time complained that they were forced to refrain from completing any corporate acquisitions out of fear that they might inadvertently pursue a combination that would cause them to become the target of an FTC or Justice Department action.

Second, social control agents also can make it easy for organizational participants to travel across the line separating right from wrong. They can provide assistance to organizational participants who are predisposed and perhaps planning to cross the line separating right from wrong. For example, the FBI enlisted an Archer Daniels Midland executive to serve as an informant in its investigation of price-fixing in the market for lysine, an animal feed additive. Then the informant participated in the arrangement of price-fixing deals between ADM and other lysine manufacturers (Eichenwald 2000). Social control agents even can entice organizational participants who might not otherwise engage in wrongdoing to perpetrate wrongful acts. In 1982 John DeLorean was indicted for his role in a scheme to raise money for his failing automobile company, a scheme that entailed the selling of a large amount of cocaine. DeLorean's involvement in the scheme began when he received a call from a convicted drug dealer who proposed the plan at the behest of federal agents, who arrested him before the plan was consummated. Two years later, DeLorean avoided conviction by successfully arguing that he was a victim of government entrapment. At the time, his lawyer reportedly stated, "This was a fictitious crime. Without the government, there would be no crime."

THE CREATION OF SECOND ORDER WRONGDOING

Social control agents also can create wrongdoing in a more elliptical way. The contest between social control agents and potential wrongdoers over the labeling of one of their behaviors as wrongful can cause organizational participants to engage in other behaviors that social control agents label as wrongful. That is, the contest between social control agents and potential wrongdoers can cause organizational participants to engage in wrongdoing that they otherwise might not have perpetrated had the contest between social control agents and potential wrongdoers not existed. When this occurs, social control agents create what I call "second order wrongdoing." Below, I describe three ways in which social control agents can create second order wrongdoing.

First, social control agents can motivate organizational participants to perpetrate wrongful acts that reduce their risk of detection and punishment for perpetrating other behaviors that they believe social control agents might label as wrongful. Martha Stewart violated laws that prohibit impeding a federal investigation in an attempt to avoid conviction for insider trading (Thomas 2006). Similarly, Arthur Anderson partner David Duncan pleaded guilty to, and Anderson was convicted for, shredding documents that were related to their involvement in questionable accounting practices at Enron and might have served as the basis of prosecution for that involvement. Ultimately, Anderson got off on appeal and Duncan was allowed to withdraw his guilty plea when the Supreme Court ruled that the trial judge's instructions to the jury were too vague (Flood 2005; Houston Chronicle 2005). But in many cases, convictions are obtained and penalties are issued for this sort of second order wrongdoing even when convictions and penalties are not handed down for the first order wrongdoing that the secondary wrongdoing was intended to obscure. For example, several prominent athletes have been convicted, sentenced, and served time for lying about their use of performance-enhancing drugs, although they were not punished for their use of the substances (Schmidt and Wilson 2008).

Second, social control agents can motivate organizational participants to engage in wrongful behavior that makes other wrongful behavior in which they are engaged possible, and that would not be necessary were the other behavior not labeled as wrongful. As noted in previous chapters, some believe that Lance Armstrong and some of his fellow U.S. Postal team members used banned performance-enhancing substances, most notably EPO. Floyd Landis, who rode with Armstrong and U.S. Postal, has alleged that the team paid for their supply of EPO by selling bikes provided by their team sponsor, Trek. Federal officials are now investigating the possibility because the sale of sponsor-donated equipment for the purpose of sustaining an illegal doping program could constitute fraud (Albergotti and O'Connell 2010). It seems reasonable to conclude that the team would not have had to resort to selling sponsor-donated equipment (if the team in fact did sell the bikes) if EPO was considered a legitimate competitive resource. If that were the case, then the team could have raised money to support the EPO program from another sponsor, perhaps a pharmaceutical company.

Third, social control agents can cause the organizational participants that they pursue to develop self-concepts that make them prone to engaging in wrongdoing. When organizational participants engage in a behavior that is at risk of being labeled as wrongful by a social control agent, or is in fact labeled as wrongful, the anticipated or actual labeling can cause the prospective or actual wrongdoers to think of themselves as wrongdoers, and then to commit additional acts that are at risk of being labeled as wrongful by social control agents. Social control agents can cause wrongdoers to develop deviant identities by leading them to develop outlooks, establish relationships, and engage in behaviors that protect them from the psychological and practical impacts of the wrongdoer label. They can cause wrongdoers to search for and embrace techniques of neutralization that justify, and thus perpetuate, their involvement in wrongdoing. They also can cause wrongdoers to develop associations with others who can provide resources (including knowledge) that help wrongdoers avoid detection and punishment. And these associations can generate group dynamic pressures (social comparison and subtle rewards and punishments) that shape wrongdoers' norms, values and beliefs, and assumptions about the world. Finally, social control agents can cause wrongdoers to engage in second order wrongdoing that precipitates the self-perception of motivation.

I think a small number of organizational wrongdoers develop a wrongful identity of this sort. For example, as Walter Pavlo became increasingly immersed in the scheme to defraud MCI and its delinquent customers, he became increasingly close to Harold Mann and his MCI co-conspirators, partly because they shared the common goal of escaping detection and punishment. In fact, Pavlo remained in the scheme after souring on the scam partly because he felt a sense of obligation to his compatriots. Further, over time he came to think of himself as a fraudster, naming a boat that he purchased with his ill-gotten gains "Miss Deeds." Nevertheless, I suspect that most organizational wrongdoers do not develop wrongful identities of this sort. For example, I doubt that Martha Stewart came to think of herself as an insider trader. Wrongdoers are likely to develop a deviant identity when surrounded by other wrongdoers. Unlike people who engage in wrongdoing outside of an organizational context, it is rare that organizational wrongdoers find themselves embedded in social interaction isolated from right-doers. However, I suspect that many potential wrongdoers develop a wrongful identity of a different sense. I consider this possibility in the final section of this chapter.

Before moving on, I present the first of two extended case analyses, which pertains to the enforcement of laws governing the prescription of pain medications. The enforcement of laws regulating pain medications illustrates how social control agents policing the line separating right from wrong can cause organizational participants to cross the line separating right from wrong. It also illustrates the subjective character of the line separating right from wrong and, more specifically, how social control agents sometimes can label arguably rightful behavior as wrongful.

The case of pain doctors and Dr Ronald McIver

Physicians who specialize in the management of pain have several treatment modalities at their disposal, one of which is medication that reduces a patient's sensitivity to pain. A physician's prescription of pain medications can be considered wrongful if lawmakers designate those medications as controlled substances and law enforcement officials judge that a physician's prescription of the controlled substances facilitates abuse of the medications. But health care professionals and law enforcement officials disagree about where the line separating lawful from unlawful prescription behavior should be drawn. Some pharmacologists believe that pain is undertreated in the

United States. Pain impacts a patient's health in ways that go beyond the discomfort it causes. It can lead to stress and sleep loss, which in turn can lead to adverse medical conditions such as heart disease. Further, studies suggest that many pain medications can be taken at very high doses without resulting in addiction, which appears to be predicated as much on a patient's genetic make-up (with respect to susceptibility to addiction) as on a drug's chemical composition.

Physicians specializing in the treatment of pain have requested the Drug Enforcement Agency (DEA) to establish explicit guidelines delineating the line separating legal from illegal prescription of specific drugs. But the DEA has refused to post such guidelines out of fear that doing so will hamper its ability (by limiting its flexibility) to apprehend law violators. As a result, pain doctors run the risk of inadvertently crossing the line separating rightful from wrongful prescription of pain medications because they are unsure exactly where the line is drawn.

The case of Dr Ronald McIver, a pain specialist who was convicted of drug-pushing charges, provides a more fine-grained illustration of how the interaction between social control agents and organizational participants can give rise to wrongdoing (Rosenberg 2007). Prosecutors contended that Dr McIver prescribed excessive levels of the pain medication OxyContin, which several of his patients (one of whom died of an overdose) allegedly used for recreational purposes or sold to others for recreational purposes. Further, they maintained that McIver prescribed elevated levels of OxyContin in order to build up his medical practice's clientele, padding it with drug-addicted and drug-pushing patients. Crucial to the prosecution's case, experts testified that McIver's approach to prescribing OxiContin was aggressive compared to existing professional standards. The experts maintained that McIver prescribed OxyContin more readily, sooner in a patient's course of therapy, and at higher doses than other physicians typically do.

But Dr McIver's defense team countered that he prescribed higher-than-typical levels of OxyContin because his therapeutic objectives were more ambitious than the average doctor's goals. He sought to reduce his patients' perceived pain to 2 on a 10-point scale (in which a score of 10 represents unbearable pain), whereas most physicians aspire to reduce their patients' perceived pain to just 5. Further, they maintained that Dr McIver's therapeutic objectives were in line with expert opinion on pain and pain medications, which holds that the average U.S. physician undertreats pain. Thus, it is possible that Dr McIver was convicted of drug-pushing because, compared to the average physician, he was more, rather than less, focused on his patients' well-being, and more, rather than less, in keeping with leading scientific thought.

Further, Dr McIver's defense team noted that Dr McIver attempted to confirm suspicions that one of his patients was abusing or re-selling the medications he was prescribing, but the DEA thwarted his efforts. McIver wrote to the DEA expressing concern and requesting information about the patient, but the DEA did not respond to his inquiry. When questioned at the trial, a DEA official testified that the agency ignored McIver's query because it feared that any response they provided might abet a crime. Presumably, the DEA had no evidence that McIver's patient was abusing or selling the OxyContin he prescribed. And it worried that any information that it provided to this effect later could be used in court as an endorsement of McIver's prescription strategy if the DEA ever decided to prosecute McIver for unlawful prescription behavior.

Implications for organizational participants

The argument that social control agents create wrongdoing by drawing the line separating right from wrong might be considered a semantic and thus trivial point. After all, when social control agents create wrongdoing in this way, they do so as a byproduct of their attempt to root out, punish, and eradicate behavior that members of their constituency consider offensive. In other words, when social control agents draw the line separating right from wrong, they create wrongdoing as defined in this book in order to eliminate wrongdoing as conceived by their constituency. But the fact that social control agents create wrongdoing by drawing the line separating right from wrong has two non-trivial consequences for organizational participants.

First, it means that organizational participants can be on the right side of the line separating right from wrong one day and on the wrong side the next, even when they have not changed their behavior from one day to the next. For example, some firms found themselves in violation of antitrust law after the Celler-Kefauver Act was enforced, despite the fact that they were completing the same sorts of acquisitions before the act was enforced. As a result, I suspect that organizational participants sometimes perceive wrongdoing as something for which social control agents are responsible, insofar as it results from changes in social control agent behavior, rather than something for which they are responsible, insofar as it does not result from changes in their behavior.

Second, the fact that social control agents create wrongdoing by drawing the line separating right from wrong means that each time social control agents draw a new line, they create the possibility for new forms of wrongdoing. Thus, the Sarbanes-Oxley Act, which was passed in the wake of the Enron debacle, defined previously acceptable accounting practices off limits. As a result, I suspect that organizational participants sometimes perceive social control agent activity as increasing their risk of being labeled a wrongdoer.

The argument that social control agents can create wrongdoing by influencing the behavior of potential wrongdoers also might be considered an academic point. I have said that the process by which social control agents cause organizational participants to cross the line separating right from wrong is most salient for potential wrongdoers, organizational participants who are forced by competitive pressures to operate close to the line separating right from wrong. Further, two of the three processes that give rise to second order wrongdoing are only salient for actual wrongdoers, organizational participants that are already engaged in behaviors that social control agents are likely to label as such. Thus the wrongdoing that these processes create can be considered a by-product of attempts to eliminate wrongdoing considered offensive by important constituencies. Finally, while I have offered illustrations of the several ways that social control agents can create first and second order wrongdoing, I suspect that the amount of such wrongdoing likely only constitutes a small portion of all organizational wrongdoing. Still, I think the fact that social control agents sometimes create wrongdoing by influencing potential wrongdoers' behavior has two non-trivial consequences for organizational participants.

First, in the context of second order wrongdoing, it means that organizational participants sometimes find themselves engaging in behaviors that they would otherwise eschew, were it not for the fact that they were at risk of being labeled as wrongdoers for their involvement in other behaviors. As a result, I suspect that organizational participants sometimes perceive themselves as having been steered into wrongdoing by social control agents. Second, in the context of first order wrongdoing, it means that organizational participants sometimes find themselves engaging in behaviors that they would otherwise eschew, were it not for the assistance provided by, and pressure applied by, social control agents. As a result, I suspect that organizational participants sometimes perceive themselves as having been helped and even pushed into wrongdoing by social control agents. I will return to the significance of these likely perceptions after I address the second main topic of this chapter: the factors that influence where social control agents draw the line separating right from wrong.

Factors that determine where social control agents draw the line separating right from wrong

Above I explained how social control agents create wrongdoing, by drawing the line separating right from wrong and by engaging in a contest with potential wrongdoers over their location vis-à-vis the line. Here I identify the factors that govern where social control agents draw the line separating right from wrong. These factors ultimately determine the kinds of wrongdoing that social control agents create. I maintain that social control agents, like all social actors, possess interests and are subject to constraints. Further, I contend that social control agents draw the line separating right from wrong in a way that advances their interests within the limits imposed by their constraints.

Social control agent interests

Social control agents have a broad interest to safeguard the welfare of their constituencies, the organizations and people they claim to represent. If they fail to protect the interests of their constituencies, their raison d'être is called into question. Thus, social control agents tend to draw the line separating right from wrong in ways that protect the interests of their constituencies. In keeping with this imperative, the state tends to draw the line separating right from wrong in ways that defend the broad public from behaviors that cause it harm, partly by meting out punishments to perpetrators of behaviors that harm the public in rough proportion to the harm they generate.

The state's tendency to react in defense of its constituency in proportion to the harm done to it is illustrated well by a comparison of the U.S. government's reaction to the Grand Teton Dam failure and the Italian government's reaction to the Viaont Dam breach. When the Grand Teton Dam failed, no organization or individual was indicted or punished for the dam's failure. When the Vaiont Dam was breached, fourteen engineers were suspended and prosecuted for manslaughter, and three were found guilty and given six-year prison terms. A comparison of these two cases does not reveal obvious differences in the culpability of those responsible for the design and construction of the dams. If anything, the designers and builders of the Grand Teton Dam would appear more negligent than those of the Viaont Dam. The Grand Teton Dam failed as the result of a rather large number of problems that were identified but not corrected by managers and engineers in the course of the structure's design and construction. However, the Viaont Dam did not, strictly speaking, fail. The accident resulted when a landslide dumped a massive amount of rock and soil into the reservoir behind it, creating a huge wave that topped the dam by over 300 feet. But the two events produced very different consequences for the people living in the vicinity of the dams. The Grand Teton Dam failure resulted in 11 fatalities, while the Viaont Dam breach resulted in over 2,000 deaths (Perrow 1999).[1]

---

[1] Certainly the difference between the U.S. state's reaction to the Grand Teton Dam failure and the Italian state's reaction to the Vaiont Dam breach were the products of other contrasts as well,

Although social control agents seek to protect the interests of their constituency as a whole, their efforts to do so are complicated by the fact that different members of their constituency typically possess somewhat different, and even conflicting interests. When this is the case, social control agents prioritize the interests of the most powerful members of their constituency. Failure to protect the interests of its most powerful constituents is more likely to undermine a social control agent's legitimacy than failure to protect the interests of less powerful constituents. Thus, social control agents tend to draw the line separating right from wrong where the most powerful members of their constituency want it drawn. Eichenwald, who conducted lengthy investigations of both the Prudential Bache limited partnership fraud and the Enron debacle, argued that power played a role in the U.S. state's markedly different reaction to these two instances of organizational wrongdoing (Eichenwald 1996, 2005). The Enron fiasco, which caused substantial losses to some of the nation's largest financial institutions, resulted in fines, incarcerations, and important changes to the legal system (most importantly, passage of the Sarbanes-Oxley Act). But, the Prudential Bache debacle, which only harmed individual (and in most cases, elderly retired) investors, resulted in only a few fines, no incarcerations, and no changes to the legal system.

Social control agents also possess a more parochial interest in taking advantage of opportunities and dispensing with threats that affect their chances of survival and growth. Their most important opportunities and threats are those that promise to increase, or threaten to decrease their access to resources. Thus, social control agents tend to draw the line separating right and wrong in ways that ensure the steady flow of needed resources. For example, the state tends to react promptly and vigorously when it is injured, as was the case in the heavy electrical equipment price-fixing conspiracy of the 1950s. This complex scheme damaged primarily federal, state, and municipal governments that were the main purchasers of the electric transformers at the center of the price-fixing arrangements (Geis 1995). Similarly, the state reacts rapidly and forcefully when it stands to gain from action, as was the case in Boston's Big Dig ceiling collapse. By bringing legal action against the construction project's general contractor and subcontractors, the State of Massachusetts was able to obtain a sizable judgment, the proceeds of which were quickly directed to offset the construction project's unexpected and politically embarrassing high maintenance costs (Estes and Murphy 2008; Estes 2008).

not the least of which are differences in the relationship between state and society in the two countries.

Social control agent constraints

RELATIONSHIPS AMONG SOCIAL CONTROL AGENTS

A social control agent's capacity to pursue its broad and parochial interests is influenced partly by its relationship to other social control agents. Social control agents frequently interact with one another in a synergistic fashion, working in consort to draw the line separating right from wrong in a rigorous way. Criminal and civil courts can punish the same wrongdoers via independent proceedings, the former issuing prison sentences and the latter imposing fines. Professional and industry associations can bar these same wrongdoers from participating in their profession or industry. And, media outlets can tarnish the same wrongdoers' reputations, and interest groups can protest against them. On other occasions, though, social control agents can operate in consort to draw the line separating right from wrong in a lax way. Paul Krimmage contends that the social control agents regulating professional cycling conspired to ensure that the use of banned performance-enhancing substances was not detected and, when detected, was not punished. According to Krimmage, the cycling federations and the cycling media coveted the favorable public attention produced by impressive chemically fueled performances, and feared the negative attention that news of positive test results and suspensions would generate. So the federations looked the other way and the media asked few questions when it was clear that top cyclists were using banned performance enhancers. As a result, cyclists faced a tough decision. They could eschew use of the banned substances and resign themselves to a career of mediocrity. Or they could use the substances and assume the risks of adverse health effects as well as the small (but for the less accomplished riders, still very real) possibility of detection and punishment.

But social control agents also often interact symbiotically, such that the line-drawing activities of one social control agent influence the line-drawing activities of another. In Chapter 3 I noted that social control agents can be distinguished from one another on the basis of their primacy; the formality of their constitution, the breadth of their constituency, and the potency of the punishments they can impose on wrongdoers. In most advanced societies, social control agents are linked in stable interdependencies, with those enjoying the least primacy exercising their influence over wrongdoers via their relationship to social control agents that enjoy greater primacy. Thus, interest groups create news for media outlets to report. Media outlets produce stories to which professional associations and the state attend. And professional associations and the state formally sanction wrongdoers.

The media occupies a particularly important role in the stable relationships linking social control agents in advanced societies. Media organizations, like all organizations, seek to survive and prosper. They accomplish this by maintaining and expanding their readership and/or viewership upon which their advertising revenues are based. And they do this by collecting information and fashioning it into compelling stories that attract the interest of readers and viewers. In the process, the media often mediates between the state and interest groups. Interest groups sometimes lack the power to provoke the state to respond to perceived instances of wrongdoing. When the media identify organizational behaviors that interest groups perceive to be wrongful, they can fashion information about that wrongdoing into a particular kind of story, a "scandal." Scandals capture the attention of readers and viewers and, as a result, put pressure on state officials to respond (Fisse & Braithwaite 1983; Molotch & Lester 1974). The state can ignore perceived wrongdoing that is not important according to its interests as long as it is not common knowledge, but it has to act for fear of being seen as negligent when perceived wrongdoing becomes widely known (Adut 2004, 2005).

Finally, social control agents sometimes compete with one another over the right to draw the line separating right from wrong in particular places. Competition can arise between comparable social control agents located in different geopolitical spaces, such as parallel economic regulatory bodies in different countries. Competition also can arise between comparable social control agents in the same geopolitical space, especially among non-state actors. For example, multiple professional associations, media organizations, and interest groups in the same country often compete with one another over the right to position the line separating right from wrong in particular places. And when competition arises between comparable social control agents, the outcome of the contest is largely determined by the relative power of the contestants. Consider the competition between the U.S. and Swiss governments over the rules governing the reporting of investment income for U.S. citizens holding assets in Swiss banks.

The U.S. government requires U.S. citizens to pay taxes on their investment income. The Swiss government prohibits Swiss banks from releasing information on their depositors' investment income, allowing U.S. depositors to evade U.S. tax requirements. For many years, the U.S. and Swiss governments engaged in a stalemated conflict over the release of information on U.S. citizens' Swiss bank accounts. Recently, though, the interests and power of the two governments shifted. The mortgage meltdown and global financial crisis of 2008 increased the U.S. government's need for additional tax revenues to offset its politically unpopular $700 billion financial crisis bank bailout. The $100 billion that the U.S. government stands to recover by taxing U.S. citizens' Swiss bank earnings could go a long way towards paying for the cost of the bailout. At the same time, the global financial crisis severely weakened the Swiss economy, the health of which rests largely on its financial sector. And when the U.S. government threatened to indict the Swiss bank UBS AG on criminal charges in a Florida court, some speculated that a criminal conviction of UBS (which just months before had paid a $780 million fine for facilitating its U.S. depositors' tax evasion) might cripple the bank and send the Swiss economy into a tailspin. Thus, the Swiss government, which previously had stood behind UBS's refusal to release information on its U.S. depositors, quickly exempted the Swiss bank from Swiss law requiring it to protect its depositors' privacy. Then it negotiated a deal with the U.S. government in which UBS was forced to provide the U.S. authorities with information on over 4,000 of its U.S. depositors (The Associated Press March 4, 2009b; August 18, 2009c; August 19, 2009d).

RELATIONSHIPS BETWEEN SOCIAL CONTROL AGENTS
AND POTENTIAL WRONGDOERS

A social control agent's capacity to pursue its interests also is influenced by its relationship to organizational participants, especially potential wrongdoers. As noted above, social control agents are linked with organizational participants in a competitive relationship. And this competition extends to questions regarding the position of the line separating right from wrong. Organizational participants search for loopholes in the rules that social control agents establish. And when they find a loophole in a rule, social control agents attempt to close it. Thus, competitive bicycle racers, with the help of enterprising physicians and chemists, search for new performance-enhancing substances that the cycling federations have not yet banned. And when the cycling federations get wind of a new performance-enhancing substance, they add it to the list of banned substances.

Further, potential wrongdoers search for evasive measures to avoid detection by social control agents. And when social control agents get wind of these evasive measures, they develop ways to circumvent them. Thus, competitive bicycle racers, with the help of physicians and chemists, search for chemical agents that mask the use of banned substances. When the cycling federations get wind of these masking agents, they add them to the list of banned substances. Finally, in the event that they are apprehended, potential wrongdoers hire high-priced lawyers to do battle with social control agents. And when they do, social control agents attempt to amass countervailing legal talent. These competitive dynamics also are evident in the more traditional business context of "aggressive tax planning" or "tax shelter" design (Braithwaite 2005).

Sometimes the competitive relationship between social control agents and potential wrongdoers has subtle effects on the location of the line separating right from wrong. For example, the position of the line separating lawful from unlawful prescription of pain medication in the U.S., as well as the clarity with which that line is drawn, is significantly influenced by the interaction between drug law enforcement officials and potential wrongdoers. Law enforcement officials consider prescription levels to be wrongful when they exceed the levels used by the typical physician. As indicated above, physicians tend to favor an overly conservative approach to prescribing pain medications because they underestimate the negative consequences of pain and overestimate the possibility of addiction. But they also favor an overly conservative approach because they fear being prosecuted for prescribing unlawful levels of pain medications.

The outcomes of contests between social control agents and wrongdoers largely are determined by the relative power of the contestants. Social control agents have the upper hand against potential wrongdoers in regards to positioning the line separating right from wrong when they possess more power than the wrongdoers. For example, the U.S. federal government acted decisively in its prosecution of TAP Pharmaceutical for fraudulent marketing practices. And TAP quickly settled the federal government's civil suit for a record fine. The state might have acted so decisively, and TAP might have capitulated so quickly, because the state possessed resource dependence-based power over TAP by virtue of its ability to remove TAP's drugs from the list of medications for which patients could receive Medicare and Medicaid reimbursement. Indeed, while the federal prosecutors congratulated themselves for their victory in defense of the public interest, TAP stated that they settled the civil suit, not because they believed they were guilty of violating the law, but rather because the penalty, as large as it was, was less than the amount of business with Medicare and Medicaid that it might have lost had it fought the charges and in so doing incurred the wrath of the state (Weinberg 2005).

Alternatively, potential wrongdoers have the upper hand against social control agents in positioning the line separating right from wrong when they have more power than social control agents. For example, the Massachusetts Attorney General settled quickly with Bechtel Corporation in connection with the Big Dig ceiling collapse that resulted in the death of a motorist, negotiating a financial settlement with the tunnel project's general contractor. But it engaged in a protracted battle with Powers Fasteners, pursuing a criminal indictment of the epoxy supplier. It seems likely that the state settled quickly and did not pursue a criminal indictment of Bechtel because it is the largest engineering firm and the third largest privately owned company in the United States. A criminal conviction against such an economically well-endowed and politically well-connected firm would have been hard to win. Further, a successful criminal conviction would have prohibited Bechtel from performing construction work for the state in the future, an outcome the state likely did not relish. It seems probable that the state pursued Powers Fasteners with gusto because it was a relatively small firm that could not afford high-priced legal talent, and the state could easily do without its services.[2]

A further examination of the social control of private security contractors in Iraq, previously discussed briefly in Chapter 3, illustrates well the role that power differentials among competing social control agents and potential wrongdoers play in the location of the line separating right from wrong. It also provides an additional illustration of the subjective character of the line separating right from wrong, in this instance showing how social control agents sometimes can label arguably wrongful behavior as rightful.

The case of private security contractors and Blackwater Worldwide

The U.S. military has made extensive use of private security contractors (PSCs) to protect personnel (e.g. diplomats and military officers) and material (e.g. supply convoys) in support of its operations in Iraq. The military authorizes PSCs to use deadly force only if their safety or the safety of the human or material cargo they are employed to protect is threatened. All other uses of deadly force are considered, implicitly, homicide. But the categorization of situations according to the danger they pose for PSCs and their human and material cargo is highly subjective.

PSC employees, the potential wrongdoers in this case, understandably favor the broadest possible categorizations of situations and thus the most restricted definition of murder. For example, they would categorize situations in which a car filled with unknown occupants approached them at high speed as a dangerous circumstance warranting the use of deadly force. The Iraqi authorities, one social control agent, equally understandably favor the narrowest categorizations of situations and thus the most encompassing definition of murder. They would categorize situations such as the one described above as benign and any attack on the approaching car as wrongful. The U.S. authorities, a competing social control agent, adopt an intermediate stance, viewing the PSCs as too often trigger happy and the Iraqi authorities as too frequently insensitive to combat realities, especially in a context in which enemy combatants are not always distinguishable from ordinary citizens by their garb.

While one could debate the merits of alternative definitions of PSC behavior with respect to the use of deadly force, the power relationships among social

---

[2] The differential treatment of Bechtel and Powers likely was due to other factors as well. One could argue that Powers was more culpable for the accident than Bechtel, although the causes of the accident were multifaceted and far from indisputable (Allen and Murphy 2006; Murphy and Estes 2007). Likely more important, Bechtel possessed deeper pockets than Powers Fasteners. Bechtel, along with its main partner in the project, Parsons Brinckerhoff, agreed to pay the State of Massachusetts $407 million. Powers eventually agreed to pay $16 million as part of a deal in which the state agreed to drop criminal charges against the firm (Murphy and Allen 2007; Estes and Murphy 2008; Saltzman 2009).

control agents and wrongdoers, rather than rhetorical supremacy, has determined which definition is actually in use in Iraq. As noted in Chapter 3, the United States negotiated an agreement with the Coalition Provisional Authority (CPA) soon after it invaded Iraq in 2003 whereby PSCs and their personnel would be monitored and controlled by a U.S. military agency situated in Iraq, rather than by the CPA. And it arranged for the agreement to be carried over when the Iraqi Interim Government replaced the CPA in 2004. The relative power of the United States and Iraqi governments likely drove these negotiated agreements. The U.S. military decimated the Iraqi government, military, and police apparatus in its invasion of Iraq. As a result, the CPA and its successor were the dominant governmental actors in Iraq, and both were dominated by the U.S. military.

Further, as noted in Chapter 3, when the U.S. military constituted the local agency charged with monitoring and controlling private security contractors in Iraq, it did so in a less than consummate fashion. It provided the agency with little in the way of guidelines distinguishing between approved and unapproved behavior. Further, it supplied the agency with few investigators to police the minimal guidelines. The PSC's power over the U.S. government likely was responsible for this state of affairs. The U.S. government sought to minimize the appearance that the war was a large-scale endeavor with numerous casualties, a desire that intensified as international and domestic opposition to the war grew. Private security contractors offered the government a way to disguise the true number of U.S. combatants on the ground and dying in Iraq because their employees were not counted in tallies of soldiers deployed and killed in the conflict. As a result, PSCs possessed resource dependence-based power over the U.S. military.

The role that competition and power relationships among social control agents and wrongdoers play in creating, or in this case not creating, wrongdoing can be illustrated in a more fine-grained way by considering a specific instance of possible PSC wrongdoing. Blackwater Worldwide was the most prominent PSC operating in Iraq. On September 16, 2007, a complement of Blackwater guards was positioned in and around Baghdad's Nisoor Square, assisting in the evacuation of a U.S. Agency for International Development official who had attended a meeting near the square. Exactly what transpired on that day is open to dispute. The Blackwater guards contend that they were fired upon by Iraqi insurgents and returned fire in self-defense. Iraqis in the square maintain that the Blackwater guards initiated fire without provocation. What is not open to dispute is that seventeen Iraqi civilians were killed and twenty others were wounded in the fusillade that ensued.

Blackwater was not under contract to the U.S. military, so its guards were not subject to the formal authority of the local agency set up by the U.S. military to monitor and control PSCs in Iraq. Blackwater was under contract to the U.S. State Department, so its guards were subject only to the more informal monitoring and control of that governmental unit. State Department officials debriefed the guards immediately after the shootings, promising them immunity from prosecution based on their statements, to increase the likelihood of obtaining a truthful account. In the end, the State Department did not pursue or facilitate legal action against the guards (Fainaru 2008).

Months later, though, after much media attention and resulting public outrage, the U.S. Justice Department indicted six of the Blackwater guards for murder. One of the guards pled guilty to the charges and received a reduced sentence in return for cooperation in the prosecution of his co-workers. But a judge threw out the indictments of the five remaining guards, ruling that the Justice Department built its case on the guards' earlier statements to State Department officials, which the court judged to be both coerced and protected by its promise of immunity (The Associated Press, December 31, 2009e).

At roughly the same time, twelve Iraqi citizens, some of whom were surviving victims and some of whom were relatives of deceased victims of the Nisoor Square shootings, filed civil suit against Blackwater and its founder, Eric Prince, in a Virginia court. The plaintiffs accused Blackwater and Prince of "cultivating a reckless culture" that allowed innocent civilians to be killed in Nisoor Square and in three other incidents. Blackwater settled the suit shortly after the criminal indictments against the five Blackwater guards were thrown out of court. The details of the settlement are not known, but unofficial reports indicate that Blackwater agreed to pay the plaintiffs a sum in the millions of dollars (The Associated Press, January 8, 2010b). In the wake of the public outcry, criminal prosecution, and civil suit, Blackwater lost its contract with the State Department, lost its license to operate in Iraq, changed its name to Xe, restructured its management, and claimed to alter its business model (de-emphasizing its security business in favor of training, logistics, and air transport work). But the fortunes of the firm may be looking up. At this writing, Xe is favored to win a major contract to provide training services to the U.S. government in Afghanistan, estimated in the hundreds of millions of dollars (The Associated Press, January 9, 2010c).

The Nisoor Square tragedy illustrates in more detail how social control agents can interact in drawing the line between right and wrong. Ultimately, the U.S. criminal and civil court systems worked in parallel to adjudicate the Blackwater guards' guilt. But leading up to the court actions, social control agents interacted symbiotically. Growing domestic opposition to the Iraq War and intensifying international opposition to the U.S. occupation of Iraq spurred the U.S. news media to transformed information about the events in Nisoor Square into a scandal. And domestic and international public opinion, amplified by U.S. media accounts, made the Nisoor Square killings impossible for the U.S. Department of Justice to ignore. Finally, multiple social control agents competed for the right to draw the line between right and wrong in this situation. Most obviously, the U.S. State Department and the U.S. Justice Department competed to render judgments in this case, while the Iraqi government was largely excluded from the contest (despite being extremely interested in its outcome). And the fact that the State Department officials ordered the Blackwater guards to testify to their actions in the square that day and offered them immunity for their testimony compromised the Justice Department's ability to prosecute the guards.

The Nisoor Square tragedy also is indicative of the fact that whether behavior is considered wrongful depends on the relative power of social control agents. The pursuit of the Blackwater guards unfolded in the context of the general power struggle described above, involving the U.S. military, the Iraqi government, and private security contractors. It also unfolded in the context of the more specific power struggle involving Blackwater Worldwide, the U.S. State Department, the U.S. Justice Department, the U.S. news media, the Iraqi authorities, and for lack of a more precise term, domestic and international public opinion.

Perhaps because of its privileged position in the U.S. government's formal organizational hierarchy, the State Department was able to reserve for itself the right to maintain a private police force (not subject to independent law enforcement control). Further, the Blackwater guards escaped criminal conviction (on what critics characterize as a legal technicality), and Blackwater escaped larger financial sanctions because the U.S. government remains extremely dependent on private security contractors to wage its wars in Iraq and Afghanistan, and because Blackwater leadership had close personal and business ties to the U.S. military establishment. Blackwater's resurrection as Xe and its continuing role in U.S. military operations would appear consistent with this contention.

But the relative power of the U.S. military and the Iraqi government has begun to shift, as the Iraqi government has gained strength and the U.S. military has progressively withdrawn troops from the country. In the wake of the failed criminal prosecution and modest civil suit judgment, the Iraqi government vowed to try the Blackwater guards in an Iraqi court. Whether they will be able to do so remains to be seen. But the Iraqis have renegotiated the U.S.–Iraq Status of Forces Agreement, which covers the monitoring and control of private security contractors in Iraq. In the future, U.S. military (although, perhaps not State Department) private security contractors will be subject to Iraqi monitoring and control. And as a result, the opportunities for PSC employees to engage in wrongdoing will increase (The Associated Press 2010a).

The implications for potential wrongdoers

The factors that influence where social control agents draw the line separating right from wrong, and that thus determine the kinds of wrongdoing that organizational participants are at risk of perpetrating, might be considered far from the topic of this book. After all, most organizational participants are forced by circumstances to take "as given" the position of the line separating right from wrong. Only a select few in the most economically and politically advantaged organizations, the senior managers of the largest corporations, ever take on the task of influencing the position of the line separating right from wrong. But I think the factors that influence where social control agents draw the line separating right from wrong have two important consequences for organizational participants.

First, as indicated above, social control agents seek to draw the line separating right from wrong in ways that advance their broad and parochial interests, and their success at doing so depends on their power relative to other social control agents and potential wrongdoers. Hence, the position of the line separating right from wrong is a political product, a reflection of the balance of power among competing interests rather than a representation of moral imperative. As a result, I suspect that organizational participants perceive the position of the line separating right from wrong to be eminently disputable and perhaps inherently suspect.

Second, because the position of the line separating right from wrong is the product of political dynamics, the position of the line moves around from time to time and place to place as political conditions change. Organizations and their members try to track and forecast the position of the line. Large organizations maintain in-house legal staffs and public affairs offices, and establish ongoing relationships with independent law and consulting firms. Small organizations contract with business service firms to obtain information about social control agent strategies. For example, doctors who specialize in the prescription of pain medications enroll in seminars run by former DEA officials to get up-to-date information on the DEA's enforcement philosophy. Of course, the largest corporations also seek to influence the social control environment through public relations efforts, philanthropic giving, political contributions, and lobbying. Still, substantial uncertainty remains about the current and prospective location of the line separating right from wrong. And I think this uncertainty has implications for the likelihood and manner in which organizational participants might engage in wrongdoing, and the sense of responsibility they feel for such wrongdoing.

The more uncertain organizational participants are about the location of the line separating right from wrong, the more likely they are to inadvertently cross the line separating right from wrong. Further, the more uncertain organizational participants are about the location of the line, the more susceptible they are to many of the processes that lead them to engage in wrongdoing in a boundedly rational manner. People find it hard to make rational decisions when uncertainty impedes their ability to distinguish right from wrong. They also tend to surrender to social influence mechanisms and defer to organizational structures when they are unsure about whether a course of action is appropriate or inappropriate. And I suspect that organizational participants who inadvertently cross the line separating right from wrong or who embark on wrongdoing in a boundedly rational fashion, like those who find themselves on the wrong side of the line after new rules are enacted or enforced, are less likely to consider themselves fully responsible for their behavior. Below I consider the consequences of these and the previously speculated implications of the social control account of organizational wrongdoing.

The creation of deviant identities

Above I maintained that the interaction between social control agents and potential and actual organizational wrongdoers sometimes causes organizational participants to think of themselves as wrongdoers and, as a consequence, engage in more wrongdoing. But, I also estimated that this causal chain is only occasionally activated. Nevertheless, I think the full spectrum of ways in which social control agents create wrongdoing, in aggregate, can cause organizational participants to develop what I call a "deviant identity." Further, I suspect that organizational participants who develop a deviant identity are more likely to engage in wrongdoing.

Above I speculated that the way in which social control agents create wrongdoing has four consequences for organizational participants, especially those who are forced to operate close to the line separating right from wrong. First, it leads them to consider the position of the line separating right from wrong to be debatable at best and suspect at worst. Second, it causes them to believe that they are not responsible for any wrongdoing that they might perpetrate. Third, it leads them to think that social control agents increase their risk of being labeled a wrongdoer. Fourth, it leads them to believe that they have been steered, enticed, and even pushed by social control agents into any wrongdoing that they might have perpetrated.

To the extent that these speculations are correct, they provide the basis of another more encompassing supposition. I think organizational participants who harbor these four perceptions about the line separating right from wrong and their location relative to the line tend to develop a cynical outlook towards compliance with ethical principles, social responsibility doctrines, and the law. Specifically, I think that they tend to view compliance with ethical, social responsibility, and legal dictates as a practical necessity rather than as a moral imperative. And as a result, they become less concerned with operating on the right side of the line separating right from wrong, and more concerned with avoiding apprehension for operating on the wrong side of the line. And this latter orientation increases the likelihood that organizational participants, especially potential wrongdoers, will become actual wrongdoers.

I do not suppose that all organizational participants develop a cynical outlook towards compliance with ethical principles, social responsibility doctrines, and the law. Undoubtedly many, even many potential wrongdoers, feel a moral imperative to behave in ethical, socially responsible, and legal ways. But I do imagine that enough organizational participants embrace this cynical outlook to support what Braithwaite (2005) calls a "market for vice," a demand for professional services of various stripes that provide organizations and organizational participants with strategies and tactics that allow them to operate near, and even beyond, the line separating right from wrong without getting labeled as wrongful. And I suspect that these professional service firms reinforce potential wrongdoers' cynical outlook and, in marketing their services, provide a supply-side stimulus for the market for vice. In this nexus, the mantra "if you are not cheating, you are not trying" rules the day.[3]

Assessing the social control account

The social control account of organizational wrongdoing embraces the alternative approach to explaining wrongdoing more consummately than any of the other explanations of wrongdoing considered in this book. As such, it represents a radical departure from the explanations of organizational wrongdoing currently most popular. The social control account allows that organizational participants can engage in wrongdoing in a mindless and boundedly rational fashion. It holds that organizational participants come to engage in wrongful behavior, not because they choose to perpetrate wrongful acts, but rather because social control agents label their behavior as wrongful. Further, it holds that social control agent labeling can be entirely unanticipated or, if anticipated, difficult to forecast. The social control account also allows that organizational participants engage in wrongdoing partly as the result of their immediate social context. It assumes that potential wrongdoers are linked to social control agents in a relationship and engage in wrongdoing partly as a consequence of that relationship. This is particularly clear in the case of

---

[3] I am indebted to James Walsh for bringing this business idiom to my attention.

second order wrongdoing, which results from potential wrongdoers' attempts to avoid first order social control agent labels.

The social control account also allows that organizational participants engage in wrongdoing in a crescive fashion. Most importantly, it holds that potential wrongdoers, in the course of their relationship with social control agents, can develop a deviant identity that makes them more prone to engage in behaviors that are at risk of being labeled as wrongful. Finally, the social control account allows that organizational wrongdoers sometimes can engage in wrongdoing despite being disinclined to do so. It holds that organizational participants strive to avoid labeling by social control agents. Further, it holds that potential wrongdoers' capacity to avoid social control agent labels is regulated by the extent to which social control agents possess power over them. This is particularly apparent in cases in which social control agents generate primary wrongdoing by making it difficult for potential wrongdoers to remain on the right side of the line separating right from wrong, and by making it easy for potential wrongdoers to stray across the line.

Conclusion

The social control agent explanation of organizational wrongdoing is the final account explored in this book. It diverges markedly from the dominant rational choice and culture explanations, by jettisoning even more than the other alternative accounts the four assumptions that underpin the dominant accounts. Further, it departs from both the dominant and the other alternative explanations of organizational wrongdoing, which concentrate on the perpetrators of wrongdoing, by focusing on those who seek to detect and punish wrongdoers. I have attempted to draw out the implications of the social control agent account for organizational participants. But, admittedly, this attempt is highly speculative. In the next chapter I take stock of the arguments advanced in the book and consider one possible critique of my approach. I also consider the practical implications of my analysis.

12

Conclusion

Introduction

I have articulated two broad perspectives on organizational wrongdoing in this book; one that views wrongdoing as an abnormal phenomenon and the other that views it as a normal one. The first perspective views wrongful behavior as aberrant (i.e. a clear departure from the norm), wrongdoers as abhorrent (i.e. extraordinary in their psychological make-up), and the causes of wrongdoing as exceptional (i.e. misaligned incentive structures and perverse cultures). The second perspective views wrongful behavior as mundane (i.e. not much different than right-doing), wrongdoers as ordinary (i.e. not much different from average organizational participants), and the causes of wrongdoing as unexceptional (i.e. the same structures and processes that give rise to right-doing in organizations).

In addition, I have elaborated two approaches to explaining the causes of organizational wrongdoing that are associated with these two broad perspectives. The first, the dominant approach, rests on the assumption that wrongdoers deliberate mindfully and rationally, in social isolation, make discrete decisions, and develop positive inclinations to engage in wrongdoing all before embarking on a wrongful course of action. The second, the alternative approach, rests on the assumption that wrongdoers often embark on wrongdoing in a mindless and boundedly rational way, subject to the influence of their immediate social context, slipping into wrongdoing in a crescive way, without ever developing a positive inclination to do so.

Finally, I have identified eight specific explanations of the causes of wrongdoing. The first two, the rational choice and culture accounts, fall under the rubric of the dominant approach to explaining organizational wrongdoing. The third, the ethical decision account, serves as a bridge between the dominant and alternative approaches. The final five explanations, the administrative structure, situational social influence, power structure, accidental behavior, and social control accounts, clearly fall under the rubric of the alternative account.

While I contend that both perspectives on organizational wrongdoing are valid, I have championed the normal organizational wrongdoing perspective. While I contend that both approaches to explaining organizational wrongdoing are useful, I have favored the alternative approach. Thus, while I elaborate the rational choice and culture accounts, I have tried to both characterize and develop the ethical decision, administrative systems, situational social influence, power structure, accidental behavior, and social control accounts.

I hope that students and scholars interested in the causes of misconduct in and of organizations will find this analysis useful. If I have done a good job, my analysis should not only increase their understanding of current theories of wrongdoing, it should also alert them to new potential causes of wrongdoing, help them organize their thinking about the many possible causes of organizational wrongdoing, and identify lines of inquiry that they might fruitfully pursue. But what might practitioners, those who manage and are managed in organizations, take from this book? And what might policy makers, those who seek to reduce organizational wrongdoing, take away from it? I conclude with a discussion of these issues. But before doing so, I want to briefly anticipate and address one possible misinterpretation of what I consider the fundamental message of the book.

An apology for wrongdoers

Some readers might consider *Normal Organizational Wrongdoing* a veiled apology for organizational wrongdoers. A good number of the descriptions of wrongdoing that I use to develop and illustrate the ideas advanced in the book are based on depictions prepared by the perpetrators of the wrongdoing in question. For example, the lengthy depiction of accounting fraud at MCI was based on a book co-authored by one of the fraud's main architects, Walter Pavlo. Similarly, the extensive description of the engineering fraud at B.F. Goodrich was based on an article written by one of the fraud's facilitators, Kermit Vandivier. It stands to reason that these depictions were biased by the wrongdoers' desire to cast their behavior in a positive light.

More fundamentally, the explanations of organizational wrongdoing that I champion characterize wrongdoers as mindless and boundedly rational, subject to the influence of their immediate social context, embarking on wrongdoing crescively, without ever developing a positive inclination to do so. In common parlance, these accounts portray wrongdoers as frequently lacking forethought, buffeted by powerful external forces, stumbling into wrongdoing, without ever developing malevolent intent. Further, in the first

269

chapter of the book I explicitly state that I have much sympathy for wrong-doers who slip into wrongdoing in this way.

Any characterizations of this book as an apology for organizational wrong-doers, though, would miss what I believe are other overriding features of my analysis. First, most of the descriptions of wrongdoing used to develop and illustrate the ideas advanced in the book were based on depictions prepared by outsiders who obtained inside information about the wrongdoing in question. And I think that many of these outsiders were unsympathetic to the wrong-doers they portrayed. All of the outsiders were subject to the fundamental attribution error, which causes observers to locate the causes of behavior within the individual who perpetrates it, rather than the social context in which the perpetrator is embedded (Nisbett and Ross 1980). Thus, they likely assumed that the wrongdoers they observed engaged in wrongdoing as the result of mindful, rational calculations or assessments that left them positively inclined to do wrong. Moreover, many of the outsiders who provided the depictions upon which I based my illustrations were investigative journalists or law enforcement officials who likely were occupationally predisposed to embrace the cost-benefit calculation and normative assessment explanations of wrongdoing. The authors of books and articles about wrongdoing craft their stories to feature good guys and bad guys, because this conforms to popular literary conventions. Prosecutors and plaintiff attorneys interrogate perpetra-tors and witnesses to wrongdoing with the desire to uncover bad intent, because the criminal code associates bad intent with guilt, and the civil code associates it with punitive damages. As a result, I strongly suspect that many of the depictions of wrongdoing that I use to build and illustrate my arguments about the causes of wrongdoing were not biased in favor of my arguments but instead were prejudiced against them.

Second, as indicated in Chapter 3, I draw a sharp line between normative and social science objectives and firmly chose to pursue the latter at the expense of the former. As a result, I have approached the wrongdoers described in this book as first and foremost subjects to be explained, rather than condemned. Thus, my analysis of organizational wrongdoing withholds judgment on the wrongdoers portrayed in this book—it does not pass verdict on them one way or the other. Finally, while I have said that I have sympathy for many organizational wrongdoers, I have not said that I consider their behavior appropriate or that I consider the consequences of their behavior acceptable. In fact, I find most of the instances of wrongdoing described in this book deplorable. The financial investment misrepresentations at Prudential Bache, the accounting manipulations at MCI, and the market manipulations and financial fraud at Enron created serious negative economic consequences for customers, employees, and other stakeholders. The underreporting of adverse drug effects at Wyeth, the obfuscation of breast implant defects at

Dow Chemical, and the chemical disaster at Union Carbide's Bhopal plant created incalculable human misery. For this reason, I conclude the book by considering prescriptions for curbing wrongdoing suggested by the explanations of wrongdoing elaborated here.

Prescriptions for eradicating organizational wrongdoing

Remedies based on the dominant accounts

As indicated in Chapter 4, the rational choice explanation of organizational wrongdoing naturally gives rise to calls for governance reform: the establishment of clear guidelines separating right from wrong, the institution of mechanisms for monitoring behavior relative to these guidelines, and the meting out of certain severe punishments to wrongdoers when misconduct is detected. As indicated in Chapter 5, the culture account of organizational wrongdoing naturally gives rise to calls for moral rehabilitation: the delineation of assumptions, values and beliefs, and norms that stipulate appropriate conduct, the socialization of employees into these cultural elements, and the training of employees to apply the internalized assumptions, values and beliefs, and norms to practical business situations.

Governance reform and moral rehabilitation are the two most popular prescriptions for curbing wrongdoing in and of organizations. Some debate the relative efficacy of the two prescriptions, with the majority of debaters at this time favoring moral rehabilitation over governance reforms. Social pressure to conform to cultural norms related to ethics, social responsibility, and the law is thought to be a more potent deterrent of wrongdoing than the threat of detection and punishment. Moreover, a focus on governance reform is thought to promote a business framing of questions of moral significance, which is believed to reduce compliance with ethical principles, social responsibility doctrines, and the law (Tenbrunsel and Messick 1999; Tenbrunsel, Diekmann, Wade-Benzoni, and Bazerman 2010). But I suspect the vast majority of academics would agree that both governance reform and moral rehabilitation can help suppress the level of wrongdoing in organizations. Indeed, belief in the efficacy of governance reform and moral rehabilitation is so strong that even authors who advocate what I have called alternative explanations of organizational wrongdoing reflexively embrace these prescriptions.

As detailed in Chapter 8, Ashforth and Anand (2003) present a theory of corporate corruption that features the role that situational social influence and administrative systems play in the diffusion and institutionalization of misconduct. But they offer prescriptions for curbing wrongdoing that, for the most part, fall under the rubric of governance reform and moral rehabilitation. Indeed, they preface their elaboration of prescriptions for curbing wrongdoing with the statement, "These means are not unknown (2003: 39)." For example, Ashforth and Anand recommend that organizations seeking to inhibit corruption develop more intrusive monitoring mechanisms, such as ethical audits, inquisitive boards of directors, and hotlines that employees can use to report wrongdoing. Further, they encourage organizations to administer serious punishments to those found to have engaged in misconduct. Ashforth and Anand also recommend that organizations socialize their employees to take moral considerations into account and to train them to adhere to codes of ethics when formulating their behavior. They also encourage organizations to hire moral experts, upon whom employees can call when confronted with vexing ethical, social responsibility, or legal dilemmas. Finally, they recommend that organizations establish cultures in which employees are assumed to be motivated and capable of pursuing rightful behavior, citing research showing that employees who feel trusted by their superiors will tend to live up to their superiors' expectations. Of course, this last recommendation directly contradicts their prior suggestion to increase the monitoring of employees, perhaps unintentionally pointing to the inherent tension between governance reform and moral rehabilitation identified by ethical decision theorists (Tenbrunsel and Messick 1999).

Also as indicated in Chapter 8, Brief, Bertram, and Dukerich (2001) present a theory of corporate corruption that focuses on the role that formal authority and a range of situational social influence mechanisms play in the diffusion of corruption. But many of the prescriptions for curbing wrongdoing that they offer also fall under the rubric of governance reform and moral rehabilitation. For example, they recommend instituting cultural beliefs that expand the definition of employee loyalty to encompass responsibility to peers, customers, and constituents of the organization's environment. In keeping with this suggestion, they encourage the promulgation of cultural norms that support "functional disobedience," which they define as subordinate scrutiny (through peer discussion) of morally questionable orders issued by superiors. Brief, Bertram, and Dukerich also advocate that organizations establish unambiguous functional disobedience goals, provide employees with the resources (such as training and protocols) needed to attain those goals, and reward employees (and certainly refrain from punishing them) for exhibiting functional disobedient behavior.

I am certain that governance reform and moral rehabilitation can help curb organizational wrongdoing. Had the savings and loan industry not been deregulated in the 1980s, reducing the extent and enforcement of legal constraints on thrift behavior, the massive looting of thrifts that followed might not have occurred. Had Enron and MCI's cultures not endorsed a disdain for establishing and following procedures, the accounting frauds that characterized those firms might not have eventuated. However, I doubt that these remedies alone will be sufficient to eradicate wrongdoing in and of organizations. As indicated in Chapter 4, it is difficult to align incentives so that they motivate right doing, without inadvertently motivating wrongdoing. Further, monitoring and punishing wrongdoing incurs costs that sometimes do not outweigh the benefits of eliminating wrongdoing, making some minimal level of organizational wrongdoing economically rational. In addition, as indicated in Chapter 5, cultures that give rise to wrongdoing sometimes are adaptive responses to enduring environmental conditions. Thus, adaptation to organizational environments sometimes brings with it the risk of wrongdoing. Finally, more fundamentally, governance reform and moral rehabilitation are based on the rational choice and cultural explanations of wrongdoing, which provide incomplete accounts of organizational wrongdoing. The rational choice and cultural accounts are rooted in assumptions about organizational wrongdoing that are not invariably valid, assumptions that wrongdoing is the product of mindful and rational deliberation, conducted in an immediate social vacuum, and that results in discrete decisions and a positive inclination to engage in wrongdoing. To go beyond governance reform and moral rehabilitation, we need to consider the practical implications of the alternative explanations of organizational wrongdoing.

Remedies based on the alternative accounts

PRESCRIPTIONS FOR CURBING THE WRONGDOING OF OTHERS

I have elaborated six explanations of organizational wrongdoing that embrace one or more of the assumptions of the alternative approach to explaining wrongdoing: the ethical decision, administrative system, situational social influence, power structure, accidental behavior, and social control accounts. Proponents of several of these explanations of organizational wrongdoing have suggested programs for curbing wrongdoing based on their ideas.

As indicated above, Ashforth and Anand (2003) delineate several ways in which administrative systems can institutionalize wrongdoing in organizations. Consistent with their analysis, Ashforth and Anand recommend that organizations incorporate moral considerations into organizational procedures and decision-making protocols. Similarly, as noted in Chapter 7, Dennis Gioia (1992) describes how the scripts and schemas that organizational participants develop to increase their efficiency and effectiveness can cause them inadvertently to engage in wrongdoing. Thus, Gioia recommends that organizations train employees to recognize moral issues so that they can better determine when it is appropriate to break from schemas and scripts and deliberate in a less restricted way about the relative normative merits of alternative courses of action.

Likewise, as indicated above, Brief, Bertram, and Dukerich (2001) examine the role that formal authority can play in spreading misconduct throughout organizations. Consistent with their analysis, they recommend that formal authority be dispersed throughout the organization, such that subordinates report to multiple superiors. In this way, the authority that a corrupt superior might have over subordinates can be counterbalanced by the authority that other potentially virtuous superiors have over the subordinates. Brief and his associates also elaborate the role that situational social influence mechanisms play in proliferating misconduct throughout organizations. Among other things, they contend that pressure to conform to small-group norms can cause group members to participate in wrongdoing in which the group's other members are involved. Consistent with this analysis, Brief and his associates recommend that persons subject to such small-group pressures take a lesson from experimental research on resistance to group pressures. This research suggests that people can resist group pressures to conform more effectively if they express their resistance in an unwavering yet flexible way, and if they justify their resistance by appealing to logic that resonates with the majority. For example, if a corrupt group's members are prone to evaluating behavior in cost-benefit terms, resistors should justify their opposition to the group's corrupt behavior in those terms.

I think the prescriptions suggested by Ashforth and Anand (2003), Gioia (1992), and Brief, Bertram, and Dukerich (2001) might help curb organizational wrongdoing. And I think the line of thinking pioneered by these authors, if developed further, will produce other potentially useful prescriptions. Perhaps if managers had designed the communication channels, technology, and division of labor at Prudential Bache to take into account ethical considerations, the firm's brokers might not have marketed risky and fraudulent limited partnerships aggressively to their retired clients who were looking for safe investments. Perhaps if power had been more widely distributed and employee loyalty more broadly defined at Wyeth, Amy Meyers would have felt free to disregard her superiors' implicit orders to alter the firm's ADE database to under-report instances of fenfluramine-related adverse drug effects.

Nevertheless, I also think that these proposed solutions and others like them will not completely curtail wrongdoing that originates in structures and processes identified by the alternative accounts of organizational wrongdoing. First, the administrative systems, situational social influence mechanisms, and power structures that these solutions attack are the substance of organizations. They are responsible for much of what is right in organizations and often generate wrongdoing as a by-product of their positive effects. As a result, these structures and processes are likely to give rise to wrongdoing even when designed with the most earnest forethought. Second, these sorts of solutions focus on the behavior of others. But, the normal organizational wrongdoing perspective championed in this book suggests that even those concerned with curbing the wrongdoing of others are at risk of engaging in wrongdoing. I consider remedies that address this problem below.

REMEDIES FOR CURBING ONE'S OWN WRONGDOING

When managers seek advice from academicians and consultants about how to curb organizational wrongdoing, they invariably seek solutions that promise to reduce the likelihood that their subordinates, their peers, and even their superiors will engage in wrongdoing. That is, they seek solutions intended to reduce the likelihood that other people will do wrong. As such, they implicitly assume that people concerned with reducing wrongdoing, people like themselves, are not at risk of engaging in wrongdoing. This assumption flies in the face of logic and anecdotal evidence. I suspect that the vast majority of organizational participants honestly want to curb wrongdoing in and of their organizations. But if the vast majority of concerned organizational participants themselves are not susceptible to engaging in wrongdoing, if it is others who are at risk of perpetrating misconduct, then the problem of wrongdoing should be quite small. Casual observation suggests that this is not the case.

The folly of thinking that others rather than oneself are at risk of misconduct also is suggested by the numerous instances of wrongdoing perpetrated by otherwise ethical, socially responsible, and law-abiding individuals. Dow Corning established a celebrated comprehensive ethics program. They elaborated a detailed code of conduct, assigned a high-level manager to oversee continual improvement and implementation of the code, and instituted a variety of programs (the most important of which were ethical audits) to ensure that employees were informed of, and complied with, the code. Yet, Dow Corning also marketed breast implants that are believed to have generated serious health problems for the women who received them, despite becoming increasingly aware of the implants' probable dangers (Byrne 1997).

Enron's chairman, Ken Lay, considered himself a value-based leader and spoke often about the importance of considering moral issues when making business decisions (cf. Novak 1996). He claimed to be a religious man (his father was a Christian minister) and to have begun many of Enron business meetings with prayer (Darden 2002). WorldCom's CEO Bernie Ebbers considered himself to be an ethical leader. By all accounts he was an intensely religious man, a Baptist, who attended church regularly and taught Sunday school. Yet both Lay and Ebbers are believed to have facilitated serious organizational wrongdoing. Lay was convicted of ten counts of fraud (but died before he could be sentenced). Ebbers sits in prison today. Both men have been vilified since their respective downfalls, with many journalists finding previously undetected predilections to wrongdoing in their past, implying that they were self-deluded at best and hypocritical at worst (cf. Catan, Kirchgaessner, Ratner, and Larsen 2003). But, I think such retrospective psychological analyses are suspect because they likely suffer from the well-known cognitive trap: hindsight bias.

Moreover, the idea that people who are concerned with reducing wrongdoing are not at risk of participating in wrongdoing runs counter to the main thrust of this book. *Normal Organizational Wrongdoing* champions the view that wrongdoers often are not unusually malevolent human beings, and that wrongdoing often is the product of structures and processes that are prevalent in organizations, indeed, the same structures and processes that produce rightdoing. This implies that if wrongdoing is to be curbed, all organizational participants, even those concerned with curbing wrongdoing, including people like the readers and author of this book, need to become sensitive to the structures and processes that can cause them to engage in wrongdoing. They also need to become familiar with and adept at using measures to blunt those forces. The cognitive psychologists who study ethical decision making have offered several useful prescriptions of this sort. And at least one social psychologist who has studied situational social influence mechanisms and formal authority has offered suggestions that we can use to construct additional prescriptions.

Cognitive psychology
Cognitive psychologists who study ethical decision making have been particularly attentive to the practical implications of their work.[1] Almost every research article in this area ends with suggestions on how people might reduce their susceptibility to the cognitive lapses identified therein. For the most part, these suggestions fall into three categories: recommendations that people become more aware of cognitive limits to ethical decision making, suggestions on how to reduce those limits, and ideas about how to blunt their effects. For example, Kern and Chugh (2009), who study the impact of framing on ethical decision making, recommend that people alternate between loss and gains framing of ethical dilemmas to increase their sensitivity to the impact that framing has on their preferences. Further, they recommend that people deliberate about ethical dilemmas in an unhurried manner because research indicates that framing effects are most potent when people have little time to mull over decision alternatives.

---

[1] Bazerman and Tenbrunsel (2011) have written a book that elaborates in greater detail the implications of the cognitive psychological research on ethical decision making for students and managers. Readers interested in learning more about the implications of the cognitive psychological work should consult this excellent monograph, which was published too late to receive adequate treatment here.

Similarly, Banaji, Bazerman, and Chugh (2003), who study the impact of cognitive biases on ethical decision making, recommend that people take the Implicit Association Test, a diagnostic instrument that reveals unconscious biases, to increase their sensitivity to the biases that they possess. Further, they recommend that people make efforts to broaden their decision making so as to blunt the impact of the biases that they hold. For example, they recommend that people employ Rawl's "veil of ignorance" strategy when making ethical decisions, asking themselves to consider the dilemma as if they were not an interested party. Finally, they recommend that people who suspect that they harbor biases expose themselves to new environments that are likely to disconfirm and thus eradicate their biases.

Likewise, Tenbrunsel and her colleagues (Tenbrunsel et al. 2010), who study the temporal dynamics of ethical decision making, recommend that people develop ways to control the battle between the "want self" and the "should self," which they contend unfolds over time in the ethical decision-making process. They suggest that people be alerted to the want/should self conflict. They also recommend that people be taught ways to manage the effects of the "want self." For instance, they propose that people forecast the concerns of the "want self" and envision resolutions of the ethical dilemma that meet those concerns (e.g. by delaying the costs of ethical choices) and at the same time conform to ethical principles. Further, they recommend that people be taught ways to enhance the salience of the "should self." For example, they propose that people set aside sufficient time to contemplate ethical decisions, focus on "high-level aspects" of decisions, and consider decision alternatives simultaneously rather than sequentially.

I think the remedies proposed by cognitive psychologists will help curb wrongdoing in organizations. If Walter Pavlo had been alerted to the cognitive bias in which people underestimate the extent to which they are subject to conflicts of interest, he might not have attended the golf tournament with Harold Mann that led him to develop a relationship with the shady businessman that culminated in the fraudulent factoring scheme at MCI. If Joseph Jett had been alerted to the framing effect in which people who frame decisions in terms of the losses they can avert are more likely to engage in unethical behavior, he might not have exploited the computer glitch that facilitated his booking of phony profits at Kidder Peabody.

With that said, I suspect the remedies proposed by cognitive psychologists, even if employed consummately, will not completely eradicate wrongdoing facilitated by framing effects and cognitive biases for at least three reasons. First, most of the cognitive psychological remedies require that people facing an ethical decision understand that they are facing a decision and that the decision has moral implications. Without such an understanding, people will not realize that it is appropriate to employ the proposed decision bias and framing effect remedies. But, as I have argued repeatedly throughout this book, organizational participants do not always deliberate in a mindful way (i.e. they do not always make decisions) before engaging in behavior. Further, as ethical decision theorists themselves point out, people do not always become aware of the fact that the decisions they face have ethical implications.

Second, most of the remedies proposed by cognitive psychologists require people to return to what might be considered a hyper-rational state, one in which people allot for themselves a sufficient amount of time to make decisions and consider a broad range of decision criteria and alternatives. But as I have argued, organizational participants often do not have the time or capacity to engage in unboundedly rational decision making. Thus, in a sense, cognitive psychologists are asking organizational participants to employ fixes that are simply not feasible in most organizational contexts.

Third, most of the remedies proposed by cognitive psychologists require people to override tendencies that they have demonstrated are pervasive and powerful. Indeed, functional MRI studies suggest that framing effects and cognitive biases are rooted in neurological pathways; that is, they are "hard-wired" so to speak (De Martino, Kumaran, Seymour, and Dolan 2006). Thus, in a sense, cognitive psychologists are asking organizational participants to employ fixes that are not likely to stand up to the deeply engrained psychological or programmed neurological processes that they are designed to override.

Situational social influence and formal authority

Cialdini's (2001) popular primer on social influence techniques used by marketers, salespersons, and other "compliance professionals" provides an excellent source of insights on how organizational participants might cope with instances in which situational social influence and formal authority (which Cialdini categorizes as a form of social influence) propel them to engage in wrongdoing. Cialdini examines how compliance professionals use commitment processes, social comparison pressures, formal authority, and the norm of reciprocity to cause people to engage in behaviors that they otherwise would eschew. Further, crucially, he sets forth strategies that people might use to blunt the effects of these forms of social influence. I draw on this second part of Cialdini's analysis to discern ways that people might resist the situational social forces driving them to engage in wrongdoing.

Cialdini maintains that people can detect the operation of social influence by paying attention to the "pit of their stomach" (p. 91). This is not a baseless suggestion. Recent studies, including rigorous laboratory experiments that employ functional MRI scans of the human brain, indicate that people begin to formulate their reactions to matters related to morality and self-interest split seconds before they conduct logical deliberations about those matters. It is unclear whether the instantaneous reactions, which have been characterized as emotions or intuition, are part and parcel of deliberate thought or whether they prefigure and dictate its outcome. Regardless, these reactions tend to be associated with physiological responses that people can monitor, in the form of what we commonly refer to as "gut checks."

Once a gut check causes an organizational participant to suspect that situational social influence processes are pushing them in a direction that they otherwise would not want to go, they can examine their situation for signs of these mechanisms. If they uncover evidence that one of these mechanisms is at work, they can summarily abandon the course of behavior on which they have embarked. Alternatively, they can adopt a more selective but difficult to implement approach, attempting to disengage the situational social influence mechanism so that the merits of the course of action can be evaluated on rational terms.

For example, Cialdini recommends that if a gut check leads a person to suspect that she has embarked on a questionable course of action, and a subsequent situational analysis leads her to suspect that she has become subject to the influence of a commitment process, she should re-evaluate her course of action. Importantly, she should re-evaluate her behavior, taking into account all of the information she has gleaned since embarking on the course of action. This implies that organizational participants whose guts suggest that they might have embarked on a morally questionable course of action, and whose minds suggest that they might be subject to a commitment process, should stop and ask themselves whether they would have embarked on the questionable course of action if they knew then everything they know now about the course of action.

Similarly, Cialdini recommends that if a gut check leads a person to suspect that he has embarked on a questionable course of action, and a subsequent analysis leads him to suspect it is because others are also engaged in the behavior, he should double check the authenticity and appropriateness of the models he is emulating. If a person concludes that the model is counterfeit or ill informed, Cialdini recommends that he re-evaluate the course of action on rational terms. This implies that organizational participants whose guts suggest that they might have embarked on a morally questionable course of action, and whose minds suggest that they might be subject to a social comparison process, should double check the authenticity and wisdom of those to whom they are comparing themselves, perhaps at the suggestion of others. For example, if someone exhorts us to engage in a course of action because everyone else is doing it, we should investigate whether many others actually are engaged in the behavior. If we conclude that many others actually are engaged in the behavior, we should further determine whether their behavior is based on good information and solid reasoning. In a sense, we should make sure that we are not following a fictitious or injudicious crowd of others into wrongful behavior.

If a gut check leads a person to suspect that she has embarked on a questionable course of action, and a subsequent analysis leads her to suspect that she embarked on the course of action in response to the request of someone she likes, Cialdini recommends that she mentally separate the affection she feels for the person making the request from the evaluation of the request the person is making. That is, he suggests she ask herself whether she would be inclined to accept the request if the requester were not someone she liked. Cialdini maintains that the need to blunt the liking effect is heightened if people on reflection conclude that they have come to like the requester more quickly than is normally the case, suggesting that the requester might have befriended them with ulterior motives in mind. This implies that organizational participants whose guts suggest that they might have embarked on a morally questionable course of action, and whose minds suggest that they might have embarked on the behavior because they are subject to the liking effect, should ask themselves whether they would have embarked on the course of action had not they liked the person who invited them to participate in the course of action.

If a gut check leads a person to suspect that he has embarked on a questionable course of action and a subsequent situational analysis leads him to suspect that he has embarked on the behavior in response to an order issued by a formal authority, Cialdini recommends that he check the credentials and investigate the motivations of the authority whom he feels obligated to obey. If he finds the authority does not possess credentials relevant to the issue at hand, or discovers that the authority has ulterior motives, Cialdini suggests the person give himself permission to disobey the authority. This implies that organizational participants whose guts suggest that they might have embarked on a morally questionable course of action, and whose minds suggest that they might be subject to the norm of obedience to authority, should double check the credentials and motivations of the authority ordering them to engage in the behavior. And if the credentials are found to be irrelevant to the matter at hand, or if the motivations are found to be questionable, they should release themselves from the obligation to comply.

Finally, Cialdini recommends that if a gut check leads a person to suspect that she has embarked on a questionable course of action, and a subsequent analysis leads her to suspect that she has embarked on the course of action partly at the request of someone to whom she owes a favor, she should investigate the motives of the person whose prior favor she feels obligated to reciprocate. If the motives of the gift giver are found to be instrumental, then Cialdini encourages the person to view the favors not as gifts to be reciprocated but rather as traps to be eluded. This implies that organizational participants whose guts suggest that they have embarked on a morally questionable course of action, and whose minds detect the influence of the norm of reciprocity, should investigate the motivations of the favor giver. And if the motivations are found to be instrumental, the favor should not be reciprocated.

I think that Cialdini's recommended defenses against the effects of situational social influence and formal authority are sensible. Kermit Vandivier participated in the writing of a fraudulent qualification report for B.F. Goodrich's A7D jet fighter brake. I argued in Chapter 8 that Vandivier co-authored the report despite having serious reservations about doing so, partly because he had become committed to writing the report through a series of small steps. Perhaps if Vandivier had trusted his gut and re-evaluated his decision to facilitate the fraud when he sat down to write the final report, he would have gone to the FBI then and there, rather than wait for the brake to fail on the plane's first test flights. Similarly, David Levine persuaded several investment bank executives to provide him with inside information about merger and acquisition deals at their banks. I maintained that Levine was able to persuade the investment bankers to provide him with inside information, partly by presenting himself as a likable person, which he did partly by emphasizing the few similarities he shared with the bankers and partly by offering them favors both small and large. Perhaps if the investment bankers had questioned why they had come to like Levine so quickly, and asked themselves whether they would provide the requested inside information to someone that they did not like as much as they liked Levine, the bankers would not have provided him with the information. Perhaps if the bankers had investigated Levine's motivation for providing them with favors, they would have come to the conclusion that his motives were instrumental, and they would have withheld the information.

Nevertheless, I think Cialdini's recommended defenses are unlikely to completely eradicate wrongdoing that is facilitated by situational social influence and formal authority, even if implemented consummately. First, by Cialdini's own account, the social psychological mechanisms he describes are extremely powerful and possibly even hard-wired, exhibiting what he refers to as a "click-whirr" character. It likely will prove challenging to mentally disengage powerful norms, such as the obligation to reciprocate favors and obey authorities. It probably will prove difficult to shut off personal feelings such as the affection for friends. It likely will be hard to resist the temptation to copy others in one's environment when the alternative is time-consuming effortful analyses of the relative merits of multiple available courses of action. Further, any behavior set in motion of one's own volition, that has become known to others, and that is costly to reverse will give rise to formidable pressures to rationalize and continue the behavior.

Second, several of Cialdini's recommended defenses require people subject to social influence to collect information that will be difficult to obtain, and conduct assessments that will be hard to carry out in an organizational context. For example, Cialdini's recommended defense against the norms of reciprocity and obedience requires people subject to these social psychological mechanisms to assess the motivations of gift givers and authorities. Similarly, his recommended defense against social comparison processes and the norm of obedience requires people subject to these social psychological mechanisms to determine the qualifications of the models and authorities in their environment. It seems likely that even the most alert organizational participants sometimes will fail in their attempts to make these determinations. For example, a subordinate might rightly conclude that his or her superior is a legitimate authority, but wrongly conclude that the superior's motivations are proper.

Finally, my analysis in the previous chapter implies that even if all of the remedies considered in this chapter are applied consummately, some wrongdoing in and of organizations will remain. Social control agents create the categories of right-doing and wrongdoing when they draw the line separating right from wrong. Given the wide variation in organizational behavior, it is highly unlikely that they will draw the line separating right from wrong in a fashion that leaves no organizational participants on the wrong side of the line. Further, social control agents are evaluated on the basis of their success at apprehending wrongdoers by the constituencies they represent. Thus they tend to behave in ways that increase the likelihood that organizational participants will cross the line separating right from wrong.

Moreover, social control agents draw the line separating right from wrong in a manner that reflects their interests and capacities. Social control agents draw the line separating right from wrong in a manner that reflects the interests of their constituency as a whole, but that privileges the interests of their constituency's most powerful members. This points to the fact that social control agents' constituencies are composed of interest groups that compete with one another over the location of the line separating right from wrong, favoring positions that maximize their narrow interests. Social control agents also draw the line separating right from wrong in a fashion that furthers their own survival and growth, most importantly, so as to insure the uninterrupted flow of resources. And this puts the state at odds with other organizational actors. It is hard for organizational participants to forecast the outcomes of these contests among competing interests. As a result, it is likely that organizational participants on occasion will cross the line separating right from wrong simply because they do not have a good idea of where the line is drawn.[2]

---

[2] Braithwaite (2002) has offered an alternative to the dominant regulatory model that promises to moderate some of these tendencies. This alternative, known as "restorative justice," has been

Summing-up

I began this chapter by reviewing my analytical objectives: generally to provide a critical review of theories of the causes of organizational wrongdoing, and more specifically to champion the normal organizational wrongdoing perspective, to advocate the alternative approach to analyzing the causes of wrongdoing, and to contribute to the development of explanations of organizational wrongdoing that are associated with my favored perspective and approach. I then briefly acknowledged and addressed one possible misinterpretation of my outlook. Finally, I outlined a number of prescriptions for curbing wrongdoing in and of organizations based on the explanations of wrongdoing considered in the book. I reiterated popular remedies that follow from the dominant explanations of organizational wrongdoing: governance reform and moral rehabilitation. I also identified a number of formulae for curbing wrongdoing that follow from the alternative accounts: some that focus on reducing the likelihood that others will engage in wrongdoing and other formulae that focus on helping us avoid slipping into wrongdoing ourselves. But I conclude that these prescriptions, even if implemented consummately and in consort, will not completely curb wrongdoing. One might wish for a more upbeat prognosis for the future. Instead, I have provided what I believe is a realistic projection of our possibilities.

Social control agents establish the line between right and wrong in the context of a political struggle. If we think the line has been drawn inappropriately, we must engage in political activity to move it to a new location. It's a messy business, but unavoidable. A plethora of forces act on organizational participants that cause them to cross the line separating right from wrong where social control agents draw it, the vast majority of which also generate right-doing. If we want to reduce the incidence of organizational wrongdoing, we need to do our best to align those forces to maximize right-doing and to minimize wrongdoing, recognizing that we will never eliminate the latter. Moreover, we need to sensitize ourselves to the ways in which the forces that give rise to wrongdoing operate on us so that we can blunt their influence and avoid unintentionally engaging in wrongdoing ourselves. I hope that this book will help readers succeed in these very practical undertakings, especially in this last endeavor.

employed with some success in his home country of Australia but so far has not been utilized extensively elsewhere.

References

Abbot, A. (2009), "What do cases do? Some notes on activity in sociological analysis," in Ragin, C. C. and Becker, H. S. (eds.), *What Is a Case?* Cambridge University Press, Cambridge, England, 53–82.

Achbar, M. and Abbott, J. A. (2004), *The Corporation*, Zeitgeist Films Ltd, Canada.

Adut, A. (2004), "Scandal as norm entrepreneurship strategy: Corruption and the French investigating magistrates," *Theory and Society*, Vol. 33, 529–78.

——(2005), "A theory of scandal: Victorians, homosexuality, and the fall of Oscar Wilde," *American Journal of Sociology*, Vol. 111, 213–48.

Agnew, R. (1985), "A revised strain theory of delinquency," *Social Forces,* Vol. 64, No. 1, 151–67.

——(1992), "Foundation for a general strain theory of crime and delinquency," *Criminology,* Vol. 30, No. 1, 47–87.

——Piquero, N., and Cullen F. T. (2009), "General strain theory and white-collar crime," in Simpson, S. and Weisburd, D. (eds.), *The Criminology of White-Collar Crime*, Springer, New York, NY, 35–60.

Albergotti, R. and O'Connell, V. (2010), "The case of the missing bikes," *The Wall Street Journal*, July 3. Available at: http://online.wsj.com/article/SB100014240527487039 64104575334812419976690.html.

Allen, S. and Murphy, S. P. (2006), "Cheaper, faster path led to failure," *Boston Globe,* December 24. Available at: http://www.boston.com/news/traffic/bigdig/articles/2006/12/24/cheaper_faster_path_led_to_failure/.

Anderson, C., Keltner, D. J., and John, O. P. (2003), "Emotional convergence between people over time," *Journal of Personality and Social Psychology*, Vol. 84, 1054–68.

Anderson, J. (2008), "Two brokers accused of securities fraud," *New York Times*, September 3. Available at: http://www.nytimes.com/2008/09/04/business/04auction.html

Appel, A. (2009), "Lawsuits accuse mortgage lenders of rip-offs," *FinallCall.com News,* March 27. Available at: http://www.finalcall.com/artman/publish/article_5726.shtml.

Ariely, D. (2008), *Predictably Irrational: The Hidden Forces That Shape Our Decisions,* Harper Collins, New York, NY.

Aronson, E. (1973), "The rationalizing animal," in Staw, B. (ed.), *Psychological Dimensions of Organizational Behavior* (Second Edition), Prentice Hall, Englewood Cliffs, NJ, 131–8.

——(2007 [1972]), *The Social Animal*, Worth Publishers, New York, NY.

Ashforth, B. E. and Anand, V. (2003), "The normalization of corruption in organizations," *Research in Organizational Behavior*, Vol. 25, 1–52.

———— and Joshi, M. (2004), "Business as usual: The acceptance and perpetuation of corruption in organizations," *Academy of Management Executive*, Vol. 18, No. 2, 39–53.

Ashforth, B. E., Gioia, D. A., Robinson, S. L., and Trevino, L. K. (2008), "Re-viewing organizational corruption," *Academy of Management Review*, Vol. 33, No. 3, 670–84.

Ashforth, B. E. and Kreiner, G. E. (2002), "Normalizing emotion in organizations: Making the extraordinary seem ordinary," *Human Resource Management Review*, Vol. 12, 215–35.

Asinof, E. (1987), *Eight Men Out: The Black Sax and the 1919 World Series,* Henry Holt and Company, New York, NY.

Augier, M., March, J. G., and Sullivan, B. N. (2005), "Notes on the evolution of a research community: Organization studies in Anglophone North America, 1945–2000," *Organization Science*, Vol. 16, 85–95.

Axelrod, R. (1984), *The Evolution of Cooperation,* Basic Books, New York, NY.

Baker, W. and Levine, S. (2010), "Mechanisms of generalized exchange: Towards an integrated model," unpublished manuscript, University of Michigan.

Baker, W. E. and Faulkner, R. R. (1993), "The social organization of conspiracy: Illegal networks in the heavy electrical equipment industry," *American Sociological Review*, Vol. 58, 837–60.

Banaji, M., Bazerman, M., and Chugh, D. (2003), "How (unethical) are you?" *Harvard Business Review*, Vol. 81, No. 12, 56–64.

Bandura, A. (1990), "Selective activation and disengagement of moral conduct," *Journal of Social Issues*, Vol. 46, No. 1, 27–46.

——(1999), "Moral disengagement in the perpetration of inhumanities," *Personality and Social Psychology Review*, Vol. 3, 193–209.

——Barbaranelli, C., Caprara, G. V, and Pastorelli, C. (1996), "Mechanisms of moral disengagement in the exercise of moral agency," *Journal of Personality and Social Psychology*, Vol. 7, 364–74.

Bar-Lev, Amir (2010), *The Pat Tillman Story*, Sony Pictures.

Bargh, J. A. and Alvarez, J. (2001), "The road to hell: Good intentions in the face of nonconscious tendencies to misuse power," in Lee-Chai, A. Y. and Bargh, J. A. (eds.), *The Use and Abuse of Power*, Psychology Press, Philadelphia, PA, 41–56.

Barnard, C. (1938), *The Function of the Executive,* Harvard University Press, Cambridge, MA.

Barrett, D. (2009), "FBI investigating 530 corporate fraud cases," *The Seattle Times*, February 11. Available at: http://seattletimes.nwsource.com/html/politics/2008732400_apbailoutfraud.html.

Bartky, S. L. (1990), *Femininity and Domination: Studies in the Phenomenology of Oppression*, Routledge, New York, NY.

Bartlett, C. A. and Glinska, M. (2001), *Enron's Transformation: From Gas Pipeline to New Economy Powerhouse*, Harvard Business School Press, Boston, MA.

Bartunek, J. (2003), "Presidential address: A dream for the academy," *Academy of Management Review*, Vol. 28, 198–203.

Bazerman, M. (2006), *Judgment in Managerial Decision-Making*, John Wiley and Sons, Hoboken, NJ.

Bazerman, M. H. and Tenbrunsel, A. E. (2011), *Blind Spots: Why We Fail to Do What's Right and What to Do about It*, Princeton University Press, Princeton, NJ.

Becker, G. S. (1968), "Crime and Punishment: An Economic Approach," *Journal of Political Economy*, Vol. 76, 169–217.

Becker, H. S. (1956), *Man in Reciprocity*, Prager, New York, NY.

——(1963), *Outsiders: Studies in the Sociology of Deviance*, Free Press, New York, NY.

Berle, A. A. and Means, G. C. (1932), *The Modern Corporation and Private Property*, Harcourt, Brace and World, New York, NY.

Boisjoly, R. (1987), "Ethical decisions: Morton Thiokol and the space shuttle Challenger disaster," American Society of Mechanical Engineers Winter Annual Meeting, December 13–18, Boston, MA.

Bookstaber, R. (2007), *A Demon of Our Own Design: Markets, Hedge Funds, and the Perils of Financial Innovation*, John Wiley and Sons, Hoboken, NJ.

Boulding, K. E. (1958), "Evidences for an administrative science: A review of the *Administrative Science Quarterly*, volumes 1 and 2," *Administrative Science Quarterly*, Vol. 3, No. 1, 1–22.

Braithwaite, J. (1988), "White-Collar Crime, Competition, and Capitalism: Comment on Coleman," *American Journal of Sociology*, Vol. 94, No. 3, 627–32.

——(1989), "Criminological theory and organizational crime," *Justice Quarterly*, Vol. 6, 333–58.

——(2002), *Restorative Justice and Responsive Regulation*, Oxford University Press, Oxford, UK.

——(2005), *Markets in Vice, Markets in Virtue*, Oxford University Press, Oxford, UK.

Braverman, H. (1974), *Labor and Monopoly Capitalism*, Monthly Review Press, New York, NY.

Brief, A. P., Bertram, R. T., and Dukerich, J. M. (2001), "Collective corruption in the corporate world: Toward a process model," in Turner, M. E. (ed.), *Groups at Work: Advances in Theory and Research*, Lawrence Erlbaum and Associates, Hillsdale, NJ, 471–99.

Brief, A. P., Dietz, J., Cohen, R. R., Puch, S. D., and Vaslow, J. B. (2000), "Just doing business: Modern racism and obedience to authority as explanations for employment discrimination," *Organizational Behavior and Human Decision Processes*, Vol. 81, No. 1, 72–97.

Broughton, P. D. (2002), "Enron cocktail of cash, sex, and fast living," *The Telegraph*, February 13. Available at: http://www.telegraph.co.uk/news/worldnews/northamerica/usa/1382962/Enron-cocktail-of-cash-sex-and-fast-living.html.

Bryce, R. (2002), *Pipe Dreams*, Public Affairs, New York, NY.

Byrne, J. A. (1997), *Informed Consent*, McGraw-Hill, New York, NY.

Burger, J. M. (2009), "Replicating Milgram: Would people still obey today?" *American Psychologist*, 64, 1–11.

Burns, J. (2008), "FBI mortgage-fraud probe is looking at big firms," *The Wall Street Journal*, June 20. Available at: http://online.wsj.com/article/SB121389023486688775.html? KEYWORDS=FBI+mortgage-fraud+probe+is+looking+at+big+firms.

Cahlink, G. (2004), "Fallen Star," GOVEXEC.com, February 15. Available at: http://www.govexec.com/features/0204/0204s1.htm.

Caro, R. (1974), *The Power Broker*, Vintage Books, New York, NY.

Carroll, G. R. and Harrison, J. R. (1998), "Organizational demography and culture: Insights from a formal model and simulation," *Administrative Science Quarterly*, Vol. 43, 511–637.

Carswell, J. (2001), *The South Sea Bubble*, Sutton Publishing, Stroud, UK.

Catan, T., Kirchgaessner, S., Ratner, J., and Larsen, P. T. (2003), "Before the fall: How, from the outset, Bernie Ebbers' character and business methods sowed the seeds of disaster," *Financial Times*, December 19. Available at: http://news.ft.com/servlet/ContentServer?pagename=FT.co.

Cavanagh, G. F., Moberg, D. J., and Velasquez, M. (1981), "The ethics of organizational politics," *Academy of Management Review*, Vol. 6, No. 3, 363–74.

Cebon, P. (2009), "Innovating our way to a meltdown," *Sloan Management Review*, Vol. 50, No. 2. 13–15.

Chittum, R. (2008), "Opening bell: Perp walk," *Columbia Journalism Review*, June 20. Available at: http://www.cjr.org/the_audit/opening_bell_84.php.

Chugh, D., Banaji, M, and Bazerman, M. (2005), "Bounded ethicality as a psychological barrier to recognizing conflicts of interest," in Moore, D., Cain, D., Loewenstein, G., and Bazerman, M. (eds.), *Conficts of Interest: Problems and Solutions from Law, Medicine and Organizational Settings*, Cambridge University Press, London, 74–95.

Cialdini, R. (2001), *Influence: Science and Practice*, Allyn and Bacon, Boston, MA.

Clark, J. W. and Dawson, L. E. (1996), "Personal religiousness and ethical judgments: An empirical analysis," *Journal of Business Ethics*, Vol. 15, No. 3, 359–72.

Clarke, R. V. (1995), "Situational crime prevention," in Tonry, M. and Farrington, D. (eds.), *Crime and Justice (vol. 19), Building a Safer Society: Strategic Approaches to Crime Prevention*, The University of Chicago Press, Chicago, IL, 91–150.

Clawson, D. (1980), *Bureaucracy and the Labor Process: The Transformation of U.S. Industry, 1860–1920*, Monthly Review Press, New York, NY.

Clinard, M. B. and Yeager, P. C. (1980), *Corporate Crime*, The Free Press, New York, NY.

Cloward, R. and Ohlin, L. (1960), *Delinquency and Opportunity*, Free Press, New York, NY.

Cohan, W. D. (2009), *House of Cards*, Doubleday, New York, NY.

Cohen, L. E., and Felson, M. (1979), "Social change and crime rate trends: A routine activity approach," *American Sociological Review*, Vol. 44, 588–608.

Cohen, T, Gunia, B., Kim-Jun, S.Y., and Murnighan, J. K. (2009), "Do groups lie more than individuals? Honesty and deception as a function of strategic self-interest," *Journal of Experimental Social Psychology*, Vol. 45, 1321–4.

Coleman, J. W. (1987), "Toward an integrated theory of white-collar crime," *American Journal of Sociology*, Vol. 93, No. 2, 406–39.

——(1988), "Competition and the structure of industrial society: Reply to Braithwaite," *American Journal of Sociology*, Vol. 94, No. 3, 632–6.

Coleman, J. (1995), "Motivation and opportunity: Understanding the causes of white-collar crime," in Geis, G. Meier, R. and Salinger, L. (eds.), *White Collar Crime*, Free Press, New York, 360–81.

Collins, R. (1975), *Conflict Sociology*, Academic Press, New York, NY.

Connor, M. (2010), "Supreme Court ruling narrows honest services law," *Business Ethics*, June 24. Available at: http://business-ethics.com/2010/06/24/u-s-supreme-court-provides-victory-for-enrons-skilling-narrows-honest-services-law/#.

Cooley, C. (1902), *Human Nature and the Social Order*, Charles Scribner's Sons, New York, NY.

Coser, L. A. (1967), *Continuities in the Study of Social Conflict*, Free Press, New York, NY.

Cressey, D. (1972), *Other People's Money*, Wadsworth Publishing Company, Belmont, CA.

Creswell, J. and Krauss, C. (2009), "Stanford accused of a long-running scheme," *New York Times*, February 28. Available at: http://www.nytimes.com/2009/02/28/business/28stanford.html.

Dalton, D. R., Hitt, M. A., Certo, S. T., and Dalton, C. M. (2007), "The fundamental agency problem and its mitigation: Independence, equity, and the market for corporate control," *Academy of Management Annals*, Vol. 1, 1–64.

Damasio, A. R. (1994), *Descartes' error: Emotion, reason, and the human brain*, Putnam, New York, NY.

Darden, R. (2002), "The Wittenburg Door interview," *The Wittenburg Door*, May/June. Available at: http://archives.wittenburgdoor.com/archives/kennethlay.html.

Darley, J. M. (1992), "Social organization for the production of evil," *Psychological Inquiry*, Vol. 3, 199–218.

——(1996), "How organizations socialize individuals into evildoing," in Messick, D. M. and Tenbrunsel, A. E. (eds.), *Codes of Conduct: Behavioral Research into Business Ethics*, Russell Sage, New York, NY.

——and Batson, C. D. (1973), "'From Jerusalem to Jericho': A study of situational and dispositional variables in helping behavior," *Journal of Personality and Social Psychology*, Vol. 27, 100–8.

Darley, J. M., Messick, D. M., Tyler, T. R. (2001), *Social Influence on Ethical Behavior in Organizations*, Lawrence Erlbaum Associates, Mahwah, NJ.

Davis, G. F. (2009), *Managed by the Markets: How Finance Re-Shaped America*, Oxford University Press, Oxford, UK.

De Martino, B., Kumaran, D., Seymour, B., and Dolan, R. J. (2006), "Frames, biases, and rational decision-making in the human brain," *Science*, Vol. 313, 684–7.

Domanick, J. (1991), *Faking it in America: Barry Minkow and the Great ZZZZ Best Scam*, Knightsbridge Publishing Company, New York, NY.

Dowie, M. (1977), "How Ford put two million firetraps on wheels," *Business and Society Review*, Vol. 23, 46–55.

Durkheim, E. (1984), *The Division of Labor in Society*, The Free Press, New York, NY.

——(1997), *Suicide*, The Free Press, New York, NY.

Edwards, R. (1979), *Contested Terrain: The Transformation of the Work Place in the Twentieth Century*, Basic Books, New York, NY.

Eichenwald, K. (1996), *Serpent on the Rock*, Broadway Books, New York, NY.

——(2000), *The Informant*, Broadway Books, New York, NY.

——(2005), *Conspiracy of Fools: A True Story*, Broadway Books, New York, NY.

Eisenhardt, K. (1989), "Building theories from case study research," *Academy of Management Review*, Vo. 14, No. 4, 532–50.

Emerson, J (1970), "Behavior in private places: sustaining definitions of reality in gynecological examinations," *Recent Sociology*, No. 2, 74–97.

Estes, A. (2008), "Big dig settlement will take quick hit," *Boston Globe*, January 24. Available at: http://www.boston.com/news/traffic/bigdig/articles/2008/01/24/big_dig_settlement_will_take_quick_hit/.

——and Murphy, S. P. (2008), "$450 million Big Dig accord expected," *Boston Globe*, January 23. Avaialable at: http://www.boston.com/news/traffic/bigdig/articles/2008/01/23/450m_big_dig_accord_expected/.

Fainaru, S. (2008), *Big Boy Rules*, Da Capo Press, Philadelphia, PA.

Fama, E. F. (1980), "Agency problems and the theory of the firm," *Journal of Political Economy*, Vol. 88, 288–307.

——and Jensen, M. C. (1983), "The separation of ownership and control," *Journal of Law and Economics*, Vol. 26, 301–25.

Federal Bureau of Investigation (2008), "More than 400 defendants charged for roles in mortgage fraud schemes as part of Operation 'Malicious Mortgage'," Press Release, June 19. Available at: http://www.fbi.gov/pressrel/pressrel08/mortgagefraud061908.htm.

Federal Trade Commission (2009), "Federal and state agencies crack down on mortgage modification and foreclosure rescue scams," Press Release, April 6. Available at: http://www.ftc.gov/opa/2009/04/hud.shtm.

Festinger, L. (1957). *A Theory of Cognitive Dissonance*. Stanford University Press, Stanford, CA.

Fiske, S. T. (1993), "Controlling other people: The impact of power on stereotyping," *American Psychologist*, Vol. 48, 621–8.

Fisse, B. and Braithwaite, J. (1983), *The Impact of Publicity on Corporate Offenders*, State University of New York Press, Albany, NY.

Fleming, S. (2009), "Greedy bankers 'just waiting to reboard the bonus gravy train'," *Daily Mail*, May 15. Available at: http://www.dailymail.co.uk/news/article-1181928/Greedy-bankers-just-waiting-reboard-bonus-gravy-train.html.

Flood, M. (2005), "Anderson document shredding conviction overturned," *Houston Chronicle*, June 1. Available at: http://www.chron.com/disp/story.mpl/special/andersen/3206167.html.

Frederickson, B. L. and Roberts, T. A. (1997), "Objectification theory," *Psychology of Women Quarterly*, Vol. 21, 173–206.

Freedman, R. D. and Burke, J. R. (1998), "Kidder, Peabody and Co," New York University, Stern School of Business.

French, J. R. P., Jr. and Raven, B. H. (1959), "The bases of social power," in Cartwright, D. (ed.) *Studies in Social Power*, Institute for Social Research, Ann Arbor, MI, 150–67.

Galbraith, J. R. (1973), *Designing Complex Organizations*, Addison-Wesley Longman, Boston, MA.

——(2007), *The New Industrial State*, Princeton University Press, Princeton, NJ.

Gaventa, J. (1982), *Power and Powerlessness: Quiescence and Rebellion in an Appalachian Valley*, University of Illinois Press, Urbana, IL.

Gaviria, M. and Smith, M. (2009), "The Madoff Affair," Frontline, May 12. Available at: http://www.pbs.org/wgbh/pages/frontline/madoff/.

Geis, G. L. (1995), "The heavy electrical equipment anti-trust cases of 1961," in Geis, G., Meier, R., and Salinger, L. (eds.), *White Collar Crime*, Free Press, New York, 151–65.

Gioia, D. A. (1992), "Pinto fires and personal ethics: A script analysis of missed opportunities," *Journal of Business Ethics*, Vol. 11, 379–89.

Glass, I. (2009), "The watchman," *This American Life*, Chicago Public Radio, June 5. Available at: http://www.thisamericanlife.org/Radio_Episode.aspx?episode=382.

——(2010), "Petty Tyrant," *This American Life*, Chicago Public Radio, November 12. Available at: http://www.thisamericanlife.org/radio-archives/episode/419/petty-tyrant.

Glovin, D. (2011), "Hedge fund insider prosecutions rely on suspects turned informant," *Bloomberg*, January 12. Available at: http://www.bloomberg.com/news/2011-01-12/insider-trading-cooperators-at-heart-of-government-prosecutions.html.

Goodwin, S. A., Gubin, A., Fiske, S. T., and Yzerbyt, V. Y. (2000), "Power can bias impression processes: Stereotyping subordinates by default and by design," *Group Processes and Intergroup Relations*, Vol. 3, 227–56.

Gottfredson, M. and Hirschi, T. (1990), *General Theory of Crime*, Stanford University Press, Stanford, CA.

Gouldner, A. W. (1960), "The norm of reciprocity: A preliminary statement," *American Sociological Review*, Vol. 25, No. 2, 161–78.

Granovetter, M. S. (1985), "Economic action and social structure: The problem of embeddedness," *American Journal of Sociology*, Vol. 91, 481–93.

Green, J. D. and Haidt, J. (2002), "How (and where) does moral judgment work?" *Trends in Cognitive Sciences*, Vol. 6, 517–23.

Greenhouse, S. (2008), *The Big Squeeze*, Random House, New York, NY.

Gruenfeld, D. H., Inesi, M. E., Magee, J. C., and Galinsky, A. D. (2008), "Power and the objectification of social targets," *Journal of Personality and Social Psychology*, Vol. 95, 1450–66.

Guillen, M. L. and Suarez, S. F. (2010), "The global crisis of 2007–2009: Markets, politics, and organizations," *Markets on Trial: The Economic Sociology of the U.S. Financial Crisis, Research in the Sociology of Organizations*, Vol. 30B, 257–80.

Gunia, B., Wang, B., Huang, L., Wang, J., and Murnighan, J. K. (Forthcoming), "Contemplation and conversation: Subtle influences on moral decision making," *Academy of Management Journal*.

Haddad, C. and Barrett, A. (2002), "A whistle-blower rocks an industry," *Business Week*, June 24. Available at: http://www.businessweek.com/magazine/content/02_25/b3788094.htm.

Haidt, J. (2001), "The emotional dog and its rational tail: A social intuitionist approach to moral judgment," *Psychological Review*, Vol. 108, 814–34.

Halberstam, D. (1986), *The Reckoning*, William Morrow and Company, New York, NY.

Hall, D. L., Matz, D. C., and Wood, W. (2010), "Why don't we practice what we preach? A meta-analytic review of religious racism," *Personality and Social Psychology Review*, Vol. 14, No. 1, 126–39.

Hambrick, D. (1994), "Presidential address: What if the Academy actually mattered?" *Academy of Management Review*, Vol. 19, 11–16.

Haney, C., Banks, W. C., and Zimbardo, P. G. (1973). "Interpersonal dynamics in a simulated prison," *International Journal of Criminology and Penology*, Vol. 1, 69–97.

Hargadon, A. B., and Sutton, R. I. (1997), "Technology brokering and innovation in a product development firm," *Administrative Science Quarterly*, Vol. 42, No. 2, 716–49.

Henley, N. M. (1977), *Body Politics: Power, Sex, and Nonverbal Communication*, Prentice Hall, Englewood Cliffs, NJ.

Herszenhorn, D. (2008), "Senator viewed mortgage treatment as a 'courtesy'," *The New York Times*, June 18. Available at: http://www.nytimes.com/2008/06/18/washington/18dodd.html?ref=todayspaper.

Hillman, A. J. and Dalziel, T. (2003), "Boards of directors and firm performance: Integrating agency and resource dependence perspectives," *Academy of Management Review*, Vol. 28, 383–96.

Hirschi, T. and Gottfredson M. (1987), "Causes of white collar crime," *Criminology*, Vol. 25, 949–74.

Hochstetler, A. and Copes, H. (2001), "Organizational culture and organizational crime," in Shover, N. and Wright, J. P. (eds.) *Crimes of Privilege*, Oxford University Press, New York, NY, 210–21.

House, R. J., Shane, S. A., and Herold, D. M. (1996), "Rumors of the death of dispositional research are vastly exaggerated," *Academy of Management Review*, Vol. 21, No. 1, 203–24.

Houston Chronicle (2005), "Charge dropped against Anderson accountant," *Houston Chronicle*, December 16. Available at: http://www.chron.com/disp/story.mpl/special/andersen/3527841.html.

Janis I. L. (1971), "Groupthink," *Psychology Today*, November, Vol. 5, 43–84.

——(1972), *Victims of Groupthink*, Boston. Houghton Mifflin Company.

Japsen, B. (2004), "TAP jury: 'Not enough proof'," *Chicago Tribune*, July 28. Available at: http://articles.chicagotribune.com/2004-07-28/business/0407280349_1_drug-samples-jurors-doctors.

Jones, T. M. (1991), "Ethical decision making by individuals in organizations: An issue-contingent model," *Academy of Management Review*, Vol. 16, No. 2, 366–95.

Jordan, J. M., Mullen, E. and Murnighan, J. K. (2011), "Striving for the moral self: The effects of recalling past moral actions on future moral behavior," *Personality and Social Psychology Bulletin*. Vol. 37, 701–13.

Kahnemann, D., Slovic, P., and Tversky, A. (1982), *Judgment Under Uncertainty*, Cambridge University Press, New York, NY.

Keltner, D., Gruenfeld, D. H., and Anderson, C. (2003), "Power, approach, and inhibition," *Psychological Review*, Vol. 110, 265–84.

Keltner, D., Young, R. C., Heerey, E. A., Oemig, C., and Monarch, N. D. (1998), "Teasing in hierarchical and intimate relations," *Journal of Personality and Social Psychology*, Vol. 75, 1231–47.

Kennedy, E. J. and Lawton, L. (1996), "The effects of social and moral integration on ethical standards: A comparison of American and Ukrainian business students," *Journal of Business Ethics*, Vol. 15, No. 8, 901–11.

Kern, M. C. and Chugh, D. (2009), "Bounded ethicality: The perils of loss framing," *Psychological Science*, Vol. 20, 378–84.

Kerr, S. (1975), "On the folly of rewarding A, while hoping for B," *Academy of Management Journal*, Vol. 18, No. 4, 769–83.

Khurana, R. (2007), *From Higher Aims to Hired Hands*, Princeton University Press, Princeton, NJ.

Kipnis, D. (1972), "Does power corrupt?" *Journal of Personality and Social Psychology*, Vol. 24, 33–41.

——(2001), "Using power: Newton's second law," in Lee-Chai, A. Y. and Bargh, J. A. (eds.), *The Use and Abuse of Power*, Psychology Press, Philadelphia, PA, 3–18.

Kohlberg, L. (1969), "Stage and sequence: The cognitive developmental approach to socialization," in Goslin, D. A. (ed), *Handbook of Socialization Theory*, Rand McNally, Chicago, IL, 347–480.

——(1981), *The Philosophy of Moral Development: Moral Stages and the Idea of Justice*, Harper and Row, San Francisco, CA.

Kouwe, Z. (2010), "Insider's admission deepens Galleon case," February 10, *The New York Times*. Available at: http://www.nytimes.com/2010/02/09/business/09insider.html.

——and Slater, D. (2010). "2 Bear Stearns fund leaders are acquitted," *The New York Times*, November 11. Available at: http://www.nytimes.com/2009/11/11/business/11bear.html.

Krainin Productions, Inc. and WGBH Educational Foundation (2000), "The quiz show scandal," *The American Experience*, Transcript.

Krimmage, P. (2007), *Rough Ride*, Yellow Jersey Press, London, UK.

Kulik, B. W. (2005), "Agency theory, reasoning and culture at Enron: In search of a solution," *Journal of Business Ethics*, Vol. 59, No. 4, 347–60.

Lacter, M. (2008), "Toy story," *Los Angeles Magazine*, http://www.lamag.com/featuredarticle.aspx?id=9924.

Lange, D. (2008), "A multidimensional conceptualization of organizational corruption control," *Academy of Management Review*, Vol. 33, No. 3, 710–29.

Langer, E., Blank, A. and Chanowitz, B. (1978), "The mindlessness of ostensibly thoughtful action: The role of 'placebic' information in interpersonal interaction," *Journal of Personality and Social Psychology*, Vol. 36, 635–42.

Langer, E. and Moldoveanu, M. (2000), "The construct of mindfulness," *Journal of Social Issues*, Vol. 56, 1–9.

Langewiesche, W. (2003), "Columbia's last flight: The inside story of the investigation and the catastrophe it laid bare," *Atlantic Monthly*, November. Available at: http://www.theatlantic.com/magazine/archive/2003/11/columbia-apos-s-last-flight/4204/.

Lee-Chai, A. Y., Chen, S., and Chartrand, T. L. (2001), "From Moses to Marcos: individual differences in the use and abuse of power," in Lee-Chai, A. Y. and Bargh, J. A. (eds.), *The Use and Abuse of Power*, Psychology Press, Philadelphia, PA, 57–74.

Lemert, E. M. (1951), *Social Pathology*, McGraw-Hill, New York, NY.

Lev, M. (1990), "Hazelwood's acquittal clouds the Exxon case," *New York Times*, March 28. Available at: http://www.nytimes.com/1990/03/28/us/hazelwood-s-acquittal-clouds-the-exxon-case.html.

Lewis, M. (1990), *Liar's Poker*, Penguin Books, New York, NY.

——(2008), "The end," *Portfolio.com*, November 11. Available at: http://www.portfolio.com/news-markets/national-news/portfolio/2008/11/11/The-End-of-Wall-Streets-Boom/.

Lipton, E. (2009), "Ex-leaders of Countrywide profit from bad loans," *The New York Times*, March 4. Available at: http://www.nytimes.com/2009/03/04/business/04penny.html.

Litchfield, E. H. (1956), "Notes on a general theory of administration," *Administrative Science Quarterly*, Vol. 1, No. 1, 3–29.

Luhby, T. (2009), "Predatory-lending lawsuits on the rise," *CNNMoney.com*. Available at: http://money.cnn.com/2009/10/08/news/economy/Predatory_lending_lawsuits_increase/index.htm.

Lysiak, M. and McShane, L. (2009), "Bernie Madoff recalled as a lousy tipper by those who served him," *New York Daily News*, March 15. Available at: http://www.nydailynews.com/money/2009/03/14/2009-03-14_bernie_madoff_recalled_as_a_lousy_tipper.html.

McClelland, D. C. and Burnham, D. H. (1976), "Power is the great motivator," *Harvard Business Review,* 54(2), 100–10.

McDonald, L. G. and Robinson P. (2009), *A Colossal Failure of Common Sense: The Inside Story of the Collapse of Lehman Brothers*, Crown Publishing Group, New York, NY.

McLean, B. and Elkind, P. (2004), *The Smartest Guys in the Room: The Amazing Rise and Scandalous Fall of Enron*, Portfolio Hardcover, New York, NY.

Macur, J. (2006), "Two Ex-Teammates of Cycling Star Admit Drug Use," *The New York Times*, September 12. Available at: http://www.nytimes.com/2006/09/12/sports/othersports/12cycling.html?ex=1159070400anden=4939180e12448375andei=5070.

March, J. G. and Simon, H. (1958), *Organizations*, John Wiley and Sons, New York, NY.

March, J. G. and Sutton, R. I. (1997), "Crossroads—organizational performance as a dependent variable," *Organization Science*, Vol. 8, No. 6, 698–706.

Margolis, J. (2001), "Responsibility in Organizational Context," *Business Ethics Quarterly*, Vol. 11, 431–54.

Mechanic, D. (1962), "Sources of power of lower participants in complex organizations," *Administrative Science Quarterly*, Vol. 7, 349–64.

Merton, R. K. (1938), "Social structure and anomie," *American Sociological Review*, Vol. 3, No. 5, 672–82.

Messick, D. M. and Bazerman, M. H. (1996), "Ethical leadership and the psychology of decision making," *Sloan Management Review*, Winter, 9–22.

Messick, D. M. and Tenbrunsel, A. (1996), "Behavioral research into business ethics," in Messick, D. M. and Tenbrunsel, A. E. (eds.), *Codes of Conduct: Behavioral Research into Business Ethics*, Russell Sage, New York, NY, 1–10.

Mezias, S. J. (1994), "Financial meltdown as normal accident: The case of the American Savings and Loan industry," *Accounting, Organizations and Society*, Vol. 19, 181–92.

Milgram, S. (1963), "Behavioral study of obedience," *Journal of Abnormal and Social Psychology*, Vol. 67, 371–8.

References

Milgram, S. (1965), "Some conditions of obedience and disobedience to authority," *Human Relations*, Vol. 18, 57–76.

——(1974), *Obedience to Authority*, Harper and Row, New York, NY.

Milgrom, P. and Roberts, J. (1988), "An economic approach to influence activities in organizations," *American Journal of Sociology*, Vol. 94, S154–79.

Mintz, B. and Schwartz, M. (1985), *The Power Structure of American Business*, University of Chicago Press, Chicago, IL.

Mintz, M. (1972), "A Colonial Heritage," in Heilbroner, R. (ed.), *In the Name of Profit*, Doubleday and Company, Garden City, NY, 60–105.

Misangyi, V. F., Weaver, G. R., and Elms, H. (2008), "Ending corruption: The Interplay among institutional logics, resources, and institutional entrepreneurs," *Academy of Management Review*, Vol. 33, No. 3, 750–70.

Molotch, H. and Lester, M. (1974), "News as purposive behavior: On the strategic use of routine events, accidents, and scandals," *American Sociological Review*, Vol. 39, 101–12.

Moore, D. A., Tetlock, P. E., Tanlu, L. and Bazerman, M. H. (2006), "Conflicts of interest and the case of auditor independence: Moral seduction and strategic issue cycling," *Academy of Management Review*, Vol. 31, No. 1, 10–29.

Morgenson, G. (2008), "Countrywide to set aside $8.4 billion in loan aid," *New York Times*, October 5. Available at: http://www.nytimes.com/2008/10/06/business/06countrywide.html.

——and Story, L. (2009), "Banks bundled bad debt, bet against it and won," *The New York Times*, December 24. Available at: www.nytimes.com/2009/12/24/business/ 24trading.html.

Mundy, A. (2001), *Dispensing with the Truth*, St. Martin's Press, New York, NY.

Murnighan, J. K., Cantelon, D. A., and Elyashiv, T. (2001), "Bounded personal ethics and the tap dance of real estate agency," in Wagner, J., Bartunek, J. M., and Elsbach, K. D., *Advances in Qualitative Organizational Research*, Vol. 3, Elsevier/JAI, New York, NY, 1–40.

Murphy, S. P. and Allen, S. (2007), "Coakly rules out more indictments in Big Dig, but sources say talks are critical," *Boston Globe*, August 26. Available at: http://www.boston.com/news/local/articles/2007/08/26/coakley_rules_out_more_indictments_in_big_dig/.

Murphy, S. P. and Estes, A. (2007), "Wide risk, wide blame," *Boston Globe*, July 11. Available at: http://www.boston.com/news/local/massachusetts/articles/2007/07/11/wide_risk_wide_blame/.

Nadler, D. A. and Lawler, E. E. (1977), "Motivation: A diagnostic approach," in Staw, B. M. (ed.), *Psychological Dimensions of Organizational Behavior* (3rd ed.), Pearson Education, Upper Saddle River, NJ, 25–36.

Nagourney, A. (2010), "Senator Dodd will not seek re-election, democrats say," *The New York Times*, January 6. Available at: http://www.nytimes.com/2010/01/06/us/politics/06dodd.html.

Nielsen, R. (1988), "Limitations of ethical reasoning as an action (praxis) strategy," *Journal of Business Ethics*, Vol. 7, 725–33.

——(2010), "High-leverage finance capitalism, the economic crisis, structurally related ethics issues, and potential reforms," *Journal of Business Ethics*, Vol. 20, No. 2, 299–330.

Nisbett, R. E. and Ross, L. (1980), *Human Inference: Strategies and Shortcomings of Social Judgment*, Englewood Cliffs, Prentice-Hall, NJ.

Novak, M. (1996), *Business as a Calling: Work and the Examined Life*, Free Press, New York, NY.

Nussbaum, M. C. (1999), *Sex and Social Justice*, Oxford University Press, New York, NY.

O'Fallon, M. J. and Butterfield, K. D. (2005), "A review of the empirical ethical decision making literature: 1996–2003," *Journal of Business Ethics*, Vol. 59, 375–413.

Opotow, S. (1990), "Moral exclusion and injustice: An introduction, *Journal of Social Issues*, Vol. 45, No. 1, 1–20.

Palmer, D. (2008), "Extending the process model of collective organizational wrongdoing," *Research in Organizational Behavior*, Vol. 28, 107–35.

——and Maher, M. (2006), "Developing the process model of collective corruption in organizations," *Journal of Management Inquiry*, Vol. 15, 363–70.

——— (2010), "A normal accident analysis of the mortgage meltdown," in Lounsbury, M. and Hirsch, P. M. (eds.), *Markets on Trial: The Economic Sociology of the U.S. Financial Crisis*, Emerald, Bingley, UK, 219–56.

Paolini, M. and Vacis, G. (2000), *The Story of Vajont*, edited and translated by T. Simpson, Bordighera Press, New York, NY.

Pasztor, A. and Karp, J. (2004), "How an Air Force official's help for a daughter led to disgrace," *Wall Street Journal*, New York, NY. December 9, p. A. 1.

Pavlo, W. and Weinberg, N. (2007), *Stolen without a Gun*, Etika Books, Tampa, FL.

Perrow, C. (1967), "A framework for comparative organizational analysis," *American Sociological Review*, Vol. 32, 194–208.

——(1972), *Complex Organizations: A Critical Essay*, McGraw-Hill, New York, NY.

——(1999), *Normal Accidents: Living With High-Risk Technologies* (2nd ed.), Princeton University Press, Princeton, NJ.

Perrow, C. B. (2007), *The Next Catastrophe: Reducing Our Vulnerabilities to Natural, Industrial, and Terrorist Disasters*, Princeton University Press, Princeton, NJ.

——(2010), "The meltdown was not an accident," *Markets on Trial: The Economic Sociology of the U.S. Financial Crisis, Research in the Sociology of Organizations*, Vol. 30B, 309–30.

Perry, S. and Dawson, J. (1985), *Nightmare: Women and the Dalkon Shield*, Macmillan, New York, NY.

Pfarrer, M. D., Decelles, K. A., Smith, K. G., and Taylor, M. S. (2008), "After the fall: Reintegrating the corrupt organization," *Academy of Management Review*, Vol. 33, No. 3, 730–49.

Pfeffer, J. (1981), *Power in Organizations*, Pitman Publishing, Boston, MA.

——(1992), *Managing with Power: Politics and Influence in Organizations*, Harvard Business School Press, Boston, MA.

——(2010), *Power: Why Some People Have It and Others Don't*, Harper Collins, New York, NY.

Pfeffer, J. and Davis-Blake, A. (1989), "Just a mirage: The search for dispositional effects in organizational research," *Academy of Management Review*, Vol. 14, No. 3, 385–400.

——and Salancik, G. R. (1978), *The External Control of Organizations: A Resource Dependence Perspective*, Harper and Row Publishers, New York, NY.

Pinto, J., Leana, C. R., and Pil, F. K. (2008), "Corrupt organizations or organizations of corrupt individuals? Two types of organizational-level corruption," *Academy of Management Review*, Vol. 33, No. 3, 685–709.

Pizzo, S., Fricker, M., and Muolo, P. (1991), *Inside Job: The Looting of America's Savings and Loans*, HarperCollins, New York.

Platt, J. (2009), "Cases of cases . . . of cases," in Ragin, C. C. and Becker, H. S. (eds.), *What Is a Case?* Cambridge University Press, Cambridge, England, 21–52.

Pulliam, S. (2003), "Ordered to commit fraud, a staffer balked, then caved," *The Wall Street Journal*. Available at: http://online.wsj.com/article/0,SB105631811322 355600,00.html.

Radcliffe-Brown, A. R. (1965), *Structure and Function in Primitive Society*, Free Press, New York, NY.

Rauch, J. (2006), "Merrill Lynch Fined $5M for Call Center Violations," *Jacksonville Business Journal*, March 15. Available at: http://www.bizjournals.com/jacksonville/ stories/2006/03/13/daily21.html.

Raven, B. H. (2001), "Power/interaction and interpersonal influence," in Lee-Chai, A. Y. and Bargh, J. A. (eds.), *The Use and Abuse of Power*, Psychology Press, Philadelphia, PA, 217–40.

Razzaque, M. A. and Hwee, T. P. (2002), "Ethics and purchasing dilemma: A Singaporean view," *Journal of Business Ethics*, Vol. 35, No. 4, 307–26.

Rest, J. R. (1986), *Moral Development: Advances in Research and Theory*, Praeger, New York, NY.

——Narvaez, D., Bebeau, M. J., and Thoma, S. J. (1999), *Postconventional Moral Thinking: A Neo-Kohlbergian Approach*, Lawrence Erlbaum, Mahwah, NJ.

Reuters (2009), "Satyam chief quits as fraud scandal slams shares," *Reuters, UK*, January 7. Available at: http://uk.reuters.com/article/2009/01/07/uk-satyam-idUKTRE5061W020090107.

Roethlisberger, F. J. and Dickson, W. J. (1947), *Management and the Worker*, Harvard University Press, Cambridge, MA.

Rogers, P. and Weinstein, F. (2002), "The outsider; Doug Durand blew the whistle on his drug firm—and got $79 million," *People*, 6 May, Vol. 57, No. 17, 139–141.

Roitsch, P. A., Babcock, G. L. and Edmunds, W. W. (1979), *Human Factors Report on the Tenerife Accident*, Airline Pilots Association, Washington, DC.

Rosenberg, T. (2007), "When is a pain doctor a drug pusher?" *The New York Times Magazine*, June 7. Available at: http://www.nytimes.com/2007/06/17/magazine/ 17pain-t.html.

Roy, D. F. (1959), "Banana Time: Job satisfaction and informal interaction," *Human Organization,* Vol. 18, 158–168.

Ryle, G. (1949), *The Concept of Mind*, University of Chicago Press, Chicago, IL.

Salancik, G. (1977), "Commitment is too easy," *Organizational Dynamics*, Vol. 6, Summer, 62–80.

Salancik, G. and Pfeffer, J. (1977), "Who gets power and how they hold on to it: A strategic contingency model of power," *Organizational Dynamics*, Vol. 5, Winter, 3–21.

———— (1978), "A social information processing approach to job attitudes and task design," *Administrative Science Quarterly*, Vol. 23, No. 2, 224–53.

Saltzman, J. (2009), "Big Dig contractor Modern Continental pleads guilty," *Boston Globe*, May 8. Available at: http://www.boston.com/news/local/breaking_news/2009/05/modern_continen_2.html.

Sayles, J. and Smith, G. (1998), *Sayles on Sayles,* Faber & Faber, Boston, MA.

Scannell, K. and Emshwiller, J. R. (2009), "Countrywide chiefs charged with fraud," *The Wall Street Journal*, June 5. Available at: http://online.wsj.com/article/SB124414278536586095.html#.

Scharff, M. M. (2005), "Understanding Worldcom's accounting fraud: Did groupthink play a role?" *Journal of Leadership and Organization Studies*, Vol. 11, No. 3, 109–18.

Schein, E. H. (1961a), *Coercive Persuasion*, W. W. Norton and Company, New York, NY.

——(1961b), "Management development as a process of influence," *Sloan Management Review*, Vol. 2, No. 2, 41–50.

——(1985), *Organizational Culture and Leadership*, Jossey-Bass Publishers, San Francisco, CA.

——(1995), "The role of the founder in creating organizational culture," *Family Business Review*, Vol. 8, No. 3, 221–38.

Schmidt, M. S. and Wilson, D. (2008), "Marion Jones sentenced to six months in prison," *The New York Times*, January 12. Available at: http://www.nytimes.com/2008/01/12/sports/othersports/11cnd-jones.html.

Schminke, M., Ambrose, J. L., and Noel, T. W. (1997), "The effect of ethical frameworks on perceptions of organizational justice," *Academy of Management Journal*, Vol. 40, 1190–207.

Schmitt, R, Christensen, K., and Reckard, E. S. (2008), "400 charged as U.S. cracks down on mortgage fraud," *The Los Angeles Times*, June 20. Available at: http://articles.latimes.com/2008/jun/20/business/fi-mortgage20.

Schneiberg, M. and Bartley, T. (2010), "Regulating and redesigning finance," *Markets on Trial: The Economic Sociology of the U.S. Financial Crisis, Research in the Sociology of Organizations*, Volume 30A, 281–308.

Schroyer, T. (1975), *The Critique of Domination*, Beacon Press, Boston, MA.

Schur, E. M. (1971), *Labeling Deviant Behavior: Its Sociological Implications*, Harper and Row, New York, NY.

Schwartz, G. (1991), "The myth of the Ford Pinto case," *Rutgers Law Review*, Vol. 43, 1013–68.

Scott, W. R. (2002), *Organizations: Rational, Natural, and Open Systems*, Prentice Hall, Newark, NJ.

Shiller, R. J. (2005), "How Wall Street Learns to Look the Other Way," *The New York Times*, February 8. Available at: http://www.nytimes.com/2005/02/08/opinion/08shiller.html.

Shrivastava, P. (1991), "Union Carbide Corporation," in Sethji, S. P. and Steidlmeier, P. (eds.), *Up Against the Corporate Wall*, Englewood Cliffs, Prentice Hall, NJ, 383–8.

Simpson, S. S. (1986), "The decomposition of antitrust: Testing a multilevel, longitudinal model of profit-squeeze," *American Sociological Review*, Vol. 51, 859–975.

——(1987), "Cycles of illegality: Antitrust in corporate America," *Social Forces*, Vol. 65, 943–63.

Simpson, S. and Leeper Piquero, N. (2002), "Low self-control, organization theory, and corporate crime," *Law and Society Review*, Vol. 36, No. 3, 509–48.

Sims, R. R. (1992), "Linking groupthink to unethical behavior in organizations," *Journal of Business Ethics*, Vol. 11, No. 9, 651–62.

Sims, R. R. and Brinkmann, J. (2003), "Enron ethics (Or: Culture matters more than codes)," *Journal of Business Ethics*, Vol. 45, No. 3, 243–56.

Singhapakdi, A., Marta, J. K., Rallapalli, K. C., and Rao, C. P. (2000), "Toward an understanding of religiousness and marketing ethics: An empirical study," *Journal of Business Ethics*, Vol. 27, No. 4, 305–19.

Smith, A. (1991), *The Wealth of Nations*, Prometheus Books, New York, NY.

Soble, R. and Dallas, R. (1975), *The Impossible Dream. The Equity Funding Story: The Fraud of the Century*, G.P. Putnam's Sons, New York, NY.

Sonnenfeld, J. (1981), "Executive apologies for price fixing: Role biased perceptions of causality," *Academy of Management Journal*, Vol. 24, No. 1, 192–8.

Sorenson, J. (2002), "The strength of corporate culture and the reliability of firm performance," *Administrative Science Quarterly*, Vol. 47, 70–91.

Spivak, C. and Bice, D. (2008), "Case Study: No wrongdoing in writing loads," Milwaukee Journal Sentinel, September 21. Available at: http://www.jsonline.com/watchdog/32504054.html.

Spurge, L. (1998) *Failure Is Not an Option: How MCI Invented Competition in Telecommunications*, Spurge Ink! Encino, CA.

Staw, B. M. (1976), "Knee-deep in the big muddy: A study of escalating commitment to a chosen course of action," *Organizational Behavior and Human Performance*, Vol. 16, 27–44.

——and Szwajkowski, E. (1975), "The scarcity-munificence component of organizational environments and the commission of illegal acts," *Administrative Science Quarterly*, Vol. 20, 345–54.

Steiner, G. and Steiner, J. (1994), "Union Carbide Corporation and Bhopal," in Steiner and Steiner (eds.), *Business, Government, and Society*, McGraw Hill, New York, NY, 161–74.

Stewart, J. (1991), *Den of Thieves*, Simon and Schuster, New York, NY.

Stewart, T. (2004), "Governance: Managers look for the moral dimension," *Financial Times*, August 27 Available at: http://royaldutchshellplc.com/2008/09/08/european-frauds-such-as-vivendi-royal-dutch-shell-and-parmalat-demonstrated-that-corporate-scandals-were-not-confined-to-the-us/.

Stone, J. and Yohn, T. (1992), *Prime Time and Misdemeanors: Investigating the 1950s TV Quiz Scandal*, Rutgers University Press, New Brunswick, NJ.

Story, L. (2008), "In Bear Stearns case, question of an asset's value," *New York Times*, June 20. Available at: http://www.nytimes.com/2008/06/20/business/20Marks.html.

Sudnow, D. (1965), "Normal crimes: Sociological features of a penal code in a public defender's office," *Social Problems*, Vol. 12, 255–76.

Swartz, M. and Watkins, S. (2003), *Power Failure: The Inside Story of the Collapse of Enron*, Doubleday, New York, NY.

Sykes, G. and Matza, D. (1957), "Techniques of neutralization: A theory of delinquency," *American Sociological Review*, Vol. 22, No. 6, 664–70.

Taibbi, M. (2009), "The great American bubble machine," *Rolling Stone*, July 9, 1082–83.

Tavaris, C. and Aronson, E. (2007), *Mistakes Were Made (But Not by Me)*, Houghton Mifflan Harcourt, Orlando, FL.

Tedeschi, B. (2007), "Mortgages; The NAACP vs 11 lenders," *The New York Times*, September 23. Available at: http://query.nytimes.com/gst/fullpage.html?res=9B0CE0DB1539F930A1575AC0A9619C8B63.

Temple-Raston, D. (2008), "FBI sweep reveals new twists to mortgage fraud," *National Public Radio*, June 20. Available at: http://www.npr.org/templates/story/story.php?storyId=91755465.

Tenbrunsel, A. E., Diekmann, K. A., Wade-Benzoni, K. A., and Bazerman, M. H. (2010), "The ethical mirage: A temporal explanation as to why we aren't as ethical as we think we are," *Research in Organizational Behavior*, Vol. 30, 153–73.

Tenbrunsel, A. E. and Messick, D. M. (1999), "Sanctioning systems, decision frames, and cooperation," *Administrative Science Quarterly*, Vol. 44, 884–707.

Tenbrunsel, A. E. and Smith-Crowe, K. (2008), "Ethical decision making: Where we've been and where we're going," *Academy of Management Annals*, Vol. 2, 545–607.

———— Chan-Serafin, S., Brief, A. P., Umphress, E. E., and Joseph, J. (2010), "If it ain't broke, should you fix it? The tension between the informal push to do wrong and the formal pull to do right," unpublished manuscript.

The Associated Press (2009a), "Mattel fined $2.3 million for toy hazard," *MSNBC.com*, June 5. Available at: http://www.msnbc.msn.com/id/31129127/ns/business-consumer_news/.

The Associated Press (2009b), "UBS: 47,000 American clients avoided taxes," *MSNBC.com*, March 4. Available at: http://www.msnbc.msn.com/id/29514602/ns/business-world_business/.

The Associated Press (2009c), "U.S. seeks reduced term for Swiss bank witness," *MSNBC.com*, August 18. Available at: http://www.msnbc.msn.com/id/32463035/ns/business-world_business/.

The Associated Press (2009d), "UBS to divulge more than 4,000 account names," *MSNBC.com*, August 19. Available at: http://www.msnbc.msn.com/id/32474087/ns/business-world_business/.

The Associated Press (2009e), "Judge tosses Blackwater shooting charges," *MSNBC.com*, December 31. Available at: http://www.msnbc.msn.com/id/34645192/ns/world_news-mideast/n_africa/.

The Associated Press (2010a), "Iraqis outraged as Blackwater case thrown out," *MSNBC.com*, January 1. Available at: http://www.msnbc.msn.com/id/34660136/ns/world_news-mideast/n_africa/.

The Associated Press (2010b), "Blackwater settles civil lawsuits over Iragi deaths," *The Los Angeles Times*. January 8. Available at: http://articles.latimes.com/2010/jan/08/nation/la-na-blackwater8-2010jan08.

The Associated Press (2010c), "Xe Services aims for $1 billion Afghan deal: Re-branded Blackwater bids to train police forces despite legal woes," *MSNBC.com*, January 9. Available at: http://www.msnbc.msn.com/id/34778920/ns/world_news-south_and_central_asia/.

Thomas, L. (2005), "Deals and Consequences," *The New York Times*, November 20. Available at: http://www.nytimes.com/2005/11/20/business/yourmoney/20jail.html.

——(2006), "Martha Stewart settles civil insider-trading case," *New York Times*, August 7. Available at: http://www.nytimes.com/2006/08/07/business/07cnd-martha.html?dlbk.

Thompson, J. D. (1956), "On building an administrative science," *Administrative Science Quarterly*, Vol. 1, No. 1, 102–11.

Toffler, B. L. and Reingold, J. (2003), *Final Accounting: Ambition, Greed, and the Fall of Arthur Anderson*, Random House, New York, NY.

Tom, P. A. (2009), "Recession increasing insurance fraud," *Insurance Journal*, April 14. Available at: http://www.insurancejournal.com/news/national/2009/04/14/99585.htm?print=1.

Trevino, L. K., Weaver, G. R. and Reynolds, S. J. (2006), "Behavioral ethics in organizations: A review," *Journal of Management*, Vol. 32, No. 6, 951–90.

Tversky, A. and Kahneman, D. (1974), "Judgment under uncertainty: Heuristics and biases," *Science*, Vol. 185, 1124–31.

——— (1981), "The framing of decisions and the psychology of choice," *Science*, Vol. 211, 453–8.

Van der Heijden, K., Ramirez, R., Selsky, J., and Wilkinson, A. (2010), "Turbulence, business planning and the unfolding financial crisis," Ramirez, R., Van Heijden, K., and Selsky, J. W. (eds.), *Business Planning for Turbulent Times: New Methods for Applying Scenarios*, 2nd edition, Earthscan Publications, London, UK, 261–282.

Van Kleef, G. A., De Dreu, C. K. W., Pietroni, D., and Manstead, A. S. R. (2006), "Power and emotion in negotiation: Power moderates the interpersonal effects of anger and happiness on concession making," *European Journal of Social Psychology*, Vol. 36, 557–81.

Van Maanen, J. (1995a), "Style as theory," *Organization Science*, Vol. 6, 133–43.

——(1995b), "Fear and loathing in organizational studies," *Organization Science*, Vol. 6, 687–92.

Vandivier, K. (1972), "Why Should My Conscience Bother Me?" in Heilbroner, R. (ed.), *In the Name of Profit*, Doubleday and Company, Garden City, NY, 3–31.

Vaughan, D. (1996), *The Challenger Launch Decision: Risky Technology, Culture, and Deviance at NASA*, University of Chicago Press, Chicago, IL.

——(1999), "The dark side of organizations: Mistake, misconduct and disaster," *Annual Review of Sociology*, Vol. 25, 271–305.

——(2009), "Theory elaboration: The heuristics of case analysis," in Ragin, C. C. and Becker, H. S. (eds.), *What Is a Case?* Cambridge University Press, Cambridge, UK, 53–82. *MSNBC*.

Vennochi, J. (2007), "Big Dig collapse: Mistake or accident," *Boston Globe*, July 12.

Verhovek, S. H. (1988), "After 10 years, the trauma of Love Canal continues," *The New York Times*. Available at: http://query.nytimes.com/gst/fullpage.html?res=940DE6D9143CF936A3575BC0A96E948260.

Wagner, S. C. and Sanders, G. L. (2001), "Considerations in ethical decision-making and software piracy," *Journal of Business Ethics*, Vol. 29, 161–167.

Wang, L. and Murnighan, J. K. (forthcoming), "On greed," *Academy of Management Annals*.

Weber, J. (1990), "Managers' moral reasoning: Assessing their response to three moral dilemmas," *Human Relations*, Vol. 43, 687–702.

——and Wasieleski, D. (2001), "Investigating influences on managers' moral reasoning: The impact of context, personal, and organizational factors," *Business and Society*, Vol. 40, No. 1, 79–111.

Weber, M. (1946), "Science as a vocation," in Gerth, H. H. and Wright Mills, C. (Translated and edited), *From Max Weber: Essays in Sociology*, Oxford University Press, New York, NY.

——(1978/1922), *Economy and Society: An Outline of Interpretive Sociology*, University of California Press, Berkeley, CA.

Weick, K. (1990), "The vulnerable system: An analysis of the Tenerife air disaster," *Journal of Management*, Vol. 16, No. 3, 571–93.

Weick, K. E. and Roberts, K. H. (1993), "Collective mind in organizations: Heedful interrelating on flight decks," *Administrative Science Quarterly*, Vol. 38, No. 3, 357–81.

Weinberg, N. (2005), "The dark side of whistleblowing," *Forbes*, Vol. 175, No. 5, 90–8.

Wilber, D. Q. (2010), "Charges dismissed against Blackwater guards in Iraq deaths," *The Washington Post*, January 1. Available at: http://www.washingtonpost.com/wp-dyn/content/article/2009/12/31/AR2009123101936.html.

Williamson, O. (1983), *Markets and Hierarchies: Analysis and Antitrust Implications*, Free Press, New York, NY.

Wimalasiri, J. S., Pavri, F., and Jalil, A. A. K. (1996), "An empirical study of moral reasoning among managers in Singapore," *Journal of Business Ethics*, Vol. 15, No. 12, 1331–41.

Woodward, J. (1965), *Industrial Organization: Theory and Practice*, Oxford University Press, Oxford, UK.

Zhong, C., Ku, G., Lount, R. B., and Murnighan, J. K. (2009), "Compensatory ethics," *Journal of Business Ethics*, Vol. 92, 323–39.

Zimbardo, P. G. (2007), *The Lucifer Effect: Understanding How Good People Turn Evil*, Random House, New York, NY.

Zucchino, D. (2010), "Iraqis settle lawsuits over Blackwater shootings," *The Los Angeles Times*, January 8. Available at: http://articles.latimes.com/2010/jan/08/nation/la-na-blackwater8-2010jan08.

Index